Peculiar Passages

PETER LANG
New York • Washington, D.C./Baltimore • Bern
Frankfurt am Main • Berlin • Brussels • Vienna • Oxford

Carol Dawn Allen

Peculiar Passages

Black Women Playwrights, 1875 to 2000

PETER LANG
New York • Washington, D.C./Baltimore • Bern
Frankfurt am Main • Berlin • Brussels • Vienna • Oxford

Library of Congress Cataloging-in-Publication Data

Allen, Carol Dawn.
Peculiar passages: black women playwrights, 1875 to 2000 /
Carol Dawn Allen.
p. cm.
Includes bibliographical references and index.
1. American drama—African American authors—History and criticism.
2. Women and literature—United States—History—20th century.
3. Women and literature—United States—History—19th century. 4. American drama—20th century—History and criticism. 5. American drama—19th century—History and criticism. 6. African American women—Intellectual life.
7. African American women in literature.
8. African Americans in literature. I. Title.
PS338.N4A425 812'.4099287'08996073—dc22 2004020875
ISBN 0-8204-7620-X (hardcover)
ISBN 0-8204-7619-6 (paperback)

Bibliographic information published by **Die Deutsche Bibliothek**.
Die Deutsche Bibliothek lists this publication in the "Deutsche Nationalbibliografie"; detailed bibliographic data is available on the Internet at http://dnb.ddb.de/.

The paper in this book meets the guidelines for permanence and durability of the Committee on Production Guidelines for Book Longevity of the Council of Library Resources.

275 Seventh Avenue, 28th Floor, New York, NY 10001
www.peterlangusa.com

Printed in the United States of America

For my Aunts on the other side:
Amy, Edith, Elise, Fannie, La-La, Mary, Nita

CONTENTS

ACKNOWLEDGMENTS

I express my sincere gratitude to the parties that helped make this book possible. I thank Long Island University for granting me the time to work on the project; I appreciate as well the assistance given at the University's Library, the Schomburg Library, Rutgers University Libraries, the Free Library of Philadelphia, and the New York Public Library. To my colleagues and supporters who have given me critical feedback on the project, I owe my sincerest regards. And, to all those in the field of African American Drama, I am deeply humbled by your commitment, perseverance, and artistry. In particular, I have been inspired by Wesley Brown, Cheryl Wall, Abena Busia, Elin Diamond, and Ed Bullins as well as the writers featured in this work. Peter Lang's editorial assistance and support has been invaluable.

Most importantly, I give homage to my wonderful family, immediate and extended, for your patience, love, example, and faith.

♣ INTRODUCTION

WHEN I initially conceived this project on African American women playwrights, I was naive in thinking that I could limit my study to the primary works and the attendant criticism and then construct a meta-text based on that labor. What I have discovered is that assessing African American women's relationships and contributions to the stage requires an extensive exploration of various intersecting histories that have not been viewed, heretofore, as necessarily interrelated. For instance, while one can claim that black women came to the American theater relatively late, circa 1870, proving this statement demands that we define "theater" exclusively as the controlled material space set aside for the public consumption of entertainment. One could counter legitimately that the slave auction and the plantation fashion a "show business" of sorts. There is no clear place to begin. That realization liberated me, allowing me to glide through time and space, peering here and there with the constant call to revision not interfering with the urge to "pass it on."[1]

Shakespeare; opera; Greek drama and myth; African dance, song, and ritual; European folk traditions especially Irish and Welsh; Asian style and flare in combination with Native American ceremony have shaped America's theater. Yet to apportion how much each has added would be imprecise and, ultimately, rash because there is no pure or authentic origin; American theater is a combine, not an efficient one but one rife with unequal power relations, constant coups and battles for ground, one that is held together by mere geographic proximity, not ideological consensus. To extract from this maturing discipline the contributions made by African American women is an act of triage that will force any scholar to relegate some portion of the American theater's convoluted saga to the shadows, but the effort is worthy because African American women's voices, projections, and scenarios have been ignored too often in order that other depositors to the pool could be extolled.

Heeding this caveat about slicing off a limb from the body, we know that Africans transported pieces of their various cultures with them to the Americas, retaining significant fragments, some of which centered on religious and secular ritual, myth-making, dancing, musicality, cooking and linguistic patterns. These modes were wed to those of other future citizens. However, while African Americans have traded with their fellow patriots, rarely have these exchanges been equally reciprocated or just. As James Snead points out, "…the entire history of blacks in America has been the history of whites taking from, rather than giving to blacks" (*White Screens* 127), and this applies especially to the entertainment industry, including the fine arts. We see this propensity for race-marked cooptation very early on in the theater as "the black" was transformed into a stock repository that captured and reflected European discomfort with what it considered to be an encroaching alien culture: a 1769 piece, *Padlock*, featured a West Indian slave named Mungo, who established the paradigmatic stereotypic darky, and, by 1795, American audiences were introduced to Sambo through a production entitled *The Triumph of Love* (Peterson, *Early Playwrights* 2). By the time that minstrelsy galvanized the public during the mid-1800s, racial typecasting had been circulating by way of the traveling show for close to a century, which indicates that the time span when representational blackness had not been appropriated to provide varying degrees of psychological assurance to bolster white "new worlders" was either brief or nonexistent.[2]

Generally, sources do not acknowledge the role that African American women played in the various informal performance networks that developed prior to the Civil War, nor is there adequate documentation of women's participation in and contributions to religious rituals, another probable outlet for black female dramatic creativity. Regardless of our inability to provide a comprehensive account for African American women's innovations in performance style before 1870 (beyond a few preachers), we can fairly confidently assert that they involved themselves, in some manner, in the activities that would form the nation's burgeoning popular culture markets that began to concretize and expand after the Civil War. Sustained printed reference to black women in the professional theater emerges during the late nineteenth century, coinciding with the minstrel craze's crest that lasted approximately from 1848 to 1890. Hence, there are connections between mass popular culture's overpowering expansion, Sambo entertainment, and black women's recorded arrival on the national stage.

To unravel how these trends intersect, we consider that minstrelsy triggered a still-present split along racial lines in venues for entertainment that assume black culture. Increasingly over this fifty-year period, two prominent performance spheres faced each other and then diverged: black theater for mostly black viewers and black entertainment for white patrons (with perhaps a segregated section for some black spectators, but the black viewer is not factored in as significant enough to dictate tastes).[3] The latter arena served as a selling floor, where black peculiarity was peddled to the ticket purchaser, and the former became something of a sanctuary, where inhibitions might be released and challenges could be lobbed at wretched social conditions. I note that, while these home arenas thrived outside of commercial channels somewhat, their locations were only marginally sheltered against marketplace intrusion as potential theft constantly threatened their integrity, and some black promoters were more than pleased to model their shows after mainstream norms in order to boost receipts. In spite of their vulnerability, there were times when black performers gathered and enjoyed song, dance and drama beyond the specular light of dominating eyes. Further subdivisions played out in the twentieth century, which generated a competitive local black theater movement that was and is today often steered by black visionaries who do not view profit-making as the bottom line, subsisting instead on donations, funding, and modest gifts. On the opposite pole, Broadway reigns over America's standard live theatrical entertainment, a hegemony that is orchestrated by corporate-like machinery that caters to an affluent white audience who can pay hundreds of dollars for a single show. To these divergent contemporary avenues, we add one further development: a dollar-centered black theater network of traveling fare that attracts a black working-and lower-middle-class clientele.

Conceding that predominately black venues are not monolithic, nor have they remained free entirely from the floating racism and sexism found on the mainstream stage, we can still delineate them from conventional theater, especially in terms of the relationship between the viewer and the mobile field. Specifically, the attendees enjoy an entitlement because their vocal and physical commentary enhances the performance, a key interchange that becomes integral to the form itself. Look at the Apollo Theater in Harlem, for example. The audience's "back sass" determines a piece's success. Under this dispersal of authority that flows easily between the contrivance and the patron, criticism is immediate and rests in the crowd's hands, not those of an appointed official from a periodical or newspaper. This difference alone is sufficient to distinguish between conventional theatrical models that look to an expert's sanction for endorsement and African American theatrical spaces in which a democratic, instantaneous evaluative mechanism operates. In a similar vein, Pawley finds African Americans local, regional artistic conglomerations driven by a desire for freedom and often typified by a relaxed, open, democratic style that encompasses and encourages the maximum verbal and physical participation (312). This quest for liberty through cultural invocation combined with West African ceremonial didacticism engenders a theater that builds upon a propensity to involve, even though it may put the audience—or parts of it—on trial. Another way to define this dynamic is to say that this type of play calls for debate: many voices and views.

While both black noncommercial and black-owned profit-making groups share this formal aspect that empowers and invests those in the stands with the responsibility for determining a piece's merit, these two houses differ in thematic range and aesthetics. Community centers promote oppositional and or re-visionary offerings that tend to be more experimental in form and far-reaching in message, but the profit-geared industry relies on what has prevailed financially: comedies, musicals and formulaic dramas that reinforce spiritual transcendence over social ills. Because there is less emphasis on redressing preexisting racist and sexist images in these black-run commercial vehicles, stereotypic elements, especially in the musicals and comedies, continue to circulate far more frequently than in the other venue.

We observe these diverging strains as early as the 1920s when racial uplift organizations such as the NAACP and Urban League sponsored plays that would elevate, enthuse, and educate black people, particularly the youth just as revenue-based houses like Theatre Owners Booking Agency (TOBA) emerged simultaneously and made no secret of the fact that they intended to accumulate as much capital as possible. These high-profile promoters were less likely to censure uncomplimentary displays although they too paid attention to and eliminated some overly fawning or licentious characterizations. Still around today, this black commercial circuit supplies a rich pipeline of gospel plays, comedies, musicals and light drama, what Henry Louis Gates has labeled disparagingly "the chitlin circuit."[4] Of the three outlets, African American female playwrights have had more luck producing their work in noncommercial theaters within black communities.

Much has been written about the manner in which white entertainment has so grossly distorted and exploited black images. Loften Mitchell has observed that, in general, American theater centers on fantasies and wish fulfillment (185). One of these projections that the dominant culture barely attempts to mask is that black people, "remain unimprovable, static and timeless" (Snead, *White Screens* 139), and that black women come across as "eternal, unchanging, unchangeable" (Snead, *White Screens* 3). The implication is that American culture, including its fine arts, functions as a containment field to resist the push for independence by actual black women. "She" has to be refigured through representation continually in order to root her to prescribed psycho-social geographic locations. This conditioning is imprinted through the ritualized performance of her alleged contentment at being fixed in time and also through a constant dramatization of what would happen if she moves off the squares designated for her.

Mammy and Sapphire are the projections that have been most comforting to the nation's imagination, either a black woman who is nurturing, plump and asexual, or her antithesis, the overly sexual, sometimes castrating Sapphire, who lives for the hunt and her voracious appetites. Both are inclined to impulsiveness and a non-reflective, unmediated connection to the world and experience, not an intellectual in the bunch (Hatch, Introduction 13). Both figures sing, dance, shout, and further insinuate their way into the audience's emotional core by acting out prescriptively an unspoken nostalgia for an irresponsible, uncomplicated life, where a master's higher power is always on the scene to correct any snafus, wrong turns, or social gaffes. In essence, as first set by the minstrel in drag, her presence on the boards mirrors that of a charmed, colorful early adolescence. This overarching social role is anchored by the repetitive, ignominious delegation of black actresses to maid or temptress/prostitute and is further ensconced by their absence from leading roles that move beyond the mundane, an invisibility that results in "...the idea that blacks belong in positions of obscurity and dependence" (Snead, *White Screens* 6). Because black selves have been marginalized by, but contained within, a relentless national fantasy, African American playwrights have taken on the responsibility of creating roles that can accommodate a more lush, ridged and often politicized black subject, while conceiving alternative theatrical forms in which these "beings" can thrive and be fully and freely engaged. As David Krasner points out, "...black theatre evolved as a reappropriation and redefinition of white-controlled theatrical images [including those that are absent] of African-Americans" (*Resistance* 15).

In spite of the impediments that block African American women's access to the playhouse: restrictive formal choices, imminent industrial packaging, and far-reaching, objectifying, free-floating racial and gender pre-classification, African American women writers entered the workspace anyway, knowing that the "...American theater was just not ready for black women to write plays" (Hine and Thompson 236). The manner in which black women had been scripted first by minstrelsy, then by the Uncle Tom shows and later down the line by vaudeville, Broadway, and film could have intimidated and discouraged inventiveness, but it had the opposite effect. Artists pivoted off this wall of dehumanization to improvise novel constructs that could reflect their perspectives on world events and developments that impacted on black folks' everyday existence. Accordingly, African American women experimented with dramatic structure in order to establish choices that could reflect their actual historical circumstance and their dream to expand the reflective acreage of the American stage to accommodate them. Partially in response to these obstacles erected by the mainstream and partially stimulated by an admiration for the patterns of black vernacular modes, especially rhythmic music, these female playwrights construct fields where the performers traverse various positionalities, sometimes passing through different facets of one persona and, at other times, migrating through several selves with little orienting guidance from the dialogue. Borrowing from Hatch and Shine (*1935–Today* 492), I call this aspect of African American female theater "quick-change artistry," signifying on the manner in which African American women playwrights create subjects that often slip on many coats, bundling up when the audience is cold but shedding layers as the rituals move closer to home. Hence, the performance platform is transformed into several daises, a trait that this tradition shares with the multi-ring circus, but the design is not meant to astonish or delight but to inform, teach, and break down facile acquisition. In this tradition, culture is not an object to be consumed but becomes a product that is in continual formation as the audience should shape it as well with its own assortment of tools: lively verbal commentary, shout outs, and other animated methods like toe-tapping, head movement, and snaps.

Not an authentic or sealed site, noncommercial African American theater is striated by the confluence of thematic revision that embraces colliding allusions combined with formal properties that stimulate the participants by eroding the division between performance and audience, a trait that critic Kimberly Benston recognizes distinguishes black theater: "...a shift from drama—the spectacle observed—to ritual—the event which dissolves traditional divisions between actor and spectator, between self and other" ("The Aesthetic" 63). This thematic multidimensionality and the inclusiveness and ceremonial expanse of the conveyance place non-profit black theater in contrast to the traditional Western dramatic style that builds upon acts, scenes, and curtains that serve to divide the play into a text that is palatable and consumable (Dickerson, "A Womanist Theater" 118). The history, then, of black drama in general and that of black women in particular is also the story of how a practice that aims for the greatest involvement from its attendees becomes transformed into and resists dominant normalization. So, in lieu of converging on stereotypes, we target the manner in which this looming normalization impacts on the tradition's formal and thematic contours. What happens, for instance, to the improvisational, often highly individualized (signature) but staunchly communal codes that local African American performance depends on when it is redesigned to fit a more segmented and regimented theatrical space? What is lost, what remains, what resists, and what submits, and how does this process reflect on both interior and colonial penetrable sites?

To explore these queries in greater depth, I turn to William Wells Brown's influential nineteenth-century play (1858), *The Escape; or, A Leap for Freedom*, a work set before the Civil War. Melinda, a slave woman who must flee for her life, comments, "'Oh, how I would that those who think the slave incapable of the finer feelings, could only see our hearts, and learn our thoughts,—thoughts that we dare not utter in the presence of our masters!'" (41). On the surface, these lines purport that African American drama will hinge on revelation, a display of private sentiments and insights, prime pickings for eager markets. Drawing a parallel between Melinda's situation and that of the playwright, it would appear that to construct a black humanity for the American state, the artist must bare black souls, but Brown eludes this mandate because he anticipates that his audience will be a mixed group, some sympathetic and others not, some in line with slavery's philosophy and some runaways themselves. Thus several tiers of intimacy are encoded into the script. We may even go so far as to argue that the line "thoughts that we dare not utter in the presence of our masters" refers not only to the actor who portrays the slave owner but to certain aspects of the American stage that threaten to imprison through formal regulation the drama itself. To the black writer who quests after open communication and democratic ritual, the prevailing Western theatrical space is off-putting, controlling, confining yet altogether viable because it can be redesigned to fit aims other than those that it professes. So Melinda's words may be loosely decoded to mean "I wish I could reveal my innermost thoughts, but the time is not conducive to full disclosure and will not be until social inequalities are replaced by more egalitarian conditions. In the meantime, however, I can reveal these desires under a utopian list's protective guise." Melinda's dream, spoken out loud, is analogous to African American drama at large for it, too, seizes on a performance space where strong yearnings for freedom can be alluded to—held in utopian escrow—while the business of resistance and submission play out, forcing the piece to travel and look beyond the imaginings of its current historical moment (sometimes progressing by going back). I should add that these spun voyages are rarely linear and prefer to zigzag and cloak themselves to shield the vulnerable dreams that comprise the vision's core.

So, African American theater is a place where red herrings abound, where the act of doing is surrounded by feints and diversions that lead rapacious consumers astray. While diverting imperial intrusion, these same treatments inscribe subtextual instructions, guides, and meanings. Racial stereotypes are often a crucial part of this oscillating dramatic design, as ofttimes they are converted into critical tools. On the one hand, they sparkle as the master's ultimate fetish collection, but, on the other, their polarities can be deflected to shed light on their creator instead of on the object that they seek to imprison. African American women playwrights are exceptionally adroit at nodding to what has been made of them while they explore various facets of life from their unique position as spectacle and unimagined (unread) spectator. This rotation provides room for the artist to tunnel inside preexisting dramatic conveyances to create pocketed platforms, shifting them on sub-levels that become part of the performance space. What we find is that like Brown's Melinda, African American female dramatists' characters speak and communicate in overlapping aesthetics, with sublime nuance and deflection sewn into their utterances and physical gestures. The overall impact of this multi-spectral reach is embedded theatrical fields where selves rather than a self are implanted in characterization (if we can still call it that). Thus, the fulcrum point is shifted away from a single limelight on a prime role and toward destabilization: stimulating the audience to grow conscious of the numerous facets that construct subjects and the conditions that the subjects inhabit at various moments. Revolving the paradigm in this manner allows for fresh and unexpected plot twists, sightings, and events. Stereotypes engage with each other and with subjects; symbols encounter aesthetic poses; groupings of female characters take on systemic violence, even the very violence of the entertainment industry from which they materialize.

This marbled, swirling dynamic requires an equally sensitive critical approach. Correspondingly, I suggest that we foreground two assumptions. The first is that, when we assess plays written by black writers that have become acclaimed hits and have merited national attention, we consider that in many instances these works speak to an idealized audience/participant group. So, while the drama unfolds before spectators of various ethnic and racial backgrounds, the playwright often embeds a more streamlined group of imaginary "in-house" celebrants within the play's textual boundaries, creating an effect whereby the work speaks in multiple frequencies.[5] On one level, these pieces address a broadly defined kinship group, and, on another, they manipulate the traditional audience that absorbs the product/display rather than augmenting it. The second point is that, even though there is far less documentation on performances that are situated and produced within predominately black communal institutions, critics should read back through the contemporary moment to participate in and study artistry that continues to be initiated by African Americans for primarily African American groups.

Doing so will allow reconstructive glimpses into how these rituals signify historically, a labor that is crucial to an understanding of what constitutes black theater and, by extension, large components of American culture. "In-house" sites that remain active and influence the African American dramatic tradition are black churches that routinely mount Sunday School pageants and religious plays; predominantly black colleges that inspire new drama and revamp old scripts; black clubs like sororities and fraternities that sponsor amateur skits and variety shows to raise funds for charitable services; and elementary and secondary schools that showcase entertaining educational pieces about black history. Drill teams, double-dutch rope jumpers, marching bands, step shows, stump speeches, basement soul train lines, debate clubs (formal and informal), fashion shows, house parties, outdoor sports and countless other sources drive and shape black styles and aesthetics as well, a collection of activities that provide the material that black playwrights blend into their own often avant-garde models.

From this list of possible sources and inspirations, it becomes clear that African American drama is a hybrid, bringing in various innovative media under one roof. So, noncommercial African American theater, for the most part, does not settle into an easy groove but draws its energy from bouncing assorted topical and formal choices off each other, strumming them as one would toy with a musical instrument. African American women playwrights adhere to this experimentation and volatility, as they, more than male dramatists, fall into quick-change modes. I further suggest that in the case of the women's tradition, this impulse to transform follows an approach and retreat pattern, a pulling away as the action is maneuvered toward the audience. This seemingly paradoxical shifting is perplexing, for why would these female bards invite and repel the viewer, a pattern which is akin to a seductive dance? This formal structure that runs through much of the tradition, I believe, reveals an inherent distrust of the genre, even though—for whatever reason—the artist has selected it over other options. It also tells a great deal about how the composer perceives her audience, never sure how strong the intimate circle will be, never entirely convinced that her product can be properly read because of the weighty and prevalent circulating images, representations, and narratives that have scripted previously the black female presence as "eternal, timeless and unchanging."

To delve further into this conundrum, we have to consider minstrelsy's impact on American culture. When white actors drew on burnt cork, they created a fictional Sambo as mediating identification. This symbolic mask beckoned the audience and became a way for the viewer to orient and judge his world. Blackface became something of a perverse mirror that could reflect for the attendee the qualities in himself that he knew he possessed and enjoyed but tried his best to hide in public. The darky was all the things that the audience did or imagined doing in the dark. In the United States, these taboos became racialized, which is why racial profiles run rampant and continue to validate the structure that holds contemporary America's social schema in place. Furthermore, because these minstrels never fully represented material black bodies, they were inexpensive, and it was easier for the general American consumer with only a few cents admission to own them. In essence, Sambo could be purchased and become anybody's best pal, a cultural singularity that, in many ways, extended another form of slavery (representational and symbolic) well into the twentieth century.

This made-up, racially charged clown was never intended to encase or project a self-governing persona. When black women came to the national stage en masse during the 1870s and thereafter, they broke the identificatory hold between spectators (mostly white males) and minstrels (mostly white males in colors) that epitomizes a hollow receptacle for relieving anxiety-producing thoughts, opinions, and yearnings. The black female stage presence that came first in the form of dancers, singers, and comediennes interrupted this process because it called for the differences between viewer (we assume a dominant white male gaze) and cultural product to outweigh the commonalties. Here was a new exhibiting body that looked nothing like the men in drag who had played her for years. Sambo and his darky band were old acquaintances, but these new creatures were as unfathomable as a locked ornate box. There simply was no place for the typical minstrel connoisseur to hang or attach versions of his warring selves on the vibrant and energetic black female form. Rather than bonding with her as a black, albeit inferior, twin brother, they found themselves fascinated by her exoticism.

Exoticism categorizes an appealing strangeness that resides outside and beyond the domestic sphere. Impulsively, we could label exoticism as sexual energy that destabilizes a previously safe space but that relays only part of the story. When black female performers dared to sashay on stage without a minstrel veil, they instantiated a public self who was both other and "already full," a force that had to be contended with like the face-off of the tango or the black bottom's whirling motion. In this move away from a simple collapse between minstrel and unsanctioned (by the state) but highly pleasurable desire, a black womanly presence forced a theatrical model where the object could no longer be assumed or completely consumed without mediation (recognition of difference). This shift opened up performance space. In other words, because of black women's novelty and unassailable internal dynamism, the traditional minstrel-fed white viewer was literally and metaphorically pushed back from the viewing field, and, as a result, all kinds of activity could enter the relationship between act and audience from contemplation to longing, to appraisal, to high anxiety, to lust, engagements beyond minstrelsy's capabilities. Reflection (no matter how base) was ushered into the rapidly expanding American public sphere: what (if not who) were these black women?

Black female performers attempted to capitalize on this novelty by controlling this exotic/erotic power. Unfortunately, history has shown us that these pains were largely transitory as their innovations were quickly engulfed by capital markets, markets that did not channel wealth to the many black female dancers, singers and comediennes who labored at the task. So while this surfacing black female visibility and physicality radically transformed the American stage, reversing its polarities from acting out fantasy to creating it, the material condition of black women was not improved significantly by the expanding entertainment business. In fact, by the mid-1920s, the rigid, over-processed chorus line had all but nullified the black female performer's improvisational or circular communicative designs.[6] The selling floor had suppressed the multifarious, bustling power of black female expression.

So, even though the addition of black women to the American stage caused a revolution in what the theater, especially its popular strain, could do, in hindsight, we realize that the mere addition of darker women to commercial entertaining circuits would not enhance African American civic, economic and social autonomy. Instead, it would carve out new but distinct holding cells. If this major shift had been allowed to follow a course that granted black female entertainers more control over how their talent would be represented, then things might have turned out differently. Unfortunately, as black women entered the American theater, segregation as a standard was gaining in strength and popularity, which led to a cultural appropriation that James Snead has deemed "exclusionary emulation": "…the power and trappings of black culture are initiated while at the same time their black originators are segregated away and kept at a distance" (*White Screen* 60). Under this system, raw talent is tapped and then siphoned off to satisfy trade requisitions. So, those who actually design steps, songs, arrangements and styles are disconnected quickly from their inventions as middlemen and polishers reconstruct and pare down "the original" in order to peddle it. In this manner, black female energy (and certainly that of other underrepresented groups) fed vaudeville, Broadway fanfare, and Uptown nightspots that featured yellow chorus girls and sultry black singers but barred black patronage. Ironically, African American women writers, directors, and artistic visionaries were not invited to participate in this scene either, even though they stoked its vitality, nor did these sites acknowledge, understand, or esteem the manner in which African American women in the audience enliven and sculpt black performances with their critical feedback.

As uplift intellectuals witnessed "exclusionary emulation" intensifying during the early twentieth century, they realized that America's theater would not do black people justice; therefore, they would have to establish their own traditions and institutions. So there was an implicit understanding that even though the national arena had been corrupted by racism, sexism and vulgar trade, the fine arts held potential, that it was not the whole of the discipline that caused the trouble but the manner in which certain white male fantasies had gained economic and representational supremacy. Suffocated, frustrated, and denigrated by conventional vehicles, black artists and leaders set out to recover a time where those in the stands could join in, where the lushness and precision of black dance did not feel chained, where music, drama, and comedy did not have to be segmented into discrete portions. Subdivisions such as musical, drama or comedy made little sense in regard to the more fluid African American folk forms like storytelling and testimonials that move in ringed fashion. Artists from this early period up to the contemporary moment began to redraw the boundaries by applying vernacular-based motifs to their work, a gradual transformation with many tributaries inscribed along the way.

The quick-change modes that I have mentioned are a means to resist cultural imperialism, especially when this methodology is applied to formal as well as thematic aspects. For instance, incorporating musical genres has become a mainstay for African American female playwrights to the extent that, according to Margaret Wilkerson's keen observation, when black music with its complex rhythms and reliance on improvisation exists in a play, the very notion of text is changed and becomes only marginally useful ("Music as Metaphor" 74). Serving as more than mere background to the dialogue, black music often commands a pivotal role that authorizes speech, not just reinforces it. Simply put, African American women playwrights refuse to privilege language over music and other communicative channels that include dance and costuming. Music's encroachment on the script crops up repeatedly across this tradition as numerous and various creations have a broader range because they submit to musical patterns and hold them against what is uttered and exhibited on stage, an extra layer that insists on a dialogue between modes. Spirituals, ragtime, blues, jazz, and funk riffs greet each other while they also look down onto the panorama below as a puppet master would follow her handiwork. When activated, these musical metatexts transform the drama from immediately accessible realism, opting instead to evoke lived experience by pricking the audience's memories, especially those triggered by familiar sounds. Combining this reliance on music with the exotic "otherness" of black female physicality, African American female dramatists guide the room toward contemplation through a dynamic repartee between stage and audience. Superseding minstrelsy's lure, easy and eager grasping through identification, the African American female writer prepares a collation that is as textured as possible.

Another explanation as to why African American women playwrights adopt flexible, even prickly, structural conveyances proceeds from the rationale that black invention, in its various guises, precedes its appropriation: forces initiate black play long before monetary gain or the need to redress negative images became chief impetuses. We ponder, for instance, why those Africans paused to fete in the eighteenth century in spite of overwhelmingly dire circumstances. Why did African American women continued to compose stage pieces throughout the twentieth century with little hope that they would reach production beyond, perhaps, a limited run at a local library, church, school, or club? (Perkins 4) Critics have argued that this faith stems from a connection between entertainment and learning in West African practices. Terry-Morgan observes that, "the preferred style of blending a didactic purpose with entertainment values is a long-standing tradition in the history of African-American dramatic art" (677), a slant that may stem from the storytelling circles that Africans reintroduced in North America on plantations and in the church during testimonial hour. Acting out or punctuating a lesson to be passed from mouth to mouth ensured that the participants would remember the message and be more inclined to repeat it, and a vibrant raconteur could gain favor with a cherished style and charisma. The most respected performers could incorporate history, myth, literature, symbols, dreams and inspiration (Dickerson, "A Womanist Theater" 111). Improvisation, dexterity, and breadth of reach are the standards for this sport as the artiste must invent constantly and rapidly to demonstrate her worth.

The idea that pedagogy and theater are often one and the same underpins black dramatic traditions, and it explains why dominant and communal strains of American live art have diverged so deeply. More often than not, mainstream directors and producers have ignored this vital component of African American theater, peeling off and discarding it. Evidence is readily available. One need only recognize how African American religious and educational centers have sustained black drama, especially around the turn of the century leading up to World War II. During this period, play construction by African American women was fairly prolific. Sunday school teachers, drama and elocution coaches, uplift intellectuals, anthropologists, community activists, clubwomen and musicologists heeded the call and seized the pen to elevate the race through cultural/educational intervention. In tandem with these goals, *Crisis* and *Opportunity* magazines held contests that encouraged black artistry in several fields, spurring on a renaissance in play composition by black writers that was already underfoot at the Dunbar School in Washington, D.C., and across the nation at various black colleges and universities and at public libraries and social clubs.[7] Furthermore, the black church was known for mounting Christmas and Easter pageants that featured young children, teaching them religious doctrine assuredly but also instilling in them the confidence and masking skills that would facilitate their survival. In black folk culture, imprinting is not considered enlightening; rather, learning develops from friction, dialogue and interaction. When mainstream commercial channels tapped African America's folk base, they eliminated this schooling function because it conflicted with the market's demands. As Snead observes, in the modern West we have a cultural hierarchy that draws from its common/everyday foundation and repeatedly codifies its yield. In the contemporary moment, Broadway extracts talent from street theater (much of it urban and African American inflected) just as during the first half of the twentieth century it siphoned off routines, gimmicks, moves and actual bodies from both roving and established black theater companies such as the Lafayette Players and the American Negro Theater. Similarly, during the turn of the century, vaudeville and broad musicals reached back to Harlem and other major city cabarets for fuel, sites which, in turn, borrowed from backwoods juke joints and shouting shanties that sampled liberally from rural areas. These local spots were not pure factories either but depended on sub-group local creativity that spliced dance moves with singing, oratory (especially down-beat recitative styles), comedy and instrumentals.

A reliance on music, sagacity, and pleas for democracy are traits that both African American men and women share when it comes to composing drama, but gender differences arise in the relationship between the female artist and the female subjects that she constructs. African American women playwrights are archly aware that in Western entertainment, the black female body often registers as a text that dominates over black female writing and/or dialogue, so pieces composed by African American women feature more complicated and assorted roles for black actresses and performers, artistic vehicles that insist that both body and speech generate meaning (alongside the musical and choreographic text). Intellectuals have debated frequently how and what the female body in general can signify. One theorizes that "the female body, always present in the theater, is in fact absent because it is the bearer of a desire which is not hers.... The erotic theatrical language is always male, even when it is totally impregnated by female forms" (Maraini 153). Maraini posits that public displays of the female physique are circumscribed by male constructs because that feminine form undulates and answers to a sexual auction that supplies men's needs, one that does not recognize women's utterances, gestures, or attitudes beyond those regulated by a masculinist order. Honor Ford-Smith extends this line of argumentation and compares traditional theater's mechanism in relation to female bodies to science's penchant for objective reality (193). In her view, the theater has become a discipline complete with intricate protocols that process elements that appear chaotic into more recognizable and systematized data. Once these catalogued bits have been registered, anything that falls outside of the systemization can then be corralled back within its borders through association. What happens in the round, then, is that circulating types become akin to scientific categories. For black women, this means that Mammy and Sapphire (perhaps the repressed middle-class lady, Topsy, and the tragic mulatto as well) share the spotlight with the black female actors/bodies that perform: body type alone is sufficient to relegate an actress to one of these "objective" holding pens. Therefore, if the one who takes on Mama Lena Younger from Hansberry's *Raisin in the Sun* looks like Mammy, then the dominant theater apparatus makes it so, and if Shange's feisty *colored girls who considered suicide* resemble Sapphire, then they too are yoked facilely under that designation.

Other scholars are more optimistic that the female body can reform the theater. Ford-Smith views the traditional realistic play as a means to further silence women, but she predicts that women artists and performers will locate ways to upset and challenge dramatic form, to end its current disciplining repression (193). Sue-Ellen Case claims that the female body on public display is subversive because her implied sexuality "brings disorder to the social body" (20). Judith Butler, inspired by Beauvoir, situates this depolarizing energy in the fact that the body dramatizes and reproduces an historical situation (272). Whether the disorder or subversion stems from a sexual subtext or history's awakening at the behest of the body's physical posture, gesture, and costuming, the female body in performance is, to these scholars, a polyvalent site, not a mere reflection of male wishes. Following this logic, feminists argue that skilled execution combined with women's writing and directing can lead to a re-appropriation of the auditorium, forcing it to reflect women's designs and yearnings.

The genre may be transformed only after the female form/role has been recast as a subject in lieu of an object. According to Forte, that idealized female subject would also "…[clash] in dissonance with its patriarchal text, challenging the very fabric of representation by refusing that text and posing new multiple texts grounded in real women's experience and sexuality" ("Women's Performance Art" 254). To foster competition over the female body's signification is the first step toward liberating the theater from its male-fantasy-based core. And, this conflict has to be reflected on stage to indicate difference from the conventional. If this departure is too subtle and therefore undetectable, then it may collapse into a patriarchal offering because, according to Maraini's warning, male desire is so entrenched in modern culture that it finds ways to envelop even those subversive efforts scored by women. So the device that brackets a departure from the norm may require underscoring. In this vein, Elin Diamond points out that Brecht's alienation effect can be adapted as a feminist tool to "resist fetishization" and establish "a position for the female spectator" ("Brechtian Theory" 83). A breaking moment and sign that doubles back on what has become naturalized and reveals, therefore, the artistic vessel's artificiality can be deployed by women who wish to divert the theater away from its propensity to regulate female difference.

These concerns apply to the black female dramatic tradition in several key ways. African American women playwrights, including those from the nineteenth century, grapple with whether women can reclaim the public sphere and make it speak through, to, and for them. Certainly Brecht's proposition that the theater has to be fractured and reexamined so that the audience can perceive how it factorizes experience coincides with the goals that African American dramatists have set, a practice of trial and transformation that is necessitated by the historical circumstance that when African American women arrived on the national stage in the last three decades of the 1800s, their roles had been limited largely to no more than three or four recognizable types.[8] These stock characters had been enacted first by white men in drag and blackface and later by black men and white women. Dislodging this widespread mocking subjugation of black female signification demanded not only charged, rupturing moments but also alternative images, dialogue and physical suites that could showcase a complex and sovereign African American female subjectivity.

In spite of the daunting task at hand to redress an entire series of misconceptions that reside, unfortunately, close to the nation's psychological center, African American women script writers have incorporated, since the nineteenth century, the same strategies that Case and Butler have recently proposed: figuring the body to reflect history and featuring a women-authored sexuality, or more precisely sensuality, to complicate traditional Western dramatic form and to confound the viewer's grounded expectations. Harnessing the play so that it can point to alternative interpretations of the past and present that may contradict very common histories and exploring female erotic energy to see if its heat can break apart and reset the theater into a site where female desire is conceivable are strategies that African American women artists turn to repeatedly as this study will reveal.

Venue selection becomes pivotal too for African American dramatists. After desegregation, choosing a performance's operational base becomes a political act (before segregation ended, this decision was dictated by legal and informal policy). In the contemporary moment, when the playwright locates her platform in black communities where churches, social and service clubs, schools, correctional institutions, and libraries launch shows, she finds, more often, that she is at liberty to create a panoply of substantial and complex roles and may build on topics drawn from an assortment of referents including the Bible, myths, and chronicles. Folk heroes (Harriet Tubman is a favorite), urban sophisticates, rebellious anarchists, tricksters, lovers, ceremonial leaders, malcontents, and a whole slew of vigorous, multi-dimensional subjects parry and dally in front of delighted, empowered and vocal fellow ritual-makers, who are not afraid to project their opinions and enter into the performance space with their personalized moves.

While certainly energizing, this preference for the local arena results in trade-offs because newspapers and periodical reviewers with greater subscription rates rarely visit these productions, a reality which restricts the piece's influence. Then again, it is possible today for African American women to address directly Western forces in the very locales that have assisted in engendering and extending race-and gender-based oppression. With a corrective mission in mind, the bard may opt for national or international circulation and mostly mainstream houses in addition to or in place of the community forum. Of course, as in the first alternative, this one also entails sacrifice as the core audience (from black communities) that supplies so much of the fuel and texture to live black art may be lost or muted, resulting in offerings that are less able to defy commoditization. Post-desegregation, location selection reflects more on who the writer places as her implied viewer, what overarching messages she hopes to transmit, and how her play's formal properties imbue her general artistic strategy. Therefore, by the twenty-first century, site preference carries the added burden of naming the writer's politics (whether the playwright prefers it or not).

The African American play writing tradition hovers around multiple, implied platforms and both retreats from and approaches the very social chambers that it builds; furthermore, the subjects travel and seldom cohere into unified selves although subjectivity as a concept is confirmed. It holds as well that this body of work does not rest on disclosure or coming to a conclusion as is the case with conventional Western drama but rests on limited (temporal and physical) dreamscapes of what a black self could be if it had not been trapped by the conditions of modern life that render that self invisible. Similar to briefly raised daises that feature ghostly projections of parallel utopian worlds, the black female subject is alluded to or gestured toward and then removed. Highly self-conscious, almost intrinsically absurdist, African American female drama takes the form's dishonesty as a given and brackets and highlights that quality with sustained moments of stepping out of the shadows, what Brecht would call pointing to the box. Building in the mode of imagistic fissures that slip around and call to mind what can be read by the audience as they take their seats and what they may well learn to read as the visual and aural novelties develop on stage, African American female playwrights spring off and between the present, the absent, the hoped for, and those ambient specters (like Mammy) that wait invariably in the wings for their turn to shine. Needless to say, this handling of imaginative space highlights bustling, exaggerated, often speedy, new world nomads, an apt metaphor that fits many black women's so-called real existence, dashing from location to role, switching approaches and guises according to the surroundings.

While numerous precursors have stimulated African American female drama, two sources stand out: minstrelsy and William Wells Brown's *The Escape* (1858). Brown's piece impressed Pauline Hopkins, a late nineteenth- and early twentieth-century playwright, novelist, short story, and nonfiction writer from Boston, who began her career after winning a essay contest sponsored by Brown. Her *Peculiar Sam, or The Underground Railroad, A Musical Drama in Four Acts* (1879) revises Brown's ingenious dramatic-comedy about escaping slaves and their quest to be recognized as Americans and as human beings. In the foreword to his piece, Brown admits, "This play was written for my own amusement, and not with the remotest thought that it would ever be seen by the public eye. I read it privately, however, to a circle of my friends" (37). That black Americans seek amusement evidences that their capacity far exceeds that scripted by the physical economy of slavery that defines them as chattel. Reading rests on the presupposition that the recipient is refined enough to appreciate a genre that works on a cerebral level, not on mere visual and aural stimulation. Hence with his booklet/play Brown substantiates that black people can think and be delighted simultaneously. Hopkins follows Brown's lead and writes musical dramas in the late 1870s for an implied warm circle that shares in her view that black citizens had earned the right to full inclusion; however, in contrast to Brown, she had the temerity to prepare her work for the popular market. She wanted to have it all: a profitable, portable piece and one that uplifted the black community. Then again, the times dictated that, to accomplish this ambitious feat, Hopkins would have to contend with minstrelsy, at that moment, the nation's most galvanizing and espoused live art form.

Blackface saturated American culture in the mid-nineteenth century so deeply—securing the right to authenticate racial representation—that an artist who painted anything but all-white scenarios encountered, without question, this monolith. Minstrelsy branches out from the ballad and comic operas that ran earlier in the nineteenth century, genres that introduced musical and dance numbers that could be shuffled and mixed (Southern xiii). To this basic template, entertainers added a variety of rapid-fire, kinetic presentations that mirrored presumably certified black folk practices: songs, jigs, walk-arounds, skits, horrendously garish costuming and tortured dialogue. These practices became props that distorted but steered black creativity into nothing more than white-owned fantasies of teetering proportions. Typical shows at mid-century starred seventeen to a company including the interlocutor and the end men, Bones and Tambo, all in blackface with grotesque, enlarged lips (Sampson 2–3). "The comic black wench [often Mammy], originally played by white men [then black], was also a staple of the minstrel show, thus establishing the first black female stereotypes" (Peterson, *Early Playwrights* 5). By the end of the century, white women had joined the party and smeared on burnt cork and donned curly wigs to delight the consumer with renditions of "down home black gals" (ladies being too feminine and adult a description).

In order to reach America's platform in 1878, Hopkins had to confront minstrelsy. So she signified on it, borrowing parts from it to make her musical palatable and recognizable, therefore, viable, while her uplift goals drove her to modify it sharply. Setting out to revise the Sambo exhibition as radically as she could without offending those who would purchase a ticket, a mixed audience that could easily turn violent and sullen, Hopkins spliced the formal aspects of minstrelsy and its free-wheeling, rapid pace with the thematic lessons found in Brown's play, a synthesis that planted leaping for liberty as her ever-present trope. On top of that twist away from but staying within a variety show's boundaries, the dramatist centered both African American female and male trickster figures with highjinks and capers, scenes that recall an underlying racial progressivism, even as the characters vamp and prance before the audience. She aimed to balance out both the stabilizing message that black bands have to labor together to attain civil rights against another bit of advice: that pleasure elicited by music, comedy and dance is warranted and a chief reason why liberating enterprise should exist. Siphoning off the corked-up buffoon's intense physical mobility and animated delivery, Hopkins mines it to supply her own artistic revelation that debunks the non-thinking darky motif, reworking both male and female stereotypes. Of special interest to this study is the manner in which she treats her female figures, deconstructing Mammy and the Tragic Mulatto with a third element: an empowered female rogue who, "plays to and for her own amusement."

Perhaps the greatest innovation of this romping musical is that it sparks a sexy charge. Frisky and sassy, provocative and flirtatious, Hopkins's *Peculiar Sam* hinges on courtships rituals and the sensually permeated interplay between various wooing couples; even the elderly are in pursuit of a partner. This underscoring matte is in direct contrast to the minstrel text that features disagreeable, castrating black females and foppish, incompetent males. If minstrelsy subverts black-on-black love, Hopkins's vehicle celebrates it, is steered by it. Here the audience encounters something that was and still is fairly novel to the American stage: black bodies whose delight springs from their own quest for intimacy, not the grotesquely displaced erotic desire of the minstrel tradition where the most attractive object on the stage is a chicken or a watermelon.

I can not overemphasize how vital this moment is to America's cultural development. After African American female performers and writers reached the theater, carrying with them sensual panache, white men in drag no longer had the same allure. Moreover, historians "…attribute the demise of minstrelsy to women's emergence in popular entertainment" (Watkins 97). Perhaps this claim is a bit premature as minstrelsy continues to color the public sphere, but we can argue that this black womanly visibility began to compete with, sometimes superseding, the older form's penchant for bleeding black desire onto inane markers; instead, these new black female public players returned desire—now more autonomous—back to the site of the black body, mind and spirit. In addition to enhancing and redirecting the theater's erotic polarities and adding a collective advancement theme, Hopkins follows the contours of in-house African American performativity in the sense that she settles on an elastic and improvisational passage to build and sustain a close community while she also pokes fun at the dominant society (especially those post-Civil War reactionaries who were nostalgic for slavery). She maintained this multiplicity by keeping more material on hand than could be offered during any given engagement, thereby enabling her to recombine her segments under an assortment of orders (Shange would adopt this methodology a century later). Illustrating this flexibility, her notations include a book of musical numbers along with the script, making it possible for the director or actors to select unique combinations each night, guided by the audience's and the artists' proclivities. So, dance routines and comic skits could be elaborated on or abbreviated according to the cast's talents and any hints that they receive from the viewers' verbal and nonverbal responses.[9] These conversations between attendee and actor characterize black-community "show rooms" even in our contemporary moment as black people continue to talk back not only to live events but to film as well.[10] In fact, this right to launch an opinion during an actual presentation is not taken as an affront but as part of the group's duty. One of the worst reviews that a show in a home venue (across most of the African Diaspora) can warrant is one where the rafters remain abnormally quiet.

Having established the ground work for a tradition that strives to rectify the gross misrepresentation of black people, especially women, and one that endeavors to educate its viewers and win them over to adopt a progressive posture, Hopkins infuses her heady labor with a fun-filled current. This synthesis of pleasure with uplift imperatives would mark African American entertainment over the next forty years, as much of it incorporates music, dance, and comedy with dramatic elements. Notable works that characterize this frenetic period are the *Creole Show* (1895) that featured Sam Lucas, Bob Cole, Billy Jackson, George Williams, a female chorus, a female interlocutor, and an urban setting; *The Octoroons* (1896) that highlighted black women leads and dancers; *Oriental America* (1896) that revised the musical by combining an operatic slant with the burlesque format (the Hyers Sisters had done this twenty years prior); *Black Patti's Traveling Troubadours*, a roving company that was led by one of the first African American female stars, Sissieretta Jones; A.L.G. Field's *Darkest America* (1896), which dramatized black history from the plantation through Reconstruction on to modern, urban sophistication; and Cole and Johnson's *A Trip to Coontown* (1896), a seminal musical that would set the tone and format for many all-black productions for years to come. (Sampson 5–7, Tanner 39, Woll, *Black Theater* 4–5).

By 1916, we observe a shift in American theater with the advent of the first sponsored race or problem play. Angelina Weld Grimké's *Rachel* replaced light patter with a sustained concentration on racial violence. Furthermore, by this decade, ragtime had unseated plantation tunes; vaudeville had replaced minstrelsy, to some extent; black women now had a permanent place on the stage (chiefly dancing in the chorus); and, most importantly, strong civil rights organizations that upheld black leadership had been established. These organizations would stimulate the arts by funding theatrical productions and literary contests, searching earnestly for serious works that dramatized the social issues that faced African Americans and colored people around the globe. Take as a case in point that "as a result of support from the NAACP, between 1910 and 1930 blacks owned and operated approximately 157 theaters" (Brown-Guillory, *Their Place* 2). These houses staged shows ranging from broad musicals, comedies, classical tragedies, and melodramas to historical pageants.

By the early twentieth century, black comedians had facilitated and molded popular aesthetics as well. Moms Mabley, Della Reese and Josephine Baker (she used comedy to catapult her career) are just a few of the more recognizable humorists. James Hatch reminds us that these artists bolstered America's growing reputation as "the entertainment capital of the world" by providing the material and innovative styles that would feed trendy markets. He further observes that white comics such as Eddie Cantor, Al Jolson and Jerry Lewis borrowed liberally from Bert Williams, Pigmeat Markham, Flournoy Miller, Aubrey Lyles and others (18), just as their black choreographic counterparts like Ethel Williams were heading to Broadway to teach white chorus girls select dance moves (Woll, *Black Theater* 56). Amateur stock companies such as Russell and Owens toured the country, paving the way with printed bills that advertised attractive photographs of company members, promising even more pretty girls on the day of the show (Sampson 13). By 1915, more stationary and professional troupes launched their wares. These companies include The Lafayette Players, The Krigwa Players, and later, the Rose McClendon Players and the American Negro Theater (ANT).

Given this flurry of theatrical activity, we should not perceive of Grimké's *Rachel* (1916) as an anomalous event. As one of many experiments, it would query the many available paths the African American play should take from commercially successful musicals that ran before mixed and all-white audiences to historical pageants that aired in front of black school children to heavy-handed problem plays. Thematically and formally, *Rachel* is a syncopated ride through this field of possibilities, which adheres to quick-change modalities, especially polemical emotional states that act as a prism to portray how modernity has taken up the veil of the ordinary or commonplace to hide its pagan core. *Rachel* was the first production to be backed by the NAACP's drama committee, debuting in New York on March 3, 1916 (Wilkerson, *Nine Plays* xv). This precedent tethered uplift ideology incontrovertibly to the black theater, an association that would further cast the African American female dramatic tradition, just as a strong desire to revise minstrelsy had set it off in one direction during the nineteenth century. The other major development that this bond between the NAACP and *Rachel* solidified is that Washington, D.C., would become the major contributing hub for African American play writing (even though Grimké's piece opened in New York, the drama committee that sponsored it was attached to the D.C. branch of the NAACP). Brown-Guillory confirms that, "Nearly all the early black women playwrights are connected with the Washington D.C. area" (*Their Place* 4). This nucleus's geographical location is significant because it stands in close proximity to the South but also faces the North; District writers were prone to include rural and urban, southern and northern tableaus, providing the tradition with a well-rounded flavor that did not lop off the South as an historical and contemporary field of interest.

By the mid-1920s, the division between mainstream, popular offerings and what were being called problem or race plays conceived by uplift-minded black artists widened to the extent that critics could more securely map out the contours of black self-expression as opposed to American versions of what Stuart Hall would recognize as media-driven alterity. In this case, the intervening talisman (alterity) is the darky who performs a diversionary function to alleviate the threat of insurgent black activism that could force a return to Reconstruction or demand newly designed social and economic restoration programs to rectify the mass exploitation of African Americans. Uplift artists, who were committed to equality, identified the Sambo and other racial straw figures as the enemy, proclaiming that if these images were removed, then white America would have to face and respond to actual dark citizens. Culture became a means to secure this victory because it reflects and sustains deeply-rooted beliefs. If the new play could make the black buffoon appear unnatural and perverse, then it had done its job.

During this period, African American women writers angled their art toward acquiring civil rights and were not seduced by potential profits from the lucrative entertainment business. In fact, not one commercially successful play could then be attributed solely to a black female dramatist, even though some had a hand in creating and maneuvering such pieces to production. Zora Neale Hurston, in particular, aimed for the popular stage but had no luck.[11] So, this period is typified by an odd phenomenon: While actual play writing by African American women increased, the financial compensation for these works decreased as did the dramatists' expectations that they could make a living from their art. African American female playwrights could anticipate recompense from only a few limited sources including donations or patronage, a modest admission fee, and/or payment from literary prize contests sponsored by journals like the *Crisis* and *Opportunity*. This state of affairs explains why there were only six fairly well-publicized productions of works by African American women between 1918 and 1929 (Hatch and Shine, *The Early Period* 132).

In lieu of capital-driven venues, black women dramatists selected "semi-public" sites for a showing of their work. They may have even preferred the familiarity of library basements, church halls, lodges, school auditoriums, and even kitchens, parlors and backyards (Wilkerson, *Introduction* xv) because in these places they could reach readily black women, children and men. Then too, of course, Broadway was not interested in the displays that black women constructed because their work charted such thorny issues as lynching, whether blacks should join American war efforts, and folk culture's role. Domestic concerns were deemed too heavy by Broadway, and the truncated forms that black women selected during this age (mostly one-act installations) did not satisfy the public's thirst for broad, sweeping, segmented, whimsical romps. As Brown-Guillory asserts, "They did not write for a Broadway audience that brought with it monetary remuneration" (*Their Place* 4).

As this was an age of cultural territorial dispute over black creativity, one way to imagine the period between 1916 and World War II is to say that the African American female dramatic tradition limns geographic space and queries what constitutes a safe zone, what is permeable, and what is completely beyond the control of the home community. Hence these works audition turf, searching for the sites that could launch a bid for full African American citizenship. Combining a formidable indictment of social ills with an affirmation that African people and their many cultures will flourish, this span traces everyday resistance to despair and persecution. In these plays, ironing one's favorite dress and/or reading the signs left by tea leaves become rituals that can stave off madness and nihilism. Using this rubric, I examine pieces by Georgia Douglas Johnson, Marita Bonner, Zora Neale Hurston, Eulalie Spence, May Miller, Shirley Graham, and others.

By 1938 the Rose McClendon Players had formed, and two years later The American Negro Theater invigorated the scene, a company that would nurture Alice Childress, a pivotal and leading figure. She would insist on bringing a black female-owned voice to the nation's mainstream cultural houses as she captured the concerns that faced all post-war, civil rights era Americans. Over all else, Childress attacked easy binaries, calling for complexity to rule her mise-en-scène. Love, for example, often resided where the state prohibited it (*Wedding Band)*; class further divided ethnically and racially marked communities but not neatly (*Wine in the Wilderness*); and subalterns including invisible black women often had much to say. Childress examines the American Dream from various angles, making sure to repudiate egregious typecasting while she confirms that many overlooked subjects exist, think, and conspire to pilot their own lives. Often, she dramatizes these concerns by combining music, sound and a more fluid physicality to truly "speechified texts" that assure black actors substantial lines. Because she began her career as an actress, Childress tweaks her script, obliging her cast to emote with subtle, studied movements that mimic the manner in which African Americans dance lively to press on and upward. Returning repeatedly to this early training, Childress, throughout her four-decade play writing career, brings to life black female figures who know how to manage and restructure their environments by using improvisation and keen observation as fundamental tools, an attentiveness that includes knowing how to dispatch powerful sensual and erotic messages to enhance the script, sometimes making speech ironic or superfluous. This crackling dialogue—verbal, sublingual, musical—suffuses Childress's oeuvre and continuously disrupts stark oppositional constructs. The writer also entrusts this cross-fertilizing density with the responsibility to formulate corridors that allow her subjects to make incursions into "white" and "male" territory, raids that will abet them in planting critical questions that, en masse, will lead optimistically to Jim Crow's and sexism's dismantling.

Lorraine Hansberry also mulled over how to dramatize emerging black stories that they had been circulating within home groups but had not yet become perceptible to the white majority. As Margaret Wilkerson points out, Hansberry's more rebellious black female subjects such as Beneatha from *A Raisin in the Sun* and the African dancer who opens *Les Blancs* orbit the text's periphery, framing the dramatic action with a budding Afrocentric and womanist insurgency that places more emphasis on the African cultural remnants in the African American construction ("Diverse Angles"). More precisely, both Beneatha and the dancer resist European cultural imperialism by opting for African-based aesthetics in dress, physical movement, and hair style. Recovering myths, symbols, and even mass social organization from pre-colonial Africa places Hansberry's writing squarely in the modernist tradition because, to her, change and revolution require a—at least a temporary—step back. While Mama Lena Younger and her son, Walter Lee, from *Raisin in the Sun* debate a contemporary dilemma: deciding whether to integrate a white neighborhood, an argument that is rooted in the belief that property ownership can define value, Beneatha, the daughter, dreams about a spiritual bridge that will link Africa and America and accelerate the process that was put in motion by the Middle Passage. That is, she yearns for restorative soulful rituals drawn from her Africa heritage while Mama and Walter Lee trail after hard currency to purchase a business or a residence. What makes *Raisin in the Sun* a tragedy, perhaps, is Hansberry's calling to our attention that Beneatha's spiritual quest cannot be situated in the drama's core and has to be marginalized to make room for "more pressing" Western matters.

Similarly, Adrienne Kennedy searches for the spirit or spirits by returning to African traditions, but, distinct from Hansberry, who implies that these lost moorings will be replenishing and corrective, Kennedy portends that these forces may be wild and uncontainable. In my chapter on Kennedy, I assert that her offerings affirm a clear Afrocentric bent, a characterization of Kennedy's work that has not been commented on nearly enough. On the contrary, the critical majority that treats Kennedy's drama deliberates over colonialism's and racism's psychological impact on the black subject and on how the ensuing fragmentation is borne out in the artist's aesthetics. Certainly, this engrossing study on the internal mechanics of the self in a highly volatile and hostile environment is an important aspect of the playwright's opus, which has been camped under both the absurdist's and deconstructionist's archways. However interesting, unfortunately, this approach has so saturated the critical terrain that other takes on Kennedy's pieces have rarely surfaced and, when they do arise sporadically, they are granted spare follow-up response. Since many reviewers and scholars from the sixties and seventies aligned Kennedy with the absurdists (she studied with Albee and certainly shares some formal aspects with this aesthetic), she has been excluded from the Black Arts Movement and has been painted as a mere fringe member to this widespread school of thought. This classification and misplacement are limiting and regrettable because Kennedy's work frames the absurd as predating the colonial condition as she points her imaginative vector toward West Africa and the Middle Passage, a grounding that many Black Arts Era adherents hold in common with Kennedy. Furthermore, her installations exemplify that rare gift of adroitly projecting a highly individualized associative stream with a keen gaze at national and global conditions. Not mere claustrophobic reflections of middle-class black angst, Kennedy's early offerings, for instance, have far more in common with Amiri Baraka's piercing indictments of Western culture than have been previously recognized.

In addition to the first wave of reviewers, a second generation of deconstructionists and psychoanalytic specialists has taken a great interest in Kennedy, a preoccupation that led to a revival of her work from the late eighties through the mid-nineties. While these probes are certainly more intense and measured than those of the initial respondents, who seem taken up by the mere thought of a black woman delving into experimental form, there is still a greater need to connect these theoretical-driven assessments to the specific historical and cultural frameworks that engender the texts. For instance, I suggest examining further how Kennedy's poststructural proclivities are coupled with what is African-American and female in her plays. The other unfortunate repercussion of the direction that Kennedy scholarship has taken is that while it has stirred a resurgent curiosity about the writer and her art (mostly from the academic community and New York's intellectual tribe), her offerings have not reached the mass black audience for which, most likely, they were conceived. Because "expert" commentary estranged the relationship between black writer and black audience before it could be established, few theatrical homes within black communities recognize that the playwright's issue belongs to them. To restore this contract between audience and artist, the foregone critical terrain has to be adjusted or at least held up to scrutiny. Merely changing the assumptive base and positing that Kennedy does, in fact, belong to the Black Arts Movement, as I do, opens up numerous alternative critical questions. More precisely, I re-categorize Kennedy's plays from fringe theater to black America's eager ambassador/emissary, who transports notes and fragments of experience gained from many voyages over distance and time. Once these postcard plays are collected, they are packaged by Kennedy and sent back to the people who sustained and justified that travel.

I divide Kennedy's artistic body into three periods: early, middle and late. During the early period, she, like Baraka, dismantles the Negro to instruct through negative example which values will sustain liberation struggles. *Funnyhouse of a Negro*, Kennedy's first play, is comparable, then, to Baraka's *The Dutchman*. The second phase positions the black female subject as a spy/detective who must prophetically and consistently decipher her surroundings: "the smoke," as Kennedy calls it. Watching, tracking, unlocking clues, withstanding horrifying epiphanies and atrocities, undergoing enormous, sometimes brutal, physical changes (often against their will), hiding, voice throwing, splitting subjectivity by using "quick-change" artistry, and redressing misconceptions and untruths without offering a truth are the actions that history forces black women to take in Kennedy's world. Notably, this list encompasses many of the tools that deconstructionists embrace; however, I believe that the major variation from this school and the role that black women take on in Kennedy's second phase of increasing black female empowerment is that black female figures do not need to propel themselves out of binary thinking and binary modes because they collectively do not belong to an historical/cultural group that views the binary as the original norm. Instead, their world/symbolic order begins in involvedness, begins with interrogatives that are then extended over life. Thus, there is always more to engage, rather than to know, a philosophy that renders the notion of conquering an object obscene. Kennedy inserts this worldview into a landscape drenched in a colonialist fog. The resulting impact is drama that runs off of numerous mini-clashes, the warfare of everyday existence, where various perspectives collide. If this second period remains tentative but is more aggressively assured than her first, then Kennedy's most recent transition evidences a major revolution in tone and is characterized by black women retaking their position as myth-makers. Certainly revisionary, but also predictive, there is nothing provisional or hesitant about this third phase. Anger has driven black female subjects, often speaking from the position of Mother, to reset the human course, even if that means doing so from apocalyptic scenarios.

Ntozake Shange returns full circle to the late nineteenth century and the productions mounted by Pauline Hopkins and the Hyers Sisters. Shange's choreopoems, which restore dance, musicality, lyricism, and a much more improvisational dramatic structure, are reminiscent of the melodramatic ballad operas from which minstrelsy and vaudeville derived. Along with the marked variation in style, Shange's work breaks from the calcified racial uplift ideology that had shaped African American art for nearly a century. Akin to Toni Morrison, who explores in the novel the rift between proper black mothers and defiant, "soul-seeking" black daughters (*The Bluest Eye, Sula, Song of Solomon,* and *Paradise*), Shange restores what Ishmael Reed would refer to as the "hoodoo barbecue" to America's theater. What she enacts is extremely bold and daring: she recovers the revelry that braces minstrelsy while renouncing those parts that have become implicated in structural racism and sexism, a dangerous undertaking, indeed, because the line between dancing, singing, and carrying on to achieve a higher consciousness and the potential repackaging and selling of these very moves is a thin one.

Even in the nineteenth century, Hopkins was aware of this precariousness and chose to bracket "Negro peculiarity" while calling for its death.

Shange, having the benefit of a century's distance and hindsight, devises other ways to approach America's strange racialized fetishes. First, she links African American women's experience to that of other women of color, muddying race from its binary white/black dominant United States' signification to a more mobile array so that she can readily exchange African, Caribbean, South, Central and North American forms. This is a show of force as it bridges several ethnicities and nationalities. In aggregate, this tactic points out the ludicrousness of American racial stereotypes. For instance, if most of the hemisphere prefers to sing and dance during its rituals, then, perhaps, that is "normal," not a Puritanical repression of physicality. Shange's pieces reveal colored women's power as a collective strength in other ways as well. Extending from the body out through the intellect, she locates a female sensuality that begins with loving the self and owning one's woman's parts, and, only after such a declaration, does one dare to envelop lovers. Her overarching artistic challenge awakens colored women who have been taught to see themselves as objects and victims to their full talents and to the practices that represent these gifts.

In terms of theatrical form, Shange revels in ritual, using its participatory properties to foment conversations between mother and daughters, across geographic sites that may often span temporal locations. This formal foundation results in an open-ended theater, as if the house could go on all night if that is what the audience requires. Therefore, we can say that she encodes a democratic intimacy within her form's structure that makes it elastic and popularly inviting. This welcoming, conversational strain extends as well to the manner in which Shange speaks to other playwrights with her offerings that are densely intertextual, as she uses her poetry to correspond with those who have comprised the African-American female dramatic tradition. But, make no mistake about it; this interwoven dialogue is anything but mannered and measured. At times joyous, terrifying, unapologetic, confrontational, lush, incongruous, contentious, anything but nihilistic, Shange's noise arrives at a plateau that Hopkins reached for in 1880, a theatrical moment when the stage would become a place for black women to feel full[y].

NOTES

[1] The phrase, "pass it on," is borrowed from the last line of Toni Morrison's *Beloved.*

[2] I should note that, in spite of the widespread propensity to mock the African that extends back to the 1700s, there were varying degrees of racial inclusiveness in the new world through out the early colonial period. For example, during the eighteenth century there were numerous fetes, pageants and informal dances sponsored by blacks and whites which were open to the general public and were ethnically and racially integrated. Unfortunately, this democratic eighteenth-century revelry set the stage for intensely aggressive and violent commandeering of black expression in the nineteenth century. See Lhamon.

[3] While minstrelsy became a phenomenon during the mid-nineteenth century, Lhamon points out that its roots stem from the 1700s and may have originated in port/market areas such as Five Points in New York, where street performances, including those by black Americans, circulated regularly.

[4] See Gates' article, "The Chitlin Circuit."

[5] Daryl Dance coins the expression "in-house" to refer to black performances at primarily black venues.

[6] One of the few mega-stars to rise above the chorus line's regimentation was Josephine Baker. She did so by splicing dance with raucous comedic breaks.

[7] Georgia Douglas Johnson's 'S' Street Literary Salon nurtured and promoted several playwrights, including May Miller, Marita Bonner, and Willis Richardson.

[8] Judith Williams argues that these black female types stem directly from the numerous productions of *Uncle Tom's Cabin* that circulated around the country during the second half of the nineteenth century (*Uncle Tom's Women).*

[9] The Hyers Sisters Traveling Company, who added Hopkins's plays to their repertoire, transported them across the United States. These works showed in front of racially and ethnically mixed audiences in major towns and cities from coast to coast. The only place where the company did not spend a great deal of time was the Deep South.

[10] During the eighteenth and nineteenth centuries popular entertainment was a noisy sphere, regardless of the racial and or ethnic composition of the audience. It is only in the twentieth century that silent observation has become the norm. Those who speak out during a show today—outside of black communities—are considered rude.

[11] The story of Hurston's *Mule Bone,* a play that she co-wrote with Langston Hughes, is especially telling. Conflict over ownership led to the project's preproduction demise. It was not presented as live entertainment until 1991 when it appeared at Lincoln Center in New York.

ONE

Peculiar Juno: Staging Black Female Pleasure

MUSIC critic Eileen Southern alleges that Pauline Hopkins's *The Underground Railroad* (1879) is littered with formulaic plantation roles: male fieldhand, elder, a Topsy-like female fieldhand, and a female house slave (xxv). Southern's assessment accounts for the dearth of criticism attending this musical. Scholars, following Southern's lead, discount it, perceiving it to be an anachronistic throwback that belongs to late nineteenth-century America's perverse pining for the antebellum period, retrogressive longings that elicit artistic productions that materialize from staid, broad racialized types.[1] From their heyday in the mid-1900s, these figures—Sambo, Mammy, the tragic mulatto, Sapphire, and the black dandy—have been exercised continuously within Western culture and now cover a global media gamut, a dispersal that can be traced to nineteenth-century dramatizations of Harriet Beecher Stowe's *Uncle Tom's Cabin*. Relying on these caricatures, the "Tom plays" gained acceptance, became lucrative, and traveled international and national circuits. Minstrel and other tent shows also amply furnished "darky" entertainment. Pauline Hopkins, a young black playwright from Boston (only twenty when her work was copyrighted in 1879), dared to take on these insulting phantoms that sullied the American stage, not by way of the incremental steps that Booker T. Washington's famous plan proposed that fixed economic improvement as the first rung toward racial progress but from one bold socio/cultural interruption.[2] Thus Hopkins's *The Underground Railroad* aims to educate, or lead out from the bondage of black buffoonery to a new dramatic form that embraces the attitudes of a newly freed and forward-thinking country that is ardent about welcoming its black citizens.

In Henry Louis Gates's much-used phraseology, Hopkins signifies on minstrelsy as she banishes it to an historical detention chamber. Her play is an ambitious stab at retiring the outlandish, offensive plantation show while protecting the overarching tenet that performance should center on enjoyment, pleasure, celebration, and largely unencumbered frivolity. Entertainment, according to the Boston trailblazer, should impart an anecdote to overly codified and institutionalized rituals. To carry out this leap into a new artistic order, Hopkins writes a musical that distills the exuberance and improvisational speed from the day's popular live amusement as she incorporates the then-rising formative and formidable racial uplift ideology to steer her piece away from dangerous ghettos. In opposition to entrenched theatrical contrivances, we find that her Uncle Tom is a consummate trickster; her house wench becomes a spirited refugee, who would rather escape than accept a forced marriage; her Topsy is a grown woman with sexy moves and a confident style; her Mammy is not overbearing but has ceded the way to a new generation of striving African Americans, and her gospel music does not connote resignation but is about defeating and transcending impediments. With humor, music, structural innovation and aesthetic appeal, Hopkins blurs the lines between melodrama and comedy, between entertainment and history, combinations that destabilize authenticating mimesis, nineteenth-century America's premier mode of transacting sentiment and thought.

Subversive and seething with the hopes of a people who are demanding an acknowledgment of their worth and their rights, *The Underground Railroad* (or its alternative title, *Peculiar Sam*) launches its challenging mission to redirect America's course by addressing the mass audiences that most often viewed stock, racially marked characterizations, or, as Hamalian and Hatch claim, "…she employed the current minstrel dialect as well as song and dance to engage her audience in the serious subject of emancipation" (31). Hopkins seasons her work with wit and music, breaking down the defenses of her viewers by serving them robust (but affordable) mead. Sojourner Truth, Hopkins's contemporary, shared this approach as Truth's speeches were often a "…complex medley of tough talk and humorous delivery…" (Painter 128). Certainly this period with its unfinished Reconstruction and its wavering commitment to African American's and women's rights lent itself to cultural forms like Truth's lectures and Hopkins's disruptive musical, platforms that could issue forth ongoing, charged static or "back sass."

Comedy becomes a crucial tool for artists from oppressed groups because it allows a critical voice that would be otherwise prohibited. Yet, the drawback to pivoting around wit, as Nell Painter points out in regard to Truth and by extension to other black speakers and performers, is that while the artist's message may be shrewd and sharp, because it comes wrapped in a humorous delivery, it permits some of its hearers to dodge the meaning [and the messenger] (128). This is the obvious pitfall of securing one's representation to a comedic base: those it is intended to chastise and/or awaken may elude its full import because it invites light responses and only reaches a deeper emotional and intellectual level if the participant takes the time to reflect on its embedded meaning. Conscious of this problem, Hopkins builds triggers into her musical drama, clues that will, she hopes, stimulate more measured and revolutionary interpretations during this age of Jim Crow's menacing shadow. Because the age mandated that artists from subjugated groups to secrete subversive communiqués within the text, contemporary scholars are obliged to dig beneath and between the codes, locating those places where the playwright deviates from conventional themes and structure, buried sites that reveal what Mel Watkins has called a "rich underground spring" with a "sardonic bite"—the crust that has framed the black stage (153).

One way in which Hopkins navigates the boundaries between safe/sanctioned and potentially threatening fare is by shifting the comedic polarities from minstrelsy's self-destructive lampooning that eviscerates the "darky" and reduces him to mere tatters to humor that faces outward to deliver more direct and scathing social commentary. Although the shift in comedic thrust from racialized self-depreciation to brittle verbal and stunt-based combat that attacks contemporary and past social ills is the principal means by which Hopkins spars with the hegemonic minstrel tradition, there are a myriad number of ways that her show veers away from nineteenth-century popular expectations. Some of these revisions are glaring and others not.[3] The more notable departures are that no one wears burnt cork; women take roughly half the key roles; the scenes, except for the first, migrate out from the plantation; and dialect, while employed as the drama advances, is abandoned by curtain fall. More subtle changes reside in the musical selections that ostensibly evolve from the sentimentalist school that often equates black vocalists and their melodies with a childlike simplicity but underneath reinforce an earned utopia and an eventual deliverance from suffering. For instance, featured tunes such as "Didn't My Lord Deliver Daniel," "Gwine up," and "The Gospel Train" imply grandeur, mobility and a belief that liberty can be attained on earth and in heaven, racial uplift's major aspirations. Musically, the audience is predisposed to look beyond the limitations of the day and become enthusiastic about joining the movement for a greater and realizable tomorrow. In fact, because they are performed in route to the Promised Land, even songs that can be associated with plantation life ("Home Sweet Home" or "Old Kentucky Home") are enclosed within the overriding announcement that an exodus from the past is warranted and will be regenerating indeed.

Hopkins's bold costuming constitutes another variant strain. She adds shorter hems and polished gentlemen's clothing to her repertoire, fighting minstrelsy's penchant for enrobing black figures in rags, clashing, wild colors and ugly frocks for the cross-dressers (male performers as Mammy, Sapphire, and Topsy). In addition to rejecting the shambling, outrageously fashioned minstrel, Hopkins sexualizes her figures with her tasteful costumes, an act that challenges head on the manner in which black sexuality had been twisted (male) and obliterated (female) by American culture. She strives to restore pride and self-determination to the body and souls of African Americans by transforming blackness's conceivable representational range. Hopkins maintains that the African American is entitled to name his/her full expressive scope that comprises body, mind, and soul and does not need to prove her humanity to a white audience. Instead of a yet-earned goal, African American dignity stands as a treasure that is under siege, the very ideological posture that many Harlem Renaissance artists would refine and advocate through their literary, critical and visual texts forty to fifty years later.

While I am suggesting that *The Underground Railroad* branches out from America's usual nineteenth-century popular offerings, the piece does not burst forth from an historical vacuum. Its production began, in terms of material pre-condition, around 1871 when the Hyers Sisters, two African American performers from San Francisco, began a national tour and achieved fame as opera singers (Peterson, *Early Playwrights* 7). By the mid-1870s, they had adopted Boston as their home, discovering that within its enriching hub they could acquire formal operatic training. 1875 was a propitious year for them as they "…formed a traveling troupe called the Coloured Operatic and Dramatic Company to produce plays about the black experience" (Hine and Thompson 189), adding drama to their musical catalog (Peterson, *Early Playwrights* 7). So, a situation existed where skilled black women artists were in search of a black playwright, and a dramatist was in need of a professional troupe; thus was born the seminal relationship between the Hyers and Hopkins, a union that would bring together some of the day's noted black talent and a rising, socially conscious writer. In 1879 Hopkins would copyright *The Underground Railroad*, which became the most widely produced of several theatrical compositions that she devised.

Briefly, the plot revolves around a band of escaping slaves who must outwit the master's black agent, the overseer Jim, who pursues them. They pause at various stops along the Underground Railroad to regroup, belt out numbers, and step lively. In addition to the overarching goal of reaching Canada safely, several subplots steer this human train: Sam and Virginia intend to marry but are prevented from doing so because the master wants Virginia for Jim; Mammy is lampooned as being ever fearful but becomes rejuvenated after she reunites with an old friend named Caesar (they marry in the end); Juno, who becomes a teacher, spars with Jim and the modest Virginia breaks free from her domestic service job and finds work as a singer. Needless to say, good professions and enjoyable sexual interaction (broadly named as marriage) expand independence's definition beyond securing civil rights. The writer maintains that the ability to live without an invasion into and a blurring of privacy's parameters, a respect denied the slave as part and parcel of his/her objectification, are just as vital as the right to vote, own property, attend school and conduct business without fear of intimidation.

While *The Underground Railroad* is the most recovered script that Hopkins composed for the Hyers, at least two of her other plays circulated by way of the sisters' national tour. One, *Aristocracy* (1877), focuses on the budding black middle class and the economic and social advantages gained during Reconstruction (Southern xxiii). This is the most blatantly uplift-oriented piece that Hopkins would offer in dramatic format (she would return to it in her novels). The play was later renamed, *Colored Aristocracy*, a significant point because various stage offerings and movies from the late nineteenth and early twentieth century either share this title or vary from it slightly.[4] In any event, beyond Hopkins's earnest treatment, this concentration on the acts and sometime shenanigans of the black middle class has become a staple of both in-house black entertainment and that offered to a mixed audience, a thematic touchstone that is, in part, a rewriting of minstrel skits that expose black dandies as pretentious and grossly grasping for an illusive whiteness that can never be obtained. Another work by Hopkins, *Urlina, the African Princess* (which may have had another title as well) completes a trio of musical dramas that were readied for production in a fairly short time. Hopkins may have actually been working on these plays over a longer span because we know that she had been writing for at least five years, winning an essay contest sponsored by William Wells Brown when she was just fifteen. This piece about an African princess rounded out the Hyers Sisters' excursion that reached all the way to San Francisco, where they performed it at the Bush Theater, an occurrence that Jo Tanner cites as the, "first black theater company to stage a musical set in Africa" (26). This, too, would become a major theme for black theater: shifting the setting to Africa to recover a lost past. Unfortunately, this specific thrust became one of the most woefully and egregiously mishandled topics of the twentieth century. Harlem Renaissance writers jumped into quicksand by trying to describe a land and people with whom they had limited contact. While we can debate the ways in which African Americans wrote over Africa, we can also observe that these artists searched for connections and retained an interest in their ancestry.

Critics most often reference *The Underground Railroad*'s stint in Boston during the summer of 1880. However, the Hyers Sisters transported it out west with them for the 1879–1880 season (Tanner 26–7), a white-owned troupe auspiciously called Sprague's Underground Railroad Company aired it in the Midwest from March to June of 1879, traveling throughout Illinois, Minnesota, Wisconsin, Michigan, Iowa, Kansas, and Missouri, hitting major towns like St. Paul and Chicago more than once (Southern xxiv). It ran at two venues in Hopkins's hometown of Boston: the Opera Hall of Boston's Young Men's Christian Union on December 8, 1879 and again for nine shows between July fifth and tenth at the Oakland Gardens, a Boston amusement park (Southern xxiv). The December show was performed by Hopkins's own troupe that she had shaped from family members that included Hopkins herself (soprano) and her parents, The Hopkins Coloured Troubadours. The July 1880 run was a reunion of sorts and brought together the Hyers Sisters and Hopkins's group with noted minstrels Sam Lucas and Fred Lyons (what would have been a star show by that era's standards). The combined performances were heavily attended, favorably reviewed, and won Hopkins the Playwright's Award from the Congregational Publishing Society of Boston; in fact, an extra show had to be added that drew over 10,000 people (Southern xxv, Perkins 3, Hamalian and Hatch 40). After the run, Sam Lucas's fame continued to increase and the Hyers toured until 1883. Hopkins, on the other hand, seemed to disappear as her family's company disbanded, but she continued to write as she worked as a stenographer. She resurfaced at the helm of the *Coloured American Magazine* by the turn of the century, drawing on her finished and incomplete plays to supply her with the raw material for four novels. *Winona*, for instance, was the title of an early Hopkins play; she later composed a novel with that title (Hamalian and Hatch 96).

Taken together, this information leads us to conclude that this musical comedy is more influential and far reaching than documenters have noted. For over a year, it played America from coast to coast, a musical that featured black performers, including black women, and no burnt cork yet still managed to amuse and delight. To claim that it prepared the way for vaudeville is something of a misstatement, for it hurdled over the brief skit format and insisted on full acts with plot development. In many ways, it is more akin to contemporary, popular black theater, a tradition that often combines humor, music, dance, and drama with an inspiring theme.

It's a shame that *Peculiar Sam's* descent into relative obscurity may be due to its broad appeal, which links it to working-class people and not the high-brow literary establishment that some intellectuals laud. Its comedic bent alone (not to mention its frolicking sexuality) would have made it suspect in some bourgeois circles. Unfortunately, these same artistic choices are still dismissed summarily because too much cutting-up can mark a play as thematically and theoretically naive in spite of its ideological undercurrents and overall gravity. Hopkins would continue to wage class wars throughout her career, inserting wise folk characters in all her novels, subjects who are undervalued and misjudged even today,[5] and reminding her fellow club members to face the deplorable social conditions that visited black communities (*Famous Men and Women of the Negro Race*).

The other major explanation for this work's neglect can be attributed to its headlining an assertive female co-lead. American culture has been preoccupied with male-centered products, absorbed especially with the black male body in both absence and presence. As Paul Gilmore states, "The minstrel show was obsessed with the 'black' male body" (745). This statement does much to explain why we may read and watch various treatments on minstrelsy, an all-male revue until the 1870s but can locate few works on early black female dramatic productivity beyond a brief nod to the general community of black chorus girls, choreographers, singers, writers and comedians. Even today, only those truly exceptional performers and artists receive scholarly study. Who were the black female playwrights, lyricists, directors and creative backers who contributed to American culture during this formative era? For the most part, a gaping documentary void stands in for the activities of black stage women before the 1920s. Relatively recent treatments by Jo Tanner, Donald Bogle, Cheryl Wall, Wesley Brown, and Daphne Harrison have begun to fill this vacancy, but it is doubtful that—no matter how diligently scholars attempt to uplift these artists—women such as the Hyers Sisters or Hopkins will gain the stature and receive the respect given to, for example, Cole and Johnson. To the general public and within the nation's annuals, black women in the theater between 1880 and 1925 are viewed en masse: a long-legged chorus who swing the black bottom or otherwise kick their way to glory. Hopkins's piece, then, is significant because of her introduction of three major black female characters, all different, that ostensibly represent certain types, as if the artist leaped in the midst of the mundane and stimulated it from within to such an extent that she allows new selves to break free on the stage.

From its very title, we are warned to expect mutability in *Peculiar Sam or The Underground Railroad, a Musical Drama in Four Acts*. Not definite about whether to set in relief an abolitionist cornerstone or a folk hero, uncertain as well about whether it will showcase singing or acting, Hopkins's piece toys with interception, fuels up on indeterminacy and agility. The emblazoned "peculiar" in the title indicates the piece's polymorphous aspect, signifying on the nineteenth century's pseudo-scientific/ethnographic discourses that studied subgroup behavior, schools of thought that included scientists (biologists, eugenicists and zoologists) and regionalists and local colorists who transcribed their own little corner to the world. Peculiar, under this rubric, refers to cataloging, tracking behavior that extends outside and beyond the normalized ideal citizenry in terms of race, class and gender markers. So, at first glance it appears that Hopkins has aligned herself with the plantation writers, but she will rotate out from and break this associative link in much the same way that Charles Chesnutt will undertake a few years later with *The Conjure Woman* (1899). Both depict the invisible insiders/evaluators as suspicious and the visible outsiders/objects as comparatively sane and rational in the midst of this race-marked anthropological making/unmaking.

In addition to insinuating the image of middle-and upper-class white Americans peeking under the trousers and skirts of their less-fortunate brethren to locate and determine what constitutes difference from the standard, "peculiar" implies that which is quaint, homey and most likely disappearing to be replaced shortly by a rampantly approaching urbanism and cosmopolitanism.[6] Hopkins's Sam does land under this generalization because he personifies the old submitting to the dictates of the new as he migrates from slave to senator over the course of four acts and six years. Yet, Hopkins twists this rubric and furnishes "peculiarity" with a slightly altered connotation: Sam's ability to adapt does not chart a mere transition from one age to the next but a sophisticated richness that combines old and new world views, a position that stems from his knack for remembering and incorporating his slave past into the modern era while checking any ensuing self-destructive impulses from a recollection of that past. This packed, but porous "peculiar" quality is akin to what Cornel West refers to as the tragic comedic base for black culture and resistance ("Black Strivings" 89).

Evidence substantiating this claim about Sam's symbolic potential arrives quite early during the very first scene when he stands apart from the other laborers because he prefers to dance and let his body submit to music's powerful pull, as Sam exclaims illustratively: "Take kar dar, de spirits a movin' in me, Ise comin" (101). This connection that Sam owns ties him to a procreant "family of the universe" and marks him as a transcendentalist like

Thoreau, who greets the elements knowing that they can provide him with a mystical succor: give him one more ride. We may also deem Peculiar Sam's testimony as summoning a new world shamanism that is conceived by way of the Middle Passage's forced merger of multiple and multiplying traditions, ethos, cosmologies and rituals. Sam conceives of himself as a product in formation just as his dream country exists as mostly promise. The individual's responsibility under this worldview coheres around combining these protean scraps into "peculiar" (signed) artistic products. Sam, then, takes stage as an exemplar because, without doubt, he is a modern magician who will mold something fertile from the cast-off residue from civilization's instruments of torture.

Midway through the piece, Sam taps once again into his faith, amassing the forces that will steel his intentions, "Dars been suthin' a growin' an' a growin' inter me, an' it keep sayin,' Run 'way, run away, Sam. Be a man, be a free man" (105). Liberty is associated with locomotion, not just in the obvious sense that his feet will take him to Canada but that his prancing, strumming and warbling (which in Western African and African American cultures is often circular) can lead to an enhanced consciousness: motoring on progressively enlightened sacred and secular stones. That his spiritual engine, which he manifests through his joy in stepping and rotating his limbs and torso is reinterpreted in the dominant market as nothing more than a humorous and odd habit, one to be routinely derided, exposes Hopkins's foremost challenge: her show must be multi-edged in order to break through rooted formulas and receive a fresh hearing. Yet, the playwright is careful not to alienate her audience by pushing them into the realm of revolutionary theater; reform is sufficient. Therefore, a bit of the commonplace to ensnare the consumer is a concession that Hopkins is prepared to make.

"Peculiarity" in this dramatist's hands becomes a hook that she shapes to double back on its vernacular nineteenth-century meaning, changing the subtext from that which implies an exhibition-worthy, slightly off-kilter grotesque but absorbing object to a state of mind that revels in the unexpected, a physical arc that a love of life can engender, a clear rejoinder to minstrelsy, which co-opts black expression to disarm it. What she does—like Sam's physical machinations—is nothing less than a reversal of polarities that takes Jumping Jim Crow, who was himself borrowed and repackaged, and rearranges him once again, wrapping him in the tricksters' robes.[7] In total, the work is just that and more: a new world Anansi (the spider of African-based myth), who plays the consumer while he rolls around for them. Those who recognize the slide away from the buffoon and toward the skilled artist will join the playwright's intimate circle, and those who do not will still enjoy the piece and pay for it but will be relegated to the communal outer circle, and, therefore, become spectacle to the participant intimates, who not only watch the stage but each other.

The curtain descends with Sam once more vibrating his body to the natural and metaphysical sounds that compel him. In this final act, Sam symbolically synthesizes the playwright's vision for the future: a political sphere that is tempered by a transcendentalist, element-praising base as Sam has become an elected official who enjoys raising spirits through dance and song. Sam's political victory argues that it is possible to be a dignified, respectable citizen and be peculiar, to retain and cherish that bit of autonomy and highly differentiated eccentricity that becomes the signature for a specific individuality. As a civics lesson, this musical drama calls for relaxed notions of national symbology. If Uncle Sam, a rather tall, bearded and silent fellow who does not resemble surely the majority of Americans can define our country, then so can Peculiar Sam with his penchant for besting others with his quick mind and handy barbs; his love of celebration, toe tapping and snappy tunes; and his adroitness at adapting over a short time span.

In addition to modifying the dimensions of key nineteenth-century discourses, Hopkins's work supports racial uplift ideology both formally and thematically. The mere title alone, *The Underground Railroad*, indicates that her program is steeped in abolitionist, reformist doctrine that will identify and accentuate a series of procedures that can lead to enhanced civil rights and personal liberties. It insists as well that pleasure need not be abandoned as a trade-off for social and economic advancement. Sam states the case as he turns to the stands immediately before the end and implores: "…I hope you will excuse me for laying aside the dignity of an elected M.C., and allow me to appear before you once more as Peculiar Sam of the old underground railroad" (123). Although Hopkins's text precedes Brecht, we can discern that this final aside is analogous to Brecht's alienation effect because Sam steps outside of his given role and comments on his awareness of and his reaction to both the act's artifice and its borders. Certainly, some of the Sam's disaffection with his character stems from the manner in which it parallels the minstrel, but the performer who enacts Sam, as directed by the script, is conscious that he is compelled to walk in Sambo's rags to deconstruct him. Sam's statement—both a direct appeal to the audience and his own internal mandate—etches a popular convention and his subversive variation on it.

Furthermore, this epiphany is not an instance of despair nor is it blues-like in nature even though Sam is mindful of the grim reality that he cannot overcome entirely racial typecasting. In lieu of tragic undertones, this moment stands as one rich in possibilities, contemplation and outreach as Sam pulls the curtain down on the figurative notion that historical time can be revamped and made to loop around through reinterpretation, a strategy that broadens space beyond the capabilities of a nod to "new" aesthetics. Thus this finishing movement is about progress, climbing upward, but also about return, about locating the inner spring that propels the soul, arguing as well that an individual's highly personal quest can be (must be) shared with a group. Peculiar Sam operates on the participants that come to this play like the storyteller of African and African American lore who entertains to educate; in this sense, the moral hinges on bringing the viewer along to an enhanced appreciation for his/her environment, viewing it as a fecund and dense forest that awaits the magician's eager hand, a response that ridicules, ultimately, puritanical fears of the wild region beyond the community's perimeter.[8]

If Sam represents a model male citizen who has learned to remold the past into ritual—a game that the performer controls, draws strength from, and relishes—guiding the audience somewhere else in time, then Juno, his sister and co-ruler, serves an equally vital function.[9] Stepping back, we bear in mind that there are three female roles scripted for this musical: Virginia, who is Sam's intended, a former house slave and the soprano; Juno, who is irreverent, witty, sensual, and strong and the alto; and Mammy, who is comparatively reserved and atypically dependent on her children for leadership. While all three parts represent a divergence from stock characterization, Juno embraces female self-reliance more vigorously than Virginia or Mammy. As feminist critics have maintained, female playwrights need offer bold departures to break and resist masculinist theatrical patterns; Hopkins's Juno is one such radical charge.

Southern aligns Juno with Topsy, the girl-child of Stowe's *Uncle Tom's Cabin*, who in her theatrical reincarnation became a blackface character that was played by a man or later a white woman who put on a braided or curly wig and shabby clothing rolled her eyes and emitted loud noises. In her "barbaric" innocence/experience, Topsy symbolizes the unrestrained mayhem of an untutored brat, foil to the angelic white child, Eva. Hopkins's Juno, to the contrary, is a grown woman who is forceful and self-confident (she restrains the irascible overseer Jim), wears sexy, short red dresses that are cinched at the waist according to Hopkins's costume list, and keeps the company marching along in its quest toward advancement. The play makes it clear that Juno is a leader, as opposed to the more conventional Virginia and

Mammy. One need only look at a photograph of Emma Louise Hyers, the contralto who played Juno at various times, to receive a sense of how this role may have played before Hopkins's contemporaries. Hyers is a beautiful, petite, brown-skinned woman with deep-set fiery eyes and a poised attitude. She looks to be a woman not afraid to explore new terrain, a model of the pioneering spirit (she is from California), nothing Topsy-like about her.

I have argued elsewhere that Juno's major contribution to the stage stems from her electric, physical humor, which she uses to deliver black female sexuality to the public forum so that at least some of the desire displayed on the stage is self-generated, not a mere reflection of the black female body filtered through various master texts and gazes. Just to touch briefly on this inscription of black female power, during the last act when Sam announces his Brechtian distance from America's nineteenth-century racial codes and the cast has reunited in Canada six years after the Civil War, Hopkins splits the visual field by circling around to the other characters' reactions to black progress and a hope that a new inclusiveness would usher in a solid, more honest America. Juno, for instance, is very much invigorated by and prepared for the challenges that will greet black Americans who have decided to return to the United States. Animated by this news and the announcement that her brother and Virginia will soon wed, Juno demands that, "Somebody hold me, or I shall bust. I'm so full. Come on boys and girls, let's have an ol' Virginia, it's the only safe exit for surplus steam" (123). While post-War Sam concentrates on controlling his image, post-War Juno locates the expressive means that will allow her to reveal the full extent of her joy, what William Wells Brown's Melinda could only conceive of as utopian projection. Viewing this as one of the first intertextual moments between dramas scripted by black writers, Hopkins links one major black female figure with another, bridging her text with one from the pre-Emancipation era. What Melinda could merely imagine, Juno anticipates, even celebrating its immanent arrival.

One additional illustration of Juno's departure from known theatrical conventions will concretize the writer's devotion to showcasing black female pleasure and gratification. To value fully Juno's final pronouncement of her satiation, we have to explore how Hopkins bisects the minstrel to unearth its complicity in bracing the state's economic interests. On the one hand, the bard provides, in the Sambo-like figure, Jim, state-sanctioned chattel whose nineteenth-century marketability fills capitalist coffers, an emblematic role that gestures toward the nation's highly active, semi-feudal, slavery-based shadow economy. In other words, the darky retains feasibility by keeping a system in place that depends on the subordination of black labor. As long as the black worker is subjugated by being made to appear loutish and, therefore, not entitled to a decent wage, the manager and owner of his labor may take a greater share of the profit from that black worker's productivity. As an effigy in service to this dynamic, Jim carries out his overseer's duties by tending unapologetically the master's interest, even accepting the clown's mantle when that is required. Verification for my assertion is found in the costume list that instructs Jim to wear immense false feet and garish clothing. Furthermore, his dialect is atrocious and evidences no hint of the wit inherent in the other characters' speech, nor does he question authority or fight for his own community. To subvert Jim and the economic arrangement that he endorses, Hopkins introduces Sam, a black entrepreneur who will forge his own fiscal development model by skimming energy/value from this deeply entrenched feudal operation. We are made aware of this bifurcation as Sam appears briefly as a buffoon but quickly reveals his trickster's soul and bests (along with Juno) the darky extraordinaire, Jim. Sam and Juno arrest Jim (Sambo) and keep him in check, an act that will liberate both the cultural sphere and the marketplace from feudalism and unethical (in the sense that money is gained from dehumanizing a particular group of people) profit-taking.

Ironically, along with the allusion to economic and social reform that Sam and Juno's apprehension of the minstrel stands in for, the scene where they collar him is filled with erotic double entendre. For instance, while Jim's freakish feet align him with the European harlequin, in African American folk humor, large shoes indicate sexual prowess. Even as Juno and Jim square off literally as captor and prisoner, their encounter reads simultaneously as charged foreplay. Midway through the piece, after Sam trounces Jim, disarms him and marches him back to the camp, Juno volunteers to guard the reprobate. A kinky seduction scene unravels that includes Jim, Juno, and the master's sidearm (which Jim has borrowed):

> Juno: (*Walks around Jim, and plays at shooting him. Jim rolls his eyes in terror*) Ef you move one har, yas ef you wink, I'll shoot dem feet clean off ob you. (*Keep this by-play through remainder of this scene*). (116)

Juno atomizes the hall with sensuality by keeping the light on her strutting and cross-stepping and Jim's kinetic masculinity as both alternate between approach and retreat. We follow Juno's pistol-waving, phallic hand that motions toward Jim's enormous appendages. All in all, this scene proffers a crackling air that suffuses the drama, which, in general, thrives on hetero-sexual "by-play," a clear rejoinder to minstrelsy's inherent homoeroticism (which doesn't altogether disappear but shares the stage with male/female encounters). So, Juno's declaration in the last act, "I feel full," may be interpreted as an acknowledgment of sexual satisfaction or at least the expectation of it at the behest of Jim's return in the last scene, a scene which reintroduces the same frisky banter that Hopkins introduced in the previous act (neither has forgotten the other after six years).

Considering the period in which Hopkins produced *Peculiar Sam*, we may rate more accurately the impact that her scripting and enactment of black sexuality had on a nation that, over the course of the slave era, had been trained to either stifle or render it obscene. To live without tyranny, Hopkins broadcasts, is to enjoy, and she demands that this basic—to her, natural—right be upheld.[10] She arrives at this conclusion after witnessing minstrel and tent shows that mocked black male sexuality by rendering it excessive and monstrous while erasing any inkling of black female agency. Given the choices in popular culture that surrounded her, Hopkins's erotic pulse makes perfect sense: restore what has been obliterated. What she could not have foreseen, however, was the manner in which black sexuality would become commercialized beyond the vulgar economic exploitation of slavery, media processes that were amassing as Hopkins dispatched her revisionary play across America. She could not have predicted the high yellow chorus line that would serve mostly white clients, nor could she have imagined that black women would be limited largely to music and dance for decades to come and would have to fight for a few meager dramatic roles (Hopkins combines all three art forms). She could not predict our contemporary video and pornography industries that extract fetishes from black women's body parts. Hopkins optimistically calculated that drawing desirable African Americans, wrapped in a mildly spicy and sensual dramatic underbelly, could translate into enhanced civic rights because a theatrical display of frivolity and joyous romping could verify black humanity and forge common bonds across gender and racial lines.

Accounting for the historical context, we commend the playwright's forceful inauguration of black female and male pleasure. While the musical braces uplift's directives by showcasing scenes that could prompt white America to recognize black interiority, an interiority that was just as concerned with romance as with commercial and civic progress, making this case would not be easy because Victorian discourses linked the black female body to prostitution. So, the dramatist had to safeguard her vision by ensuring that her piece's heretofore uncharted, public black female-authored whimsies and flirtations fell within propriety's boundaries. She had to ascribe to nineteenth-century tenets of true womanhood such as a respect for marriage, or her work would assuredly reproduce racial stereotypes.[11] To head off any potential correlation between her underground romp and those sordid myths that circulated about black female promiscuity, Hopkins concludes her event with conventional domestic configurations: Mammy and Caesar jump over the broom and Virginia and Sam intend to tie the knot. Yet, we observe as well that even though convention is upheld in the form of marriage, all the young people including the women are employed outside the home. Thus sexualized black women who enter the labor force are heroines, not aberrations, just as motherhood, the nineteenth century's prime symbol of feminine virtue, cedes authority to the daughters and their carefully selected paradigmatic "womanly" merits such as perseverance, creativity, wisdom, adaptability, and a strong commitment to education and self-betterment. To underscore this point, we recall that as the play closes Mammy is the only mother standing, and she is consigned to the background so that her two figurative daughters can revel in the spotlight. At one point, Hopkins even dares to have Mammy admit her retrogressive position vis-à-vis her children, "Good-bye ole home, de place whar my chillern war born, an' my ole man am buried. Ise ole now, I may neber see you 'gin, but my chillern's gwine, an' I'm boun' to go too" (108). With this lament, Mammy realizes that she is a relic who ought to surrender to new representational models of black womanhood because her loyalty to plantation life cannot co-exist with her daughters' passion for emancipation. Perhaps the playwright's determination to displace motherhood's centrality implies that other "womanly virtues" must come first: valuing the imagination, embracing one's lush sensuality, and discovering a solid career that evolves from one's signature talents.

Hopkins hypothesized about how to best build a stronger America during an age of rampant national formation and was determined to redefine gender roles under a newly reformed state sign, revised categorical functions that were not so much wish fulfillment but reflected real African American material conditions and experiences.[12] Broader, more fulfilling and active roles for all American women, not just those of color, would invigorate the American landscape. So, her decision to feature fiery black women is more than a mere introduction of black women to the stage but also a seating of increased female self-sufficiency in the nation's cultural heart.

With Juno, Sam, and the entire cast, America's wit, sensuality, pleasure, maneuverability, female agency, upward striving, and self-respect filtered through the multifarious prism of humor—peculiarity—played the United States, at least for one year between 1879 and 1880. Hopkins's subversive characterization, skilled deployment of comedy, and remarkably fresh black female roles redressed her backward-facing contemporaries who had taken to regional and plantation drama and fiction to alleviate their fears about change. *The Underground Railroad's* form also departs from other late nineteenth-century offerings. Unveiling a tableau that grafts various modes atop one another, the bard rivets a progressive motif at the base, an ideology that is mirrored by the drama's narrative action in the jumping from act to act, which captures incrementally more pleasurable states of fulfillment. This successive field is then cut into by comedic and eroticized undertones that transmute the primary text like a woven basket, where one pattern informs the next. This mat, then, rotates as the stage, full to the brim with dance, song, and wit, divides into competing visual sectors. The result is reminiscent of ragtime and early jazz and allows the playwright to be flexible within guidelines, to speak to a diverse audience, and to interrupt any facile identification between attendee and character or star.

Hopkins composes a work that splits the arena so that the gaze is released and becomes ambulatory. She manages this revival by way of several techniques. The panorama hums with multi-faceted activity pockets that partition the audience's attention. Note that Peculiar Sam is not always the focal point (Hansberry will employ this device in *Raisin in the Sun).* In fact, the play is loaded with jostling subplots and physical stunts that intermittently burst forth. Humor sustains this radical form, resulting in something like a circus but without the obvious material signs that separate each ring. In place of highly recognizable markers like rims, perimeters and spotlighted sectors, Hopkins partitions space with her decision to skillfully pit comedy, music and drama against each other while interweaving them as well. It's the old notion of repulsion and attraction in the hopes that the colliding forces will elicit startling and engrossing combinations, a structure that differs from the controlled chaos of minstrelsy, where subdivided skits are looped together in clearly discernible segments.

In addition to revamping theatrical structure, the play's piecemeal configuration has an additional practical purpose because it can highlight the talent of performers from any number of troupes, professional and amateur. If, for instance, the tenor in a specific company is the finest vocalist but does not dance well, then the piece can be tailored to fit that immediate situation. In other words, it is planned for portability, yet it has enough stability to resist any homogenization into a minstrel format. This piece thrives on its ability to collapse the tent and raise it again under new direction. Its architecture is echoed in the title because the play operates like the Underground Railroad: escaping detection by changing paths, re-designating safe houses, substituting labor, and knowing when to disappear when the heat grows too intense.

Keeping in mind the work's built-in mutability, for the sake of exploration, we momentarily separate *Peculiar Sam's* generic components. Comedy is the means by which Hopkins adds depth to what looks to be an amiable and simple drama. Humor directs the work's semi-buried rebellious and radical comments to the surface, interrupting the conventional cover story that avails itself of the nineteenth century's many circulating autobiographical and fictional slave narratives, including William Wells Brown's *The Escape* and Stowe's *Uncle Tom's Cabin*. More precisely, Sam and Juno rely on the witty aside to re-narrate events and advance alternative interpretations. Ultimately, wit refashions the show from slave narrative to a picaresque tale about the search for lost black sexuality. In addition, comedy highlights how language works on concurrent planes, and these various levels become the trickster's instruments and purview.

If banter and physical comedy limn normalcy's edge, the music reinforces the progressive element, bolstering the uplift theme while adding two major variations to it. First, it comments that social and economic striving can be festive, not deadening, that amusement can reside beside and within conflict and that mass advancement need not be a bland social, political and economic movement but may be converted into a spiritual journey won by motoring through music's ephemeral realm. Furthermore, song adds a communal quality to performance, especially numbers that galvanize both audience and cast. Choral in design and participatory in function, Hopkins's incorporation of spirituals, gospels, arias and popular tunes radicalizes high and low culture, targeting, specifically, plantation-born melodies and opera. In essence, she endeavors to involve both quarters to democratize and elevate black "authored" music to a national level, a neoclassical step surely, as she borrows from the African, Greek and Elizabethan theatrical choral traditions that insert a respondent body into the form's fabric, a body that invites and encourages greater audience investment.

Contrasting the funny quips, physical shenanigans, banjo playing, heel kicking and strong vocal renditions, the pathos-ridden, dramatic elements are the most conservative because they are indebted to nineteenth-century sentimentality and operate under the auspices of implied domestic order. Under this convention, nineteenth-century viewers would have been conditioned to feel rage when Sam and Virginia are prevented from marrying, the most naturalized American religious and secular social formation, and Mammy's appearance as a sympathetic character is thrown in to ameliorate the more threatening comedic undertones. These nods to current nineteenth-century notions of dramatic authentication are contained and remarked on within the text, not allowed full sway without some serious reflection as if Hopkins is cognizant that the very entrenched and familiar models that she relies on to maneuver her dream to production are outmoded and faulty. But, she could not comment on their stilted irrelevancy unless she employed them. So, Mammy, for instance, is undone by her own inflexibility and inability to break open on the stage and produce a new self.

As we have explored how these pieces function separately, we return them to real time and their interweaving disposition within the text. Often, as in Juno's pursuing Jim in both the second and the last acts, the Boston dramatist inscribes overlapping physical activity, which results in various viewing fields that resist a potentially concretizing master gaze. This attempt on the artist's part to reduce specularizing would warrant it the label of postmodern pastiche with a competing modernist undertow in our contemporary critical parlance. I add the modernist qualifier because, while certainly sniffing around the perimeter of staid stylistic boundaries—a totally unexpected hodgepodge of activities—this work does have a mission beyond mere surprise or novelty, an overarching ambition that is evidenced by its four linear acts, not the disconnected skit format of minstrelsy (which, I argue, becomes extremely contrived even within its seemingly chaotic guise by the late nineteenth century). Nevertheless, some musical numbers are expendable and easy to shuffle both in terms of arrangement and in performance order. Dance numbers can be added, shored up or eliminated, as the dramatic force can be similarly suppressed or raised. So, a dialogic relationship between actor and spectator runs through the work as the viewers' reactions and verbal remarks demand and merit immediate and significant changes, an aspect that aligns the musical with the sacred/secular call-and-response motif (Traylor 51). Inserting a call and response mechanism allows the writer to mesh her role as playwright with that of educating race worker, who elevates the flock's consciousness and brings them to epiphanies: those in the body respond to the scenes, which are nothing more or less than the leaders' words, voice, and vision. In turn, this interaction converts the membership into vital and ignited co-creators. Laughter, hissing, cat-calls, loud murmuring, singing-along and restless movement constitute some of the more polite means by which the paying attendees can convey their antiphonal feedback, thus embarking on a voyage between stage and seat that alchemizes both authority and contributor. Voices float and make noise together, a forum-like arena that is still channeled by the writer/director toward a specific set of social reform goals.

Beyond its ability to create an empowered consumer, *Peculiar Sam*'s call and response mechanism breaks the identificatory link between spectator and character that blackface invites. Corking up created "home-grown" American faces or what Alice Childress would later identify satirically as white America's formula that locates blackness within the comfortable sphere of a white-owned domestic economy: a far-reaching exploitative design that fixes the black citizen in service positions where she is also perversely considered "one of the family," not a wage laborer.[13] The minstrel, the paradigmatic vassal who lives to entertain, grew so comforting that some Americans were affronted when actual African Americans did not act correspondingly (sing, dance, or shuffle on demand). Lynching, in addition to being execution that intimidates others, can be attributed, in some measure, to white America's inability to conceive of black autonomy.[14]

Part of minstrelsy's acumen at building and conveying familiarity resides in the form's structural design that, while projecting the allusion of ribald commotion, is actually tightly controlled. Certainly, by the late 1870s, the minstrel show had become standardized and introduced seventeen men in garish costume, blackface, and white or red exaggerated lips. Tambo, the end man, and the Interlocutor or master of ceremonies were the two most important roles, the first seemingly irrepressible and the latter serving as warden and foil to the others' antics. The first segment usually featured jokes, song, and dialogue, ending with a light-toed strut that mimicked the cake walk. The second part offered stock, sentimental songs, sketches and recitations (Sampson 2–3). Because this emphasis on brief snippets that run over and into each other (a forced clumsiness) does not gel around key social themes (beyond chicken stealing and melon eating),[15] the viewers perceive that bona fide black folk, as represented by the minstrels, stumble and stagger because they have difficulty thinking in straight patterns. Thus the overlapping dialogue between the blackface performer that is a misreading of African poly-rhythms and the topsy-turvy transition from singing to instrumental music to humorous skits and speeches regularize the conception that black culture is discernible in its incoherence; even its jocularity can be reproduced and mastered.

Hopkins's play, on the other hand, resists closure and domination while it demands lucidity. An audience has to get the point that the subjects have survived the greatest odds, have made contributions to the nation, that they have searched for a sense of well-being and joy and have found it, but this journey has not concluded by curtain fall. As there is no sense of a firm exit, there is no place to fix the "Negro" in *Peculiar Sam* because the African American subjects reconstruct and redefine themselves continually. Existing as unfinished vessels, these figures embrace unequivocally a dynamic operability: Sam's "I'se coming." One is not left with the sense that we can grasp Sam nor can we guess his next step; instead, we are left with the overwhelming impression that the production is commenting on its own ingenious rejection of conventional American realism, for what can we say about this gyrating, crooning senator who slides into dialect as easily as he transmigrates out of it? Subjectivity is confirmed but becomes inconclusive as a discursive category because it is in constant flux.

Similarly, the dramatic structure adheres to a travel motif, riding from station to station, a formal choice that mirrors the playwright's postulation that reform should be personal and public and that part of the growth process entails experimenting with the environment, manufactured and natural, to locate the resources that can help procure these substantial leaps across psychological, physical, and spiritual distance. In breaking from minstrelsy's overly stylized, contrived bedlam, Hopkins dismantles an easy identification between viewer and character, supplying instead the more participant-oriented call and response mode that places the viewer as an integral, junior member of the ritual, placing him/her in the unique position of being consumed by the pageant as he or she absorbs it. Here we see a collapse in the standard Western stage rules of the period that rest on a masterful aficionado to fix the theater into recognizable sectors because the audience is deemed paramount over the production. In Hopkins's imaginative world, power is redistributed so that the performers' surveillance of the crowd also determines the drama's course. From this foundation, the composer builds a structure that is controlled by a linear chain of events, but she allows for several encrypted, improvisational eruptions. The end result is that Hopkins transforms the stage to reflect the sacred choral interplay of call and response while she shapes it into a potential instructional, motivational guide that, on occasion, drops its formal reins and falls into unfettered revelry. Teaching the eye to expect and respect diversity while building up from an evident political stump, the playwright combines, therefore, two vital African American discourses: spirituality defined as dialogue between an engaged authority and a receptive body and education through entertainment (primarily storytelling). These modes interpenetrate and are sustained by her decision to juggle mobile artistic forms: music, dance, comedy and drama.

A review of several textual moments will concretize these points. In the first act, first scene, which is set on the plantation, Sam calls on his band (fellow male slaves) to relieve some stress after laboring in the field. This set up provides a great segue for Hopkins to begin her assault on minstrelsy as the setting mimics that genre's location of choice; once again we are faced with a group of black men from the fields who, in the process of unself-consciously entertaining themselves, will provide ancillary enjoyment for the audience, which supposes that it is watching a dissection of Negro life. Hopkins immediately turns on these stock presumptions with the following song:

> One night as the moon was beamin' I lay fas' asleep a dreamin':
> That the sun was shinin' bright, In the middle of the night
> And the darkies had assembled to have a little fight.
> I woke an' the banjo was soundin'
> An' the bones through the air were boundin':
> How happy I did seem, I was married in a dream,
> In an ole Virginie mudscow floatin down stream. (102)

The lyrics trip along like stream of consciousness notations and bestir imagery reminiscent of an unending nightmare where all that is pleasant lies beyond reach as Sam croons about physical resistance and marriage, both prohibited by slavery. In contrast to various late nineteenth-century regionalists, who were wrapping the plantation in nostalgia's comforting blanket, the Boston playwright renders it as an opium-induced hell that can not be colored real via representation; it can only be a place where all is an illusion, a painful "untouchability." That Sam's phantasmagoric slave "state" has him drifting further south indicates as well his descent into an historical vacuum. The lyrics speak of loss and an inversion of the natural and civic spheres.

What makes this particular theatrical moment "peculiar" or indeterminate is that these yearnings are not delivered melodramatically as convention dictated but are inserted into a banjo-accompanied frolicking melody, the kind of song that was reserved by the minstrel to tell of his love for the good old slave days. But, in place of the wistful yet carefree pining for a patriarchal past that secured the Negro within a feudal domestic economy, this rendition chronicles—with nimble accompaniment—the manner in which an entire block of history and people has been ontologically removed from the nation's memory, if it ever resided there in the first place. In an absurdist vein, Hopkins builds in a tension between the song type and its lyrical content, exposing the complicated roots that inform American culture. Certainly she addresses commoditization as a major factor that impacts on black subjectivity because Sam and his friends must harmonize odd, off-center lyrics within the packaged form of the plantation melody. On the other hand, she argues through the proof of this keenly critical musical text that black America is not only aware of its negation but also ready to speak about the consequences of this injury, whose scars are deep and jagged. During this late nineteenth-century moment, the nation's cultural arena supported products that projected slavery as an incantation that seduces. Hopkins resists this lure and exposes how deeply implicated most American popular expression has become in defending an underlying slavery-based model.[16] The writer's decision to begin with this disruption that bores inside a familiar musical air is a bold one that signals right from the outset that her theater will feature black difference through thorny and cagey responses and odd juxtapositions.

The next musical selection is equally telling and passes from disorientation to action. Titled "Poor Juna," this melancholy tune frames a Mississippi slave woman who requires deliverance from the plantation because the master's sexual exploitation of her (along with the other uses of her body) is imminent. A subjective voice promises to release her, "Tell her that I will break the chains, That bind her to the gate" (Southern 152). It is no coincidence that the liveliest female role, Juno, is a slight derivation from Juna. This small detail indicates that Juna's status is crucially symbolic. Traveling from Juna to Juno, from dependent (Juna waits to be rescued by others) to proactive firebrand who secures her own freedom while also defending her loved ones, implies a departure from rigid nineteenth-century gender roles, a reformist avenue that parallels the overarching break with entrenched racial codes. In short, the writer inscribes another internal scopic field where litigious worldviews square off and the subaltern's will prevails. Here we detect the first psychological step on this Underground Railroad, even though the characters have not yet physically fled the plantation. In a moment reminiscent of Frederick Douglass's great fight with Covey, resolve precedes action. This song and Juno's emergence from it are so bold and unambiguous that they may be interpreted as a metaphor for the African American performer cracking the minstrel shell to throw off the impediments that would reduce her range.

Within these musical numbers that are designed to alternatively relax and stimulate the audience, Hopkins implants a stacked progressivism that, when assessed in total, rings forth as a clear departure from plantation fiction and minstrel theater. Hence while the play's interior textual space is segmented, its comprehensive impact broadcasts a scathing indictment of cultural products that install sanitized widespread illusions that shield slavery's and racism's continued brutality. Hopkins opens the door on a new archetype for popular theater that could include gospel tracks, popular tunes, physical stunts and humor but would avoid the objectification of black bodies and the intentional obfuscation of history. This cultural reform would dictate that cutting-up or peculiar dance, speech, and or regional acts ought to be framed by a forward-thinking ideology: No more inert, "realistic" slices of life that strive to authenticate various ethnic and racial groups. Structure, to Hopkins, should reflect an unfolding web of intimate and associative interconnections that do not allow the viewer to identify with theatrical ghosts. If any mirroring is to occur, then it should happen between the participant/viewer and ideas or stances or becomings (Juno and Sam).

Humor is yet another means by which the artist complicates her play and undermines the authority of set traditions. Undoubtedly, minstrelsy thrived on comedy, using it to broadcast social critique from within the veiled space of a grotesque shell that also houses alleged black inferiority. Hopkins liberates blackface humor by overturning its reliance on "accidental delivery." Note that Sambo, a purportedly "genuine" Negro, unwittingly makes the crowd laugh, and we see that part of minstrelsy's "charm" is that the darky figure is unaware that he is amusing the much more sophisticated connoisseur with his malapropisms and unintentional stumbling into jocular territory. *Peculiar Sam* reforms this contrivance and puts the words and the artistry back in the black subject's mouth and mind. Obviously, unmasking the actors indicates the work's departure from the minstrel mold. By dropping the corked façade and allowing the actors to step out on a platform to address directly the powers that have limited their full potential, Hopkins's script creates an opportunity for the performer to regain control over the text and subtext to more readily manage an arena that is diverse, perhaps even, at times, hostile to the emerging, improvisational black independence that the piece awakens. Relinquishing blackface during the height of the minstrel craze is in itself an audacious move. Yet, Hopkins proceeds further and employs black female humor to galvanize her creation, a force that, in her expert hands, is not self-deprecating but socially conscious and rejuvenating to the black figures that enliven it. For example, Juno "feels full" because she has been "playin' tricks" (117) for four acts. With this bragging self-assessment, Juno maintains that black female wit is entitled to a role in the public sphere. Juno's announcement recovers as well a cultural means by which she can circulate and propagate black female ingenuity, a discovery that she had to foster because other aesthetic forms at that moment could not house her daring insinuations. Mimetic regionalism, for instance, offered a haven against cosmopolitanism's encroachment, standing in its stead representation of a nation safely divided into bracketed and sealed peculiar geographic pockets. Juno's chicanery resists any attempt to stave off mobility by fixing social and economic order.

In redefining "peculiarity" to signify a hybridized active playing field that does not settle into strictly definable space, Hopkins resists compartmentalization. Each time new voices, aesthetics and semiotic codes enter the theatrical arena, they further inform community, shedding easy identifications from viewers, forming, ultimately, something akin to a staged version of what Stuart Hall calls a politics of location.[17] Bear in mind that radical audience members can align themselves with Juno as she contains the accommodationist Jim, but the reaction to her prancing around in a short red dress and aiming lightheartedly at Jim's feet will vary according to each viewer's race, class, gender, and sexuality—any number of factors. So the stage is broken open additionally in terms of how and where the audience will stand in relationship to the multiple events. These innovations lead to a more dynamic spectator that is forced to assess and reassess its position.

Less fluid, certainly, than our contemporary moment when racial uplift ideology is itself debated and diverse, Hopkins's musical still calls for a restless eye and spirit while the piece strives to lead the masses to support policies that would enhance further national Reconstruction, curb mob violence, and extend legal protections. Hopkins breaks with the status quo, with a minstrel tradition that did not thematize or structurally reflect black-owned desire. Stylistically, she transported Americans from thinking about their fellow countrypeople as transparent and ingenuous to considering how black shamanism could bend rhetoric, sound, word, and choreography to carry out its own processed aims, a mission that can be thought of as a lesson about the complexity of black interior space, consciousness that can tap into various expressive tempers. Accordingly, the structure of her musical represents its option-filled interiority that is flexible enough to select, shape and interweave song, dance, drama, and humor while rotating out from a clear focal point. Using a ragtime aesthetic to predict modernism's paradoxical experimentalism and its adherence to mastery, Hopkins's *Peculiar Sam* also predicts postmodernism's preoccupation with fragmentation and overlapping, encrusted textual terrain.[18] This is a work that strains its own boundaries, pushing out from the traditions that it debunks and the new traditions that it attempts, with wit, to suggest.

NOTES

[1] Martha Patterson argues that Hopkins rotated out from the minstrel tradition but that her work was limited by her reliance on stereotypical characters ("Remaking the Minstrel").

[2] Booker T. Washington's dream for racial uplift is spelled out in his Atlanta Exposition Address, where he concedes that racial progress should be incremental. The Negro, according to Washington, should forfeit his bid for social equality—at least temporarily—in order to gain economic security and a solid capital base.

[3] Martha Patterson argues that Peculiar Sam is a trickster figure who, "…signifies upon the racist tropes of white minstrelsy" (14).

[4] See Peterson's *Early Black American Playwrights and Dramatic Writers* for a list of titles and play synopses from this formative period preceding the first Great War.

[5] Kristina Brooks maintains that one of the older black female figures from Hopkins's *Hagar's Daughter* represents an absence: "…[Aunt Henny's] rolled-back eyes indicate a deviation from rationality, a lack of control, and her literal inability to see or possess 'the gaze' that marks one kind of subject position, while her silence confirms her status as an object…(142)." Aunt Henny, far from being silent, retains the folk practices that have helped her people to endure. She is a seer, a midwife, and a survivor. In fact, it is Aunt Henny's bloodline that outlives the tragedies that unfold narratively, while the more decadent upper middle class is slow to adapt and therefore perishes. Hopkins is so enamored with the aunt and her communally based power that she inserts her all over her oeuvre, often at a crossroad when a difficult decision must be made or when things have gone awry. Rather than object, she is anchor. Thus we can read Aunt Henny's rolled eyes as additional insight that others do not share, for she can look inward for answers as well as outward, and she can use this tool to signify on conditions that do not meet her approval by turning her eyes in, an act that "speaks" without expending too much of her vital energies.

[6] I refer you to Sander Gilman's article on the Hottentot Venus to glance into the manner in which, during the nineteenth century, physical traits came to connote character and social propensity.

[7] While Martha Patterson argues that Peculiar Sam is a trickster figure as well and that Hopkins revises the minstrel tradition, I disagree with her conclusion that this play is nostalgic for the plantation. I read it as much more subversive in terms of trying to undermine regional writing as it calls for redefinitions of art's role, an effort that she hopes will play out on a national, rather than a local scale. I also emphasize that Sam's love of music and dancing should not be read as a mere plea to white audiences that had been fed on black highjinks, but should be appreciated as an encoding of a new-world site of cultural production that locates power in the body and its expressive range, its ability to reach a heightened metaphysical state.

[8] To appreciate the manner in which the dark space or the wilds are demonized in Puritan culture, review much of Hawthorne's work, especially *The Scarlet Letter* and "Young Goodman Brown."

[9] Juno is named for the Roman goddess who rules beside Jupiter. She is also a protector.

[10] There are numerous scenes through out Hopkins's texts where this sexual banter holds sway. For example, *Contending Forces*, certainly the most staid of her four novels, features a

scene where an older black woman and her young paramour ride together on a bicycle, another allusion to sexual activity: "'All this spring he's been a-ridin' me on his bike down in the kitchen every day…'" (366).

[11] See Claudia Tate's *Domestic Allegories of Political Desire* for a sound discussion of the manner in which black women used domesticity and sentimentalism to win political influence.

[12] See my *Black Women Intellectuals* that argues Hopkins's admiration for nation-building, even though her model differed radically from actual Western countries that were defining themselves largely through colonialism, using "others" to delineate a sense of national unity. Hopkins's utopian society was a combination based on merging ancient and modern epistemological systems which would then be connected to a spiritual base that recognized humanity's common ethnic source.

[13] Childress wrote a satirical column about an African American domestic worker in the fifties that was modeled after Langston Hughes' Jess B. Semple series. These works have been collected in a single volume, *Like One of the Family*.

[14] Scholars from Lott to Lhamon have argued a complex relationship between audience and the ebon cover, generally proposing that Americans turned to the minstrel as a sort of catch-all to collect their fears, libidinal wishes, and aspirations for freedom. While complicated and comprising admiration as well as disdain, assessing minstrelsy's formative power is a tricky slope because an entire ethnic/racial group is evacuated out to promote this national cultural fixture that has become a place of national stability, a site to travel to that provides comfort in the guise of a well-rehearsed reverse reflection, what Morrison has described as "playing in the dark with whiteness."

[15] I grant that there was some social commentary embedded within the malaprop-ridden stump speeches that were part of the minstrel repertoire. However, the ignorance of the orator detracted so much from these critiques that it immobilized the performers' ability to persuade. Rather, these orations served as additional proof that black America was not yet ready for or entitled to full citizenship.

[16] Hopkins's first novel is titled *Contending Forces*. (1900)

[17] Hall asserts that identity politics (racial ethnic, gender based) are no longer sufficient to navigate the contemporary civic field because there are no guarantees that specific ethnic groups will either think or act in predictable ways. In modern times, one is much more likely to encounter situations where one has to throw one's hat in with a diverse combine to lobby for a given interest, and the composition of these reformist blocks will change so that the citizen will travel across and make alliances with various civic communities given his diverse needs over time.

[18] I am using Houston Baker's definition of modernism here. See *Modernism and the Harlem Renaissance* (50–51).

TWO

Bridging the Modern: Neurotic Sentimentality Encounters Racial Uplift in Angelina Weld Grimké's *Rachel*

ANGELINA Weld Grimké's *Rachel*, first produced in 1916, is, if anything, decidedly controversial, drawing heated responses from major black leaders and artists such as W.E.B. Du Bois and Alain Locke. Whatever one's estimation of it, the drama is one of the more significant stimuli that invigorated the Harlem-based black cultural proliferation during the twenties and early thirties. It was a key historical marker along the lines of Booker T. Washington's Atlanta Exposition Address and Du Bois's *The Souls of Black Folk*. In terms of the African American women's play writing tradition, I situate Grimké next to Hopkins, a practical convenience that obscures the massive social and political changes that transpired between Hopkins's 1879–1880 *Peculiar Sam* and 1916. Entrenched colonization in Africa, Asia and the Caribbean that would lead to numerous armed conflicts coincided with vast innovations in the manufacturing, communication and transportation industries. On the home front, economic upheaval, Western expansion, Native American insurgency/resistance, immigration, urban instability, mob violence, race and gender-based discrimination all collided with the American Dream. Black America rallied to face this chaotic and often—to it—painfully volatile era by forming its own institutions to fight for the rights and liberties promised to and deserved by the people. The NAACP, one such organization, certainly the most influential by the 1920s, spearheaded the battle against injustice and prejudice on several terrains. As its legal arm identified cases that could set precedents for judicial reform, the cultural branch promoted representation that would set the record straight about black potential and black donations to the world's library of masterpieces. In 1916 under Du Bois's leadership, the NAACP launched a long-term project to redress the maligning of black citizens and sponsored a drama contest to identify a piece that could, among other things, counteract D. W. Griffith's *The Birth of a Nation* (Anderson 3). *Rachel* triumphed and became the first official Race Play (some would argue because her father Archibald was on the NAACP board).

The fact that this production was tied to the NAACP's propaganda campaign would dictate its critical reception for years; only recently have scholars begun to assess it through different lenses. Yet, while we can certainly approach the text today through various theoretical apparatuses, we would be remiss if we did not grasp the manner in which the work and the institution that endorsed it co-created each other. In many respects, the NAACP's development and Grimké's melodrama are intertextual entities. Certainly, what *Rachel* has signified and is likely to continue to project is circumscribed, to some extent, by racial uplift discourse, defined here as the general imperative to enhance black people's quality of life through legal and civil intervention and to rectify racist distortion and to positively inform on black life and contributions. These objectives can be reached by way of united action but also through stalwart deportment on the individual black citizen's part. Culture enjoys a crucial role in most improvement schemes as it, arguably, verifies the displaced African's worthiness by parading his or her intellectual capability, talent and ingenuity for the world to observe. Racial uplift adherents predict that once impediments to black advancement have been removed, there will be no limit to black America's collective giving, envisioning, for instance, that efforts charted by black trailblazers (as various as Du Bois and Garvey) will eventually steer the political system toward a global governing body that views human rights as the top priority.[1] Major tools to fulfill this mission include a zealous faith in education, entrepreneurial acumen, and black leadership training across all fields. So when the NAACP sponsored this contest, it demanded a work that could exemplify its political and social thrust to improve conditions by staging a realistic performance of sanitized model, modern black patriots who were concerned about violent intimidation and deeply rooted racial stereotyping and profiling. Only a mimetic rendition of "real" black figures facing "actual" adversities could remedy the pressing demands levied by Americans who did not feel protected by the law or the government. If Grimké's composition did not meet uplift constructors' (northern, urban and male) exact specifications, then it would be remade, via criticism, to fit the requirements.

Responding to the directive that the play blossom under black progressivism's guiding auspices, *Rachel's* first wave of evaluators, who were associated with the movement, ignored the glaring gender issues that the piece raises and billed it a slice-of-life portrait that explored the barriers that faced the budding black talented tenth (and by extension, through a trickle-down process, the rest of black America). Until the last twenty years or so, the womanist aspects of Grimké's drama have been overlooked in sacrifice to more strictly defined masculinist parameters that in many instances fix black males' plights as essential, while the concerns pertaining specifically to black women are judged to be secondary. My revisionary examination will heed these womanist leanings but recall as well that the piece was commissioned by a powerful civil rights organization, making it, at times, a chimerical product that strives to satisfy numerous deeply held objectives.

The conflicting tensions over whom to reach and what message to prioritize bore their way through the dialogue, action and structure, leaving the interpreter to study how Grimké manages the fissures and recoil of these diverging and competitive political demands and imaginative leanings. I believe that the drama's main strength resides in the writer's resolution not to seal over the contradictions wrought by these various expectations but let them stand, an artistic choice that delivers a modern, allegorical dramatic design. In lieu of realism, the work opens a corridor to what Paul Carter Harrison would recognize as "the supra-universe of myth that reveals the form of things unknown" ("Praise/Word" 5). [2]

Evidence to support my observations comes from the early commentators who realized that something about the play was off kilter because it did not follow naturalism's strict codes, but they did not articulate what that variation from the convention may have insinuated. So, instead of rating the work's properties according to its own logic, critics labeled it failed realism, not living up to what it was intended to execute. Locke and others even charged that Grimké's work won undeservedly because her father was on the NAACP board, an accusation of corruption that provokes still relevant debates about whether the masses or the talented tenth should steer social reform and reconstruction plans.[3] Not surprisingly, this production and its handling elicited censure that was aimed at the emerging black bourgeoisie. Debates about gender, class and aesthetics within black communities and black culture surfaced with Grimké's ambitious show, topics that would drive the Harlem Renaissance's intellectual vitality as various trailblazers vied to promote curative models that privileged a single sector of America's multifaceted black experience over others.[4]

Centered is the Loving Family: Mary (mother) and her two devoted children, Rachel and Thomas, who reside in a small apartment in a northern city with secondary characters that include Jimmy Mason, a four-year-old whom Rachel has befriended, and John Strong, Rachel's beau. The action results from a double lynching down South (Mary's husband and son). After that horrific event, Mary migrates North with her remaining children but decides not to share the murders with her offspring to spare them an extra psychological burden in addition to the one that they have to manage as African Americans during the first decade of the twentieth century. Late in the first act, Mary divulges this gruesome secret after ten years of silence, a decision which alters dramatically both siblings' perspective on life. Rachel ends an engagement and forgoes marriage because she does not want to bring an infant into a savage environment that has no consideration for black life, and Thomas steels himself for revenge. Poverty, inadequate housing, brutal domestic work, employment discrimination and racism in the schools and churches round out the list of social issues that the subjects condemn over several hours (representing a four-year span). What is refreshing, however, is that, although the dramatic scenario is quite bleak, the dialogue challenges these seemingly crushing circumstances. A counteracting power resides in communal and domestic relationships, especially Mary's rapport with her surviving children, which forms the backbone for the care and nurturing that suffuses the play. Grimké is most successful at designing a montage that highlights how the mundane and simple conversations between people can be steeped in affection. For instance, the mother sustains her family with daily rituals and small acts such as listening to them patiently, amusing them, and handing out advice, practices that were not deemed sufficiently dramatic by any standard during the early twentieth century.

Not only does this compilation of small-scale loving gestures extend out to immediate family members, it blankets those who live in the near-by community (defined here as the apartment house and the neighborhood). Kindness begets kindness across and within gender lines as there are special mentoring relationships between Jim and Rachel and between Thomas and John (John serving as a surrogate father figure for Thomas). Furthermore, although Rachel decides not to marry John, their courtship is respectful and tender just as there are indications that Mary's marriage was fruitful, caring and passionate. We surmise from these details that the text explores polarities: tenderness and encouragement versus destruction and alienation.

Conceding that the elements of *Rachel* that I have provided thus far do not fully justify my generic re-categorization, I argue additionally that, in spite of its three linear acts that imply typical realism, Grimké's use of vernacular expression and her introduction of a hodge-podge of interpolated forms including children's games, stories, singing, tearful outbursts, and grand, teetering speeches combined with an oscillating emotional range inscribe an oppositional undercurrent, a subversive strain that renders the drama comparable to the medieval Passion Play that features a number of figurative, highly recognizable binary forces such as good and evil, mercy and retribution that emote and plead their case on the stage.[5] Wickham encapsulates these religious pageants as requiring the entire community's involvement so that the Bible could spring to life, "...in everyday attire to be recognized as a recurring reality throughout eternity" (90–1). The parallels between these ancient outdoor fetes and Grimké's uplift forum are clear as the characters' names, Mary, Rachel, Thomas, John, and James. We should view them as moral figures, spirits that a folk familiar with Biblical lore would recognize.

Other aspects of Grimké's offering fall in line with the medieval Miracle Plays, entities that evolved from the Passion Play and spun out from a concentration on Christ's life to a preoccupation with the saints. Rather than merely listing divine instructions for day-to-day existence, saint-centered theater introduced the ordained, enigmatic outsider who may walk amongst the common people but has been imbued with a visionary compassion. This anomalous dignitary fights for the communal good through tremendous sacrifice and would become the model for modern heroism. Often these virtuous paradigms protect and carry talismen that we associate with specific powers, a practice that many Christian and syncretic religions continue to observe (Catholicism, Voodoo, and Santería, for instance). In Grimké's hands, Rachel is transformed into a saint over the three acts, a conversion that fits her with her own iconography (rosebuds), outsider status, and sacrificial tendency. Not directly reflecting reality, the drama's overwhelming atmosphere is thick with questions concerning original sin, a fall from grace and attempts to recover a lost Eden through faith and good acts, making this piece more modernist in design and theme than Victorian. In fact, a parallel to Harlem Renaissance staples like Jean Toomer's *Cane* and Countee Cullen's neoclassical poetry and drama is obvious because all three writers revive and even reshuffle Biblical tales by rotating them through the prism of various African American modalities and experiences.

Rachel premiered at the Myrtilla Miner Normal School in Washington, D.C., on March third and fourth, 1916 (Perkins 8), then moved to the Neighborhood Playhouse in New York City for a showing on April 26, 1917, and concluded its run at Brattle Hall in Cambridge, Massachusetts, on May 24, 1917 (Archer 114). Cornhill of Boston published the play in 1920, an event which increased its reach and enhanced the esteem afforded it because the work received more and better reviews when published than it did as a live production (Perkins 9). In spite of its relatively short run, the show galvanized black America, drawing thinkers, artists and cultural workers from the three urban centers that would contribute the most to African American intellectual thought and creativity during the forthcoming

Renaissance years. I would go so far as to assert that, notwithstanding that fewer Americans saw this work than Hopkins's *Peculiar Sam*, its impact has been much more absolute because it catalyzed and unequivocally shaped contemporary racial discourse, especially the path that African American cultural resistance would take. Primarily, even though the reception to it was mixed, *Rachel* fostered debate, pricking discussions on how to respond to lynching, whether black art should be primarily propaganda or organic expression, whether urbanity or a regional/rural core should constitute the basis for black art, how class difference should or could be explored imaginatively, whether sentimentality still held significance as an discursive source and which rights and social roles were available to women.

The drama's deeply rooted, ground-breaking impact has much to do with its production history. It was the first theatrical work to be sponsored by a national, secular black institution that did not set out to be a financial success. Carving out a niche that combated commercialization, this originating official problem play was meant to be "acapitalistic," running outside the marketplace's reach. A cooperative effort would sustain it through ticket sales, and those receipts would either fund its future or that of other pieces that the NAACP would mount or go towards institutional and programming needs not in the arts. Du Bois's revolutionary insistence for a theater about, by, for, and near us is echoed in *Rachel's* launching ("Krigwa Little Theatre" 135); therefore, it set a precedent for local black theater situated in a black milieu that would foment ideas and elicit constructive solutions to various social, economic and political predicaments.

Leaders expected and insisted that Grimké ascribe to racial uplift themes. However, while the NAACP and others were calling for propaganda, they were not actually sure about which forms would best serve that purpose. Realism was often touted as a necessary rejoinder to racism, yet Du Bois privately favored the elaborate historical pageant over naturalistic displays.[6] Controversy extended as well over which core audience to address. Should art be designed to inspire and challenge black people, and, if so, which ones? Middle class? Working Class? Urban? Rural? Men? Women? Or, should it persuade white Americans to alter their attitudes and behavior toward their darker fellow citizens? The first strategy, created in nationalism's kiln, advocates a separatist culture that takes as its main goal enacting African American wellness through art by providing installations through which black people could form healthy identifications that would, in turn, stimulate pride and growth. The other model takes off from abolitionism and places white America in a "loving" hot seat so that the performance space becomes a cradle for massive social reform.

Du Bois, the great architect of black theater, was not definite about which direction to take or whether one avenue had to be subordinated to the other. His commentary on *Rachel* reveals just this inconclusiveness: He thought the many monologues in the drama succeeded in pricking white consciences and inciting African American emotions (Hay 23). The only clue to his evaluative ranking in this review comes from Du Bois's listing "white consciences" before "African American emotions." So it would seem that, while he had proposed on separate occasions that black drama should directly serve black people, in his assessment of Grimké's work, he locates the black artist's chief responsibility in building humanitarian bridges across color lines. The reasoning is that once practices that are bounded by the ideology of whiteness cease, racism will disappear. Du Bois was not yet prepared to stand behind a distinctive African American culture that was not facing a white audience (double consciousness). The great leader would continue to wrestle with this matter.

In response to reviews, Grimké clarified that she wanted to persuade white women to organize against lynching, rationalizing that motherhood was the most rhetorically convincing tool at her disposal (*Selected Works* 413–4). If she could convince white women of lynching's far-reaching destructiveness, how it shattered home life and perverted family bonds, then she could prevail upon them not to collude in the bestial vigilantism that was sweeping the country, the mob violence whose number-one justification was the alleged mishandling of white women by black men. Without white women's testimony—official and unofficial—lynching could not be justified. The drama, then, is designed to lead America toward empathy and to evaluate whether sentimentality was a rhetorical tool that could cross racially segregated lines in 1916. Sentimentality is placed under the microscope as the tried method that had reshaped history half a century previously when abolitionists had deployed it successfully to mobilize northern white women to join their cause.[7]

In spite of both Du Bois's and Grimké's naming of an external focus for black art that extends out to dominant society, *Rachel* is not just dramatized oratory that pleads to white America. If that comprised the entire scope of its impact, then it would be far more melodramatic along the lines of *Uncle Tom's Cabin*, where Tom's links to family and life have been completely and unremittingly forfeited by curtain call, but this does not happen in *Rachel*. Instead, the last scene exhibits a new social order where a certain wildness (Cornel West may even call it nihilism) deconstructs the "naturalized" domestic field and offers in its stead an engineered version of social relations as Rachel takes on the mantle of mother but renounces her role as a biological parent.[8] Therefore, the play subverts both its author's and its influential critic's stated intentions. While offering itself as a problem play that petitions white America, the work spins out from this political platform through a series of redefinitions and re-codings. Ultimately, this drama comes off as more tinged by black separatist discourses than by American reformism because Rachel becomes an icon for black self-sufficiency and black decision-making in much the same way that the Statue of Liberty represents open opportunity to immigrants.

The domestic front becomes the staging point for this new nationalism.[9] Grimké carries out her charge to incite an era of black strength and excellence by creating saintly iconography with a black female face, a pivotal emblem that will bridge the gap between domestic disharmony and political action. Furthermore, Rachel's metamorphosis from ordinary, black teenager to exemplar of race-proud values occurs because she is exiled from and "dispossessed" of the domestic center by racism. In the end, a black nation becomes her only viable home as she is forced to reject the then-standard Western role for women because she rationalizes that without major social, political and economic reform, black children born in the United States become targets for lynch mobs, psychological murder, and economic starvation. Given these conditions, black parents who do nothing to enact their release from a neo-slavery system doom their children to a cycle of terror. Therefore, traditional gender roles for black citizens had to change and broaden to win greater civic freedoms. I should note that the playwright is not encouraging African American women to stop having children, but she is calling for them to tap more often into the saint's path that often calls for delayed gratification, rapid adaptability, a focused vision, and heroic efforts: stalwart striving.

Grimké is cognizant that her forward-seeking African American attitude will result in certain losses. For instance, the saint-like role that Rachel acquires has the added consequence of alienating her from her time period as she becomes something of an alpha and omega signification, one that does not physically reproduce but is consistently reproduced by culture. This quality allows her, by the final act, to float above the events that transpire on stage, especially the violence, condescension, humiliation and fear brought on by unequal social conditions and irrational hatred and panic. However, as she rises and looks toward the heavens, she becomes more estranged from the tight family unit that granted her succor as the curtain opened on the first act. The drama's final note affirms that even though Rachel's broader vision costs her separation anxiety and tears, her position as an entity that transcends the community that she serves by way of her extreme departure from social norms grants her the insight to lead a rebellion by way of symbolic power. This is the trade-off. By taking on the mantle of a super-maternal figure that does not engage in adult intimacy, a weeping, black virgin myth-maker who guides little children through racism's fire, a figure akin to what the emblematic mother of black nationalism might look like if rendered artistically, Rachel must release her connection to domesticity and move away from her beloved mother, brother, and boyfriend.

Grimké's play secretes its more threatening black state-building leanings within a milder outer layer that presumably appeals to white America. This structural choice developed from the understanding that white patrons and contributors to the NAACP would certainly see and comment on the production as well as less empathetic white viewers who could block future uplift art. Equally germane to her project was the fact that by 1916 black radical sentiment was in the process of being resuscitated and modified, reinterpretations that would tap into ideas set down by Nat Turner, David Walker and Martin Delany. Grimké's play fell on the outer edge of this revival, a course that would be brought full circle by Cyril Briggs and Marcus Garvey during the twenties. So, even though Grimké does not provide Rachel with a specific, razor-sharp platform, her canonization transmits the message that a revamped radical ideology is immanent. Rachel stands for what will later be defined as a vehement departure from accommodationist practices. Thus the piece wraps itself in several veils as it struggles to illuminate the strongest conduit for black America to reach its aims. Toying with reform while it leans toward nationalism, seemingly realistic but actually delving into ancient repositories of rousing, polar passions, planting one foot in nineteenth-century sentimentality to watch its reincarnation with variation in the twentieth, predicting modernism's preoccupation with circularity and relational historicism and elevating black women even if she has to locate them partially underground, Grimké reaches for a dramatic foothold that will imprint and inspire black progress. *Rachel* radiates like an enlarged dramatic star that stirs black folk to action, no matter how difficult the trail.

In contrast to Du Bois and Grimké who were willing to claim the race play because they believed it could restore America, knowing full well that the pieces that they wrote and sanctioned were also engaged in other "covert" missions, Locke dismissed the form categorically. He insisted that sentimentality and problem-oriented themes reduced black theater, which he thought should explore the totality of black experience without excuse or defense (Sanders 9). To him, the problem play's aesthetics impinged on black expression's full breadth. *Rachel* stood as an exemplar of the stiff theatrical stuff that Locke abhorred, and he was not too fond of the overwrought emotive tone of it either. Preferring folk plays and sexier urban dramas (perhaps Locke was most offended by the lack of funkiness in the problem play), he demanded that the ordinary man's rendition of black life motivate the live arts.[10]

In any case, the period between 1916 and 1936 witnessed serious (in contrast to merely commercial) black productions that are rife with references to the Bible, mothers' missions and courtships, while they explore social environments and reflect vernacular speech patterns and contemporary—rural and urban—aesthetics, all characteristics that fall under *Rachel's* net. Yet, a distinct division between Grimké's installation and later works by Harlem Renaissance writers, Willis Richards and May Miller, for instance, continues to dominate critical perception.[11] As a case in point, Brown-Guillory warns that, "A contemporary audience might find the sentimentality in *Rachel* objectionable, but one must bear in mind that Grimké was born in 1880 and grew up with Victorian influences" (*Their Place* 6). In linking Grimké to Victorian mores and style, Brown-Guillory denies the writer's conscious attempt to shift to a twentieth-century sensibility and vibe: setting her vision in an urban apartment, supplying the characters with urbane chitchat and informal phrases such as "Jiminy Xmas" (126), and revealing much about the characters' personal lives and their passion as in the mother's confession to her children about her first marriage (for the most part, such revelations were kept hidden during the Victorian age—at least until someone stumbled across them—and only veiled references were made to a sexualized past). Not complying with Victorian rules about decorum and speech, this melodrama strives to unearth repressed personal and national memories. It dares to address every social ill prevalent during the early twentieth century from work discrimination to racial epithets and lynching to the limited roles available to black women and men. It is even about sex, or rather the lack of it that is caused by unrelenting social pressures. Bear in mind that Ma Loving's husband is dead (lynched); Rachel decides not to marry John because she refuses to bring more children into a abysmal world and birth control is not an option, and Thomas is too busy searching for a job and restitution to worry about a social life. If the sexual landscape is barren, then perhaps that is the broad picture that Grimké is painting of her American moment that she views as appallingly sterile. We do know that in her poetry, she treats lesbian sexuality in spite of its being forbidden.[12]

As she was not afraid to represent the body or the spirit in its full complexity, I propose an alternative rubric. Rather than categorizing this dramatist as a strict nineteenth-century sentimentalist who was overly preoccupied with proper/fixed gender roles, we place her next to someone like Tennessee Williams, who is also adept at uncovering the neurotic underground stream that seeps through Western culture. Grimké proclaimed that her show examines how a highly-strung girl reacts to strong social forces (*Selected Works* 413). The intensely sensitive woman who stands out against a staid social backdrop is common to both Grimké and Williams. Like Williams, Grimké casts a net where neurosis is gendered female, exaggerating the space between male/rationalist discourse and female silence/unintelligibility to highlight how women have been confined by domestic and social constraints, but, in spite of the limitations, their imaginations allow them to build alternative worlds/spaces. Because she lives on several sliding planes (certainly her own and that of a master text), Rachel, like Williams's Blanche, Maggie, and Amanda, is ahead of her time and, therefore, foreign to the present/contemporary moment.

We should not, however, read this heightened but detached state as pure tragedy under either Grimké's or Williams's guiding hands because, while the female subject's self-constructed reality may be as debilitating as it is often chaotic, it is also empowering in its intense ardor, a fervor that can change or at least challenge a traditional discursive/dramatic course. Both dramatists craft a theatrical environment where the zeal generated during old-world rituals that predate America is drawn on to reinvigorate and shape contemporary theater, resulting in forms that implicitly chart the continuity and difference between ancient representations of emotion that hinged on fluid, demonstrative, excessive figurations and modern representation that contains these same passions within a splintered, subterranean mat, defined by porosity, erratic nature, and volatility. This working definition of neurosis as an agile, quick-change emotive trope mirrors the high-pitched, jagged tone found in these writers' works.

Furthermore, Grimké and, I would argue, Williams take an additional step and figure the neurotic as a modern-day saint, offering the view that a compassionate visionary today would be out of sync with the demonstrative hub of her surroundings that tend toward sterile indifference. In other centuries, these anomalous emissaries were celebrated in the Miracle Plays and set up as exemplars of civil disobedience. By the twentieth century, because modernity reinvents and invests in the trial to dispatch with "abnormal" or extreme behavior, the saint becomes marked by various discourses (primarily medical, legal, and psychiatric). Thus these figures, especially the female ones, continue to stand apart from their surroundings, but that distance is no longer read as triumph but as an aberration that requires containment. To elude capture and to make meaning beyond that which is sanctioned by state codes, these rebellious female figures are forced to concoct their own myths, narratives, and imaginative realms to contextualize their existence beyond the truncated and often distorted apertures provided by dominant discourses. As the drama unfolds, female characters are caught in a parallel process of conjuring communicative vehicles right on the stage. Often this eerie, echo-like cross-current is delivered by way of the women's verbal asides that include songs, chants, refrains, nonsense phrases, children's rhymes, and/or babble that is loaded with subversive marginalia.

Perhaps it was easier for reviewers and scholars to label *Rachel* Victorian melodrama than to grapple with and explain its disturbing temperamental polarities and odd interpolated narrative snatches and tunes that surely must have enervated and exasperated the audience. Consequently, critics contrast it to the hip, sleek, sometimes gritty plays that Locke promoted, often favoring these smoother folk-based displays that ran high on cool aesthetics. Delving deeper into the debates on Black Drama, we know that Locke, Du Bois, and their disciples distinguished between what they considered to be two promising schools: race play and folk play. Despite the antipathies, from our historical distance, we observe that Locke's folk play (or what I call hyperrealism) and Du Bois's problem play were linear in form with straightforward plots, identifiable characters, and believable predicaments. In fact, one of the few innovations that separates one subgenre from the other is that the folk dramatist has no intention of parading black role models, preferring instead the endemic subject whose actions and thoughts dictate the plot; therefore, these works tend to stay afield of characterizations that are clearly and vulgarly manipulated for ideological purposes (their subjects are exploited more subtly). On the other hand, conventional problem plays exhibit black figures who uphold the race through dignified action and resolute demeanors. So, hyperrealism is, in black art's case, a depiction of scenarios where the subjects fall short of perfection and therefore must return to culture to explain and explore the gap between idealized vision and raw experience. As a result, there generally tends to be more tea reading, dancing, singing, and alternative practices circulating around and within hyperrealism's conceptual fame. Other than this dissimilarity, both modes adhere to traditional Western dramatic structure but incorporate undercutting black aesthetics.

Grimké's piece has been placed squarely under Du Bois's wing, Sanders distilling it to "…a melodramatic exposition of the traumatic effects of racial persecution…on a respectable middle-class…family" (23) and Brown-Guillory claiming that, "…she merely mirrors life for blacks in American society at the turn of the century" (*Their Place* 6). Even Molette, who argues that the work has been undervalued, reads it as strict realism: "Here was a woman attempting to portray Black people as she knew they existed and not how the white playwrights of that era, such as Eugene O'Neill and Ridgely Torrence, envisioned them—exotic and inarticulate creatures" (30). Disputing the critics who categorize the piece as prototypical naturalism that simply promotes the black middle class, Grimké avows staunchly that Rachel does not epitomize the average African American woman of her day but is a figure that charts liminal formations. Granted that the writer's claim is not the ultimate or even primary authority when it comes to interpretation, in this case, Grimké's statement seems valid because from the first scene, Rachel's fragility and earnestness infuse the performance space: she is either out of sync or over the top, so much so that it is difficult to identify with her in the manner that realism typically facilitates. How can the audience relate to a character that sloughs off her earthiness to become a saint? Certainly Rachel's audacious denouncing of biological motherhood during this time period is reason enough to view her as an enigma, which strongly affirms that the play moves beyond strict mimetic boundaries.

Some other elements prick us to resist a naturalistic reading. Even with three linear acts, time loops around to the anniversary of the lynching and the memories associated with it. Moreover, while we greet an average middle-class black family, each member battles with demons born from racism in much the same way that the saints were commandeered to fight evil by almost viscerally tussling with its existence. And, while she paints "traditional" gender roles, she freezes them as relics, just as a cameo would capture a lost bubble in time. These combined structural departures create an impressionistic field of static, ghosts, and seething and palpable anger coinciding with tender exchanges between loved ones, bringing on stage a communal, nightmarish vault that houses many war stories.

A few additional distinctions need to be made. *Rachel* dramatizes an emotional unraveling where the threads of nineteenth-century "womanly duty" separate into flashes of shrill energy, but the work is not a character study or a single psychological profile as critic William Storm has proposed. Rachel is figurative, and her state of being should not be separated from the vast historical surroundings that produce her. More exactly, she magnifies the social context, divulging how political and ideological forces can act on the self. If Rachel becomes odd, then the explanation for the change in her behavior is external. We must view this drama, in spite of its title, as a work that does not glorify a single subjectivity over relationships. As I have argued, the package features a number of formidable characters who all have a chronicle to share. In truth, Mary's revelations are more crucial to the show's combustible engine than those of any other character. Her resolve to impart the atrocity that destroyed and splintered her family initiates the events that propel the plot. Mary's fulcrum position emphasizes life's relational, woven patterns that inherently resist dissecting scientific discourse. In this sense, Grimké's work is modern and foreshadows Williams, Faulkner, Morrison, and Hansberry. Thus, the symbol/saint Rachel can only rise because of the social net that manufactures and then buoys her.

That Mary is named after the most famous mother in the Christian lexicon draws our attention to her pivotal placement. We confirm her significance as we encounter her in the first scene, sewing a white dress in a green and white apartment, imagery associated with nurturing, growth, fertility, and innocence (124-5). Like many a parent, she watches worriedly by the window because her children are late in returning, an anxiety that is exacerbated by the trauma she carries from her husband's and son's dismemberment down south. Time takes stage as a major entity as well; a clock sits on the mantel, and the plot's gears revolve around the anniversary date of the killings on October sixteenth. In place of the spiral progressivism that Pauline Hopkins depicted with *Peculiar Sam*, Grimké adopts repetition as her fundamental guide, continually returning to this family's wounding. Taking into account the mother's significance and circularity's structural dominance, we realize that this work will concentrate on generational and affiliation concerns. Should all memories be passed down? Can they be? What happens if they are, but those images and narratives render the recipient unfit for survival? Is adaptability—quick change—preferable to repetition both in cultural and domestic configurations?

While these queries are dramatized across gender lines, I isolate the relationship between Mary and Rachel. In the first act, Rachel is bent on duplicating her mother's life, stating that, "…and a voice said to me…'Rachel, you are to be a mother to little children'" (134).[13] It is worth mentioning that Grimké paints Rachel's early decision to be a mother as acquiescence to disembodied instruction, a choice that argues that the contemporary ideological edict states that women value themselves in terms of their reproductive capability. This stood as the norm for all American women across race and ethnicity, and, while slavery had transferred black women's "biological imperative" into a vast, exploitative economic network, by the late nineteenth century, social rules stipulated that past atrocities be forgotten. Black women were to start afresh with the nuclear, patriarchal, single-race family model and forget their white relatives who resided outside legal/legitimate designations. They were also to forget/disremember the gruesome and violent acts levied on black citizens and forge a commitment to a largely unfamiliar and unsustainable domestic structure. Pledging allegiance to the nuclear family became a condition of their citizenship.[14]

Ma Loving awakens from a ten-year slumber during which she guarded and censored the past, a repression and hibernation that parallels the manner in which the nation requires African Americans to deny history to join the civic body. Significantly, she begins to resurrect her formative years in the South at the behest of her son's ghost, who manifests himself in the guise of a neighborhood child: "Rachel, he [Jimmy] is the image of my boy—my George!" (148). This reincarnation buttresses the repetitious motif that permeates the play as bodies, faces, images and sounds circulate around and within African American domestic space, a cultural phenomenon that is reminiscent of the intense search for family that obsessed late nineteenth-century African Americans, a period when friends would bring news that, over the course of their travels, they had seen someone who "favored" "so and so's" kin. Informal and formal networks scoured the landscape, hoping to discover any physical resemblance that could reconnect children, parents, aunts, uncles, and grandparents. Descriptions could also help to reunite lovers and mates. These genealogical searches not only resulted in actual physical reunions but also sparked the recollection and declaration of submerged memories. Ma Loving ponders whether to answer the call to retell—what Morrison would view as "passing on"—both the terrifying stories of murder and of cherished conviviality, all of which are bordered within the Middle Passage's broader context. Ma Loving weighs the impact of her disclosure, "I have been trying to make up my mind for some time whether a certain thing is my duty or not.... I see you ought to be told." (144). The irony is that in the recount, a circular rite that brings together past and present, Ma precipitates the ensuing break with the domestic space that Rachel feels she must carry out to overcome their brutal past and present. So, in direct contrast to the oral narrative's usual function, which is to bring the circle closer, Mary's tale is so abhorrent that it disperses the network, igniting an exodus toward other social configurations.

We find nothing less than a redefinition of motherhood. The Biblical Rachel endures, overcomes, rises to leadership, and then dies giving birth. Here the same pattern ensues up to the point of the biological birth and then diverges from that sequence in a manner that is so antithetical and radical to the age's prevailing norms that it literally petrifies the audience. Even late twentieth-century reviewers find this play somewhat repugnant; for example, Trudier Harris argues that Rachel's decision not to have children is genocidal and self-indulgent ("Before the Strength" 30), a charge similar to those levied at Grimké when the play was first produced (Perkins 9). The writer fought back by arguing that Rachel was just one neurotic girl, and, therefore, her decision did not promote "race annihilation." Yet, the fact that Grimké had to defend her speaks volumes because during the early twentieth century, the standards yoke giving birth and motherhood. Illustrating an alternative path, Rachel does not abandon her intention to raise and defend black children along with her decision to forego marriage: The last line of the play is "Ma Rachel loves you so" (209). While she does select a virginal life, Rachel becomes, for all intent and purposes, a nun on par with Mother Teresa. *Rachel* posits that she who gives up something precious to guard and love her community/race typifies motherhood, not the biological act of giving birth.[15]

Rachel's decision voices her agency, but during the final act, the Lovings become increasingly concerned about Rachel's health, labeling her depressed (198). Casting aside the medical terminology for a spiritual frame of reference, it is conceivable that we perceive of the character's estrangement as a rebirth. On one side we locate Rachel, the daughter, sister, friend, and playmate to the neighborhood children and, on the other, a heroine, who grows through suffering before her eventual writing off the dais/page. Corroboration that she undergoes a self-induced transmutation comes from her destruction of the rosebuds that have been given to her by her suitor (198). This crumpling of the buds may represent a symbolic barricading of her sexuality: Rachel takes the fate of her hymen in her own hands because that is the only way that she can surpass the gender roles that have been laid out for her by not only the dominant culture but by the leaders of her own community. Not a personal sacrifice nor meant to mirror the actions of actual black women, this gesture becomes a comment on social cause and effect. More specifically, Rachel's jettisoning of her sexuality and her awareness that she has pursued this option lead to a resultant, splintering neurotic pulse, a tone that begins to invade American culture more generally during the early twentieth century.

Winding its arms around American theater certainly, but other institutions as well, including the self-help industry, psychology and advertising, neurosis takes shape as both a condition and an atmospheric entity. By emphasizing this new teetering modality, Grimké distinguishes between the nineteenth century, when women had not fully perceived that the female body was something that Western culture had selected to trade for progress (if women became aware of this barter, it was justified as part of the natural design) and 1916, when it becomes possible to trace what happens when a female subject awakens to the realization that she is forgoing her own gratification for a greater cause. In the early twentieth-century model, anger, bitterness, and resentment coexist with Rachel's very conscious denial of self. During an era when mob violence and the mutilation and disposal of black bodies was the norm, Rachel with the foresight of future anguish, selects community over her own pressing needs.

While separated by two ruling world views, progressivism (Hopkins) and compression (Grimké), the pair are in conversation across time, Hopkins locating a safe arena for an aesthetics of pleasure and Grimké arriving at the bleak conclusion that representations of black joy have not only become packaged but have been minted into weapons that further assail darker citizens. Chiefly, dominant myths had determined that the alleged uncontrollable lust of the black man compels him to attack white women and the so-called "hot nature" of the black woman prevents her from establishing domestic security, limitations that blocked rapid black assimilation into the dominant group. Not naïve about these devastating circulating myths, Grimké removes black joy from the cultural sphere, fostering the birth of a painful cultural era that is penetrated imaginatively by the governing trope of madness (defined here as competitive parallel worlds). So, while she may use her art to mourn this forced revamping of the public sphere, Grimké views repression as a political necessity.

Given forty additional years of Jim Crow, intimidation, and pervasive racism, this young uplift writer walks a disturbing, black female heroine across the boards mainly because the atmosphere was ripe for producing her. If critics find themselves taking issue with Rachel, then perhaps it is the concept of a heroine as an outsider/protector that is so needling and requires study. Is the kind of sacrifice that so separates a subject from the communal hub that the subject warrants subsequent or alternative categorization ever worth it? This is the philosophical question that the play raises, expecting that the audience will debate and formulate their own conclusions on the matter because when Rachel declares herself "Mother" at the end of the performance, she not only affirms her right to re/name herself, she brings this implicit inquiry to the fore. Will, can, or should the audience accept this altered Rachel as their champion? The reviews/critiques indicate that a great deal of anxiety continues to reside in doing so. Rachel emanates as a shipwrecked hermit whose great martyrdom is still largely misread as a self-indulgent act rather than a noble gift, interpretations that probably have much to do with the manner in which black women continue to be scripted.

Black heroines are still uncommon. Ask for a list of African American female leaders, and one is sure to receive Harriet Tubman, perhaps

Sojourner Truth, and Ida B. Wells, women whose public persona is vocal, strong, determined, practically impregnable. Unfortunately, artistic renderings of these figures rarely extend beyond a prescribed set of parameters, but, as revisionary historians are redefining these greats, we are coming to realize that vulnerability, frustration, and a certain degree of social rebelliousness (hence distance from the social center more often than not) distinguish these black female leaders. With its emotion-laden dramatic housing, *Rachel* problematizes the act of documentary reconstruction (especially heroism); for in this play, we follow a guardian who appears to be disintegrating at each step because of her growing separation from the norms that she must defend. Rachel is so harried by curtain fall that we anticipate a final gut-wrenching cry as the stage darkens. The playwright's directive stipulates that—similar to a torch singer—the actress has a voice full of pent-up longing, heartbreak, and hopelessness (189). This broken song represents an early instance of a black female dramatist incorporating the blues into her text, a fragmented chanting and lamentation that swaddles the play within a blues-based ethos where the atmosphere has begun to erode the existing basic social plane, both materially and metaphysically. Culture returns to "build up the sand bar" and ward off this incursion on the soul. We find this type of weary labor reflected in the drama's circular form that turns back on itself to return continuously to the site of the original bereavement. Thus *Rachel* epitomizes a variation in the African American female theater tradition, a turning away from a progressive ragtime beat to more weight-bearing blues keys.

While Hopkins hangs her hopes on contentment (even bliss) and its ability to reinvigorate liberation discourses and Grimké uses her piece to define historical space as disintegrating and open to the reemergence of the most polarized and mythic forces, they do share, paradoxically, the faith that a theatrical fullness can be achieved, a conviction that drama can at least partially reconfigure the audience as a community that can be sated/stimulated by the spectacle. Grimké strives especially to revolutionize the manner in which her imagined recipient either watching the piece or reading it values domesticity, defined in the nineteenth century as the mundane and the sentimental but redefined by this play as a complete range of competing and compelling high-pitched states. In her production, it comes to the fore that neither family nor feeling will ever be whole or singular again, that porosity is a condition that we will have to live with in the modern age. But, this eventuality as displayed on the stage may be comforting to the viewer because it reflects, more accurately, life's imbalances.

Another vital aspect of Grimké's message is the manner in which the natural world is redefined: nurturing not procreation governs our survivalist instincts because biological reproduction (depicted here as a series of necessary accidents) is less important than what happens to the child/adult in a social environment. *Rachel* argues that without care and positive reinforcement and fortification, the young can be dehumanized to the point of non-being: lynching can either be a physical or psychological murder. For instance, the script recognizes no difference in intensity between the stringing up of Rachel's father and brother and the taunting of young Jimmy with the word "nigger." Hatred can turn both word and rope into a rattler's coil. Rachel uses the rosebud to explicate her case: "If you are good to them, they'll grow up into lovely roses, won't they? And if you hurt them, they'll die" (178). This may seem like an obvious point in our contemporary self-help era, but, in 1916, it was quite novel. A black female intellectual had the temerity to dramatize that addressing the private sphere should form an integral part of any uplift program. And, by extension, if black women ruled over the domestic realm, then their contributions to freedom-fighting efforts were invaluable. So, she mounted a work that was sponsored by the NAACP, which then had mostly all-male leadership, and, with it, she chided the board for overlooking or making secondary the concerns and distress of black women and the places where they "live."

The playwright also collapses Victorian distinctions that sharply divide public and private into specific quadrants because what happens on the home front impacts on open ground and vice versa. Pressing a social/psychological model where subjectivity formation determines humanity rather than legal or biological terms, her drama demands that homes, schools, churches, and other community-based institutions take responsibility for their often tyrannical and harmful attacks on black minds and spirits. A number of interpolated accounts stress this point: Ethel Lane, a little black girl, has been stunted by racism at school and at church (173–177); Tom is snubbed by his white school friends (142); Rachel complains about segregation at the theaters (170); and John Strong has to wait tables in spite of a college education (164). These everyday insults compound and do as much long-term damage as the image of strange fruit in Southern trees.

Grimké strives to shape racial uplift discourse and the very institution that was willing to recognize her as a creative artist but not as a strategist for black liberation. Thus in many respects, *Rachel* is Grimké's contribution to the NAACP policy board, her interpretation of the past and how it has constructed her present, and her response to these amassing forces. Ultimately, she sought to broaden liberation policies to include semi-private institutions, what Raymond Williams would identify later as the ideological state apparatus. The playwright illuminated the sites where psychological racism is levied, and she provides the implements that can remedy these strikes (primarily loving relationships). Therefore, I disagree with Brown-Guillory that "…there is no call for action" (*Their Place* 6). Antidotes are hidden in the alternative language/codes that the women use: visions and dream talk, singing, children's rhymes and games. *Rachel* is rife with such breaking and breaking in utterances as lullabies that feature sailing babies and sweet little fellers (132–133), tears of joy and anguish, Ma Loving's recurring dreams that resuscitate the bracing, vivid memory of her loved ones (147), and Rachel's song to John that explains her thoughts and feelings (203). Together, these dialogic elements that interrupt the strict dramatic narrative line transform the piece into a poly-rhythmic exhibition that incorporates various ranges, making it subliminally choral in the way that Hopkins's *Peculiar Sam* operates more overtly, for where this is a call (pain) in *Rachel*, there is a response (song/game/protection).

A fine illustration of what I have just described occurs in the third act. By recounting a fable about two boys who live in an abusive household but are visited by a good fairy who provides direction to the Land of Laughter, a place where happiness, gaiety and good will preside, Rachel pacifies young Jimmy, who has just felt racism's first nettle. In the fantasy, the two lads are tempted by riches, power, and fame but maintain their course and eventually reach a lush place where people treat each other with warmth and compassion (183–187). This interpolated narrative operates on several levels, the literal one being that Rachel arms Jimmy by elevating the cultural arena that could be inhabited by African Americans during this period when very few could attain fame, or economic and social security. In its place, the land of laughter is a manifestation of creativity, channeling pain into aesthetically appealing traditions, rituals and codes, the exact process that Rachel's myth-making follows as she warms Jimmy's dejected spirit. On another level, this story is inherently gendered; the alternative paths not taken are masculine, but this land of laughter is an interior space that bridges both genders. I see Grimké's racial uplift blueprint: to draw on the cultural and psychological facets of black life that already protect and tend the soul and use that ground to spring off into the public sphere. Health begins at home, home here defined as an oasis that includes "green trees and grass," "singing birds," softly murmuring, welcoming people, easy sleep, and folk "growing old with laughter" (187). Because this world is offered up as dreamscape, it reveals the writer's best hope for combating the many ills that faced black citizens. She comments that a people's gains and prosperity would be short-lived without a firm, fertile interior life that could help brace the black self when infringements are made on it. Money and renown without a firm stake in "the land of laughter" would only lead to the mimicking of oppressive dominant systems. The little fellow's journey to that smiling country represents as well the artist's attempt to introduce black male leadership to the domestic sphere's centrality, especially in regard to policy making and resource distribution. Civil rights steps that did not entail bolstering black people's psychological well-being alongside legal, economic, and political maneuvering would fail. Furthermore, black men in the home space—living in it and emerging from it with the lesson of laughter intact—are crucial too.

By the third act, Rachel begins to safeguard this realm, but the irony is that while she blankets her little charges with wholeness, she is herself fragile, spinning out from the traditional role that her mother has bequeathed her into the more nebulous territory of African American female myth-maker and guardian. Perhaps Rachel's uneasy stretch into uncharted waters parallels what Grimké may have felt about her role as "the uplift dramatist" and male leadership, including her father, who selected her work as the NAACP's first official play. Surely she must have encountered some discomfort related to stepping out from the domestic arena and entering the public sphere as "the cultural representative" of the first major, national black organization. Undoubtedly, she may have been preoccupied with how to transmit her message but not offend or seem overly critical of black men. Quick change, or in this case, a breaking emotive subtext characterized by Rachel's intermittent sobs as the last act winds down becomes an ingenious way to retain a non-threatening (to men) posture while also directing these male leaders as to how to establish and design their program. Employing a dynamic that approaches and retreats from authority, the play appears to submit to a male-authored agenda but turns and highlights a female visionary. Reflect for a moment on the manner in which Tennessee Williams's female characters galvanize the stage/screen and gain power with their tears and ranting—even if their influence only flashes temporarily and in fits and starts. Rachel functions in much the same way, but, in contrast to Williams's women, her deeply felt fatigue stems from the jettisoning of her sexuality, and it also emerges from her disquiet about securing and sheltering the dream of a safe environment for America's black children. Grimké's emphasis on the psychological health of black youth is prophetic. Unfortunately, her call for a shift in uplift institutions' priorities went unheeded until men like Alvin Poussaint, James Comer, and others raised it later in the twentieth century and made it a national issue.[16]

Questions about rearing sound African Americans and about gender and authority are not the only subjects raised by this production. For instance,

Rachel comments implicitly on how the black female body in performance dispatches meaning concurrently with the written script. Audiences view a kinetic, attractive African American actress in the prime of her life, who all the while projects heavy speeches, conveys involved bedtime stories, sings to family and lover alike and, for much of the stage time, frolics and romps with little children. This role, in terms of physical execution, emits sensuality. Akin to Hopkins's prancing Juno, Rachel commands the boards through movement, for the other characters, except for the youngsters, are still in light of Rachel's exhausting activity. She throws off a potent sexual vibe that contrasts with her relatively staid lines. Rachel's sensuality is disconcerting, especially to the heterosexual men in the audience because after a few hours of this supple mobility, she then renounces all plans for romance and sends her lover away. To these viewers, *Rachel* is a tease: three long acts of inviting body play and barely a little kiss by curtain close. Frustration alone was enough to make some male reviewers walk away from the piece thoroughly annoyed: Willis Richardson vowed to get something more from the theater even if he had to write the script himself. Perhaps this explains why Grimké's published text received better reviews than the theatrical production did (Perkins 9). Without the "distracting" black female body, readers could digest the speeches carefully and pay attention to their full import.

While the ending, most likely, exasperated quite a few members of the audience who had been trained to expect a happy conclusion, there are several explanations for Grimké's suspension of black female allure in an unattainable balloon that hovers over and around the stage. Perhaps the playwright's decision boils down to a show of female power, given the limited options that presented themselves to women during this period. More specifically, regardless of the fact that she will, in the end, cross over into sainthood, whilst in the midst of the wooing game, Rachel and *Rachel* can make male heads and hearts turn, certainly a means to finagle some control during a male-dominated age. Similarly, by rebuffing Strong, Rachel could at least make a choice that allowed her to control her environment despite the forfeiture of her own enjoyment. Perhaps Grimké struggles to hold onto and display black female desire but is compelled by propriety to bracket it within representations of martyrdom and care-taking. How, for instance, would the NAACP board have reacted to love making on stage in its first official race play? Whether we assign a subversive subtext or a materialist condition to her rationale for drawing such a captivating black female lead and then not allowing her sensuality to bear fruit, this aspect of the drama renders it enigmatic, charged, and covertly aggressive, certainly not what race leaders envisioned for black uplift theater.

I raise this final point about how Grimké's piece could not comply with the prescription for uplift drama because it reveals the competing notions of theatrical "fullness" that we have uncovered thus far, Hopkins defining hers as pleasure and Grimké shedding light on the burden of fighting racial oppression. In spite of all the rhetoric that jockeyed back and forth, black leaders were unsure about what they wanted (or needed) from the stage. For example, when those who advanced the problem play were supplied with role models, propaganda, and symbols of strong race work in *Rachel*, they were not content because they where drawn to the theater's prerogative to house desire and fantasy. Thus Grimké's contemporary black and striving audience was not able to overcome its yearning to experience pleasure via the communal space of theater, Du Bois's elaborate pageants with ornate costumes and tons of participants being just one illustration. The race play unadorned was not satisfying enough, and *Rachel* lost before it started, even though it tilted its own professed aesthetic form on its end and mocked it with its fretful, sobbing, sensual breaking elements. It became, for many years, a grand experiment against which other artists would find the motivation to conceptualize their own projects.

Yet we know now that rather than serving as a mere foil to more rounded works, *Rachel* warred against formal containment. We can appreciate as well its questioning of sentimentality and its ultimate decision not to dispense with it but to chart its ebb and flow in a modern world where Victorian gender lines were being challenged by real experience, especially those who lived outside of the mainstream. Thus in her deconstruction of Victorianism, Grimké uncovers a new current in Western culture: a rising, anxious subtext that represents how the "feminine" often imprisons women and how female subjects concoct resistance to thwart this socially constructed cell. Accepting the birth of neurosis, the playwright alchemizes this particular energy into clay that she manipulates to build an African American saint whose power resides in learning how to navigate precarious ground: commoditization by a dominant consumer culture on one side and masculinist uplift ideology on the other.

Ultimately, even with reservation, Grimké selects the black institution as a springboard for reform, hoping that her alliance with it will enable her to expand the organization using her position and vantage point as a strong female outsider/savior (parallel to Rachel), who would shift uplift's focus from excursions to the land of riches, power, and fame to a sound program that spotlights black psychic and spiritual health, spinning all efforts out from that hub, an accentuation that would prepare African Americans for the onslaught of twentieth-century terror that would come in the form of egregious lynching but also via the flooding of black communities with drugs and alcohol, the warping of black self-perceptions through intense media campaigns that elevated all things white, and the continuous policing of black territory (exterior and interior) through both psychological and geographic segregation. So while Grimké claimed that her piece was designed to address white women and change racist perceptions by appealing to a universal Motherhood, its most salient message is transmitted to African Americans and the thousands of African American homes in the country during this time. Her creation sings to, soothes, and reminds black America, in blues style, that even during a time of increasingly vicious violence and Jim Crow, there are those who are willing to relinquish their own needs to protect the greater good, especially the cultural arena that these black communities form and inhabit. Therefore, because of the play's emphasis on a heroine/saint-in-the-making, we should not read *Rachel* as tragedy but as a complex, ridged, performance that documents the way that resistance mutates to fit historical circumstance, a play that dares to make "super-drama" from the absurdities that impinge on interior black space. In terms of what it did for the African American playwriting tradition, it opened the public/cultural forum to black female voices during a period when black men, because they had been silenced for so long themselves, dominated the public sphere (at least that slim portion of it that allowed black visibility). Rachel arrived, even if she had to quick-change into tears, the vamp's veil, and, ultimately, a habit to get there.

NOTES

[1] For excellent instances of progressive race men's and women's connecting humanitarian causes in the United States to events happening across the globe, see the numerous articles in the *Crisis* on nationalism and the first two Pan-African Conferences. The *Crisis'* official correspondent on these events is Jessie Fauset: "Nationalism and Egypt" (April 1920, 310–316), "Impression of the Second Pan-African Congress" (November 1921, 12–18), and "What Europe Thought of the Second Pan-African Congress" (December 1921, 60–69).

[2] The compunction to force the drama under realism's sobriquet came about because that was the form that race men thought would be best suited to fight the skewed, racialized characterizations depicted in American film, literature, and in the media and advertisement, fields that were expanding exponentially. *The Birth of the Nation* and regional literary works from Joel Chandler Harris, Norris, and others were particular targets that race leaders named as requiring rectification.

[3] Alain Locke was an outspoken critic of the contest and the play and attempted to postpone announcing the selection. When he did not succeed in convincing the committee to reconsider, he resigned from the board (Hay 81).

[4] Marcus Garvey, for example, delivered rhetoric that was geared specifically to working-class black people and focused on black men taking charge of their destiny, while Du Bois, during this period, leaned toward the educated elite. Locke rooted his hope in culture while socialists like Cyril Briggs demanded that workers unite across racial lines.

[5] Wickham notes that the Passion Play that featured Christ's sacrifice and later the Miracle Plays, which were based on the lives and works of saints, brought together entire communities comprising, perhaps, the first major form of popular entertainment: "What started simply as a procession had, by the end of the century [1300s], been elaborated to include plays on Old and New Testament subjects performed by laymen as well as churchmen, in the vernacular instead of Latin, and subsidized as heavily by civic promoters as by the Church itself. Christ's passion became a central feature, frighteningly and pitiably realistic in the detail of its re-enactment...Passion Plays caught on in France, Germany and Spain; Miracle Plays in England, which often lasted several days by the fifteenth century" (76–77).

[6] Even before Grimké's production, Du Bois had written and staged his own theatrical extravaganza, an ornate historical pageant called *Star of Ethiopia* (1913), which had several well-attended airings at the National Emancipation Exposition in New York from October 22–31, 1913; in Washington, D.C., on several dates in October of 1915; in Philadelphia in May of 1916; and in Los Angeles in June of 1925. His extensive tableau featured the Negro's gifts to the world, an endeavor that employed from three hundred to twelve hundred performers per engagement. In addition to this rousing work, there are several manuscripts in Du Bois's papers of pageants that never came to production (Hatch and Shine, *The Early Period* 87–88).

[7] It makes sense that Grimké would at least audition the sentimental, reformist strategy of the previous century because her own relative, Charlotte Forten Grimké, was a staunch, white abolitionist who had devoted her life to the cause.

[8] West defines nihilism as "...a natural consequence of a culture (or civilization) ruled and regulated by categories that mask manipulation, mastery and domination of peoples and nature" ("Nietzsche's Prefiguration" 208).

[9] Claudia Tate has argued convincingly that controlling their destiny from within the domestic space became an important component of black female agency during this late Victorian, early modernist period. Refer to her *Domestic Allegories of Political Desire.*
[10] While Locke evokes the same notion of the mundane as Du Bois and Grimké, he validates this common pool with a different social sub-strata, seeking out the folk, rural and urban, as the primary source for artistic renditions of black life, a world in contradistinction to Du Bois's and Grimké's models that center on the upwardly mobile black middle class. I would argue that all three are a bit dishonest about their desire to represent *objectively* a cross-section of African American life because each one selects, from a variety of sites, that location that he/she believes authenticates black experience, not acknowledging that black subjectivity spans numerous overlapping positionalities. Locke encourages drama set at least partially outside the domestic and labor arenas (street life) that could "master" what he considered to be the core of black living, Grimké grounds her ontological field in domesticity, and Du Bois, in his own creative work, chooses a mythological historical space to make a collective black presence known. This contestation over an ideal representational geography masks the fact that a similar strain runs through each one's conceptualization of black theater; that is: it should portray communal codes, everyday objects, and strong emotions, but the artist has the right to rearrange these aspects according to ideological partiality and offer this simulacra as either truth or utopian promise. It should be noted as well that black modernists' quests do not end necessarily in clear revelation but, often as not, lead to a revised symbolic range that embraces aspects previously coded as unreachable or unseen.
[11] Richardson claims that he decided to become a playwright after attending *Rachel.* He was so disappointed by the production that he convinced himself that he could do better (Sanders 21-22).
[12] See Gloria Hull's *Color, Sex and Poetry.* Christine Gray notes as well that Grimké's other play, *Mara,* focuses on romance and a young girl's budding sexuality.
[13] All quotations for *Rachel* are from the *Selected Works.*
[14] The extended family has served as the norm for African Americans rather than the nuclear patriarchal model. Much has been written on this extended structure. See Carol Stack's *All Our Kin* and work by Patricia Hill Collins (especially *Black Feminist Thought*).
[15] We see this Africanized redefinition still holding sway today as some predominately black churches refer to the most sacrificing and giving female parishioners as "Mother" followed by the woman's name. Mothers may even wear special dress to designate their status in their church communities.
[16] Some of the first major psychological studies on race and self-image targeted how black children responded to a choice between a white or a black doll. Overwhelmingly the children selected the white toy. Although the disparity has been reduced, recent studies prove that black children still prefer the white image. Poussaint and Comer suggest ways to counteract this psychological oppression in their instructive volume, *Raising Black Children.*

THREE

Houses Against Violence: Early-Twentieth-Century Black Women Playwrights

No Matter how hard the folks wear and tear and worry you. Set up and don' spill the things He [God] give you to keep for him.

— Marita Bonner, *The Pot Maker*

GRIMKÉ'S *Rachel* marshaled in a new era for African American playwrights. It epitomized as well the paradoxical strands that would characterize the Harlem Renaissance: artists' demands for aesthetic and thematic freedom bounded by an expanding popular market that benefited from exotic demonstrations of blackness, both tensions thrown against a jostling contest for ascendancy by would-be race leaders. Pockets of partially formed schools of thought on African American issues were springing up in New York, Washington, D.C., Baltimore, Atlanta, and Chicago, a piebald mat that was concretized by the various journals that vied for readers, legitimacy, and black genius. Magazine editors, who where often backed by organizations such as the Urban League or the NAACP, offered a savvy array of topics that included political exposés, gossip columns (or the equivalent), historical pieces, visual arts and literature. Germane to this study, the *Crisis, Opportunity*, and, less often, *The Messenger* along with other regional papers outside of New York sponsored literary contests and otherwise championed African American art, each one endeavoring to confirm that African Americans were indeed gifted. Given this mutual aspiration to launch black talent, what distinguishes each publication from its peers is that each uses its literary offerings to elevate and authenticate a particular type of black citizen: Du Bois at the *Crisis* aggrandizing purified texts with sanitized black subjects and Locke, operating from a Washington, D.C., base, scouring the drafting boards for works that featured ordinary folk.[1] Amid this fanfare and encouragement, plays by black writers flourished if we merely count the number of scripts published between 1918 and 1938; yet, alongside this proliferation of written material arises a singular phenomenon because more drama was printed than produced, especially that composed by African American women, designating this period as one that invites the historian even though its midwives failed to carry to fruition their self-professed objective of establishing a long-standing black community theater, a dream that both Du Bois and Locke shared in spite of their philosophical antipathy.[2]

Neither leader made much headway in founding an inspirational and permanent national black theater that would draw on various local neighborhoods as its base because, in sharp contrast to the comparatively modest magazine prizes sponsored by black journals, the real funds that supported the live arts were collected on and disseminated from Broadway and the commercial traveling circuits. Not only did Manhattan's Midtown District lord over New York's theater scene, its great magnetism spun off imitations that fed profit-taking roving networks. There simply were not enough finances, human resources, or potential viewers to go around; therefore, black visionaries had to settle for mapping out what they hoped would be forthcoming. Regardless of their inability to secure a permanent dwelling for black-controlled versions of the dramatic arts, the passion and commitment that Du Bois, Locke, and other race men and women put into establishing a home for black theater is commendable, a noble undertaking that stemmed from their staunch commitment fueled by the overwhelming obstacles facing America: segregation, lynching, employment discrimination, and violence from a myriad number of sources and in a variety of grisly forms.

Narrowing this encrusted field of woes to the humiliation that was levied by the American theater, intellectuals identified several sub-genres that paralleled and reinforced the more flagrant economic and physical barriers to black advancement. Over all other modes, the exponentially popular musical comedy tainted and impinged on African American sovereignty and ingenuity. These works evolved from vaudeville and demonstrated an array of racial types from the shucking coon to the citified dandy to the chorus girl, an assortment that could be summed up under what Henry Louis Gates refers to as "happy-go-lucky, overly sensual bodies" ("A Tragedy" 17), physiques that could be masked in and written on with flamboyant make-up and accessories.[3] Du Bois reasoned that musical comedies in the early decades of the twentieth century required retooling to foster pride and self-esteem instead of fortifying deleterious typecasting (Hay 20). In his own staged extravaganzas, Du Bois wagered on the grandiose documentary pageant with fine music, very light on comedy but packed intensely with choral arrangements and transcendent black voices.

The other subgenre that disturbed race-proud activists was the dramatic work conceived by white playwrights about black life. Often these pieces called for exotic and primitive characters and elevated the so-called affects of the black body over the black subject's intellect and spirit. Practitioners such as Eugene O'Neill, Paul Green, and Ridgley Torrence portrayed black milieus as "pre-civilized" jungles, church halls, and plantations, settings that differed drastically from the modern cities in which these plays aired. Stage works such as *The Emperor Jones*, *In Abraham's Bosom*, and *The Rider of Dreams* lifted the Negro out of the present and relocated "him" in theatrical cages that allowed for his exhibition as a relic from the past, an act that further segregated dominant and black culture.[4] African American critics and artists were less prepared to resist this more subtle colonizing because the roles offered by these scripts appeared to be a step up from the more blatant and vulgar musical comedies in the sense that they rarely called for the more obvious minstrel-laden accouterments such as the buffoon's tawdry fashion or exaggerated movements (the oddity of their costume lists is much more subdued). Furthermore, these productions were inclined to construct the Negro as universal, although when given a second glance, they too continued to corral him within all-too-predictable holding pens. Ongoing debates still challenge whether there might be some advantage in black aesthetics taking on the mantle of exoticism or primitivism and that establishing cultural difference from the mainstream—even in non-threatening, banal and solely physical ways—is, in and of itself, a revolutionary and, in the end, a liberating act. These issues were raised in the twenties and thirties by artists like Zora Neale Hurston, Langston Hughes, and Josephine Baker and have not been fully resolved because we see the same kind of language, frames, and representational containers from the twenties being applied to contemporary black athletes and to those in the music/video industries.[5]

Whether one interprets this coding of blackness as pre-or supra-Edenic, the plays that naturalize and map skin color onto a highly visible primal (but completely contrived) backdrop generate a special set of problematics for black entertainers. According to Harrison, "Black performers ...responded... to a performance ethic that subordinates social ideology to performance opportunity, revealing an artistic ambivalence that would have them surrender their gifts in the service of the dominant culture's demand..."("Crisis of Black Identity" 570). Harrison further observes that, in spite of white writers', directors' and vehicles' efforts to dictate black images, this age stimulated dazzling black actors, the ones who could outmaneuver performance instruments that offered little more than representational shackles.

So, resistance to mainstream packaging was at least twofold. We identify the black cultural Vulcans who labored to initiate an alternative black community theater, and we acknowledge the skilled black performer who took dominant products and refit them through signification, employing inspired skill to surpass the role's boundaries. Surprisingly, there is very little overlap between these two spheres other than the fact that sometimes agents from downtown would visit Harlem and other regional companies searching for "talent," siphoning off what could be turned into profit. But, the big names like Williams and Walker, Cole and Johnson, and Miller and Lyles were not returning to small stages in black locales to nourish budding, independent, and ambitious upstart—and usually short-lived—serious-minded black companies or the theatrical schemes that spun out from uplift theorists and their institutions.

In the midst of this extremely sharp socio/cultural bifurcation, African American female playwrights had little choice: Broadway would not back their problem, folk, satiric or historical dramas. Therefore, their production venues were restricted to black high schools and colleges, church halls, library basements, the spaces commandeered by nomadic black theatrical companies and those provided by black lodges, sororities, fraternities, and service organizations. Hatch and Shine identify these female dramatists between 1918 and 1929 as mostly school teachers whose work was published in periodicals. If these writers' scenes did make it to the boards, they had limited runs in local forum with amateur actors. To generalize, "All were original voices that were unwelcome in the commercial theater of the 1920s..." (*The Early Period* 132). However, we should not view this dismissal by the capitalists as a hindrance because African American female theater workers navigated around these material constraints and concentrated on building the home-grown centers that could procure a better future for both the arts and for black people generally. Their challenge revolved around turning the living arts into a vibrant and healthy source for the overarching racial uplift mission. Consequently, their focus on the interior spaces of black society as a creative anchor led these artists to cultivate significant American cultural sub-genres: the literary play and the play as community labor.

There were numerous African American women dramatists during this time span. I concentrate on a sampling that includes Mary Burrill, Alice Dunbar-Nelson, Georgia Douglas Johnson, Marita Bonner, Eulalie Spence,

May Miller, Zora Neale Hurston, and Shirley Graham (Du Bois). From 1905 until 1944, Burrill devised her pieces while she taught English and Drama at the famous M Street School (renamed Dunbar) in Washington, D.C. The Dunbar school, under Burrill's guidance, sponsored a lively program that showcased historical, dramatic and comedic plays. In her role as teacher, she also mentored maturing playwrights such as May Miller, James Butcher, and Willis Richardson, protégés who would invest in and help sustain the tradition for another half-century. Finding opportunities to mount her offerings as well, Burrill staged *They Sit in Darkness* in New York with the assistance of several small theater groups, and she produced *Aftermath* with the New York branch of the Krigwa Players, a black company conceived by Du Bois that oversaw chapters in various cities. Du Bois also entered the play in the David Belasco Little Theater Tournament of 1928. In addition to these original compositions that treated, respectively, inadequate birth control and lynching, Burrill directed other writers' compositions including Maeterlinck's *The Blue Bird* and J.M. Barrie's *Quality Street* (Perkins 55, Hatch and Shine, *The Early Period* 175–6).

Alice Dunbar-Nelson is better known as a poet, short story writer, and diarist, but she completed several dramas to round out her repertoire. Her *Mine Eyes Have Seen* questions whether African Americans should participate in the First World War, a passionate tragedy that was published in the *Crisis* and was performed at Delaware's Howard High School, where Dunbar-Nelson taught English. Georgia Douglas Johnson is one of the more prolific playwrights from this age, but of her nearly thirty works, not all have survived or have been published. The notable ones that have been produced and/or issued in print are *Blue Blood, Plumes, Frederick Douglass, William and Ellen Craft, Safe, Blue-Eyed Black Boy, and A Sunday Morning in the South* (Hatch and Shine, *The Early Period* 232, Brown-Guillory, *Wines in the Wilderness* 12). Most of these are compact, one-acts on such themes as lynching, miscegenation, black historical figures, and the national impact of Southern mores and practices. In contrast to Johnson's naturalistic displays, Marita Bonner adopts an allegorical motif for her concepts, designing three visions during the twenties that are, undoubtedly, the most structurally experimental conceived by African American women during this era. *The Purple Flower*, *Exit, an Illusion*, and *The Pot Maker* round out Bonner's dramatic roster (she turned exclusively to short story writing by the thirties) and allude to Biblical, revolutionary, and existential concerns. Unfortunately, none of these worthy pieces has been produced, which Kathy Perkins attributes to the allegories' complex technical requirements (190). However, all were published: *The Pot Maker* in *Opportunity* and the other two in *Crisis*, where they won first prize for best play.

Eulalie Spence is the only member of this group who is a first-generation immigrant. She accompanied her family to New York when they moved from Nevis Island in the Caribbean in 1902 (Perkins 105). Spence remained in New York for most of her life, teaching English, elocution, and drama at Eastern District High School in Brooklyn from 1927 to 1958. She, like Johnson and Miller, crafted numerous plays over the years, and many found their way to the theater. Spence studied with the Krigwa Players for several years (1926–1928) and saw *Fool's Errand* and *Her* performed by the troupe in New York. Later, she directed the Dunbar Garden Players at St. Mark's Theater on lower Second Avenue (Brown-Guillory, *Wines in the Wilderness* 39). Often satiric and tastefully disapproving of social hypocrisy, Spence hit the notes that were close to the heart instead of targeting the national and sometimes international thrust of the race plays. Yet in their seemingly less ambitious reach, she engages the deep-seated human foibles that influence broad-scale social formations. Set in apartment houses, living and dining rooms, Spence's sharp-witted, dense one-act pieces embrace modern modalities but do not constantly gesture toward horrific conditions; racism merely surrounds characters who are more interested in wending their way through the pitfalls of relationships with family, friends, and neighbors. *Her, Fool's Errand, Undertow, Foreign Mail, the Starter, the Hunch, Episode, the Whipping, Help Wanted, Wife Errant, La Divina Pastora* and *Hot Stuff* represent but a portion of her collection.

If Spence is an undervalued powerhouse from the Harlem Renaissance, May Miller is her twin. Miller composed steadily too. Her drama evidences a devotion to capturing the soundings of black life. While she buoyed her student charges (Frederick Douglass High School in Baltimore), Miller remained active in the various arms of the theater by joining the Baltimore Krigwa Players. Four of her historical works, *Sojourner Truth, Samory, Christophe's Daughters* and *Harriet Tubman,* are featured in the *Negro History in Thirteen Plays*, which she collected and edited with Willis Richardson. Richardson, Miller's good friend, also compiled *The Plays and Pageants of Negro Life*, a collection that was designed specifically for school groups from junior high through college, a volume that includes Miller's *The Bog Guide, Riding the Goat,* and *Graven Images*. As one can imagine, many of Miller's works were performed at her own Douglass High and at other educational institutions across the country. Her thematic interests range from class conflict in black communities to lynching as in *Nails and Thorns*, one of the few plays written by an African American woman during this span that requires an interracial cast. Scholars Perkins, Brown-Guillory, and Hamalian and Hatch mention that Miller wrote across sub-genres and was equally at ease with historical biographies, satires, and high tragedy. Her dexterity is certainly indicative of the quick-change motif that encapsulates the African American female dramatic tradition.

Zora Neale Hurston's name is the most recognizable one on the list, but she is better known as a novelist and anthropologist, not a playwright. Privately, she admired the dramatic form over all others, notwithstanding the disappointing reality that she was largely thwarted in steering her more than twenty plays to production. Only *Fast and Furious* that she co-wrote with nine other artists and *The Great Day* had favorable runs (*Mule Bone* by Hurston and Langston Hughes was staged finally in 1991 at the Lincoln Center in New York). Despite the frustration, Hurston's devotion to the fine arts endured. Consider that she attended Howard University to study theater under Alain Locke (Perkins 77) and that she continued to compose and peddle plays throughout the forties. In the thirties, Hurston joined the Federal Theater Project but could not persuade its directors to stage her scripts; still, she did not submit to defeat and took a position as head of drama at North Carolina College for Negroes in Durham from 1939 to 1940. The following year she worked for Paramount Studios in the vain hope that the executives would option one or more of her texts for film (Perkins 78). We can mourn the great cost of this rejection not only in terms of Hurston's personal disappointment but also because it has deprived America's cultural repository of invaluable contributions. At least, many of Hurston's plays have been preserved, archived and documented, regardless of the sad fact that there is no production trail to follow. Her performance pieces that often combine music, comedy, and drama include those mentioned above and *Color Struck*, *The First One*, *Spears, De Turkey and De Law*, *Jungle Scandals*, *Singing Steel*, *Fiery Chariot*, and *Polk County* with Dorothy Waring. Hurston's texts stand apart from those by other African American female playwrights of the era because she dared to exhibit the racier inner-group dynamics of black working-class figures, characters that enjoyed their sensuality as much as they did fine music, dance, and tasty food. Perhaps her training as an anthropologist prompted her to search out these facets of black life over the more sedate aspects targeted by her more sharply discipline-bound contemporaries.

Commencing as a trained musicologist with a master's degree from Oberlin, Shirley Graham introduced another perspective to the stage, concentrating on African music and dance and the remnants of it in African

American culture. This topic comprises the backbone for her ambitious first piece, *Tom-Tom* (1932), an opera in three acts that maps black aesthetics from Africa to the United States. Between 1936 and 1938, Graham led the Federal Theater Project's Negro Unit in Chicago and produced Charlotte Chopenning's *Little Black Sambo* and a version of *The Swing Mikado*. The last few years of that decade ushered in Graham's remaining original suites, three elaborate numbers (the days of the one-act were winding down) *Dust to Earth*, *I Gotta Home*, and *It's Morning*. A radio play about railroad porters quickly followed, *Track Thirteen*.

William Wells Brown, a nineteenth-century black playwright, confessed that his *The Escape; or, A Leap for Freedom* would be nothing more than recitation (37), or what Henry Louis Gates would refer to in the *Signifying Monkey* as a talking book. Black women of the early twentieth century realized as well that their theatrical works would, in all probability, be more often read than beheld. Magazine prizes and strong editors guaranteed that their texts would have a forum, but the outlets for full-play production beyond the school or community library auditorium were extremely rare. For example, Alice Dunbar-Nelson, Ruth Ada Gaines, Ottie Graham, and Marita Bonner published in the *Crisis*, and Georgia Douglas Johnson and Marita Bonner saw their works printed in *Opportunity*. Mary Burrill issued her pieces in the *Birth Control Review* and *The Liberator*. Other sources included *Ebony and Topaz* and *Fire* for Hurston and three vital anthologies: *Negro History in Thirteen Plays* (Miller and Richardson) that featured texts by May Miller and Georgia Douglas Johnson, *Plays and Pageants from the Life of the Negro* (Richardson) that published theatrical compositions from Thelma Duncan and May Miller, and *Plays of Negro Life* (Locke) that published work by Eulalie Spence. This cooperative link that bound together the journal or the targeted drama collection with uplift-oriented female playwrights impacted on both form and content in the sense that the ideologies set forth by the magazine's or volume's oversight boards often dictated which works would be selected and, consequently, promoted via publication. At each major journal, the editors, including Du Bois, Jessie Fauset, James Weldon Johnson, and Walter White at the *Crisis* and Charles Johnson at *Opportunity*, subscribed to progressive imperatives and selected texts that would corroborate the publication's overarching principles. *Opportunity* chose folk works a bit more than the *Crisis*, which concentrated on the problem play, yet, in either case, this creative output was designed to be an antiphonal response to the dominant entertainment markets. Anthology producers Miller, Locke, and Richardson also included entries based on the criteria that they redress, in some measure, insidious and pervasive grotesque black images.

As a matter of fact, in response to the commercial theater's hegemonic control over the comedy and the musical, black assessors rated ribald humor, singing, and wild dancing as suspect and would not allow these styles to cross over into "serious" black theater until very late (Hatch and Shine, *The Early Period* 193). So, there are clear formal distinctions between the age's popular offerings, the extravagant fanfare that brought in large revenues, and these literary plays that had to be supported institutionally. An additional class-based chasm was developing as well because the black "literary" play was often conceived by and intended for an upwardly mobile African American middle class in which the members were either on their way to acquiring or had attained a high school diploma and/or college degree. The bond between drama and education in the case of works composed by black women/teachers is so strong during this period that these scripts are considered, by both writer and consumer, to be an extension of the schooling process. Each of the figures that I spotlight in this chapter—Burrill, Dunbar-Nelson, Johnson, Bonner, Spence, Miller, Hurston, and Graham—was an educator at some point.

In addition to emerging from and influencing secular didacticism, many of the plays composed by African American women during the twenties and early thirties (and even today) are indebted to religious establishments and, accordingly, follow these organizations' indoctrination processes. This component of the African American female theatrical tradition is rarely acknowledged. We owe this slight to several causes. Plays and pageants written by Sunday school leaders were not often defined—even by their composers—as literary artifacts but as mere elaborations of Biblical text. In essence, God is attributed authorship; so, the women and men who adapt Biblically based narratives for the stage tend to stay humbly in the back because they view any claim of proprietorship on their handiwork as arrogantly rivaling Divine promulgation. Marita Bonner captures this discomfort that religious artists experience in regard to signing their literature or oratory in the *Pot Maker* when Nettie Jackson proclaims to her son who has decided to become a preacher, "You is called of God and He aint asked you to set nothin' down He aint writ himself" (*The Opportunity Reader* 243). Another reason that the religious writers' contributions are difficult to trace is that few churches issued standard journals that record the parishioners' artistry although there are exceptions (especially in the African Methodist Episcopalian faith). And, most importantly, African American Christians have been especially wary about allowing dubious entertainment in the sanctuary: a Sunday School show is one thing, but a worldly commercial exhibition put on by the congregation more than likely would be strictly prohibited. Even labeling a spiritual pageant as "playing" would be considered alarming. So, in spite of the fact that various black churches loaned out their auditoriums to secular theatrical organizations, a line was drawn between local outside drama groups and the church itself—they were to remain discrete but occasionally mutually supportive organizations. Scholars should observe, however, that notwithstanding this strict territorial separation, the black church and the black theater are often involved in similar endeavors, the primary one being to prepare young people to meet a challenging future. Both secular theater and the Sunday School outreach program emphasize deportment, elocution, and confidence building, and both provide an encouraging audience that affirms their charges' worthiness and talent.

Switching gears for a moment, we return to the script as written matter and find that in their "readerly" guise these plays are meant to enter some of the more intimate spaces in black spheres. Beauty and barber shops, doctor's offices, homes, schools, and social centers all subscribed to the new race-proud journals and, if possible, purchased the illustrious black anthologies because these documents announced African American progress while broadcasting crucial information. Merely exhibiting copies of these serials and bound artifacts bore witness that a business and its owner were up and coming, sophisticated, and forward thinking. Thus, a play written by a black woman could travel through neighborhood channels without ever reaching the stage, confounding our estimation that the theater is primarily a public forum and that the printed text is a private one. An appreciation of this body of work produced between 1918 and 1938 as printed media is imperative as these bound vehicles extended its potency. On paper, these plays chronicle the abundant issue of numerous African American playwrights during this span, and they attest to the writers' zealous respect for and deep understanding of how the local and the worldly intersect, specifically the manner in which broad policies impact on domestic order (and then ripple through American social and cultural channels). In aggregate, then, these publications confirm that a strong intellectual current fueled a great deal of the in-house dramatic activity during this period, mainly by African American women, who were concocting ways to extend theatricality's power to cover and reach across black community strata including the reading group, the classroom, the head shop (beauty parlor and barber), and the professionals' waiting area, the major sites where discussion and debate is fostered.

Cognizant of the manner in which this body of texts on parchment could walk into the homes and circles of black citizens, the writers hoped that they could easily transmogrify back into live entities. Certainly, teachers discovered scenes in magazines and anthologies that they could draft for their drama club, an event that the writers counted on as they sometimes indicated on the play itself the skill or grade level that would be suitable to stage the work.[6] Hence, there is a sense of dexterity, generosity, and common purpose that guides this period of African American theatrical production. This compelling quick-change mechanism that enables a play to shuttle between book and stage provides a conveyance for playwrights without capital, especially for those who may have desired the publicity that patronage could provide but did not wish to see their visions repackaged to meet the distorting machines of dominant mills. Arguably, traveling between print and modest in-house venues extended the range of these dramatic texts that otherwise would have become obscure notations tucked away in composition books or gently shared readings at literary circles.

In regard to production history, the major venues/organizations that upheld black theater during this period are the New York branch of the Krigwa Players that mounted some of their shows at the 135th Street Public Library in New York (the library also welcomed the Harlem Community Players) and St. Mark's Theater on Second Avenue in New York that hosted the Dunbar Players. The Negro Art Theater was the brainchild of sponsors from the Abyssinia Baptist Church of New York (Mitchell 88). Howard University and Dunbar High School in Washington, D.C., had outstanding drama programs as did Dillard University in New Orleans, Morgan State University in Baltimore, and Frederick Douglass High School in Baltimore along with many other traditionally black high schools, colleges, and universities. Alice Dunbar-Nelson's *Mine Eyes Have Seen* debuted at Howard High School in Wilmington, Delaware (Hatch and Shine, *The Early Period* 169). Both Johnson (*Blue Blood)* and Spence composed works that were mounted by the Du Bois-backed Krigwa Players in New York City (Hatch and Shine, *The Early Period* 198, 232): Spence's *Her* ran at the 135th Street Public Library and *Fool' s Errand* at the Frolic Theater for the National Little Theater Tournament. Johnson produced *Blue Blood* under the auspices of the Harlem Experimental Theater and again at Howard University in 1933 (Perkins 22). Mary Burrill found an outlet at Howard as well, christening the Christmas season annually with her original composition, *The Other Wise Men*. Many of May Miller's theatrical constructions were staged at colleges including Howard, Morgan State, Dillard, and Saint Augustine and at little theater groups throughout the country (Perkins 143,

Brown-Guillory *Wines in the Wilderness* 62). Shirley Graham mounted a spectacular black opera, *Tom-Tom* that "…premiered in June 1932 at Municipal Stadium in Cleveland, on a huge three-dimensional stage before an audience of ten thousand people and with an all-black cast of five hundred…" (Hamalian and Hatch 235). In each case, the play's run was relatively contained in terms of both span and reach, except for Graham's libretto that enjoyed a huge venue and healthy audience but only ran for a few performances.

This borrowing of community real estate and labor does not deflate the merit of the dramatic output by African American women during this period because necessity led to innovations in form. For instance, many dramas by African American women during these years are distilled one-acts with simple sets and uncomplicated stage directions as if their creators built them to cater to the high school drama club or the amateur group who found little time to rehearse after long days in the classroom or at full-time jobs. Except for *Tom-Tom* and some of Hurston's more ambitious products, the cast members are few and the costumes are easy to assemble. Considerations such as these lent this period, as it pertains to the African American female tradition, a modest, understated quality in spite of the relentless dictates of white America's exotic exhibition of blackness that was represented by ostentatious plumage, ornate costuming, and over-the-top sets. Almost in direct contrast to the Downtown spectacle, we find that black women playwrights were speaking softly but solidly, firmly advancing the cause of equality and liberty by democratizing popular theater, bringing it to the places where rituals could be born, where they could flourish even in stringent times.

To fully value these plays' collective impact on American culture, we deliberate over what they accomplished, not whether they made it to the Great White Way. African American artists who were committed to serious drama outlined and bracketed community or what remained of it after its implosion brought on by the slave trade. Their staged visions also knit together debris from lost terrains by inserting a conduit into America's cultural substrata, an alternative path to the one provided by the nation's segregated and violent social turf. Thousands of African American boys and girls found sanctuary in the arts that granted them a means to translate worldly observations and concerns that were pertinent to them. Actors, designers, musicologists, directors, elocutionists, singers, dancers, choreographers, and fundraisers banded together to not only put on a show but to disseminate indispensable skills and lessons about self-determination and independence from racism and its ideology. This homespun theater also afforded an opportunity for the participants to be relieved, at least temporarily, of double consciousness's burden. During the show's span the performers and the audience were able to communicate without fear of reprisal from a hostile audience. So, in many ways, the black theater during this era served as a crucial after-school program, rivaling the church and social club for youth's attention. With easily transportable, concentrated scripts, high school and college drama teachers could ensure that their students had a healthy and demanding outlet beyond the street and a narrowly defined domestic sphere. I use the qualifier "narrowly defined" because, in many ways, this in-house theater became an extension of the domestic space (in fact, many plays are set in the home). In addition to bridging the public and the intimate sphere, these works promote a volunteerism that bridges the gap between the household and the labor sectors, a facet of black culture that could be seen as early as the days of Richard Allen and Frederick Douglass, continuing into the twentieth century with the club movement, masons, sororities, fraternities, and drill teams, organizations that, although often striated by class, sprang up across the various sub-sections of black social topographies.

In light of this relative independence from the marketplace's harsh, explosive eyes that fixed the boundaries of Negro representation by latching it to exoticism and primitivism, black community theater offers an alternative from the mechanical commercial menu. In lieu of the trendy, broad-based profitable musicals and comedies that ran under electric banners and larger-than-life Downtown producers, three major staples comprise the African American female tradition's chief tropes for the years between 1918 and 1938. First, as a body, the plays trace an imaginative mapping for displaced Africans who, even after four hundred years in the New World, continue to search for home/homes, a pilgrimage that, often as not, ends in a blues song of resolve and resignation. Second, as staged pieces, they unroll a series of impressions that contemplate visual imagery's growing significance to Western civilization, certainly predicting what would become the film industry's immense totalizing influence.[7] They counteract the pervasive national dependence on depictions of alleged black inferiority that have come to define and stabilize American identity.[8] Black female artists portray tableaus and mobile subjects who invade, offset, and deconstruct Western theatrical forms. More specifically, African American texts showcase ordinary black figures who are induced to become heroic over the work's course, theater that dramatizes a pugilistic stance forged by the tremendous risks that the subjects must take to overcome the pressing and dire conditions that face them. These in-house plays cast a mass visualization of black autonomy and self-actualization that challenges the blues-like thematic core that often wends its way through the act or acts. Tensions vie for ascendancy with monologue and dialogue often railing against visual representation to rule and define any given piece. Just as in *Rachel*, this formal upheaval arises from the playwrights being at odds about how to fulfill uplift mandates and still provide pleasure to a group of Americans who surely preferred to watch displays that appealed to their own vanity and need for assurance. No matter how bleak the plot, African American viewers responded positively to spotlights on whole, reflective, and noble black characters: nobody's fools. Finally, these plays can be overwhelmingly confessional and revelatory because they expose black communities' private matters, often placing these domestic machinations under a microscope, not to condemn but to make these institutions, rituals, and traditions more viable. Using Hurston's favorite imaginative positionality, these offerings speak and form judgments from the porch about daily activities and current events—global, national or local—that impact on black life,[9] observations that disappear in dominant products. Thus, African American women scene builders insert platforms in their acts that allow a space to debate that which would, could or should, in time, improve or harm their earth, country, community, and brood.

It is understandable that black women dramatists used their genre of choice to search for security when black soldiers who were returning from the First World War were being dismembered by their fellow citizens, and job discrimination continued to plague those of a darker hue in spite of the fact that many black people were pursuing an education, often by way of previous generations' tremendous sacrifice. Voting rights were also routinely denied as was any demand for social equality. The vast migration of African Americans from rural areas to larger towns and cities proves that scores of black people were in transit, seeking a release from intolerable conditions toward a safer, saner life. In general, what is reflected in the drama during these years is a vast acknowledgment that domestic bliss is unattainable but that in its fragmentary and often illusory state, home is a dream worth having, even if it merely serves to guard against psychological street/state violence. Home hangs somewhere within song and tradition, ritual and history. Taking into account these remarks about the travel motif's significance, it is important to anchor the impetus for the exodus as well as concentrate on the arrival, and the plays by black women from this period reflect that subtle difference. For the most part, they highlight potential and longing and are open ended accordingly. Moreover, no one site shines through as the definitive incubator for progress and stability; the investigation of several possible nesting grounds is aired; so, imaginative settings include the American South, Biblical/mythical environments, urban locales, Africa and the Caribbean, and the generic black settlement. These various geographies are performed by the text, shifted, scrutinized, shaped, stretched, collapsed, rolled across the scrim like favorite marbles with latent but ignitable interior worlds.

The arduous journey motif and the philosophical handling of what sanctuary might mean for a people driven to inspect thoroughly their relationship to nation, citizenship, domestic space, street, neighborhood, and zone is explored in many works by black women over this Modernist age. Often weaving imaginative projections in with actual historical events (many of them moments of intense cruelty), black female playwrights search after the strongholds that grant an indispensable orientation in an irrational world. Moving away from the rising pitch in Grimké's *Rachel*, the writers name, struggle with, and sometimes survive their anguish: alternately resigned and rebellious. This blues-based attitude—the language of the exile—can take on several shapes. To some artists, the journey is primarily a psychological and spiritual one and is more about withstanding the challenge of upheaval in an extracted metaphysical sense. To others, the road is comprised of real earth and the institutions that humans build such as nations, churches, and schools. In these imaginative offerings, home becomes tangible structure, whether attained or yet to be acquired. Finally, some playwrights muddy the lines between a largely symbolic versus a materialist quest and turn to culture or the displacement of both figurative and fleshy desires onto inspired expression to best embrace that succoring feeling that is the nearest thing to a complete acceptance of self and life.

Early on (1918), Alice Dunbar-Nelson sets the tone for this often wrenching exploration of the Modernist's exilic condition when she targets how lynching forced a nomadic life-style on many African Americans who were terrorized into fleeing the South because of racist intimidation. Her *Mine Eyes Have Seen* peers across the national terrain in hopes of pinpointing a place to establish both a sense of belonging and economic and social roots, but it also charts how these hops across sand can mutilate the spirit even though the flesh may eventually find some respite from impending to less-imminent hostility. Chris, a young black male character, queries, "Haven't you had your soul shriveled with fear since we were driven like dogs from our Home?" (171). By centering fear as the Great Migration's primary spur, Dunbar-Nelson frames this crossing as a debilitating retreat from atrocity, an extended psychological civil war within the country's borders while it battles with others abroad. It is interesting that this part of the Great Migration narrative that is now routinely taught in history class has been "dis-remembered," as the mass movement of African Americans is usually compared to and subsumed within immigration narratives: forward-seeking, noble folk who voluntarily seek a brighter future. However, Dunbar-Nelson zeroes in on the pain that spreads from forced relocations caused by gentrification schemes carried out by economic and social threats and bullying. Displacement and defeat color Dunbar-Nelson's vision.

Of special interest to this discussion is the manner in which Dunbar-Nelson's assessment of her historical moment is set in contradistinction to the giddy gaiety that prosperous white America was foisting on black America, a blanketing that was cast in bronze by the exotic urban night club scene, principally in Harlem. Standing these two cultural arenas akin to each other, Nelson's forlorn reference to an unrecoverable Southern residence and the white patron's pulsating, lush cabaret draws our attention to how schismatic these disparate times must have seemed to white and black. Black migrants, as etched by Dunbar-Nelson, were grieving over and coping with the rigors of banishment and had not acclimated to intimidating urban conditions. In the midst of grappling with perforated communities and wounded selves, they had to conjure up for the selling floor/club an illusionary wholeness that alchemized the site of blackness into simplistic gestures all glued to primal sets, a process that caused the black performer to reduce her own subjectivity to near-invisible levels. In order to survive economically, black people had to appear, for the span of the commercial show, shallow and unencumbered.

One of the tasks that African American playwrights face is how to render this specific condition, described by Du Bois as double consciousness, via the theatrical arts. Staging home as a jewel at the end of or beginning of a mass exodus is one way to interpret artistically a double consciousness because the lost spirit of unitary bliss stands in for that moment—be it psychological, historic, or geographic—when the self is not split into competing factions that face outward and inward. Home becomes a time and space when the black self can follow its own dictates, where even racial markers cease to register as intelligible. Therefore, the mass black migration in its entire mournful, water-laden cadence also contains a martial effort to overthrow double consciousness, to not only own and control again one's personal performances but, as Dunbar-Nelson would put it, grow the soul and release its fears. If this resistance is not levied, then dominant representations of blackness will become the only choice, as Shirley Graham warned in her Africanist Opera, *Tom-Tom*, where African and African American culture is destroyed/devoured by a synthetic package/totem: "Out from the crowd springs a cabaret dancer in African costume. He raises his spear and sinks it into the Voodoo man's chest" (284).

Eulalie Spence continues Dunbar-Nelson's investigation into how inquiries about geographical space can alleviate black crises with a 1927 one-act mystery entitled *Her*, which is set in an apartment building and illustrates the psychological impact of migration to metropolitan centers. By this time, city living had become unavoidable for many African Americans who could not afford to reminisce about what the South might have been. A middle-aged black couple and the white absentee owner of the building take center stage, but this spirited one-act revolves around the haunted upstairs apartment that the owner once denied his innocent mail-order bride, confining her instead to a small room downstairs because he planned to increase his revenue by leasing out the top floor. She commits suicide and moves into the upper apartment as a ghost, chasing away any would-be renter with clanks and bumps. A young couple, after observing some strange doings, comment, "This ain't no place fer comfort!"(140). Comparing this play to Dunbar-Nelson's 1918 work, we see that the migrant's attachment to the South has begun to erode, but the city is no haven either. In fact, a wayfaring nation of transplants had been hoodwinked into abandoning clay hills and green grounds for some supremely unnatural buildings. Introducing an anti-domestic theme to show that comfort has evaporated into the tenement's crawl spaces, Spence argues that relocation to the ghetto had not led to a firm foundation for living. Unfortunately, the apartment house stands for a mere pit-stop on the way to more functional and compassionate social cradles, a dramatic interrogative that counter-poses the linear optimism of both an improving civilization and increased racial harmony (or at least racial tolerance) that was being lauded by Broadway's swinging musicals and upbeat variety shows.

According to Spence, instead of dancing all one's cares away, city dwellers should carry out massive reforms to shift the core ethical system away from materialism to sensitivity and concern for others. Learning from past mistakes is still an option for Spence, whose sanctuary resides in a belief that the dead talk, that the universe is capable of righting itself beyond man's selfish impulses (a corrective Gothicism). Yet, because the play's heroine is a ghost, Spence reveals the fragile plane on which her reformist leanings are based. If dead spirits have more power than live black citizens to challenge and ameliorate social conditions, then the migration is nothing more than a death march where the body has to be ceded to the natural environment for it to effectuate change, a classically Romantic take on suffering and social order.[10]

If Spence's vision is guarded but evidently Romantic, then May Miller's is downright bleak. In her 1930 production, *Stragglers in the Dust,* which is set entirely in Arlington National Cemetery, she imagines that a black veteran rests in the Unknown Soldier's Tomb. Symbolically, the tomb is a collective lodging for the black citizen's unfinished pursuit after dignity and parity, as the dead man's mother comments, "Ah ain't got nothin' at home. All ah got is heah [in the cemetery]" (146). Looking back on an ethereal meadow of vanishing dreams, Nan (the black mother) conjures up a wished-for sanctum that is nothing more than an ancestral field of bones and stifled narratives. Even the belief that comfort can be achieved once the house has been swept clean, as presented in *Her*, is unimaginable here. Instead, tunneling through history becomes the sole instrument for attaining the utopian peace that reigned before the slave trade's massive disfiguration that continued through the Civil War and the many upheavals that followed, the one fresh in Miller's memory being the great disappointment that occurred when the returning Black troops from War World I met intensified barbarism in the United States. This play is about dead souls like Spence's work, but these spirits do not transcend their earthly existence. Whatever condition they found themselves in while alive continues through death, unless the poet succeeds in reexamining the subject's significance. In this work, however, that recount contains indeterminacy (the mother's insistent claim that her son lies in the tomb is never confirmed). Supporting Hortense Spillers' theory that discontinuity marks African American culture and life (half-taken steps, retreats, fissures, and disjunction),[11] Miller's black mother mourns her son and, metaphorically, the hope that black people will ever become a coherent historical force because phantom stories, stereotypes, and intentional mis-readings co-mingle with and around individual and collective black self-narrativizing. Given this condition, it becomes the artist's job to record the heroic moments of a devastatingly underrepresented and maligned group and at least attempt to insert alternative suggestions into the cut. So, part of the imaginative conveyance need contend with the knowledge that the past, eternally lost, can only be held as allusion, acknowledging that once the performance ends, or the magazine is returned to the table, dissonance and fragmentation return. We are left, at the end of the sojourn, in rows of sealed-off and silent bodies.

Miller's disillusionment is shared by Mary Burrill, who also wrote a one-act play that converges on the returning black soldier theme. However, the difference between the two is that Burrill puts her tragedy in the active mode, while Miller relies on reflection, intimation, and dreamscape to convey her message. For example, Burrill highlights a vibrant black veteran in her 1919 *Aftermath*, whose "...War Cross is pinned on his breast. On his sleeve three chevrons tell mutely of wounds suffered in the cause of freedom. His brown face is aglow with life and the joy of homecoming" (179). Sadly, over the drama's course, this stalwart figure discovers that his father has been lynched in his absence. The curtain falls on the veteran's rushing out [of home] with guns blazing to settle the score, surely a suicidal mission. Hence, there is a sense of futility in this piece that matches that in *Stragglers in the Dust*, but the fact that Burrill would grant physical form to this symbolic African American collective push for equality can be read as a forward-looking choice in an otherwise inexorable depiction of national injustice and betrayal. I highlight the difference between these two pieces because it reveals the subtle shift in tone over this period for black women playwrights. The black body removed from Miller's drama, conceived more than twenty years after this similar play by Burrill, argues a growing cynicism for African American female playwrights. Resignation continued to seep into black America's veins, so by the thirties, hope had collapsed into a deep longing for a reconstructive history that could be the lone passable road to a "resurfacing of home." One has to burrow through time and recollect black selves by way of re-imaginings and then dramatize these stories and attitudes, practices that one imagined would staunch the Middle Passage's mass mutilation. Tradition molded through cultural activities that rest on a form of ancestral recognition urging the ritual-goer or reader to speak across generations follows the repetitious arc of the blues: going back to make sense of the present's painful conditions.

While the journeys in the plays that I have just discussed are largely imaginative, there are other works that explore more concrete figurations of home, defining it as nationalism, either a faith in America, African American life, or Pan-Africanism. The pieces written by black women playwrights that affirm the United States' ability to overcome its racism and eventually cherish her black patriots are few, and when this position is investigated, it is often undercut by irony or reserve. It is also noteworthy that when an attachment to the country does appear, the work is more often set in the South, not the North. For instance, May Miller's 1933 *Nails and Thorns* features an interracial cast (one of the few) and concentrates on a Southern town where a lynching is brewing. The only black character in the play is Annabel, the housekeeper to the sheriff's family, who proudly asserts, "I knows mo' 'bout this town 'n you does, Mis' Landers, 'cause mah mammy nursed mos' o' these folks. She say one haf them's related an' those what ain't has got relatives what is" (317). As local griot, Annabel not only records the entanglements of her own immediate/legitimate family but that of the village as well, which she perceives to be an extension of her own clan. To her, the mob's bestiality is a form of genocide levied by distant and close white relatives. In the midst of mayhem, Annabel's healing abilities stabilize the situation, especially in relation to the sheriff's inexperienced wife, who has just become a mother and becomes unhinged, at the end, by the bloodlust that the town delivers. Overwhelmingly, this drama is about the interconnectedness of America's social fabric and the utter ludicrousness of segregation that cannot possibly legislate or overturn centuries of mixing. Therefore, if a black cousin is killed, then his white cousin/executioner is murdered by the act as well.

Those who advance Pan-Africanism with their works are more convinced that their aspirations can be realized without having to wait out the massive reform needed to steer the United States back on course. Furthermore, these plays tend to predict that a final resting place on earth for the black masses can become a reality without any armed conflict or the resurrecting of old bones. Shirley Graham's ambitious *Tom-Tom*, a musical opera in several acts, rotates out from a compelling fascination with Africa. Both the mother figure and the spiritual leader (the Voodoo Man)—a 1930s African American Adam and Eve—affirm what impels them to seek relocation, at least culturally if not physically, in Africa. The mother proclaims: "Our girls will be safer in the jungles of Africa than they are right here on the streets of New York. Let us board this ship of Zion, let us sail across the troubled seas and let us reach our homeland which for us will be a land flowing with milk and honey" (256). Alarmed by the incessant sexual exploitation of black women, the mother asserts that the "removal of the body," a flesh-liberating act, will also enhance the spiritual and emotional well-being of the black self.[12] The Voodoo Man evokes a cultural and imaginative return to the Motherland: "I only want my people to love Africa. I only want my people to go home" (269). His suggestion that African Americans welcome the traditions and rituals of the Continent echoes Garvey and anticipates the Black Arts Movement. So both an actual mass emigration and a cultural revolution are billed as equally significant in this complex musical that not only centers on how the material world influences migratory patterns but also reincorporates music and dance into serious, "high-brow" black theater. A tradition that had set out in the early twentieth century to counteract popular musicals was now coming full circle, using

Diaspora moves and sounds to liberate the stage from cultural imperialism. The fact that Graham chose this form when so many other black female playwrights had restricted themselves to dramas and satires reveals her buoyancy in the midst of caution. Daring to reach out to Africa and relinquish her claim to the West's webbed circles of oppression, Graham took a bold step that aligned her with other Pan-Africanists including Garvey and her husband, Du Bois, who would go through a pronounced conversion and settle with Graham in Ghana.[13]

Pleasure, power, confidence, and unfettered vivaciousness all come together in Graham's utopian stage piece, a performance that could only be achieved once the African American turned away from the New World and faced the East. There are other black women playwrights during this era who also radiate the euphoria of Graham's dreamscape but do not steep their hopes in Africa, although the remnants from that continent's cultures that were carried to and survived in the Americas certainly shape their texts. These writers rely on syncretism in their theatrical vehicles, and certain key fixtures drawn from African American traditions are lauded as the saving grace: a strong adherence to a liberating Christianity that connects the specific historical circumstances of black people to Biblical texts (Zora Neale Hurston's *The First One*, May Miller's *Graven Images*, and Marita Bonner's *The Pot Maker*) and other allegorical treatments with mythic black folk heroes.

May Miller's *Harriet Tubman* is paradigmatic of both Christianity's and African American folklore's influence on black drama during this epoch. Under Miller's direction, Tubman, who is known as the "Black Moses," is a secondary character, taking a subordinate position to the two lovers, who are separated by slave owners and must preserve their trust across physical and psychic distance. The drama pivots around whether either will betray the other to garner favor from the master; so, two competing impulses spar off: self-preservation and self-aggrandizement against the golden rule. The couple pass the test and unite by curtain close as Tubman outlines her interpretation of sacred code: "Ah trusts the sense o' a man in love, 'cause God speaks in him then" (182). Enhancing Biblical injunction with the prophetic power of the heroine's word, Miller through Tubman elevates black folk from chattel to God's instrument. This divinity that resides in everyday action is a vocation that is enthused by a deep love for others, love being defined here as a sacred trust.

This lovers' contract is symbolic of African-American thought that views common black people as connected to God because of the firm bridge established during the slave period when bondsmen and women could only look to themselves, each other, and to the heavens for relief, ties that were not shattered by looming impediments, no matter how tyrannical or how daunting. (In the play, the runaways are hemmed in on all sides but still manage to escape.) We imagine this psychic/spiritual space as home, a haven of comfort that, no matter how difficult the moment, manages to ride over beleaguering fear. Biblical allegories by Bonner, Hurston, Miller, and others contain this same framing of home as a plane where evil may enter but will be defeated by spiritual resolve. Using lessons about the deleterious consequences of jealousy, materialism, and pride, these instructional works extend the modern Passion Play cycle that Grimké reinstated with *Rachel.* However, these offerings are about unequivocal triumph and do not waver or undercut their own power to transcend as is the case in *Rachel.* Portentous, even surly, certainly defiant, this circle of theatrical installations warns boldly against modern backsliding and the eventual consequence of such acts; they are Harlem's stump speeches, exhortations, and red-eyed flame throwers that commit to compassion, conviction, and eventual peace. Speaking with loud voices to deliver a calming message, these texts embody the spirit of African-American life, not completely new or old, merely soft or tenaciously rebellious, a world where playing the flute, as in Hurston's *The First One*, can turn quickly into knocking down the walls of Jericho.

There are several manifestations of home in the works by various African American female playwrights: the spirit-filled, African American "sanctuarians" employing allegory and historical drama, the Pan-Africanist going for the ambitious musical pageant, those mourning the loss of ancestral ties and unsettled about their return relying on concentrated one-act, open-ended dramas, and the few rallying American nationalists also employing drama but more often than not using it to cross over into dominant territory to expose social and moral hypocrisy. While the search for home is the most entrenched trope for this black dramatic tradition's meandering between 1918 and 1938, there were other crucial factors that shaped this body of work. Photography and film influenced the period's art, African American women's creativity being no exception. As I have argued elsewhere, from its emergence in the nineteenth century, film was sought after by conservatives, reactionaries, liberals, and radicals alike. Regrettably, by the twentieth century, photography had been mired in racism when amateurs and professionals used it to document lynching, making it a popular form. Many of these shots were turned into postcards and distributed via the mail across the country to share the event with family and friends. Well aware of this alarming technological reproduction of mass savagery, race leaders concluded that it would have to be engaged. Correspondingly, Du Bois urged African American men and women to snap their own pictures. In an article published in 1951 in which he reminisces about the social implications of his editorialship at the *Crisis*, that distinguished leader declared that the inclusion of prints of black people led to the journal's fame and viability: "Pictures of colored people were an innovation; and at that time it was the rule of most white papers never to publish a picture of a colored person except as a criminal…" ("Editing the *Crisis*" xxix). Du Bois insisted that the *Crisis* showcase photos that captured black faces and bodies in a pleasing and hospitable light that enhanced their humanity rather than reducing them to a "thing" somewhere between man and beast. He accepted the responsibility of rectifying the widespread misrepresentation of black America by filling the pages of his journal with vibrant black visages.

Similarly, the mobile visual tableau of serial photos and early film was incorporated into the aesthetics of African American impressionistic plays by women (the fact that most were one-acts aided in this effort). These pieces placed more emphasis on atmosphere than character development. After Grimké's *Rachel*, few works by black women playwrights before the forties featured characters that develop significantly over the course of the performance. Roles remain static and merely sketchy, falling in line with Benjamin's definition of epic theater: "… instead of identifying with the characters, the audience should be educated to be astonished at the circumstances under which they function…the truly important thing is to discover the conditions of life" (150). Certainly, this collection of works produced during these early decades of the twentieth century exposes the conditions of life, figuring everything from war to lynching to urban tenement squalor, an array of visual dramatizations that depict the dimensional surroundings of black existence. Still, it would be remiss not to note that while these artists wheeled atmospheric heartbreak across the stage, they also created competing shadows in a Du Boisian photographic vein by providing gratifying images of black selves.

A mere perusal of the costume lists indicates that black female writers concocted ways to counteract stereotypes; there isn't a rag-wearing clown or tasteless dandy in the bunch, but modesty and good taste prevail (the farthest the playwrights go is to insert occasionally a bit of Eastern flare as is the case for Hurston and Graham). Furthermore, the prevailing setting for plays by black women is interior domestic space, kitchens and parlors, artistic decisions that brand these black figures and their domiciles as familiar and approachable in opposition to the mainstream media that rarely depicted black characters as home dwellers (unless they were cleaning or serving in someone else's residence). Falling under the influence of racial uplift ideology that relied on black citizens who were honest, positive, humble, but ambitious, the sets, for the most part, and the sparse impressionist mood position black America as pensive but drawn toward motion, stoically outlasting their present harsh circumstances and ready to progress. Inspiring serial images that have been pressed on top of ugly renditions of cruelty and brutality typify the general African American female theatrical visual resonance during this span.

A sampling from various works will illustrate that there are layers of representation pasted onto the ambulatory screen. A common device is an opening moment that allows the audience to absorb a visual imprint of the "condition" before any dialogue is rendered or any motion proceeds. Contrast this contemporary dramatic staple to the nineteenth-century popular programming that offered action, singing, dancing, and hollering as the initial motif. This novel convention, alone, retards the dramatic field and allows various temporal perspectives to enter the theatrical domain. A prime moment comes from Hurston's *Mule Bone*; the first scene commences with a large, open porch that wraps around the general store. Villagers amble in and out; children gallivant nearby; men debate, whittle and eat peanuts: "…*when the curtain rises there is a momentary lull for cane-chewing*" (48). By freezing this snapshot, Hurston instructs the audience through emphasis toward the manner in which she would prefer that they imbibe her play. That is, she encourages them to join the cane-chewers, an activity that is characterized by a leisurely, thorough enjoyment of the good, ingesting only that which is sweet and worthwhile and discarding—after consideration—the tougher bits. This temporal suspension also resembles the moment when the flash burns the image to a backdrop; thus, it is the instant that the director/artist commandeers, records, and sets apart from all the other mundane, available options. As the lead impression, it colors and channels each subsequent frame. All other events that develop on the stage are held up against the first dominant indelible print of a social group that eats in tandem, a metaphor that, I would argue, renders racial uplift's essence: to work together in order to draw sustenance from the surrounding conditions. The Hurstonian spin on this notion is that this activity may actually be pleasurable and that enjoyment of life does not have to be sacrificed in order to advance as a people.

This direction, then, sends a strong message of inter-group cooperation while it places the recipient audience into a meditative state of mind, a pause that contrasts with the bustling pace that is otherwise set by the events. In effect, Hurston has scripted parallel fields atop one another. More specifically, while bluseian in terms of its thematic content and its repetitious and circular structure, the visual aspects suggest that the scene be read as pensive and mythical, and this is a general effect that *Mule Bone* shares with other pieces written by black women of this period. Recall the manner in which *Rachel's* exuberant, frolicking, nymph-like young lady fought against the sometimes grim notes that her speech conveyed. Similarly, Mary Burrill's *Aftermath* comes to light on the picture of Millie, "...a slender brown girl of sixteen, who stands near the window ironing," (137) an impression that stands out against the closing shot that captures the black Veteran John running from the house with his guns drawn to revenge his father's murder. Both Georgia Douglas Johnson's *Safe* and *Blue-Eyed Black Boy* commence with sewing/ironing images that suggest a domestic and aesthetic calm that is destroyed by catastrophe, and Bonner's *The Pot Maker* comes into focus with the mother poised stiffly on the edge of her chair (*The Opportunity Reader* 243). These portraits marry visionary progressivism to contradiction and strife as the women wait, listen, and divine the future while they make clothing and raise children. Relying on this technique, the playwrights are able to render the despair and resilience of African Americans who tackle and overcome relentless social and economic barriers. Acting in a restorative capacity, the images point toward moments on a mythical arc.

Therefore, when these treatments reach the live arena, they reinforce collectively through repetitious imagistic knelling that black America is not only surviving but is healthy, defiant, vigilant and roundly primed for action. The overwhelming number of sewing scenes, for instance, profess that, even with little time and modest material, black women will find the means to produce art, a dramatic motif that is analogous to the manner in which the African American female playwright with limited opportunity must knit together new patterns/designs in order to reconstruct "the play" into a tool that she can use. Quick-changing between literature and production, adopting an impressionistic tableau to keep the viewer stimulated during an age when the visual arts were becoming the dominant entertainment form, and further providing an assortment of contemporary, recognizable and self-respecting black subjects who, even if they do not speak a word, combat the minstrel hold-overs who were paraded across mainstream culture from stage to coffee tins, African American female playwrights respond to their dismissal from profit-taking markets with installations that are closer to the intimate spaces of black America.

In spite of Broadway's determining a piece's success, African American women dramatists were not seduced into angling their shows toward the majority's stage. So, they were relieved of the burden of considering how a white audience would respond to or interpret their plays. While constrained in terms of financial compensation and a limited reach, black women made the best of black audience engagement and repartee. Based on a more relaxed, liberating relationship between writer and audience, these dramatic texts, whether in print or performed, often disclose black institutions' strengths and their faults. Satire is the language of critique, and many playwrights employed this vehicle. Localized concerns such as color politics within black groups, the assault on black families, black women's roles as tradition makers and stabilizers, gender imbalances within the intensely patriarchal black church, the sounds and modalities of black speech, music, folk knowledge and custom; and the elegance and diversity of black and black female difference were all aired. Material and spiritual issues that mattered to a broad sampling of black people were germane and were tackled unabashedly without defense or the need to exalt black life to superhuman proportions (even the historical dramas had an element of the commonplace). In contrast to *Rachel*, these plays present heroines and heroes but do not elevate them over the society that they serve, a redefinition of heroism, praising the one who stays and labors inside an imperfect system as much more precious than the one who dismantles it from the outside.[14]

Major satirists of the period are May Miller, Eulalie Spence, Zora Neale Hurston, and Ruth Shelton (Shelton composed the award-winning *The Church Fight*). Miller's *Riding the Goat* encapsulates the most rehearsed topics that black women satirized with its illumination of a black doctor who views the lodge practices of his working-class black patients to be beneath him. He is saved from his folly by his fiancée, who wears his lodge costume in a neighborhood processional after he refuses to don it. This masquerade on her part saves him from the community's ire and a consequent economic boycott. Thus the play not only targets class divisions within black groups but courtships between black men and women and the sometimes overzealous and odd traditions of black organizations. Black establishments' foibles, specifically those of the black church, are examined as well in Shelton's *The Church Fight*, Spence's *Fool's Errand*, and Shirley Graham's *I Gotta Home.* Coupling is one of Hurston's favorite themes, and it crops up in *Mule Bone* and *Color Struck* as does an investigation into class and complexion biases within black social strata. In viewing the inequitable practices in black social groups and domestic arrangements as somewhat ridiculous and absurd, the playwrights instruct through negative example, thereby fostering a reinstatement of equilibrium and parity to those same institutions and associations.

These satires are significant because they document more closely the private spaces where black people congregate while the problem plays and folk dramas concentrate more heavily on the threats to black progress and, therefore, provide fewer opportunities to explore in depth how specifically black-owned/authored social constructions operate. In addition, the satires approximate, more than the other genres, mainstream commercial ventures as both employ wit. So they grant us an opportunity to chart any possible intersection between the dominant, popular theater and the African American female dramatic tradition during this period. If any vehicle has the potential to forage capital markets and gather resources to fuel black community theater in general, it is satire because humor renders its message less threatening. Hurston, more than the others, took up a sardonic dramatic posture (in both work and life) and used it to maneuver her pieces toward commercial production. After only achieving limited success, she relented in the forties, but her resilience indicates that she did not perceive of African American drama and American entertainment as necessarily discrete arenas. She struggled to make America see her art and not collapse it into pre-designated confining cells. That was the path that racial uplift should follow instead of insisting on a separate nationalism attended by an isolated black culture. Unfortunately, her contemporaries did not concur with Hurston, and much of her work went unproduced during her life.

Searching, revelatory, and impressionistic, en masse the theatrical works of this period empower segregated black communities by providing them with vehicles to audition, more than anything, the direction/s that could enhance the general condition of life for black people. These artists imbue their works with interesting arrangements that dip in and out of the active tropes that characterize the age. Bonner, as a case in point, pushes her plays' formal barriers to make them magically illusive but also grounds them in early twentieth-century experience, and Graham's historical pageant and other works trip along like films that can incorporate fantasy as easily as it charts a clear path to African-based salvation. Churches can break the surface almost anywhere in these offerings and at any time. So, it behooves us to examine a few samples more closely, keeping in mind the tradition's dominant ethos and patterns but also recognizing the specificity of each effort. An extended reading of several plays also grants us an appreciation for the intersecting and sometimes contrary impulses that playwrights grapple with to reach the viewer/reader but not bombard him/her with neatly concluded and trite endings that would shut down any interpretation on the participant's part.

Georgia Douglas Johnson is known primarily as a poet and a black arts proponent because of her famous literary salon in her Washington, D.C., home. Encouraging Marita Bonner, Willis Richardson, Zora Neale Hurston, May Miller, Alain Locke, Langston Hughes, Sterling Brown, Mary Burrill and many others through regular meetings, Douglas also found the time to write dramas. Margaret Wilkerson aptly describes Johnson's drama as the place where propaganda and folk art meet (Introduction xviii). Certainly *Plumes* verifies Wilkerson's claim because on the surface it reads like a brief glimpse into the life of working-class black southerners, but it considers as well colliding epistemologies and world views especially on the subject of death. It is what critics Deborah McDowell and Karla Holloway would call a mourning story. According to this one-act piece, black America and white America hold sharply divergent philosophies about the presence of death in everyday life and how that presence should be treated. Ultimately, the play centers on signs, language, and back talk in a bell hooksian guise: how black women gain control over their environment by calling out and redressing the governing social constructs without merely mimicking their linguistic and semiotic patterns, an individualized echo with its own aesthetics.

The drama begins, as Megan Sullivan has observed, in the kitchen, an important clue that this play will spotlight domestic space and how it is constituted. In this small house there are only two rooms, the kitchen and the bedroom, the social locations most often assigned black women by white America and by black men and children as well. Two friends, Charity and Tilda, contemplate whether to pay a doctor to operate on Charity's ailing daughter, a procedure that the surgeon admits has no guarantee of success, or whether to save their money to bury the child in grand style. While the women debate these choices, Emmerline decides for them by dying, a surprisingly open-ended anti-conclusion that does not authorize either approach, transforming this into a text that could certainly foster a great deal of dialogue and debate. Both sides on the issue are logical and tenable, a thematic decision on Johnson's part that places folk belief on an even keel with science. The women rationalize that mortality is inevitable and that sometimes it is better to accept it and show one's high regard for the deceased with "plumes" instead of expending energy on the delusion that man can cheat death with the knife (cut it out) and lose the little bit of dignity that God has allowed. The doctor, representing Western science, counters that every method should be tried before giving into fate and that Charity's daughter, whether she lives or not, can augment the data pool by relinquishing her body to the scalpel. The black women see the doctor as an arrogant butcher, and he sees them as superstitious and callous: there will be no reconciliation here, only a standoff that goes unresolved.

By using a polemic style, Johnson makes black female reasoning concrete, giving it a visibility that is often overlooked in the West. We know that Johnson is highly sensitive to the wholesale dismissal of black female knowledge systems. In her *A Sunday Morning in the South*, a white officer tells two black women, "Shut up. Your word's nothing" (235), an observation about white authority that Johnson shares with fellow playwright Eulalie Spence. When the white apartment owner in *Her* tells his black female tenant, Martha, "...I know they're [your words] lies or fancies" (135). Later this same landlord comes to learn—the hard way—that Martha's appraisal is accurate. Nevertheless, many discourses deny black women credibility because their observations and conclusions are constantly discounted by suspicion. African American female playwrights answer this racism by generating characters that speak out by way of their costuming choices and practices as well as words, a series of rites that we can view jointly as testimony. In the words of Sister Lucas, a figure conceived by Zora Neale Hurston, "I got just as much right to testify as you is" (*Mule Bone* 116).

A complex mixture of attitude, pronouncements, and ritual, Charity's testimonial is a rejoinder to imperial directives. When the surgeon informs her that he has to operate, she shouts, "MY Lord! Doctor—don't say that!" (29). Not only does Charity express her own view on the matter quite emphatically, she reaches into the physician's territory and asks him to rethink and retract his words; so, beyond her disapproval, Charity is also redirecting the discourse. She later informs the physician, "...there's things you don't know 'bout—there's other things I got to think about" (29). Not blindly accepting the scientist's recommendation, Charity opens channels, venting space to allow room for her own ethical system and social traditions. With this contestation and broadening of possibilities, Johnson reveals the testimonial's reach, for it takes wisdom based on personal and communal experience and inserts that into established discursive conduits in a way that the discourse cannot escape or ignore the utterance because its authority comes from its specificity to the subject: testimony cannot be disputed but can only be deflated or "disempowered" by other testimony.

In addition to Charity's "talking back" to the doctor, three additional symbolic codes contribute to the witnessing energy in Johnson's drama: the plumes, Emmerline's funeral dress, and the oracular custom of coffee-grounds divination. In tandem with her banter, Charity's artistry in the shape of the dress that she stitches for her daughter also divulges the mother's thoughts. It, in opposition to the shorter hems that Emmerline usually wore, is more akin to a gown that will cover the child from head to toe (25). Like Joseph's coat of many colors, this garment symbolizes the mother's love and pride in her youngster and demonstrates that the girl had been venerated by a family in a world where black women are routinely discounted as little more than cheap labor or bodies ripe for sexual exploitation. This raiment elevates the child and grants her a wholeness and respect, contradicting the scientific discourse's estimation that her value lies in her separate biological parts. The plumes announce pride, care and nurturing. As Charity puts it, "The plumes is what cost" (27). In other words, these decorations attached to the horses that draw the funeral casket stand for the sacrifice that the living are willing to make for the dead and are reminiscent of African ancestral reverence that requires that the dead be honored so that they can assist the living. Allowing a loved one to be interred without ritualizing their worth is asking for trouble in both a spiritual and a psychological sense. Psychologically the living must then contend with their guilt if they do not carry out the various ceremonies that document the deceased's importance (one need only recall the New Orleans wake to see the labor that is put into these funerals). Spiritually, the ancestor moves into another realm that allows him/her to continue communing with the living. If this ancestor is wronged by a stingy relative who will not grant a proper send-off, then the dead's spirit in a state of pique can cause all kinds of nettlesome bothers. This belief system did not altogether disappear when Africans were transported to the New World.

The third sign that testifies is the prophecy in the cup. Tildy divines a large gathering in the random coffee grounds that collect at the bottom of Charity's mug, and she notes that, the last time she observed such a pattern, Tildy's mother died (27). Even though the grounds are, perhaps, the most far-fetched of the omens, one must concede their clout as a meaningful text[15] in the community in which they signify. Prophetic ciphers have been seized and imbued with promise by black Americans from Nat Turner to twentieth-century figures including Marcus Garvey, Father Divine and Jean Toomer in *Cane*.[16] These readings of natural motifs are democratizing because the truth teller is not embodied in a human shape but is a sacrament that common people can tap. Interpreting the coffee seeds' splatter indicates a faith that the spirits will correspond directly through the individual rather than through an intermediary. This, then, is a reformist principle that sacred translation and analysis belong in the folk's hands. Right or wrong, these women determine their own moral course and consequent path of action, and, in the process, they testify that their decision to do so is their right. This treatment reveals a migration towards home because the black figures have found their ethics to be a comfort, something to lean on when pressured by an imposing culture. What remains ambiguous is whether clinging to these black southern rites is the soundest option. The question remains unanswered because Johnson does not seal off a single perfect ethical sanctuary as the definitive answer to black survival. The play's open-ended conclusion and impressionistic style prevent us from settling in and saying, "okay, this is it." Instead, the audience exerts itself to close or complete the play (as Brecht and Benjamin would insist upon).

An inherent call and response motif is threaded into Johnson's drama, generating a time-delayed dialogue that empowers each viewer/reader with an analytical vantage point. These extended conversations course through this age's African American female theatrical tradition and can be overt as in *Plumes*' unsolved ending or more diffuse in the case of Eulalie Spence's *Fool's Errand.* This light satire has a clear finale, but it centers on an enigmatic trial. The plot is straightforward and features a church council that attempts to ferret out who has impregnated Maza in hopes of forcing that young man to marry her. The irony is that the church has pre-judged the young woman and determined that she is pregnant simply because baby clothes were found in her home, items that, in fact, belong to her mother. As in *Plumes'* case, two factions square off: on one side, we find the level-headed Maza, a self-assured figure who feels that her private life belongs to her, and, on the other, an intrusive church judicial panel that operates under the aegis that everyone has something to hide. Their mandate entails excavating the hidden sins of others. While the moral entanglements of this specific work are indeed heady, the tone is not overly somber or grave, melding this work into that rare treat: a black comedy that does not devolve into buffoonery but discloses and condemns black community foibles, principally its reliance on gossip, hearsay, and a predisposition to draw pleasure sadistically from accusing and splattering fellow members.

On the surface, this satire shreds light on the black church's fervent attempt to control its parishioners, especially their sexual activity, but underneath it touches on the pressing questions that arise when a culture is caught between a trial-anchored and a proverb-driven base. The first rubric supposes that choice is the universe's premier marker and that nature—including man—is ruled by decision. The other, much older position, accepts that nature adheres to its own rules and, therefore, is not subject to review. Man's job, under the proverb's gleaming purview, hinges on keen sight, determining the inherent patterns that prefigure man's habitation, data that can then be converted into language in the form of the adage.

Black women's plays from this period are rife with maxims that explore these tensions and fall somewhere between proverbial knowledge and judgment. In Spence's *Her*, the wise black female tenant warns, "Weather what's good fer farmers doan help us wash-wimmen none" (133). Sister Lucas from Hurston and Hughes' *Mule Bone* contends that, "You clean round yo' own door before you go sweeping round other folks" (116), and the song refrain that begins May Miller's *Stragglers in the Dust* is, "Be shore you knows 'bout all you tells, But don't tell all you knows" (145). In these simple and elegant refrains truth is beyond reproach, and, because they are wrapped as maxims, they are general observations, not meant to malign an individual but to guide a society of hearers to sagacity. Trial, however, presupposes the eventual vilification of one or more persons. So, a proverb can find its way into a trial and be used to coerce and convince but not vice versa. We can see how this difference is drawn out in Spence's ingenious farce because the church council is convened with the following lines: "Thar's a meetin' here ter-night, Ah know yuh by *yo*' daily walk, Thar's a meetin' here ter-night" (123) [emphasis mine], a chant that implies evaluating a congregant based on the board's code of legality. In stark contrast, the play closes with a proverbial musical number from an offstage voice that all can hear: "Yuh call dat a sister? No! No! Who'd scandalize mah Name!" (131). Here the emphasis is on a generalization: She who would tarnish one's reputation should not be called sister. Hence, the refrain's goal is not to chastise particular church members but to draw out a truth that contains wisdom/survivalist strategies.

Spence may have selected a comedy for the squaring-off of these world views because in the modern era both collide and intersect, and humorous cavorting is more suitable to a blurring of the lines than the clear-cut antipathies of drama. With its emphasis on agile amusement, a satiric charade captures contemporary conditions more aptly because in the modern moment both ethical cores are active. To consider this complexity, bear in mind that in *Fool's Errand*, despite the church elect's overall mission to assign or remove guilt (the charges are recanted eventually and the busy-body, Cassie, is unmasked), this process is not drawn as entirely detrimental to the churchgoers because, during the testimonial hour, Maza learns which of her suitors really cares for her. Invaluable collateral information can spill forth, regardless of the procedure's chief objective which is to brand and control. As Foucault suggests, through its ability to regulate and normalize behavior, the trial has become an indispensable component of our social order that disciplines the individual. Yet, Spence's play points out that while the judicial process strives to define and defend conforming group behavior, the trial, just like any other performance, contains enough unpredictability to occasionally foster break-away revelations and speech. This shadowy facet of the proceedings that resists the overwhelming regulatory mechanism of the church council, which is to shape and stem the sexuality of its affiliates, salvages the board from pure authoritarian rule. An extension can be made to the manner in which African Americans are disproportionately acted on and normalized by the judicial system, but there are times when surprising testimony can elicit liberating pronouncements. Rescuing "the hearing," to Spence, means shaping the forum to allow for as much free-flowing speech as possible.

The council's convening and governance seems a tolerated encumbrance in Spence's work, a prevailing invention that has become so integral to social cohesion that even the hermit cannot escape its far-reaching discursive net. And while these "meetings" may contain the capacity for a degree of "talking-back," repartee between authority and the witness/accused, in comparison to the proverb, which Spence argues should remain black culture's indispensable touchstone, the trial is less democratic, less coded in a natural discernment that does not seat man at its core but situates him in relation to other creatures. Her fear is that a society rooted exclusively on trial to define and map out its coherent boundaries is more susceptible to abusive hierarchies. The maxim, then, becomes a way to reverse inequities and place insight back in the hands of the hoi polloi, as any subject, especially those who are not sanctioned as authorities, can mine a general pool of "truths." The necessity for these proverbs becomes concrete when we consider that Maza's directed proclamation of innocence, "Ise's tole de truth, Parson! Ah can't tell—no different!" (128) is ignored. If she adorned her affidavit in proverbial splendor, she could more readily persuade the panel.

Unfortunately, Maza's plain deposition carries little weight, which brings up gender concerns and, once again, the manner in which black women's articulations have been muted by modern channels. During the trial the council turns to Maza's father for clarification even though he is ignorant of the events and is not a parishioner. However, as patriarch, despite his stated distrust of church people and their proceedings, his word can persuade the judges (audience and church council). In regard to a female voice, only the mother's narrative is formidable enough to impact on the deliberations because only it can rival the patriarch's (in this instance that is the church itself) indictment. Woman communicating as a mother can register (and even more so when she uses the adage), but a woman recounting her story under and with her own name, from her own subjectivity, is overridden.

In a manner parallel to Grimké's *Rachel*, Spence yields to proper, state-sanctioned gender categories. However, in place of the neurosis that suffuses *Rachel*, Maza's unmitigated anger seethes as she levels one council member after the next, hurling at Cassie, "You hateful, evil-minded old hag! You sneak! How dar yuh say such a thing 'bout me!" (127), and to the Parson, (With angry scorn) "Reckon yuh's got mo' sense, Parson, dan tuh believe dem lies!"(127). Ultimately this wrath will lead to a cleft in this spiritual network, a rift that analogizes the many fissures within black social groups that are brought on by too much trial and too little spreading and upholding of proverbs. Neoclassical in its call for a return to an ancient value system, Spence's *Fool's Errand* takes seriously its mission to cajole the audience into rethinking its own reliance on sniffing out abnormalities (thereby contesting the tribunal's hegemony). According to Spence, black folk can find their road home with proverbial wisdom, following in the tracks of the Old Woman in Marita Bonner's allegorical play, *The Purple Flower*, who throws a handful of dust in an old pot (210), a symbolic act that parallels the proverb's construction: taking natural elements and distilling them to something beneficial that can be shared with a group.

With a stress on conjuration and transformation, it is not surprising that *The Purple Flower* predicts and welcomes revolution. This is indeed the most hopeful of Bonner's three plays as *The Pot Maker* is reserved and didactic, hinging on the Biblically-based aphorism that one will reap what he/she has sown. *Exit, an Illusion* is cautionary as well and is a blues-based one-act impression that is set squarely in a contemporary urban apartment. On the surface, *Exit* chronicles the implosion of revolutionary desire: accepting a loss. I argue, however, that in spite of its austere, nihilistic exterior, this work goads its viewer towards contemplation and, perhaps, fitting social redress even though the play itself offers no visible solution.

Located in an overworked room, *Exit* tackles how constrained city living presses on black migrants. In this very short piece, two down-and-out lovers have had an exhausting evening that includes the consumption of alcohol. In his inebriated sleep, Buddy dreams that he and Dot, his paramour, spar over whether she is having an affair, but her other suitor is actually the grim reaper. During the tussle, Buddy kills Dot, and the strange twist is that, on waking, he sees that Dot has indeed expired beside him in bed. Overwhelmingly, the backdrop reinforces the play's macabre events. As Bonner describes it, "The room you are in is mixed…It is mixed…Everything is mixed…Shoes mixed with dishes on the table" (200). In this topsy-turvy space, there is no focal point, no beacon back to nationalist desire or some other collective unity. The small cell has shifted events, time, and expectations on its side as in a Dali painting; the only thing that has real force or meaning is the body in two fixed positions, either on or off. Beyond that, as mid-twentieth-century existentialists will explore, is a vast graveyard of meaningless questions. During this mass exodus of black people who were leaving economically bleak circumstances (but often ones rich in environmental sustenance) for the miniscule footage of urban rental units, such considerations as whether life is futile rise to the fore.

This work is paradigmatic of drama that adopts an impressionistic motif because scene and ambiance are emphasized over character development, which is negligible. The message resonates clearly that these figures are entombed in a chamber that is bounded once by a city building and then wrapped again within a segregated nation. Thus they are doomed to repeat the death/dreamscape as though they are mannequins operated by remote machinery. In this case, the artist's light lingers on the intersection of modernity, urbanity, race and gender, a cross-road that Bonner employs to inscribe the blues as the twentieth century's foremost social signifier. Her blues variant, though, is that, instead of centering on depravation (since my baby left me), she fits murder/theft as the engine that compels the form. In other words, the blues' repository is not a mere entity that motors by way of repetition but becomes both agent and recipient (rather than a circle, we find arcs with ridges on it like gears). While circumstance (the room) distorts Buddy and Dot, Buddy responds by enacting the same frustration on Dot. So Bonner activates what Houston Baker would describe as a blues matrix (*Blues* 3). Meanwhile, an equally heady Darwinian dynamic emerges and intersects with the repetitious motif, a battle for ascendancy that is not waged by physical combat but functions in the realm of desire. He who has greater passion for living not only survives but can shape reality's contours in the same manner in which a painter would select to light and shade key features. This dynamic is also an apt description of the way in which discourse is shaped: a number of constructions meet, but power determines which notions/perspectives will lead through the subordination of the "lesser" views. Under this reading, Dot stands as a discursive choice not taken, for the audience will never fully visit her version of the events but must infer her probable stance through Buddy's and the omniscient playwright's focal points.

Beyond the obvious angst over urban space and how it redefines the social strata, a racial sub-text is grafted onto the broader philosophical plane. Dot, who is so light-skinned that she can pass for white, is courted by the white death/lover whose name is Mann (after Thomas Mann). Buddy's quarrel and subsequent metaphoric murder of Dot erupt out of his jealousy over this white rival. Holding in abeyance for a moment the drama's expressionist elements, we find a topic that is directly aimed at black Americans, that of color politics and the way that exoticism and primitivism are tied to economic exploitation, skin color, and prostitution. Skin color, for many, had become a measure of money-making potential in that the closer to white, especially for women, the better the chance for upward mobility through either marriage or selling the body in some other manner. In addition, the closer to white, the more the lines blurred between legitimacy and prostitution because the dominant culture placed darker black women outside the boundaries of propriety, branding them deviant and consumable,[17] but lighter-skinned black women could pretend "white female decorum" until the primitive heart—or I should say bottom—that they shield is bared. During at least two thirds of the twentieth century, America had granted the tan woman a mediating role as is the case in this composition.

By killing Dot off, Bonner, who was herself quite brown, dispatches with this intercessory buffer role and forces Buddy to confront his own construction of female value—the lighter the skin, the more valuable the commodity. Carried off so easily by Mann and disappearing into that "white" world, Dot represents the illusory nature of Buddy's sexualized hunger that mimics that of the primitivism and exoticism encoded by way of mainstream medium. To him, Dot is fantasy, the embodiment of an "ethnic" crossing between Puritanism and liberated expression. However, according to the play, trying to sustain this dream world of mixed-up things, actually a dramatic enactment of Buddy's interior machinations (Bonner foreshadows Adrienne Kennedy here), is akin to sitting on a balloon because the fragile synthesis between angel and whore, lady and tramp, white and black will not hold. Mann—the man—prevails in the end because, when threatened with forfeiting control over his lady/whore construct by insurgent black efforts or demands, either pulls (or passes) that representation into the white simulacra or kills it.

Pressing the implications of this allegory a bit further, we arrive at Bonner's take on America's future course. She sees no equitable way to blend the distinguishing core components of either American or African American culture because the more powerful one will devour the other.[18] Therefore, a jazz motif is unworkable here; in its stead, a blues' pattern anchors the allegory, a quick interlude that harps on the inevitability of pain and suffering, especially considering the modern world's penchant for imperialism. Thus this drama as blues' archetype mimics the prevailing nation's impulse to pull subcultures and subalterns into the center (embodied by Dot, the silent woman), a continuous process that outlines how the West Balkanizes (mixes up things) and repackages (usually as a prostitute) the other only to more easily conquer this now-separated and resealed entity at its leisure. Ultimately, after many generations and bluseian cycles of lightening-up, both metaphorically and biologically, what was once distinct about African American culture will disappear if ways to resist its wholesale consumption are not discovered. For Buddy this means taking control of his dream/nightmare and redirecting his life's course before it is too late. His continual replaying of this persistent struggle between authoritarian and subcultural leanings limits his ability to step out of the allegory's seductive pattern. To endure and mature, he must assert his difference and not be drawn into battling against an impenetrable and insurmountable exterior world (Mann).

What is on stage or in the book represents the visible portion of the blues text, that which is recorded in the lines. But the unanswered questions that the play raises and its structural design that forestalls consumer satisfaction follow the blues' sub-text or, more exactly, under-text. In this genre, thought is often implied by grunts, moans, gaps, and breaks that signal to the hearer how the more obvious articulated lines should be interpreted. This method of incorporating both the lingual and sublingual is used across African American culture and can often be found in the sermonic and testimonial traditions. For instance, saying "Well" and leaving a long pause after it implies that the narrative is not complete and that the hearer must fill in the blanks. In *Exit,* the dream sequence contains both the shaded and lit components of the blues motif, the visible tableau, but the under-text is the lesson that Buddy should learn from his nightmare, specifically to part from double consciousness.

Predictive of the Black Arts Movement and early Malcolm X, Bonner's piece counters both integrationist and double consciousness dilemmas, a thoughtful contribution that impels her reader/viewer to, as Melville would say, "untie the knot" (*Benito Cereno)*. Therefore, the racialized reading that I have just offered, certainly one of many possibilities, would call for placing this play in the same general category as Bonner's more perceptibly radical *Purple Flower* because both works imply that only drastic change will purchase the key to turn the tenement's sealed door, a metaphor for oppression and cultural death. The difference between the two allegories is that in this one the radical imperative is figured as an intellectual and mental conversion and requires that the reader/viewer push hard against the play to free herself/himself from its allure, while Bonner's *Purple Flower* features a social restitution that appeals directly to the audience's need for physical action. Therefore, the consumer is urged to identify with the *Purple Flower* but defy and defend against *Exit*.

Zora Neale Hurston's theatrical output is cousin to Bonner's in that both writers advocate an investment in African American culture, hoping that it can shelter black people. But, if Bonner alludes to and sketches the possibilities, Hurston spells them out in compelling vernacular language. Interweaving music, dance, drama and comedy, Hurston's art nods to the ebullient pleasure that Hopkins secreted in her *Peculiar Sam*. Both *Color Struck* and *The First One* braid together melodic, dramatic, body shaking, and humorous elements, a pattern that is modeled after the involvedness and "quick-change" of living black in America. *The First One* revises the Biblical story of Noah and his three sons, Shem, Japheth, and Ham. Ham's father rains down a curse that turns Ham colored, a malediction that Noah is tricked into uttering by the older brothers, who are envious of Noah's favoritism toward Ham, who enjoys singing, stepping, girding himself in attractive apparel, and strumming his harp much more than he takes to farming, his older brothers' occupation. The play ends on a bittersweet note with Ham exiled by both physical difference (his dark skin) and his estrangement from the domestic harmony of his childhood; however, in defiance of this tragedy, he picks up his harp and sings, "I am as a young ram in the Spring" (88) while his sobbing mother implores Jehovah to remedy the events. She faces the mountain, and Ham addresses the sun. A work about the origin of black culture, Hurston highlights the composite emotional core that drives black artistry, exploding common early twentieth-century views that black creativity originates from childlike pathos. In response, Hurston's performance transmits black art's emotional range and figures exile as the African American's initial state of being (as opposed to Eden). This condition is actively answered with culture, either to be faced down or overwritten, a heroics that results from resignation and an ensuing celebration of difference. As in many of her works, Hurston sets African American communities apart by insisting on their ability to eventually accept individuality (defined here as disconnection and loss), a concept the West—regardless of the rhetoric—still finds largely daunting. Culture, here, is surveyed with a broad scope as Hurston searches out mythic patterns to discover what it is about herself and her people that she admires, making this play both a personal and a communal odyssey. She will return to self-discovery and rehearsal of possible origins repeatedly, especially in her autobiographical narratives such as *What It Means to Be Colored Me* and *Dust Tracks on the Road.*

Color Struck is less about migrations and journeys than it is about an issue that challenges cooperative advancement: a couple is pulled apart by color politics. The beautiful Emmaline, who is dark brown, accuses her lighter-skinned boyfriend of having an eye for a yellow woman. Her vulnerability is augmented by the unspoken color bar that lighter is better, and the couple eventually become estranged. They reunite after many years, both regretting the parting, and it seems that all is well until Emmaline accuses John once again of favoring a light-skin female, this time her own daughter whom she conceived with a white man (the implication is that Emmaline intentionally selects a white father to give her child yellow skin). As a result of her obsession, Emmaline will not leave her ailing daughter with John while she fetches the doctor. The child dies, and Emmaline again forfeits John's love.

On the surface, this reads like outright melodrama, heavy topics that impact directly on black communities throughout the country who were grappling with racism's reach into black psychology. That Emmaline internalizes messages that uplift whiteness is the piece's painful admission. However, given this souring of life that infests various black networks, the playwright finds ways to defend against it. The cake walk competition, fellowship, and group camaraderie that are exalted in the first few scenes offset what would be an otherwise devastatingly bleak panorama and contrast with Emmaline's eventual isolation. In terms of fomenting participation through performance (or even through reading), the dance contest warms the audience's heart, not to mention its hips, and spirals toward a high-spirited climax: "[The] Fervor of spectators grows until all are taking part in some way—either hand-clapping or singing the words. At curtain they have reached frenzy" (97). Of course the spectators are both on the stage and in the seats; all are invited to partake in the festival, a unit that is counter-posed to Emmaline's utter alienation in the closing scene. By inserting this feeling of a democratizing surge that develops from individual dancers, a hyperbolic celebration of what the contestants can do that neither reduces their singular efforts nor closes off group involvement, Hurston creates a porous loop that has enough resiliency to protect and enliven black souls. Akin to the ring shouts and circle rites that course through African-based cultures from Ghana and Nigeria to the Caribbean and the United States, this outing that the writer interpolates into her piece corresponds to a home-like configuration, one that is about the present moment and exalting the self in all its aspects. The processional's transcendent power develops from an emotional investment and the full experiential range of each member, a duality that is built into the practice's architecture, for while the group forms the outer perimeter, there is space in the middle for partakers to break free and showcase their own signature steps. Once one or a subgroup has exhausted itself, they then rejoin the wider circle, and others may jump into the center. In this sense, the structure of the ring dance contains what playwright August Wilson would call "two trains running," or the ability to foster personal dynamics and still maintain group directives by upholding a tradition that declares diversity.

Like the ring shout, Hurston's *The First One* and *Color Struck* are exercises in *multiple* antiphonal calls and responses. Within the ring, drum encounters speech, swinging legs meet tears, and pride brushes against fatalism. Other African American women writers of the period also root circular aesthetics with variation and employ it as a sounding board to collect black diversity and aim it toward uplift prerogatives.[19] For instance, Shirley Graham's *Tom-Tom* includes the following lines, "In the darkness is heard the beating of a tom-tom. A distinct signal is heralded. From the opposite direction comes the answer. Now, faster the answers come from all sides" (238). Similarly, Marita Bonner features a conversation between modes: "A drum begins to beat in the distance. All the US stand up and shake off their sleep. The drummer, a short, black, determined looking US, appears around the bushes beating the drum with strong, vigorous jabs that make the whole valley echo and re-echoe with rhythm. Some of the US begin to dance in time to the music" (209). In each case, the drum invokes the circle, a vital detail because this sounding can reach beyond commercial and national boundaries to restore uniting rituals that have been sealed by centuries of slavery. But, paradoxically, while the boom resurrects the past, it forms the future as well because it prefigures and determines inner-cultural dialogue. By insisting on the tom-tom's centrality, African American women playwrights recover another variation of the call-and-response dynamic where the tom-tom displaces the authoritative leader who projects out to the witness. With a pulsating guide replacing a spoken text, the mode becomes more egalitarian because no one "voice" carries more heft than any other.

African American women's theater folds this version of the call-and-response motif that is set off by the drum inside its constructions, an innovation from the twenties that grants a new direction for black drama. With the reintroduction of the drum that coincides with African America's budding respect for West African practices, the interlocutor and the Bible are superseded (or at least challenged) by a more liberating musical/lingual initiating text that invites individualized responses to the call. Thus the tom-tom channels energies, but it is less insistent on protocols. (We see evidence of this difference in Hurston's *The First One* when the family splits into two strains, the first led by Ham's flute whose only directive is to follow the sun and the other typified by Mrs. Noah's facing a mountain that symbolizes man-made social prescriptions and rules that she dare not break even if it means denying her offspring.) By displacing order and then recombining it, percussion's addition to the theatrical forum acts as a deconstructive force so that the black writer may more readily dismantle traditional Western structure in hopes of securing a performance vehicle that he or she can own. So, Hurston's, Graham's, and Bonner's beating summons insist that rhythm should be incorporated in "serious" black drama and that music in the theater can represent black-defined modalities, not the market's canned offerings.

Black female playwrights' use of the tom-tom was especially tricky during the twenties because Broadway, traveling shows, and cabarets used drumming to announce black simplicity and primitivism.[20] In Western discourses, the pulsating snare or conga signified little more than a savage sexuality or liberation from inhibitions. Therefore, when black artists brought the drum to the theatrical arena, they had to build the context in which it sounded cautiously and skillfully to avoid the overriding association of blackness and black music with unleashed tribal spirits. Black women writers struggled to make beats connote a beckoning gesture to invite conversation. To these artists, the rhythm discharges subtle variations in tone and duration that retain the nuance of language. Graham, in particular, was extremely vigilant and studied African dance and consulted with African advisers to do justice to what she considered to be a sacred text/tradition (Hamalian and Hatch, *The Early Period* 235). The devotion and attention that Graham conferred on musical tone and pitch and to hand and foot position, for instance, redirected the vitality that primitivism strove to inveigle. She labored to transform what appeared as haphazard abandonment in dominant theater into routines that required measured craftsmanship and discipleship. Reversing the discursive plane from the dominant code of gyrating, sexualized black bodies and replacing it with a raised consciousness, an overwhelming call to reunite with pre-exilic (Eden is claimed to be in Africa by some black writers) rituals and a celebration of new variations, musical numbers inserted in serious works by black writers demanded a heightened level of audience engagement that unembellished drama could not ignite.

All in all, during this period, African American artists did not capitulate to capital and dominant naming but fought to assign meaning to rites that stemmed from African American cultural memories and experience. While Graham, Bonner, and Hurston pushed toward a complete synthesis of music with drama in a manner that would reflect that song and dance often designate blessed spaces to the members of the Africa Diaspora, Spence, Miller, Johnson, and Burrill incorporated fragments and snatches of song in their work, signaling that although they may have protested how popular musicals defamed black people, not one was willing to give up melodious sound as a device. From Hopkins's bold stab at diverting minstrelsy to Grimké's quirky insertion of children's rhymes in her problem play, to the Harlem Renaissance when a group of highly educated "teachers" transformed the data that they collected about black culture from West Africa to the Caribbean to the southern American states and its urban cities, the black female dramatic tradition labored to define the rituals of black people beyond the reductive cultural ghettos supplied by dominant venues. More than anything else, this reliance on "rhythm" ensured that their artistry would embrace antiphonal, quick-change properties, inestimable apparatuses that resisted the static roles that Western discourses held open for black female figures. Alternatively, in the circle of the step or within the harmonies of song, textured black female subjectivity could be gestured toward and approached.

The story of African American drama by women between 1918 and 1938 is one of versatility, earnestness, hope, frustration, modification, and, above all else, open-endedness, featuring a series of ongoing antiphonal queries and replies. In terms of its material mark, this period's cultural activists made headway by channeling their products to extend the educational institution. Creating roles for black performers that gave them reprieve from stereotypes but with little money to promote the talent that came from this labor, the writers made do with amateurs and volunteers who were learning a myriad number of skills that could be employed to enhance and expand black growth. So, this span leaves us with a series of contradictions: blues themes encounter progressive visual fields, bound scripts cede to limited productions, and a cataloguing of social ills resides next to a commemoration of African American epistemologies, folk practices, and modalities. Black women dramatists were proactive and reactive, somewhere in the middle of a nomad's struggle to find the star that points to home.

NOTES

[1] The ideological debates between Du Bois and Locke are well documented. See Du Bois's "Criteria of Negro Art" in the *Crisis*, October 1926, 290–297 and Locke's *The New Negro* and "Steps toward the Negro Theater" also in the *Crisis*, December 1922, 66–8. A lucid discussion of how these varying standpoints impact on black theater's shaping can be found in Hay, 1–38 and Sanders, 8–9.

[2] There were several attempts such as Du Bois's Krigwa Players to establish black companies, but the problem was one of real estate. While the bodies, talent and drive were certainly evident, the venues for full production seasons were scarce. Established black institutions such as churches, schools, lodges and public libraries did their share to mount works, but a separate "art-house" for race plays and serious black drama did not exist. Theaters in black communities such as The Crescent, Lafayette, and Lincoln in Harlem and the Pekin in Chicago on rare occasions offered serious efforts, but, more often than not, they provided the light, popular musical or comedic numbers that would make money. Woll refers to them as the "new Broadway for black theatrical performers" (54). Furthermore, the TOBA circuit, a national entertainment ring that served black clientele, marketed musicals and vaudeville/variety acts (Mitchell 70).

[3] Black actors were typecast routinely according to skin color. Darker women were barred from leading roles and the chorus and were relegated mostly to playing maids and church sisters.

[4] Major African American theater critics and historians agree that O'Neill's, Green's, and Torrence's plays, however well intentioned, reproduce far too many misshapen generalizations to elude the surrounding country-wide penchant for grotesque racial coding. For example, Sanders observes that, "In the Torrence play [*Rider of Dreams*], music becomes the signature of the simple, happy-go-lucky, but now sobered, stereotypical man-child of the Negro folk play" (31). Loften Mitchell assesses these pieces similarly, observing that they appear to elevate the black man as proletariat hero, but, in fact, reduce him to an all-too predictable "sensual body" (Mitchell 69 and 75; Sanders 55).

[5] I am envisioning the various songs and videos that zero in on black women's backsides or "back" as it is colloquially called and the comparisons between black athletes and various members of the animal kingdom.

[6] For example, May Miller's *Riding the Goat* is, "Adapted to the capacity of advanced students in high school." Her *Graven Images* is designed for "children of the eighth grade" (*Plays and Pageant of Negro Life).*

[7] I have discussed elsewhere the bearing that photography has had on black cultural formations. See *Black Women Intellectuals* and my forthcoming piece on lynching photography, *Snapping Frontiers: Lynching Photography, Then and Now.*

[8] I am thinking about the manner in which nineteenth-century holdovers such as Mammy, Sapphire, Sambo, and the Dandy have mutated in the twentieth century and have become the Welfare Queen, Black Ho, the Criminal (badly dressed), or the Pimp (well dressed).

[9] Hurston's most renowned porch scenes are in her acclaimed novel, *Their Eyes Were Watching God*, but she inserts them across her oeuvre from the short stories to plays to her non-fiction.

[10] Many Romantic texts featured ghosts that direct the discourse. Consider Bronte's *Wuthering Heights* and Wordsworth's *Lucy* poems.
[11] Refer to Hortense Spillers' "Cross-Currents, Discontinuities."
[12] In her persuasive article, "Mama's Baby, Papa's Maybe," Hortense Spillers distinguishes between the black body and the flesh, flesh serving as a site of struggle that can be recovered by the formally enslaved and their progeny: "…before the 'body' there is the 'flesh,' that zero degree of social conceptualization that does not escape concealment under the brush of discourse, or the reflexes of iconography." Stolen bodies wage high crimes on the flesh, and the flesh becomes the place where the narratives of this terror are written (659).
[13] Graham targeted liberating themes by publishing historical biographies as well as drama, compiling sketches on such figures as Booker T. Washington, George Washington Carver, Benjamin Banneker, Jean Baptiste de Sable, Paul Robeson, Phillis Wheatley, Pocahontas, and Frederick Douglass.
[14] This trend toward drawing the heroine as part of and central to a community rather than on its margins departs from Grimké's Rachel who stands as a reluctant saint who may only protect those she cares for by withholding intimacy.
[15] Gates first coined this term "speakerly text" in his seminal work, *The Signifying Monkey*. See especially his chapter, "Zora Neale Hurston and the Speakerly Text" (170–216).
[16] While the prophet has become a fixture in African-American culture, it has been satirized roundly by the likes of Chester Himes (his detective series, in particular, *The Big Gold Dream*), Ralph Ellison (*Invisible Man*), and Ishmael Reed (in any number of his parodies from *Flight to Canada* to *Mumbo Jumbo*).
[17] Consider, for example, the case of Sarah Baartman, otherwise known as the Hottentot Venus, a nineteenth-century African woman whose buttocks and genitalia were put on display, even after her death (Gilman).
[18] Later in her career, Bonner will return to the question of syncretism. Her short fiction, in contrast to her allegorical drama, concentrates on the unnamed, undocumented moments when ethnicities, races and world views collide.
[19] See James Snead's "Repetition as a Figure of Black Culture" for an apt discussion of the manner in which circularity dominates black cultural patterns.
[20] Some of the more notable Broadway productions that featured black casts are *Bandana Land, In Dahomey, Abyssinia, The Shoo Fly Regiment, Clorindy, A Trip to Coontown, The Red Moon, Shuffle Along, The Green Pastures, Runnin Wild, Plantation Revue, Africana, Dixie to Broadway, The Chocolate Dandies, and Blackbirds of 1928 and 1929.*

FOUR

When Saints Build Frames: Sacred/Secular Musical Pageantry in Alice Childress's Plays

Julia: Nobody comes in my house

—Childress, *Wedding Band*

THE YEARS between 1935 and 1950 reduced the American Theater to streamlined operations, and African American female playwrights bore the brunt of this austerity.[1] During the Depression, Broadway capital evaporated as did that for regional theaters and traveling circuits, and, while plays by African American women were not impacted directly because they had been already passed over by the commercial houses, the socio-economic foundation that sustained black community organizations was under siege as well. Dire financial times led to tighter budgets for drama programs as did a decrease in funds elicited either through donation or some manner of subscription: the live arts, even in the cellar, became an extravagance. Informal networks that stirred productivity such as literary salons and reading and writers' groups began to disintegrate too since fewer Americans felt that they could make a living at or make a difference with literature.

Of course some amateur productions and even a few professional ones survived the Depression's economic winter. The WPA's Federal Theatre Project is one of the few groups that cultivated and promoted the performing arts during the thirties; however, the conveyances that featured black casts (in sharply segregated America) were composed nearly exclusively of either white or black men. Shirley Graham was one of the few African American women to hold a position in the Project as Chicago's Negro Unit Director, overseeing runs of the *Swing Makado* and *Little Black Sambo* (Perkins 210). Joining the handful of African American women who found employment in the fine arts during these Spartan years, Zora Neale Hurston served briefly with the WPA's New York Branch as a drama coach, but she did not secure backing for any of her original scripts (Perkins 78).[2] Even with fewer resources, predominantly black high schools, colleges and universities remained the major venues for airings by black women dramatists, but these educational institutions had to resurrect pieces that had surfaced prior to the lean thirties. The only African American female playwright who managed showings of new material was Shirley Graham, who wrote and launched four compositions between 1938 and 1940 while she was in residence at Yale University (Brown-Guillory, *Wines* 80 and Barlow 239).[3]

In spite of this sharp decline in original scripts, it would be remiss to equate this fall-off over this fifteen-year mid-century span with a general creative forfeiture or complete disillusionment on the part of black intellectuals and artists. To the contrary, this transitional phase braced and fed the Civil Rights period that would erupt in full bloom by the early fifties. Consider as evidence that in 1945 the Dillard Players Guild commemorated their tenth anniversary by indicting Uncle Tom and stipulating that he be, henceforth, banned.[4] This mock tribunal establishes that a major black university's drama program was viable and feisty, and it argues that black America had grown weary of racist typecasting. The times were ripe for a national transformation at the behest of a new generation of black citizens, both men and women. What the "teachers" from the previous era had set in motion was coming to fruition, for their students, armed with technical skills, intellectual fortitude, and a craving for justice on a grand level, were completing their apprenticeships and were ready to take on oppressive structures, even Broadway.

More specifically, even though fewer were churning out new plays, many African American women aspired to be entertainers and behind-the-scenes specialists. Alice Childress materialized from this group. As an active cast member of the American Negro Theater, she appeared in such stage shows as *On Strivers Row*, which headlined at the Harlem Boys Club in 1941 and at Armstrong High School in Washington, D.C., in 1942; *Natural Man* at the 135th Street Library in New York in 1941; *Rain* at the ANT playhouse on 126th Street in Harlem during the 1948 season; and *Almost Faithful*, also in 1948 at the Playhouse. By 1949, Childress had crafted her first drama, a decision that resurrected the African American women's play writing tradition. A kindred spirit to Morrison, Childress yearned for art that carried her life observations, sense of self, and dreams from her position as a black woman in America, aesthetics and themes that did not yet exist—at least not on a countrywide level—in 1949. As Childress observes baldly, "*Gone with the Wind* is not our story. And our history is not gone with the wind, it is still with us" (*Freedomways* 16). To animate those narratives,

Childress wrote over fifteen dramatic works between 1949 and 1987, many of which were performed.

In contrast to African American women playwrights from the early decades of the twentieth century, Childress labored to see her offerings blossom on the stage and had no intention of settling for a purely literary play. "The thing," in her hands, awakened fully only under the penetrating lights of the first night's opening. She insisted, pushed, held to her convictions and utilized the networking base that she had facilitated to display her drama before the public. The end result was a long career in the performing arts that beheld and contributed to the sixties' and seventies' numerous revolutions. Over the course of her life, Childress would bear witness to the fruits of her labor: The American Theater would no longer belong exclusively to white males, nor would drama be contained within the art house because it would become popular again.

Childress's involvement with the stage began with her move to Harlem in the twenties with her grandmother, an influential woman who introduced her young charge to as many galleries, books, lectures, shows, and concerts that the two could imbibe. When she was barely beyond her teens, Childress had helped to found and tend to the American Negro Theatre in Harlem (Curb, *DLB 7* 118).[5] While with ANT, she acted, coached, directed, served on the board, and replaced the personnel director for a year in addition to holding a number of part-time jobs to provide for herself and her daughter, Jean (Harris, *DLB 38* 69). In 1949, she produced her first play, *Florence*, which she envisioned for the ANT ensemble. Kicking off in a Harlem loft that seated twenty-five (Curb, *DLB* 7 118), the venue reflected aptly the writer's goal to capture the familiar and ordinary sights and sounds of working-class black American activity. Set in the segregated South, *Florence* spotlights a bristling encounter between a white liberal and a working-class African American woman. This is the first of Childress's five major plays that include *Trouble in Mind* (1955, 1970), a treatment of racism and sexism in the theater; *Wine in the Wilderness* (1969), which confronts pretentious African American aesthetics during the Black Arts Movement; *Mojo: A Black Love Story* (1970), a blues-based romance; and *Wedding Band* (1973), her greatest work, about miscegenation in South Carolina during 1918. Minor pieces include *Just a Little Simple* (1950), based on Langston Hughes's Jess B. Simple character; *Gold Through the Trees* (1952); *The World on a Hill* (1968); *The Freedom Drum/Young Martin Luther King* (1969); *String* (1970), an adaptation of a Guy de Maupassant story; *A Scene from the African Garden* (1971); *When the Rattlesnake*

Sounds (1975); *Let's Hear It for the Queen* (1975); *Gullah/Sea Island Song* (1984); and *Moms: A Praise Play for a Black Comedienne* (1987), based on Moms Mabley's exploits. In addition, Childress has provided us with children's novels: *A Hero Ain't Nothin' but a Sandwich* and *Rainbow Jordan*; novel, *A Short Walk*; and a collection of humorous yet provocative impressions from the vantage point of a wise African American domestic worker (another tribute to Hughes's Jess B. Simple), *Like One of the Family: Conversations from a Domestic's Life.*

After her debut with *Florence*, Childress followed with *Just a Little Simple*, which was sponsored by the Committee for Negro Arts in 1950. *Gold Through the Trees* was produced in 1952 at the Club Baron Theater, performed by ANT. *Trouble in Mind* ran at the Greenwich Mews Theater in 1955 and won an Obie Award in 1956; the work was revised in the eighties and nineties and appeared in 1984 in Chicago under the guidance of the Kuumba Theatre Company, in 1987 under the HARDLEY Players of Harlem, in 1988 by the Takoma Players of Washington, D.C.; in 1990 it was presented at the Black Theater Festival in Philadelphia at the city's Theater Center; in 1992 it made its way to the Tricycle Theater in London, and in 1998 it found a home at the Samuel Beckett Theater in New York under the directorship of the Negro Ensemble Company. The Negro Ensemble Company produced *String* as well in 1969, while the New Heritage Theater featured *Mojo* in 1970. *Mojo* resurfaced in 1978 and 1982 at the Inner City Cultural Center in Los Angeles. Newark, New Jersey, welcomed Childress's work in 1969, as its Performing Arts Repertory Theater backed *The Freedom Drum*. *Wine in the Wilderness* had brief stints in the early seventies as did *Wedding Band*, which was produced by the New York Public Theater's Shakespeare Festival in 1972, Los Angeles' Inner City Cultural Center in 1977, and Hartford's John Huntington Theater in 1979. *Wedding Band*, certainly the most widely circulated of Childress's scripts, was revamped in 1989 at the Milwaukee Repertory Theater, and it was televised by ABC. Appearing on National Educational Television, *Wine in the Wilderness* is her only other dramatic vision to be televised. Other productions include *Gullah*, which premiered at Stage South in Charleston in 1977 and was revised as *Sea Island Song* for the University of Massachusetts at Amherst in 1984. *Moms* ran, fittingly, at the Hudson Guild Theater in New York in 1987 as New York had been Moms Mabley's base of operation for many years.

This list of extensive productions, however impressive, merely hints at Childress's gifts because, while she created her own energetic line of characters who would not be daunted by racism, sexism, and economic limitations, she also extended herself to her local artistic community, to racial uplift goals, and to her country as the embodiment of what America could represent: ingenuity, fairness, diligence, generosity, forgiveness, empathy and courage.[6] The critical reception to Childress, while not as far-reaching as it could be, is generally favorable, but the memorializing of her career and life has collapsed into the pedestrian casings that usually contain powerful, black female figures. Plainly put, she has been documented most often as an underrated foremother who paved the way for other talent and a realist who "mirrored" the essence of black life. Paradigmatically, Curb observes that, "...Childress is a splendid playwright, a veteran—indeed a pioneer. She has won awards, acclaim, and everything but consistent productions," (*DLB 7* 76) while Brown-Guillory refers to her a "giant in a straitjacket" (*Their Place* 28) and Mitchell laments that she, "...represents a figure that is not unknown to students of the American drama—a major talent that is rarely produced" (169). Most reviewers situate her unequivocally within naturalism's domain, Curb roundly claiming, "Childress's mode of characterization is unflinching realism," (*MELUS* 65) a belief that is shared by Barlow ("Childress has fought against racism and sexism to provide audiences with truthful depictions of the lives of African Americans, particularly women" (479)).

Given the aforementioned list of production sites, it is fairly safe to posit that the Harlem artist did enjoy at least a modicum of backing for her work; yet the claim that she did not receive the attention and accolades that her efforts deserve rings true. The rationale provided for the disparity between Childress's stature as a playwright and her need to scramble to locate sponsorship to present her scenes rests on the supposition that she was out of sync with the times, composing Afrocentric pieces during the very start of a national push toward integration and conceiving a play about miscegenation during the height of the Black Arts Movement. She would rarely go along with the programming of the moment, whatever it might be, and this led to both her martyrdom and her obscurity. Call it "dignity," (Barlow 68) a stubborn desire not to compromise, or a commitment to higher ideals, Childress held firm to the view that if she had been granted the awesome responsibility to speak for millions of black people that she would depict those stories in her own way and not concede to fashionable expectations and tastes.[7] She suffered for her convictions by having to toil continuously and contentiously to bring her plays to the stage. But, in hindsight, we should be clear that Childress was not out of bounds; the American theater afforded too few outlets for her work. Her well-crafted plays bubble with the paradoxical quick-change, open-ended, steely courage that characterizes the

African American female theatrical tradition. They are aggressive at times; at others, they purr and harp on the subtle, deep-grained emotional strings that make us all recognize our vulnerability and incompleteness. And, if she deals in heroines and heroes, then they are a new postmodern breed. The greatest compliment to Childress would be to resume production and critique of her work, ever searching for the fine-tuned variations in shade and tone that she encodes.

While I agree with Brown-Guillory, Curb, and Mitchell that Childress is underrated and underappreciated, the charge that she is a strict realist is debatable because the writer breaks apart classic naturalism with intrusive African American cultural invocations and African American steeped aesthetic frames. For instance, if we encounter the familiar beginning, build-up to the denouement, and conclusion (or a facsimile of one) in her plays, that overall structure is infiltrated by interference, musical riffs, signification, back talk, and folkloric, historical, and contemporary references that undercut the obvious linear pattern. As Brown-Guillory comments, the dramatist accomplishes this disturbance by injecting a variety of inspirational sources into her theatrical collection "…that incorporate the liturgy of the black church, traditional music, African mythology, folklore and fantasy" (*Wines in the Wilderness* 98).

In addition to the interstices created by the artist's skillful placing of rebellious, polarized vernacular impositions, she alters the traditional mimetic field by incorporating symbols that force the dramas to transcend the moments in which they are set, lifting her pieces into the time and space of legend. This reliance on a resonant figurative code impacts on her use of characterization as well because each of her major roles has both a mythic and modern subtext. I note as well that Childress brackets and examines the "paradigmatic leader" designation, and we discover that the chief figures in the playwright's major works approach and retreat from their own canonization and are, therefore, constantly in flux in relationship to the position that they would or should take vis-à-vis the communal center. This shimmering or traveling not only within form but also within character suggests a revolving property that makes it difficult to fix the writer's scenes within naturalism's more static shell. Each of these innovations such as disruptive interpolated expressive elements, semi-emblematic characterization, and overriding prismatic signs demonstrate that Childress's project entails deconstructive ambiguity, rage, and detachment, elements that are couched within a more general racial uplift shell that, under this artist's watchful eye and ear, sports a patina etched by a compounded and raspy impatience with power.

Comparing Childress to Harlem Renaissance-era African American women dramatists confirms that she reproduces many of the tradition's methods and topics, but her work charts out a novel direction. Childress's pieces are built more often on multiple acts, and the background sounds and ambiance acquire an enhanced role while character development increases in import and depth. Also, in relative terms, the general thematic range, while still highly conscious of and sensitive to racial uplift themes, spins out from the more prescriptive early twentieth-century tenets of black progressive doctrine. For instance, lynching and urban blight, two key concerns for the previous generation, are barely alluded to; furthermore, the mother's hegemony is upended as the playwright does not require her female characters to speak through a parental veil to be certified noteworthy. These details confirm the Harlem-based writer's departure from orthodox uplift ideology in terms of a shift away from the major social ills and rhetorical tools that preoccupied black leadership during the first three decades of the twentieth century. These divergences alone make it obvious that Childress's oeuvre signals a fresh era's emergence, yet she veers away from established black progressive dictates most radically in her treatment of black female sexuality as her figures have intimate lives that are connected integrally to her plot machinations. Childress's black women love men and suffer the rewards and consequences of doing so, an insistence that black female heterosexual subjectivity not only exists but is often complicated by a dominant public sphere that either wishes to deny it or render it pornographic. Childress refuses to censor her art, even beneath the looming cumulus of the prevailing (now international) lore that connects the black female presence to excess, gross pigeon-holing that prevented previous black female playwrights from openly acknowledging black female sensuality and desire, although they certainly chronicled its signature with oblique and displaced references (Juno's tricks, Rachel's romping, and Hurston's bodacious dance scenes). For Childress, naturalizing black female sexuality is radical activism.

This mid-century bard stresses how racism curbs individuality and creativity and how capitalism takes its toll by narrowing women's lives to bourgeois pretentiousness and a series of psychological impingements. The importance of intergenerational, communal struggle also rises to the fore as Childress maps out black women's roles in America, including their link to the nation's economy and how they help to construct America's identity by helping to shape the nation's intricate social patterns and systems. These stories could only be dramatized, Childress professed, by interweaving sound, folk practices, and comedy into "serious" tragedy.

From a bountiful catalog of possible additions and combinations, this Harlem artist entrusts music with its intense range to forge traditional theatrical realism into something that more faithfully reflects her thinking, experience, and observations. Accordingly, over the course of her writing career from 1949–1987, Childress subsumes the break, a master trope; travels through blues, jazz, and early hip hop/funk motifs; and fashions a tragic opera that incorporates all these functioning modes and more. Therefore, Childress, in terms of structural design, is sister to Pauline Hopkins and cousin to Zora Neale Hurston. Finally, because she realizes that global plights and conditions are linked inextricably with black women's bids for autonomy, Childress demands a broader audience for her work, not settling for the semi-private stages that the Harlem Renaissance female dramatists often utilized. And, if that meant that the world's theater would have to be revamped to accommodate her, then so be it, for her version of integration entailed full membership between the races and between the sexes—no compromise.

The playwright extends her reconstructive project by disassembling hierarchy in whatever location it may arise, using form to explore America's cultural fusion as she interlaces African American and majority patterns, often positioning the African American cultural referent as a strip that surrounds and directs how the audience should read or respond to the enclosed inner drama. Thus we detect another instance of the ring-dance structure with external and interior traveling circular chains. The difference in this mid-century iteration is that there is no exchange of individual and group expression as in Hurston's *Color Struck*. In contrast, Childress places traditional Western theater—its themes and structure—on display in the inner realm, as the outer perimeter (black modes) evaluates what is seen below, somewhat akin to the Greek chorus mixed with a modified trial. More specifically, in this artist's plays, the blues, jazz, and other musical conveyances comment on the exhibit. So we find that musical meta-texts peer into the manner in which race and gender relations work themselves out during late capitalist moments when class lines appear fluid but are becoming more acutely entrenched, resulting in a theatrical atmosphere where wise, discerning aural annotations await a rising consciousness and a corresponding reversal of destructive patterns. Childress's outer ring sings to its interior to alter itself or be enclosed perpetually within a repetitive border in the shape of a sounding/recording that loops around incessantly and seals its material fate. Note that this choral edge is not alien to the center, nor is it autonomous as it does not predate its interior's historicity but is created by it and can only speak in response to the dissonance produced by fallible human interaction. During the earlier years of African American female play writing, structure, generally, is more explicit; by the time of Childress's advent, it becomes more deeply striated (often camouflaged) and will remain so for contemporary African American female playwrights.

Another key distinction between Childress and the previous generation of writers is that most of them earned a living by teaching, and, while some may have acted occasionally in amateur productions and may have directed, not one acquired Childress's professional proficiency by devoting her career exclusively to the thespian arts. The Harlem actress composes from this location; so her drama is performance rooted. In fact, the dearth of acceptable acting roles available to Childress at mid-twentieth century prompted her to formulate her own pieces that showcase viable, complex, dignified roles. Impelled to unleash on stage black subjects who were logical and recognizable to her, Childress became preoccupied with her characters' socio/psychological predicaments, their motivations, and what constitutes the point when they move from passive observer to active agent (scripted as a perpetual query). The Harlem activist's path also determined that she would not be indebted to any specific black uplift institution, a situation that granted her more latitude than early black women artists, a new-found sovereignty that sprang from the changing social times.

Childress's association with the professional theater gave her the masterful control of the seasoned and trained practitioner. Scenes are so tightly constructed that not only does every line count but every space between, what critic Barnsley Brown refers to as her strategic and paradoxical use of silence (135). Much of the effect depends on intervals of stillness and movement and knowing when best to switch from one to the other. This component that the playwright seals into her productions is double edged: on the one hand, she is demanding that actors communicate successfully these fine distinctions, and, on the other hand, she must design vehicles that reflect in some manner the hard-bitten circumstance of black people surviving segregated America when interracial interactions call for intricate and continual feints and bobs. She insists that both material and agent wrestle with (not imitate) the mundane, which is far too habitually demeaning, and make something sentient of that localized humiliation nevertheless.

This emphasis on timing and delivery depends on transcendent performances, and it signals an important shift in the African American female playwright's tradition. Not since Grimké's *Rachel* had so much weight been placed on the female lead's shoulders. Each of Childress's major plays highlights a central, pivotal female character (the satellite roles are rich too). In addition to returning to dramatic vehicles that rest on a key role, Childress insists that her texts transmit the modalities of black speech and aesthetics. Of course Hurston had attempted to do just cause to a broadly defined black expressive base, but she did not combine intense characterization with African American linguistic patterns. Both came together under Childress's pen. Noting this variation (resisting the urge to call it a progression) is not meant to reveal the previous writers' shortcomings but to indicate that Childress had more artistic opportunity. Minstrelsy no longer loomed over the public sphere as pervasively, and white America during the fifties wanted to ignore and forget the Negro instead of flocking to primitive uptown cabarets (constructed on demand in the twenties to fill white requests). In this moment of great denial, an artist like Childress could surface because the country was so sharply segregated (by law and by fact). Because there were so few spheres where curious whites and blacks could interact, the theater, still liberal by many standards, stood as a logical springboard for a discussion of race relations. So when Childress composed *Florence* in 1949 and *Trouble in Mind* in 1955, plays that concentrate on racism and sexism in the South and in the theater, respectively, the revelation of segregation's dual ghettotization of both blacks and whites was shocking and titillating to white audiences and a call to arms for black viewers. In this space of emotional crossfire, Childress found room to insert African American cultural patterns as one means of resistance to the very delimiting social system that her work reflected.

Gwendolyn Brooks, Childress's contemporary, shares her preoccupation with transforming artistic form to mirror not the natural world but the control that must be maintained so that ordinary black citizens may ride atop of oppression's constant erosion of the self. And in both visions what lies beneath is a seething rage,[8] the very energy that will fuel the Civil Rights Movement (whether resistance is passive or visceral). As Childress proclaimed, "Who wants to live with one foot in hell just for the sake of nostalgia? Our time is forever now!" (Betsko and Koenig interview 63). A correlating amassing of forces swells through the writer's pieces that gesture toward reform and lie on the brink of revolution. For example, in each major work, frustration, anger, and annoyance lead to a temporary overturning of long-set social hierarchy, but the sparks do not result in irreversible, entirely transformational acts. So, if change is spotlighted, it is scripted as a perpetual oasis, and struggle becomes the chief motif, a strategy that brings substantial discomfort to the audience because when the supposed conclusion arrives, the play's atmospheric rage does not dissipate. The actors must labor to sustain this mood while also stretching through various simultaneous emotional tempers.

This accent on the actor, who must carry the performance's weighty emotions, may be the reason why critics have categorized Childress's drama as realism because, on the surface, it appears that she invests in character over other elements. However, the playwright deviates from the standard mimetic formula that attempts to place an individual in society and employ that self as a prism to reflect the material world. Childress disrupts naturalism's hold by several means: The most obvious is that she supplies each major subject with a multifarious coating that forces that speaking self to represent her own individuality and a piece of the African Diaspora's collective consciousness. Secondly, she redefines the heroic from its traditional Western definition as a force that overcomes adversity to win something for a home community to a pilgrim from the Diaspora who, through perseverance, applied experience, stalwart positioning, and fearlessness, learns to discard debilitating ideology to return to a more harmonious state with a wisdom that makes no conquest beyond its ability to stare down history. Childress's "heroines" arrive at the gate, stripped and naked but leaner and better prepared for the next task on a perpetual journey, an extension of what Wole Soyinka would identify as "the collective experience of the past, present and unborn (prognostic) realities": the heart of transitional being (148). As her sagas do not conclude triumphantly or even tragically, the quest motif, if we can call it that, extends itself beyond its theatrical housing. If completion is to occur, it must happen in the political and social arena. By checking art's ability to represent progress, Childress comments on realism's underlying premise that life can be captured adequately by representation.

In lieu of narrativizing, this writer constructs her plays to chronicle the Diaspora's travel records, including its many contact points with various groups, cultures, and geographies. Childress states it best when she affirms, "When the saints have gone home together, some of us will tell their story—it doesn't have to be a history of exactly what any one person did, but their story is inside of us" (Childress, "Keynote Address" 13). So, the Harlem-based visionary draws her figures with enough depth and detail so that their names and signatures will be remembered, but they point as well toward broader social positionalities.[9]

Given her basic imperative that the black character radiate mythic suggestion in the midst of trial, Childress's figures reveal themselves after a sloughing-off process that discards any useless layers to distill the subject/collective band to its elemental function. Bare-bones "saints" cut through excrescent racist, sexist and classist tradition to stimulate change and suggest a healing home space: a particular brand of primitivism where America's sludge has sealed over the spiritual kings and queens of Africa. The playwright's framing concept is unabashedly Afrocentric and like some models from that school essentializes Africa by bending it to signify all that is positive, unified, dignified and unadulterated. While I do not wish to debate the pros and cons of such ideology, which would certainly require several volumes, I can at least point out that Childress's Afrocentric leanings impact greatly on her artistic decisions as other critics have noted as well: "Numerous references are made to Mother Africa in Childress' plays" (Brown-Guillory, *Their Place* 138).

An additional specificity must be added. Saint and folk are often interchangeable terms in the writer's oeuvre, a choice that Barnsley Brown has referred to as Childress's revision of the 'ordinary' (132). From domestic service, to a so-called black matriarchy, to the black female body as commodity, the writer dramatizes the pockets of society where black women have been entombed by conquering discursive forces, and she reshapes these garrets by using characterization as the chisel. She concentrates on the hackneyed roles that dominant representation holds open to black women, and she evacuates and implodes them, granting opportunity for alternative depictions. Childress visits and plants her subversive "common people," who, standing for one, carry, through association, many. Therefore, her list of major roles for black actresses includes home workers, heads of households, entertainers, and models, choices that diagram an historic mapping of where America has labored to corral black women through repetitious representation. Using each cell as a rotation point, the artist draws a migration out from the "established" site, journeys that delineate a large-scale mytho-poetics of African American women and their connection to the world.

This emphasis on the traveling band's constant motion and return provides clues to interpreting Childress's work. Critics have generally considered that the playwright's characters evolve and that a major transformation happens on the stage because of one gut-wrenching epiphany that usually comes at the behest of some insult.[10] While this is observable, I would like to amend this view slightly and consider reverberation's centrality as a motif, a core that is anchored by the writer's use of music. So, I suggest that instead of reading these plays as cohering around a denouement that leads to a major character's conversion from folk to heroine, we consider that the play itself has been lifted from a series of unseen/underdocumented dramatic acts, defined as a collective saint's train.

Take the face-off between Mrs. Whitney (a black woman) and the condescending white liberal, Mrs. Carter, in Childress's *Florence.* Mrs. Whitney repositions herself continually and fixes her psychological and spiritual will to endure a seemingly endless onslaught of offensive attacks. Another case would be Wiletta Mayer, the black actress from *Trouble in Mind*, who stands up to the white director who would oblige her to utter lines that deny black humanity's morality and perspicacity. One receives the impression that the decision to protest debasing roles is one that Wiletta, as archetypal black performer, must evaluate frequently. In fact, in Childress's major works, we are caught, at least partially, in a blues motif, trapped in an absurd cycle of outwitting the master only to come home to him again that night. Transcendence and triumph are almost always mitigated by continuing arbitration. Therefore, if revolution is conceivable, then it will be won through a series of acts and not by one overwhelming blow because as Childress has discerned, the oppression that submerges world progress comes not only from grand trends but from those banal injustices that work on the psyche each day. One of the many reasons, perhaps, that she concentrates on female figures to illuminate both the existence of and resistance to everyday slights is that women attend to the minute distractions of daily life: "Women know a lot more about many little things than men do, because we have had to cook and wash and bury the dead and take care of births" (Childress, "Keynote Address" 13).

So, we detect another instance of the paradoxical strains that differentiate African American culture. While subjects from Childress's theater yearn for a unifying homecoming, a projection that is carried by way of African and Afrocentric cultural items like clothing, music, and totems (the mojo), a blues-based circular pattern typifies the other pole, one that traces the grim perspective that loss will recurr. Anger connects these branches, for that emotion reigns over both positionalities in the sense that the Afrocentric stance feels stymied by the impediments to the full retrieval of shipwrecked connections, practices, and values, and it experiences pique around its growing consciousness that a glance toward Africa necessitates as well acknowledging slavery's and colonialism's massive disfigurement. Anger in the blues cycle clings to its sublingual cadences from the singer's moans and grunts to the guitar plucking that exclaims a plaintive back sass. Good blues (not commercialized facsimiles) possess some degree of rage that may or may not be exorcised through the song's course. Childress's work embraces both poles, sometime spanning the range in one show. The break, a formal, heavily used African American expressive device, will enable the playwright to move back and forth along this axis, sliding between Afrocentric and blues leanings.

As I have mentioned, the playwright designs musical frames to bracket an interior field. This device allows the dramatic orators to supersede their roles and not only stand in for mythic figures but also become singers and instrumentalists who are plugged into the symbolic dictates required by specific musical genres. Childress sits on stage through insinuation shadow shapes in the form of opera divas, torch carriers, hip/hop cut-masters, jazz soloists and the like. We can think of this foundational imaginative construction of "saints who go home together" or an aural train or "traveling band" as both the griot and his/her musical entourage. To concretize this point, take *Mojo: A Black Love Story*, a one-act conversation that converges on two major characters or "ordinary saints/blues singers," Teddy and Irene, middle-aged former lovers (they had been married briefly), who, in spite of the great odds, have held onto each other, no matter how roughly, through the years. Given this straightforward plot, the drama deliberates over the break, an African American master trope derived originally from musical and choreographic traditions that has long since been secreted in various sermonic, oral, and comedic genres. The curtain rises on Teddy, who is speaking to a girlfriend on the telephone in a manner that is akin to a chant. Through this conversation we also learn that he is what can be referred to as a "player": a hustler and a ladies man. The one-sided call carves in relief that speech invariably contains gaps and lapses that are a result of language's limited ability to carry our nascent but often deeply held feelings, but these breaks can have their own rhythm. In the play, Teddy and Irene labor to surmount a multitude of barriers to reach honest, open dialogue (learning to read silence, too), which they begin to engage by curtain fall. In terms of what is required of the actors, the roles run high on rigorous control because there are substantial lines for both that pilot the actors around various highly wrought states. Irene returns to Teddy because she has been diagnosed with cancer and must have surgery. She confesses as well that they have a daughter together but that she relinquished her to a middle-class couple because both of them were living the hustler's life, and Irene did not want to raise a child in that environment.

After divulging her secrets to Teddy, Irene explains what occasions her visit: "I loved you so much, Teddy.…I'm sorry I wasn't able to say it before. When we were around each other…it was all fightin and pokin fun…mockin ourselves. I believe niggers think it's disgraceful to love one another…" (16). Irene's admission buttresses the racial uplift theme that black self-regard is a formidable component of resistance, comparable to winning political, economic, and social equality (the Civil Rights Movement is the historical backdrop for the tragedy). Follow as well the pauses between word clusters, a device that is employed throughout this intense scene. Here the ellipses suggest reflection as Irene imagines not only the past but her "self" as an agent in that past. In this manner, she has ushered on stage another character in the form of a younger, less wise phantom Irene, who would rather ridicule her life and those she holds affection for to obviate the sting that comes from the humiliation of racism coupled with poverty that steers people toward an underground and illegal economy in order to survive. The pivotal words are "love" and "nigger," which spar off as antithetical; Irene comes to understand that niggers don't love. So, if Irene does love, then she is not that thing and must figure out who she is. Certainly, there is some rage underlying this exchange because Irene and Teddy arrive at a mature relationship so late in her life, just when Irene is to undergo a major operation. All that reflection, resentment, regret, and pride at finally freeing the tongue has to be managed and delivered by the leads.

One ponders the tools that a performer would arrange to convey Irene's jump into a post-double-consciousness state. Certainly tone and range of voice, breath control, and appropriate pause assist facial expression and body posture. We can see that silence and stillness labor with and against intense speech and an emerging physical activity. During this moment, for instance, it would be logical to assume that an actor would portray Irene as planted in one spot, perhaps with a wistful look on her face or some indication of contemplation and that the revelation that she issues forth is not easy to utter. Yet kinetically, there is much occurring beneath the surface, an exercise in making the body quiet while, paradoxically, allowing it to speak. This same emphasis on noise and calm is found in the rhetorical pattern as the breaks are just as vital to an appreciation of the moment as are the actual spoken words.[11] This is a strategy that Childress relies on consistently, as actress Polly Holliday recalls, "...the writing always enhanced the suggestion. The rewriting was always done with artistry, incorporating all her knowledge of form, rhythm and picturesque speech" (64).

Breaks, moments of abatement, and a concentration of forces are the communicative protocol that Childress politicizes. I distinguish between the break and the conventional dramatic pause that is used largely for accent. Breaks contain static, sometimes indicating that which cannot be named because of immanent reprisal. Breaks can also allude to a concept or pattern that has been shared so often that it is deliberately elided to remind the group that they belong to a family that contributes to a general knowledge pool. For instance, an African American preacher might include a breaking term followed by a weighty cessation such as, "And-a—." The break occurs after the stressed "a" and signals that a key communal pronouncement/truth will ensue (sometimes the breaking phrase is repeated several times and may be accompanied by foot-patting, pacing, or some other physical gesture). In this guise, the tool reminds a besieged group that they belong to and are buoyed by a collective base, a validating cultural necessity that alleviates fear and provides comfort. Another job for the break, especially in music and dance, is to announce a new variation, therefore preparing the company for change. The break also transpires in hand signaling (made notorious by social clubs) and secret handshaking, where the code translates into "wait together to move in synchronicity." In these practices, those who do not stop for the pause are quickly branded as outsiders.

So, when Teddy tells his white lady friend, who is on the other end of the telephone, "…the reason you always measurin time is cause you a Got-dam-white-Anglo-Saxon-Protestant-American. Yall woulda held a stop watch on God-all-mighty….Never woulda give him no seven damn days to make the world…cause you too fuckin impatient,"(5) he references the alternative notion—both in speech and sentiment—of African American time which is divided into discernible commotion and calm, with an inflection on the elision. Take, for instance, the line, "Yall woulda held a stop watch on God-all-mighty…," a bold charge. Thematically, the words accuse white America of competing arrogantly with God for authority, chiefly the right to name and value the world. But perhaps, more interesting (certainly more subtle) is the sentence's structural pattern that contains built-in pauses throughout and at the end that force the hearer (both the unseen paramour and the audience) to consider carefully what Teddy has just said. In this instance he is calling into question judgment as a process and the epistemological order that links measurement to linearity. In other words, he questions whether goodness should be associated with smooth transitions and orderly progression and evil be defined in opposition to the straight course. He suggests that backtracking or "back-thinking" in the midst of forward motion is fruitful, a concept that does not necessarily carry the coding of "good" or "bad." Instead, the pearl to hang onto is creativity, a crafting that is not dependent on linearity but on the idea that the agent has to "undo" things to achieve a fuller artistic product. Teddy's suspension of sound around his word clusters alludes to the speech's nucleus: a form of conversation/discourse that clouds the field and enforces contemplation; the listener is made to peer into a density or what early hip hoppers would refer to as, "static."

In written parlance, we use the ellipses, a notation that we easily respond to as a feature of grammar. As live art, the break must work harder to capture our attention and must be overstated at times, a decision that the director bases on the audience's familiarity with it as a cultural device. Sometimes, no matter how hard the actors concentrate on its delivery, uninitiated viewers can miss the mark. It is not surprising, then, that the "official" response to *Mojo* has been lukewarm; critics have labeled it inert and excessively verbose (Kupa) and decry the characters' inability to connect (Lowell). Yet, the break as central figure gestures toward just these specific African American inventions that are spurred by living in an oppressive nation. Black expression is typified by stops and starts because the black subject is forced by circumstance to consider his/her stasis or action and speech or silence. This required contemplation that determines black survival also tends to muddy smooth, fluid dialogue. Because America has checked and often prevented African American physical, economic, social, and educational mobility, black idioms are fraught accordingly with secret passages, false starts, re-direction, and backing off—all to elude and outwit a master discourse that would lash the black uttered word to simple binaries. If Teddy simply told his white friend Berniece that he was tired of her lambasting him because of his tardiness, then the complaint would have no teeth. By publicizing that same sentiment in the manner that he did, he forces her to think about the underlying cultural differences that even their affection for each other cannot surmount, differences that Irene, who is from the same collective past as Teddy, shares with him. The overarching point is that the break is crucial because it helps African Americans figure out—through brief incubation—an appropriate course of action, both politically and close to the heart. It serves as well to democratize exchanges when the black subject is facing an imposing force either in the guise of an individual or an entrenched system that would discount and render mute his/her viewpoint.

Mojo is a very literary drama that has little central action other than that Teddy and Irene revisit their often brutal personal past and agree tacitly to help each other no matter how unprepared each is for that commitment. Of Childress's major works, it is closest to the early twentieth-century African American female dramatic tradition because it could comfortably co-exist as a radio play or dramatic recitation. Relying on Henry Louis Gates's phraseology, this play is a "speakerly text" that transverses the line between live art and book.[12] I make this observation to reinforcement the claim that the break is the structural element that brings the pensive dynamic associated with reading into a theatrical space that coheres more around responding without mediation, and vice versa, for the break can enliven a written text by predisposing the reader to think in rhythmic rather than linear patterns. The break is the trope that Childress embraces, as she wends it through her pieces in the dramatic dialogue and in the musical and comedic elements.

Trouble in Mind is the first of Childress's major works that hinges on music and, to a lesser extent, comedy. Borrowing its title from a blues song (Brown-Guillory, *Their Place on the Stage* 62), the fifties drama is a rumination over the blues in blues format, a long refrain about racism and sexism in American popular entertainment, a condition that Wiletta, the veteran actress with the lead role notes, "…wants the damn white man to be the hero and me [the black woman] the villain" (533). Annoyed about the racialized images that pose as "real," while racially marked speaking subjects barely register, Childress composes a drama that hovers close to fatalism's circular strands.[13] We see how this transpires as the writer sets up and pivots on Wiletta's refusal to "read lines" that she finds insulting, misleading, and degrading. This protest that should reveal Wiletta's heroism leads to her eventual alienation from the group that disbands at the end of the show (and before it opens). The tragedy is that during this mid-fifties period American viewers cannot see Wiletta as anything other than a standardized effigy, either Mammy or Sapphire or both. So no matter how forcefully and clearly Wiletta verbalizes her discontent, power does not shift during the scenes in any considerable manner.

The aching background music echoes the theme and envelopes the space with a cautious atmosphere, reminding the audience that pure triumph is beyond the contemporary African American's reach. A twenty-first-century spectator should be aware that her urge to applaud Wiletta's radical stand that resists frightening racialized images would not have been the norm in the fifties. The blues motif and soundings remind us of the socio-historical facts that we would do well not to ignore: Wiletta is a middle-aged black actress whose roles are restricted by not only her race and her gender but her maturity in a youth-driven market. Whether she executes the current insulting acting assignment or not, at this point in her career (and at this point in the nation's maturity), each role may be her last. So, we question whether her radical acts are inspired by a rising consciousness or by nihilism.

Support for the play's ambiguity comes from the detail that, although she fights against the entertainment industry's hierarchy and the director's imperfect vision, she does not unionize or otherwise collectively win over her fellow actors, who are also quite cognizant of the assignment's demeaning stereotypes. This point suggests that any victory will be temporary. The precariousness captured by *Trouble in Mind* characterizes the fifties when money makers rated black drama as risky because American society, for the most part, endeavored to sweep away the untidy or internally rebellious. Thus the very tenuousness of Wiletta's position situates her not as wearing heroic robes but on the borders of the absurd as any small wind could topple her, the show and her opportunity—perhaps her last—to act on the stage. Therefore, descriptions like strong and transcendent don't really apply to Wiletta, but blues emotions like enraged, fed up, frustrated, and enervated do.

While *Trouble in Mind* is clearly ensconced within a blues motif, by the time the late sixties and the seventies roll around, Childress has found more leeway in form and content, an expansion that is borne out by the therapeutic manner in which she begins to employ African American sound in her later productions. *Wine in the Wilderness*, a 1969 two-act stage piece, borrows its title from ancient African poet Omar whose dream of paradise is "…a woman singing to him in the wilderness" (9). In this multi-act drama, that clear melodious voice is juxtaposed against the feral sounds of revolution: "The tail end of a riot is going on out in the street. Noise and screaming can be heard in the distance…running feet, voices shouting over loudspeakers….The whine of a bullet is heard" (5). Notes are unleashed that combine the intricate resonance of history turning over and around a lone female aria that can radiate even in the midst of totalizing loss. Oldtimer, the symbolic sage and provocateur of the production, aptly labels this emerging musical fusion: "*(Turning the strut into a dance)* 'Wine in the wilderness…up against the wall…wine in the wilderness…up against the wall'" (10). Once again, song releases the orbiting outer frame as this play targets how culture comments on the political plane, which is depicted as: "half finished broken out walls" (5).

Set during the Harlem riots in the summer of 1964, Childress's play diverges from those of her fellow Black Arts-era writers. Not ready to unequivocally extol the movement, her panorama chronicles it as an unfinished project that lacks sensitivity. Another way to state this point is that she fears that centuries-long African American call and response modes may be drowned out by the bullet's whistle and accompanying battle clatter. Childress's offering clears ground and protects a singular aria/signature in the midst of cacophony. Certainly reminiscent of jazz, but heavier on the bass line than most jazz compositions, the production hangs on the horde's potential devouring of individualized artistry.

By the eighties, black artists would transform this voracious and competitive aural field into rap, techno, and house music. However, Childress's modes represented an exterior/interior divide that no longer lined up with Du Bois's early twentieth century variation of double consciousness in which the Negro wears a racial mask. By this tumultuous period another strain had materialized, a strand that follows the contours of a hard, unyielding revolutionary face versus feminized, emotional interiority, a division based on gendered categories, not race. According to the playwright, the emphasis had shifted in black America from undue concern about what white people make of black images to how black men see one another (Ntozake Shange will pick up this theme and refer to this condition as "fronting").

Childress postulates that nineteenth-and early twentieth-century survival techniques, famous for their slippage into various disguises (see, for instance, Charles Chestnutt's *The Conjure Woman*), begin to wear thin by this period when the movement from one site to the other (exterior/interior) has become typified by a violent wrenching of forces where the feminized emotional core is constantly put at risk by the outer facade that often equates to a nationalistic masculinist din. As an illustration, after Oldtimer's pivotal dance in the opening scene, the space is devoid of music but filled with arguments, shouting, derision, demands and misunderstandings until Tomorrow Marie and Bill make love late in the play and a few tranquil notes reenter the forum: "*Music is mixed with the sound of rain beating against the window*" (31). Unfortunately, this soothing port proves to be short lived because Tommy and Bill are soon back to disharmony with Bill, the middle-class interloper, threatening to blot out Tommy's working-class female ideas and distinctiveness. But, Tommy prevails because, even though her song can be sweet and seductive, when required, it can also wail its way up to a corrective siren, traveling the upper frequencies (as opposed to Ellison's *Invisible Man's* lower frequencies) to reset equilibrium back on its rightful course and restore call and response's sovereignty, a re-coronation that is depicted by the close when "thunder and rain" (39) coincide peacefully because Tommy has engineered a situation where she can be met half-way in her own little corner of the world (18). An uneasy truce presides both in terms of a balance between the emotional and the martial strains of black life and between the old jazz songs/solos and the new funky beats that are on the horizon just outside the window.

Wedding Band reflects South Carolina in 1918 and culminates Childress's preoccupation with African American music.[14] While her previous contributions incorporate either a single framing musical genre (the blues) or exhibit an uneasy call and response between styles as is the case in *Wine in the Wilderness* (jazz versus funk), *Wedding Band* is truly symphonic, a black concerto in two full acts. From weeping to sellers' hawking, children's games, clanking cow bells, paper and tin flutes, laughing, coughing, and testimonials to numbers from various musical traditions: spirituals, the blues, minstrelsy, war tunes, barber shop quartets, and marching bands, this play is so pregnant with auditory stimulants that it could be distilled down to its musical core and not lose much of its impact. Its very title brings to mind the manner in which matrimony binds sounds, not just people together, and it recalls that melody in all its intricate and various forms is the best mode for discerning the complexity of that coupling institution: marriage is orchestral.

To date, most critics have concentrated on the text's socio-historical and legal aspects. For instance, Billingslea-Brown foregrounds the miscegenation statutes that prevent Julia's and Herman's legal union, "…the laws enacted to exonerate white males from the consequences of cohabitation with black women are the very ones which endanger Herman's life" (43). Others have focused on the impediments to black women acquiring the state documents that legally sanction their relationships, even though they have formed full partnerships. In an interview with Rosemary Curb, Childress claims that her play is "…about black women's rights" (Quoted in Curb, *MELUS* 59). In gratitude to previous critics for establishing this vital foundation, I am liberated to reflect on the production's cross-cultural inscriptions.

One way to see *Wedding Band* is to close one's eyes and hear it. By the time the first discernible lyric washes over the audience in the first act, it has been musically predisposed by way of the outdoor murmurings of early twentieth-century South Carolina during the time of World War I: the sobs of a black girl, her mother's threats, gossip, and the warble of the shrimp man selling his wares (6–11). Given this prelude of acoustical notes, the audience is primed to receive its first aria, which comes in the form of Julia humming "Jacob's Ladder" (13) during a conversation with Lula in which Lula confides to Julia that Lula's son died because of an accident, but even after many years passing, Lula continues to bear guilt concerning it. In this instance, "Jacob's Ladder," a spiritual that forecasts victory over suffering, soothes Lula and fashions a passageway that both women can cross into friendship. This melody is bedrock in the African American Protestant tradition and is often sung to assist the wounded in riding atop painful circumstances and obstacles. As it is positioned so early on in the first act, we read it as a refrain, a musical harbor to return to when the other sounds become too grasping of attention.

Quickly on the heels of this comforting tune, we hear some boisterous and disturbing minstrel patter from a white traveling salesman, one who mistakenly thinks that his Sambo-like jig will endear him to the black neighborhoods that he serves/exploits. This sound is grating, intrusive, and unwanted by the black women who reside in this cluster of rental houses, but it is, whether they prefer it or not, part and parcel of the African American musical tradition, a branch that is set up as an antithesis to the spiritual. Secular, drenched in commercialism, the walk-around, which represents the layering of authenticating/inauthentic seeds gathered from various cultural contributions across racial and ethnic lines, is, in 1918, the popular American form that has most successfully secured the Negro as a fixture in the nation's collective imagination, a site that not only signals theft but elevates the spoils of that larceny to commodity status:[15]

> *(As he places some merchandise in front of the* WOMEN*; does a regular minstrel walk-around.)* Anything in the world…fifty cent a week and one long, sweet year to pay…Come on little sister!
> Teeta. *(Doing the walk-around with* THE BELL MAN.*)* And a-ring-ting-tang/ And-a shimmy-she-bang/ While the sun am a-shinin' and the sky am blue….
> Lula. *(Annoyed with* Teeta's *dancing with* The Bell Man.*)* Stop all that shimmy she-bang and get in the house! (14)

The supplier is most successful in seducing the child Teeta, who quickly integrates his strut into her game, but the adult, Lula, attempts to hold the line and dissuade the girl from partaking in such frolicking, an exchange that mirrors the manner in which popular culture acts on the inexperienced who are open to experimentation but have not gained the tools to contain an encroaching and manipulative discourse. Without these skills (an awareness of history, maturity, a strong sense of self), they cannot draw a line between their desire and that which is created by the marketplace. That the jig is so closely aligned with trade proves just this point because minstrelsy is comparable to the products that the Bell Man sells, items whose value has been grossly inflated. Lula's counteracting message is: say no to minstrelsy; say no to overpriced junk.

Equally telling is that this arm of American music floats around public space in the development's open square. Alternatively, the house is presented as a sanctuary, an interior space that buffers against the public bazaar. The play as a whole will root its musical expanse between these polar ends, spirituals standing in for a sort of pure Africanist space and minstrelsy harvesting an adulteration of various styles that have been yoked together to feed the capitalists. Therefore, the wedding band as an elastic conveyor belt must be equipped to move between these polar ends and cover anything in between, just as the grand metaphor "marriage" evokes a journey—perhaps circular—along many points. Indicatively, the music that is incorporated into the production slides along this axis between the spiritual and minstrel patter. The war tunes (49, 54, 59) and barbershop harmonizing (26) are near the popular pole and only borrow a few elements from the sacred, whereas the blues (22, 32) and black marching bands (55–6), while also secular forms, more readily and discernibly return to spiritually based antecedents. Unlike *Wine in the Wilderness*, the transition between and amongst these various artistic strains is not jarring or coated by impending assimilation; here, the various arms co-exist and in their viability as separate yet involved soundings combine to create the grand march, neither tragedy or triumph but a rumination over what it takes to flourish and do so without collapsing interior, feminized emotional channels.

There is an old saying that courses through various ethnic and racial groups that states that the opposite of love is not hate but absence. That adage holds sway in *Wedding Band*, for one musical type does not drown out the other, but silence can do just that. During a riveting scene when Herman, who is white, reclines illegally in Julia's bed after he has been downed by influenza, his sister Annabel and his mother arrive to take him back to their home under the cover of darkness. Herman has been rallying himself by listening to Julia sing "Jacob's Ladder" (once again). He croons as well, a secular tune that is about physical love, "…the soles of your feet are pink and brown" (40). A duet ensues with Julia urging Herman to climb higher, and Herman reminding Julia that he cares for her from head to toe, a rhythmic mobious strip of what black recording artist Rick James would call "fire and desire," sensual and earthy on one slope, turning into sublime sentiments that can overcome physical stagnation on the other. Whatever the case, each is comfortable sharing and blending harmony and discursive space, but Annabel, the would-be concert pianist, finds this display quite unsettling, "Dammit, hush. Hush this noise. Sick or not sick, hush! It's ugliness" (40). Her compulsion to silence the duet by "dis-recognizing" its concord and labeling it hideous clutter corresponds with a purist philosophy of American culture, the same ideology that divides civilization too facilely into high and low segments and codes an unadulterated plane as superior so that anything that hints at the ascendancy of or even proves the existence of syncretism may be then labeled inferior. With this scene, Childress uncovers another shrouded racialized American marker in that popular/mixed also suggests Negro/mixed.

The playwright's *Wedding Band* debunks this classification and instates a model that esteems American culture's compilation that she mints into a continuous ring dance. In her opera, American music welcomes infinite mutations and adjusts to different sounds, a case in point being that *Wedding Band* does not darken on an absolute but on the more indefinite repetitious chant of "yes," which can be interpreted as anything from a great lie, to affirmation, to comfort, to devotion, to a new birth, to a good orgasm. Thus "negroness" is akin to "yes," multidimensional signifying terms that emanate from the troubadours who invite liberating and lush interpretations, a right to create that segregation laws deny.

Breaks and music complicate and inform the dialogue in Childress's shows and are crucial to extricating their full meaning. Comedy too is folded into the whole, more so in the early works than the later for there are far fewer sardonic bits in *Mojo*, *Wine in the Wilderness*, and *Wedding Band* than in *Trouble in Mind* and Childress's *Like One of the Family*, a collection of vignettes composed during the fifties from the perspective of a black female domestic worker named Mildred.[16] This shying away from humor has much to do with the times and the advances made by the Civil Rights Movement. Before the sixties, it was often obligatory to couch key observations and criticism of harsh practices in a comedic shell—no matter how understated—so as not to draw the status quo's wrath, which could not only close a show but blackball the writer, director, and actors. As Barnsley Brown notes, "…humor is a powerful tool for Childress…since it makes her message palatable to a white audience and uplifting to a black one" (138). Given this necessity, it makes sense that many of the more stabbing barbs and passing asides in *Trouble in Mind* come from the most senior black actor, Sheldon, who is the one most familiar with the manner in which African Americans had to rely on signification to retain their dignity under cruel conditions (Sheldon is the one cast member who has actually witnessed a lynching).

By the late sixties and early seventies, Childress and other black artists no longer demand as much shelter from humor's protecting armor. However, we note that in Childress's case, she does not dispense entirely with comedy but brackets it, comments on it and, in the end, contains it. To illustrate my point, in *Mojo*, Irene confesses to Teddy, "When we were around each other…it was all fightin and pokin fun…mockin ourselves,"(15–6) an acknowledgment that African Americans have deployed self-depreciating jest to hold life's terrors at bay, to lash oneself before someone else can do it (*Mojo* 15). While this act of deflation and deflection bolstered black resilience under apartheid America, the sixties gave rise to a crucial reevaluation of its function. If black were truly beautiful, then there was no need for the black self to ridicule its own body, rituals, or expression under the rationale that self-inflicted blows can be less painful than those raining down from elsewhere. Further confirmation of Childress's internalized censure of comedy comes in *Wine in the Wilderness.* In this two-act treatment, a middle-class black clique belittles both Oldtimer, the indigent and boozing Harlemite that the groovy people adopt as a mascot, and Tomorrow Marie, the working-class black woman who they recruit to sit, unwittingly, as a model for their "messed-up-chick" portrait (10). While Tommy amuses her new friends, who she considers to be more sophisticated, they deride her behind her back, finding her humorous lines quaint and picturesque in the same manner that turn-of-the-century regional writers sometimes depicted the charming but unlettered folk. With this display, the writer dissects comedy by placing it within a break. Through close examination, Childress concludes that, while comedy itself is not essentially ideologically dangerous, it has been engaged too often by black people to acerbically depress each other and prevent other black citizens from achieving their full potential.[17] Generally, she calls into question cultural mainstays like the dozens and the witty one-liner, not out-of-hand condemning them but advising that they be held up against what Cornel West and bell hooks would refer to as the vocabulary of black self-love.[18] By *Wine in the Wilderness*'s final curtain, the middle-class black people who ridiculed Tomorrow have recognized their hypocrisy (somewhat). As indicated by the playwright, that which detracts from a full appreciation of the self and the community's potential, even if highly engrossing, requires keen appraisal, and, if warranted, reform or expulsion from the black cultural lexicon.

Clearly, Childress challenges established ideas and aesthetics, whether global, national or specifically African American. As she centers humor as practiced by black artists into a lit circle, she analyzes the concept of the "hero/heroine" as well. Critics have labeled the playwright's black female leads as champions. Brown-Guillory identifies Childress's structure as adhering to the classic heroic journey which falls into three stages: the departure, the initiation, and the return (*Their Place on the Stage* 81). I suggest a slightly different model and emphasize that this dramatist arrives eventually at the realization that the champion's narrative as it has been scripted traditionally in the West is too far afield to reflect the facets of

African American life that she explores. In place of one who rises, fights, and wins something for a home group, we find figures who must shed just about everything they are/were to discover that they can stand on their own wobbly feet. These are less plays about triumph and eventual social cohesion and more about revelation: closer to Shakespeare's *Lear* than his King Harry plays. The classical saga of gallant bravery is interrupted as well by the fact that the social body does not return to unity once the chief agent has accomplished her mission. To the contrary, we find that social groups are stretched to the breaking point by the time the stage darkens in each of Childress's major works, where we are much more likely to encounter a lone black woman who will face even greater challenges, even though the presence of others may temporarily alleviate her pain. There are no unified permanent networks, only fragmented, unstable, temporary ones, nor do the major female leads attain the typical spoils allotted to "triumphant" women in Western literature and mythology: marriage, spiritual transcendence, motherhood, or a good home.

Reflect for a moment on how each of her main works concludes: in *Florence*, Mrs. Whitney sends money to her actress/daughter in New York, but there is no guarantee of the daughter's success. *Trouble in Mind* closes with a blank stage and a show that may or may not open just as Wiletta's job hangs in the balance. As the lights dim on *Mojo*, Irene is on her way to the operating room. Even the more optimistic *Wine in the Wilderness* falls silent on a potential but extremely uneasy reunification of the black middle and working classes. Finally, Henry, we assume, dies as Julia offers her "future in the North" to one of her friends in *Wedding Band*. Any sense of unfettered victory that these leads gain during the drama's course is tempered by these indeterminate, solemn, even desolate, final scenes. So we must ask: What is Childress doing by allowing her major figures to arrive at what the audience would most likely perceive to be epiphanies but not providing these figures with the adequate means to fully elevate themselves or those that depend on them from the situations that they resist? I read this as a comment on life's irrationality, a world view that denounces, ultimately, the heroine's return. Conquest, as it is known in the West, does not exist in the playwright's vision; instead, we are provided different variations from an invisible band's repertoire of musical selections, an open-ended series of repetitions that delay and frustrate the traditional happy ending. It becomes the responsibility of those living in the "real" social strata to complete the art work and keep/reunite the saint's band.

Rather than an evolutionary entity, character becomes entwined within the strands of various songs (blues, harmony, spirituals, jazz…) and cannot be disentangled from them. Call it an added aural shadow text or a rhythmic, historicizing, and spiritualizing border, these consistent refrains and echoes limit character to a given potential range where individual motivation is checked perpetually by social conditions. Each of Childress's major figures is shown to be trapped within predetermined parameters and can only reveal a partial self within that viewing field; so, the field itself becomes a performed item. There are three major positionalities that Childress studies in this manner, using both musical and dramatic reference points or sign posts to make her statements: servant, master, and commodity, each corresponding to a site that America's national mythology has slotted for black women. Black women as master is not a literal configuration, but there are many instances in American culture where black women are figured as dominators, especially sexually. An odd transposition of the owner's fantasy, he envisions the most controlled social group as having somehow revolted and seized power, at least within the precincts of his fanciful psychological invention.

Recognizable nineteenth-century epithets such as Mammy and Sapphire bombarded the public sphere, while in the twentieth century new sobriquets have gained in popularity as others have declined in usage (in the mid-eighties, for example, the welfare queen prevailed). Yet, no matter the signifier, these markers and geographies are the ones that American discourses have assigned to black women; anything beyond is deemed random and incoherent. Childress recognizes the importance of these positionalities and revises/implodes them from within with her lyrical plays. In her hands, the maid becomes the great arbitrator who spins through several social housings, black and white and male and female, supplanting the tragic mulatto who held this role during the nineteenth and early twentieth century. The matriarch/master is transformed into a decision maker, and the black female objectified commodity becomes the potential revolutionary. Taken as a whole, Childress's major installations sever the bond between common signification and America's racial scripting, replacing it with her own reading of what black women's roles have been and are becoming in modern history.

Demonstratively, in the writer's visual array, black female mobility is connected to domestic service, especially house cleaning, sewing, and the preparation and sale of food, an association that surfaces in African American literary texts as early as the slave narratives (See, for instance, Linda Brent's Grandmother in *Incidents in the Life of a Slave Girl*). Mrs. Whitney carries a home-made box lunch in *Florence* and has raffled off a chocolate cake at a church bazaar (114), an event which allows her to solidify her friendship with the black male porter who works at the station. He will, in turn, watch her bags for free, instituting a barter of goods for services. In *Wedding Band*, Mattie, who is self-employed, sells candy. Mrs. Beverly in *String* sells meat pies and brokers a contract to supply them on a regular basis to the local bar owner. While not peddling edibles, Irene from *Mojo* starts out as a washroom attendant and learns the value of entertaining/amusing wealthy white women, a skill that she applies to segue into a career as a con woman and numbers runner. Tomorrow Marie spends some time as a maid before she is discovered by the black intelligentsia in *Wine in the Wilderness*. Childress's most sustained glimpse into the life and power of the domestic worker is her series of vignettes from the urban black woman's point of view collected in *Like One of the Family.*

In each instance, the black female figure who falls within the cook's or the domestic laborer's ken travels across social fences, a mobility which had been granted the tragic mulatto a century before (most firmly by *Uncle Tom's Cabin*). Mrs. Whitney, the cake baker, transgresses the color bar, as Brown-Guillory detects,[i] stepping over the low barrier that separates black and white space at the train station (116). Furthermore, Dresner comments that Mildred, the domestic engineer/narrator from *Like One of the Family*,[ii] travels into white territory and intercedes between the two worlds, black and white, for she is the one who can and does desegregate the nation. She is the leading offensive line of the Civil Rights Movement because she delivers information to her white clientele, ideas that will assist them in making better and more just choices about their fellow darker countrypeople, and she smuggles news out, acting as a living listening post. Her link with the home's nucleus allows her to be proactive underneath the public scrutiny that is visited on the politician or activist. Ergo, she is in a position to push delicacies, baked goods, favors, secrets, and even her loyalty to obtain leverage for her community. By and large, her role as an agent depends on her ability to read the signs (*Like One of the Family* 48–9) and rail against fixed order by questioning and critiquing it from within the nation's domestic nexus.

She guards against the incursions made on her psyche as she unleashes her conjure from within the master's house, knowing that she must keep separate her own naming and evaluative schema from that supplied by her employers. Her role as mediator and cryptologist enables her to shift the text to reveal both her world view and that which seeks to write on her. A prime illustration arises when Irene reminisces with Teddy about her days in the washroom; she conveys how she has learned to capitalize on the ciphers that invaded her life: "...a sign pasted on the mirror [reads]...'*Ladies, your tips are my livelihood*'" (9). To the patron, this sign iterates Irene's dependence on them, but, to her, it induces a mental image of a resolute black woman who will attend those in power, not mimicking their behavior per se, but transforming to her advantage what she sifts through, absorbs, and translates.

In addition to trading manual labor for information, the black female homemaker deals in commodities, especially foodstuffs, in exchange for currency and services. The covered basket is a product that is less fraught with peril than trafficking in the black female body. A black woman who can cook can defend herself better because she offers a good that does not require that she submit automatically to physical violation through economic coercion. Sometimes, the only thing standing between her and starvation or the brothel was this ability to feed either a black man who could grant limited protection or the white-owned markets that could provide her with the money to purchase partial security: a decent home, transportation, and adequate clothing. The best instance of Childress's tapping into this socially expedient operation is in *Wedding Band* when Mattie threatens her young daughter because the child has lost the quarter that will allow her confectioner mother to purchase the ingredients for her candy business (Note that Mattie's husband prepares food for the Navy as well) (6–7). During this scene, the shrimp man hawks his catch (11); thus, the playwright spotlights the manner in which culinary artistry and sales sustain this community. Another variation on this bartering occurs in *Wedding Band*, where Julia Augustine, the lead character, grows relatively prosperous by sewing elaborate shirtwaists (8), and later it is made clear that she earns enough for herself and enough to assist her lover Herman and his mother and sister (50).

Set in South Carolina during 1918, this show underscores the manner in which an upwardly mobile black working class becomes the more "genteel" white middle classes' ticket to salvation. Because they do not wish to do "negro work," white southerners must concoct ways to siphon off others' labor, others' dreams. More specifically, what is being lifted or taken, more often than not, is some form of household labor, a sub-category that entails nurturing of some kind. As in Morrison's *The Bluest Eye*, Childress outlines an economic system where care of the body and of the home is provided for cash, but the cash cannot purchase enough restorative care to equal the amount that the safekeepers must expend to execute their jobs. Therefore, love—for lack of a better word—departs from the black community and is expended and dissipated in the white; only currency (in extremely small amounts) returns to black neighborhoods so that its members can buy things like Fanny's horsehair settee or her silver tea set or less costly items like pantyhose and scarves from The Bell Man traveling salesman, (9, 13–14), but these commodities cannot replace the embracing mothering that the black laborers have exhausted beyond their own homes. So when Julia informs Herman's mother and sister, "Nobody comes in my house," (65) she not only demands control over her "owned" living quarters, she resists a trading scheme that grants white America the right to deplete black America's nurturing repository for cash. Julia stipulates that the black home be freed from vulgar commercial constraint and be returned to the private domestic sphere (which is tied inevitably to the marketplace as well but through a mediating network, not direct sale).

Placing the black domestic worker at a fulcrum position in the state's social and economic network is just one of the avenues that Childress manipulates to re-contextualize how black femaleness should signify in the nation's annals. She takes on the myth of the black matriarchy in high-handed style too. *Wine in the Wilderness* zeros in on gross mislabeling and debunks it vigorously. During the midst of a discussion between two black women, middle-class Cynthia and working-class Tommy, Cynthia takes it upon herself to inculcate Tommy with the concept that Tommy could attract men if she breaks away from the women-governed society that spawned her. Tommy reacts with incredulity and sets Cynthia and Cynthia's privilege straight, "We didn't have nothin' to rule over, not a pot nor a window,"(19) a line which parallels her previous realization that, "Everything gone. This riot blew my life. All I got is gone like it never was" (14). While ostensibly referring to the 1964 Harlem uprising, the storm that destroys Tommy/Tomorrow's past is a metaphor for the Middle Passage that obliterated African continuity, a totalizing tempest that, along with its many atrocious consequences, rendered a matriarchy unsustainable in the New World. Tommy highlights that to suggest one is preposterous. When Tommy's father abandons his family, he does not run from a monarchy that is ruled by women, nor does his desertion generate this type of kinship structure. To the contrary, he facilitates extreme poverty—that is all. By distilling the story to such skeletal proportions, Childress, through Tommy, highlights how discourse can shape widespread opinions and social policy. Sadly, this idea that black women somehow rule an invisible nation within the nation reduces Tommy and her mother to societal aberrations; it also becomes a padlock that seals her inside the black working class as respectability/marriage is denied those who allegedly hold these matriarchal leanings. Tommy is branded by this term (a New World scarlet A): any utterance that comes from her is filtered and, therefore, heard through a "matriarchal" script.

Cynthia continues her counsel and advises Tommy to return the black man's manhood (19). Tommy replies with "I didn't take it from him, how I'm gonna give it back?" (19). Tommy's question demystifies the two major suppositions that Cynthia, standing in for the myth of the matriarchy, articulates: first, that the black man has indeed lost his manhood and, second, he lost it at the hands of black women. As maintained by the play, neither appears to be true because the black male characters are fairly solidly in charge from start to finish (selecting the model, the mode of representation, elevating their desire over that of the women), and Tommy has nothing to do with the pilfering of anybody's masculinity. She is not a complete victim, nor is she purely aggressive; rather, she endures and has found ways to be innovative and upbeat in the face of formidable imperial threats. After all, she is a figure who makes new friends, jokes around, and even searches for love immediately following the complete destruction of all her worldly goods. The playwright's depiction contrasts directly with the myth of an Amazonian black female communal structure because so much falls beyond the interior group's control that the notion of black women or black men autonomously guiding their fate is illogical. What can be managed, however, are some limited decisions, rights which, at least in the West, belong to all adult citizens, even though these rights are not distributed equally or equally protected.

Disparities in entitlement surface when women assert their civil privileges, as Childress observes, "…if the woman is the decision maker as in *Wedding Band*, it is assumed the man has lost his manhood…because what happened was her decision" (*The Playwright's Art* 55). Since the exercise of her choice is read as the diminishing of the man's, women are restricted by a dynamic that turns female adulthood into female criminality (she becomes a burglar who steals male rule). Yet, if black women do not learn to make choices under the current racist and sexist systems, they are left completely vulnerable. The actuality that nearly all the black men have departed from the South Carolina neighborhood in *Wedding Band* (war, death, forced migration) forces the women, whether they wish it or not, to fend for themselves. This play is one case where we find the writer dramatizing black female ingenuity even when that means formulating options that do not center on male prerogatives. Yet, ironically, it is precisely because of white middle-and-upper class male impositions that black women are in a position that requires them to deny, at times, all male wishes. The point is that men are responsible for generating a consciousness around female decision making because without their discursive coding, black women's choices would be viewed merely as mature living rather than theft. Consider the inverse to see the construction: if men make decisions, then they are robbing women of their femininity.

Childress naturalizes a woman's claim to formulate alternatives, and these chosen paths, whether they are prudent or not, should not be subject to challenge. In each of her works, the black female subjects discern the landscape and are quite capable of acting on their assessments. So when Wiletta resolves to confront the white director in *Trouble in Mind* to inform him that the production that he is running is not only racist and sexist but nonsensical, she recovers a natural entitlement: to think through an immediate situation, link it to broader trends, and arrive at conclusions about the world. Tragically, this demonstration/revelation that black women have fully operational cognitive powers may also mean that Wiletta has put herself out of employment, but that is her choice, not an impulsive one but one that is measured by years of experience and careful reflection. Similarly, Mrs. Whitney from *Florence* sends money to her daughter in New York and does not request that she return to the South, a calculated act that stems out of rumination over the broader implications of her daughter's determination to become an actress during an age of grotesque black representational distortion. The dramatic emphasis, then, is not meant to render these responses startling, but to normalize them. It seems fitting that a mother ought to defend her children's decisions just as an artist elects not to demean herself or the people that she knows intimately; these black women are not bandits when they engage their prerogatives. So, the dramatic suggestion is that we do not view these moments as epiphanies but as the moment when the black female subject's interior world, which has been chugging along vigorously from the start, is uncovered for the audience. Therefore, it is the viewer who is charged with coming to the firm realization that what he or she is seeing on stage at the moment of choice is what they should have been thinking about the character from the start.[21]

Toppling Mammy and the matriarch, Childress turns her pen to the excessive sexuality that has been assigned to black women. In America's mythology, black women have been too frequently designated for sexual use and/or manual labor, an onus that comes out of slavery and the manner in which the black female body was auctioned. The writer's installations point out that this industry that reduces and equates a black woman with her body, a correlation that still comprises part and parcel of the global exchange system. Specifically, Wiletta the actress and Tomorrow Marie the model personify this Western tendency to treat the black woman as if she were a packaged delicacy ripe for some one else's enjoyment and capital growth. In either case, a man (one white, one black but both at least middle class) has decided how he will position and dress his black female toy to sate his purposes.

Trouble in Mind attacks the stereotypical Mammy role that aligns the black female image to the shapeless, thoughtless drone that is programmed to guard the master's domestic space, and Childress also examines exploitative labor practices in the same play. The playwright launches her offensive by dividing the audience's attention. She introduces an up-to-date, urban black woman in the form of Wiletta, who has been playing trite parts over the span of her career and learns to separate her self-image from that which she portrays. Wiletta moves in and out of character regardless of whether she respects that depiction or not, but with her current project, *Chaos in Belleville*, she sets limits as to how her talent and her body may be retained. Though willing to dress up in rags, adopt a false dialect, and sing and pray while her son is waiting to be lynched, this performer will not send him out of her cabin to meet his death. Therefore, Wiletta impedes the misuse of her body by refusing to allow it to transmit an idea that she finds abhorrent. She, even if temporarily, removes her body/voice from the marketplace. She will not be the director's marionette, or that of a country that hungers for constant reminders/renditions of black humiliation.

Tomorrow Marie's situation in *Wine in the Wilderness* compares to that of Wiletta. The only significant difference is that the black middle class has become the market's ambassador. Prospering from calls for black authenticity, bourgeois artists and intellectuals are more than prepared to frame "the black experience" in a manner that will elevate them financially and in renown, as they take the role of middleman and sell blackness to the white majority and then peddle it again to the black majority. Similar to Wiletta, Tommy resists this packaging and declares her unwillingness to sit for Bill's portrait because she questions his motives. Once she learns that she is to become, via his canvas, the "messed up chick," she refuses to have anything to do with the project. He cannot purchase her image. The only way that he can approach Tommy is if she gives in to him in the name of romance, and that is a loan, not ownership. Even after Bill "discovers" that she is a beauty-in-the-rough, Tommy is very clear in claiming her independence, "I'm not the one you made up and painted, the very pretty lady who can't talk back..." (148). After this discussion, Tommy does consent to having her portrait painted but on her terms: she will not be retrofitted to suit his agenda. Bill must capture her as she is in her complex form and with a sense of the historical conditions that produced her. It is also significant that Tommy's reclamation of her body hinges on her agility (approach and retreat). Because her rootedness within this black community does not allow a complete break from her surroundings in the manner that Wiletta may opt to leave a bad show, Tommy learns to compromise. Harlem, after all, is where she and Bill live. Consequently, she must navigate the territory, not trek away from it. So, it makes sense that there is a negotiation at the end of this work but an ultimatum—either change the script, or I walk—in *Trouble in Mind.*

The inference of both pieces, in spite of their divergent endings, is revolutionary. The black female body has to be recovered by black women and liberated from the auction. Doing so requires back talk combined with physical removal and dexterity, a re-placement which leads to a cessation of production. Mull over the fact that Mammy would be more difficult to authenticate if no black woman would take the part. So we interpret Childress's intervention as a call to action because she stimulates a transformation of American culture that is so radical that we can scarcely imagine its full implications. Envision the magnitude of tearing down the black female stereotypes on which the country has become dependent: No more welfare queens to blame, no more matriarchs to limn a so-called deviance from femininity, no more colored female bodies to do the hard labor or provide a cheap source of sexual entertainment for richer classes.

I emphasize this point to highlight how terribly vital Childress's contributions are to the Black Arts Movement and to continued bids for equality. Notably, she taps into the strategies of passive resistance to steer the revolution in the direction of social insurgency, and she reminds black men that the methods that they were adopting in the fifties and sixties were ones that women had relied on for centuries. She comments as well that the capitalist conditions that normalize the sale of bodies are also the same conditions that cause those who are tyrannized to ignite massive change to retake ownership of their mobility. One realizes that as the curtain descends on a Childress play that something has to yield.

The playwright maneuvers her audience to uncomfortable breaks, moments that stimulate critical thinking. Another manner in which she challenges her viewer to suspend and amend long-held assumptions is through her use of symbols. Brown-Guillory rightly points out that, "It is in examining symbols that conjectures can be made about the author's perceptions and perspectives about the world mirrored in the play" (*Their Place on the Stage* 52). I would add that the symbols also divulge how the writer perceives the world beyond the stage because these imaginative signs comprise another text, another play with its own logic and design that may or may not work in concert with the production's other elements. Critics of contemporary offerings by African American playwright August Wilson will recognize the symbol's centrality. From the piano in *The Piano Lesson* to the fence and horn in *Fences*, Wilson has taken up a supernumerary language with which to transcend the local politics of the setting, thereby granting his plays a mythic quality. Childress introduced a similar strategy more that twenty years prior to Wilson's arrival on the scene. The time period and the fact that she overwhelmingly highlights black women explain why her pieces have been too often consigned to a secondary tier while Wilson's have become critical and commercial successes.

In each of Childress's major works, a meta-symbol disrupts the mimetic field and provides a clue to the overarching function and meaning. The bed in *Wedding Band*, the painting in *Wine in the Wilderness*, the low railing in *Florence*, the cancer in *Mojo*, and the stage in *Trouble in Mind* all complicate a strict reading of the events as pure realistic interplay between characters.[22] For instance, the bed in Childress's treatment of miscegenation in 1918 represents the unspoken but ever-present sign that lies at the heart of segregation, an irrational fear of black sexuality on the part of white America. The writer acquaints the audience with it early on in the first scene when a dispute outside Julia's window awakens her, and she sits up; the action never moves far from this location. The fact that this operatic drama revolves around this resonant and singular piece of furniture proves its integral resonance. It houses the sexual ghosts of the South's past and its uneasy present, specifically the so-called transgressiveness of black and white intercourse. Every word becomes reflected through the bed's omniscient but rarely commented on "sinister" presence. In the United States during the early twentieth century, the mattress of the colored (black, brown or yellow) signifies lynching, dis-ease, childbirth, illegitimacy, commerce, poverty, prison, liberation, and the wild space beyond Puritanism. It, in lieu of the wedding band that Julia wears around her neck, dictates the maneuverable space in which black character can be explored, the limit to which the theater can serve as a vehicle for commentary. Beyond that line, the play would collapse into the bed and become pure object, pure pornography, and pure commodity.

This posted canopy comments on family structure as well. Bear in mind that Herman dies on Julia's bed while Julia begins to distance herself from it both physically and spiritually. This detail indicates a significant cultural difference between the two. Herman is tied to a patriarchal social pattern;

Julia, on the other hand, relies on an extended family model that includes neighbors and friends. Therefore, her positionality is not tethered to the romance theme that exists to reproduce the nuclear family unit. Herman, to the contrary, is glued to it: He will not run away with Julia because of his obligation to his mother and sister, but he will not leave Julia because of his adoration of and commitment to her. Herman is stuck (literally in bed) because he cannot imagine and uphold a more flexible version of the family. Julia grows in courage and fortitude because she can and proves it by unmooring herself and departing from romance's compelling cradle.

Set in 1964, the unpainted portrait in *Wine in the Wilderness* broadcasts the hope that the division between aesthetics and experience is, perhaps, closing. Gayle Austin inscribes an analogous view: "The blank canvas on the stage…comes to represent both the 'nothin' Bill sees in Tommy at the beginning and the clean slate they are left with at the end" (61). To me, this empty blackboard heralds a resurgent ritual-based culture that plants metaphor and communal practices (especially storytelling) at its core. Toward the end of this work, Bill repeats a phrase that Tomorrow Marie has given him, "rolling hoops and bicycle wheels," (39) a metaphor for thunder and rain that Tomorrow learned from her mother (30). This is the preferred type of art that will supplant the mimetic oil on canvas, if the aesthetic revolution is successful because, after it, the desire to secure an image to a static frame will no longer drive creativity. The artist's impetus will be to circulate modes that stimulate democratic dialogue. This is one of the Black Arts Movement's chief tenets: to recover those rituals that energize community through interactive, participatory interplay. Here the blank canvas signals just that.

Elizabeth Brown-Guillory's reading of the barrier in *Florence* is thorough and requires no further comment. She sees this symbol as indicative of "the cross-cultural trips" (*Their Place on the Stage* 56) that black and white Americans make to negotiate segregation and racism. These forays are physical, psychological, and social. Entire Southern codes of conduct cohere around the subtle machinations of folks who are barred legally from being somewhere but need or want to be there anyway. *Florence* reveals how we have become a nation of intentional interlopers who perversely erect barriers so that we can find pleasure in crossing them. Of course the amount of delight gleaned is directly proportional to the amount of control that one retains over the system that institutes the rules in the first place.

Mojo settles on an American dysfunction as well. In this play, Irene's cancer threatens her life, but she fights it with her Mojo, a faith that a collective African past and her own personal past are strong enough to carry her over the cuts into her flesh (perhaps a metaphor for the slave whip or the Middle Passage). Her disease breaks down the whole/the body, an allusion to the manner in which enslaved Africans were separated from history and a West African ancestral-based religion that reveres an open channel between living and dead kin as sacred text: one has to know and speak to one's people to feel complete. We find this sentiment mirrored by Irene's confession that she bore a child during her brief marriage to Teddy but that she handed over the baby to an adoption agency, a version of fragmentation echoed by her cancer. Irene's relinquishing their daughter and her ensuing obsession with finding her make more sense under this looming symbol of dismemberment. The play ultimately posits that even if Irene cannot find reunification in a physical manner, she can join with her kin in spirit. Art is intertwined indelibly with the search for family, a trend that African Americans have certainly employed from postbellum days. For instance, nineteenth-century African American women writers composed novels of manners and poetry where the search for lost loved ones shapes both the plot and the form.[23] In *Mojo* analogous stimuli propel the plot because the Mojo/talisman is a physical manifestation of the faith that some manner of reconciliation or healing can be achieved before it is too late.

The stage becomes the symbol in *Trouble in Mind*, a theme that Shange will treat as well. A meditation on double consciousness, this particular work looks at the manner in which subjects mask themselves to survive modernity. Therefore, because taking up the veil is not depicted as choice but a linchpin that permits civilization's continued existence, submission to discursive patterns is no longer a debatable option. Given this view, travel is defined as expending energy to transform the discourse so that a new facade may by substituted for the another but completely leaving the theater behind (Barth would call it the funhouse) is no longer possible. So even though Wiletta and her friend Henry, a seventy-eight-year-old stage hand, fire the theater anew at the play's close by turning it into an intimate dais that rests between these two knowing veterans, who have learned to esteem and reach for talent beyond cheap typecasting, they are still acting, still in character, still not sure who either is when they go home at the end of the day and no one is watching. Modernism means the death of the private sphere, and the self has to pay for this continual masking and revealing a composite face. Consider that in *Trouble in Mind* Wiletta delivers the closing speech, but the lines that she spews forth are not her own, but from *Psalm 133* on "dwelling in unity" (542), an odd pronouncement given that the preceding events have charted how difficult that endeavor would be for twentieth-century actors (black and white) in a market-driven culture and economy. It seems, then, that the only role left to her beyond the Mammy that she refuses to perform is that of transparent oracle.

If we extract these major symbols and read them as a general guide to Childress's mytho-poetics, the bed, white canvas, fence, cancer, and stage collectively name a tension between a modernist and a postmodernist perspective: What, I would argue, represents an entrenched bi-polarity in African American culture, with modernism being associated with the tendency toward Afrocentrism and postmodernism lined up with the propensity to incorporate all that came before in a new, sliding, spirited representational field. African American culture, according to Childress, is often expressed paradoxically in both manners because the will to return to what is often perceived as a unified psychological and cultural state in Africa coexists with the Middle Passage's demand that histories and myths are constantly discursively mobile. Imagine, for instance, these major symbols providing the motivation for a painting or a musical score. There are shades reminiscent of the concrete, physical world like the bed, picture frame, and fence intermixed with more intangible signs like cancer and the acting process.

The playwright/artist settles nowhere, but she holds the door open to those who attend her productions and to those who will mount and direct them. What is interesting is that in her suspended status, she manages to unleash the general feeling that a race is on, as though African Americans have been challenged to find a return route to a stabilizing cultural home, even if that past has to be resuscitated from scraps (primarily musical, aural ones) before a disassembling postmodernism makes actresses of us all, black women perhaps having a bit more practice with these rites because of the all the camouflaging required to survive slavery and widespread racism and sexism. And, if it is inevitable that we become actresses (and that likelihood is highly probable), then the writer implies that we should at least proceed in this enterprise as often as possible on our own terms.

Turning to quick-change methods to flip the surface between these divergent modes, one that anticipates a return home and one that forfeits that prospect and strives to master by riding atop of representational nuance, Childress plants one foot in the Black Arts Movement and a prescient one in what we have come to think of as the hip hop era. That she has not been associated with either school rests on the fact that she insists on highlighting how black female figures toil with and inside these philosophical states. The Black Arts Movement and current hip-hop modalities have been regarded overwhelmingly as black male movements that articulate black male rage. Childress reminds us that women have had an integral part in constructing these aesthetics, so they are not alien to black female imaginations, nor do they automatically check female agency. Thus, we read Childress's art as a four-decade-long break that inserts meaning between Black Arts policy and vernacular practices that black women have been instrumental in building, even though their labor has not always been accredited to them. The playwright argues as well that African American women's integral contributions to the country's development have been overlooked. So rather than mirroring black life, Childress's drama lands on obfuscating acts, a continually deconstructive and self-consuming theatrical attitude that employs repetitive choral arrangements that prompt the audience to discern more minute details of the abstraction and its theft with each iteration. In tune with Morrison's and Faulkner's fiction, character is filtered by sound and atmosphere; reality is sifted through a monstrous underground but has extremely material echoes and vibrations, and yet this cacophony is formed into art largely by a band of black female musicians along with *their* relationships to others, a black female aesthetic that is soulful, searching, funky, assertive, nimble, pained, resilient, enraged, wise, and often estranged, lonely and mythic but rarely just plaintive.

Since the popular entertainment industry from its inception has trained the consumer to see that which is associated with domesticity, care and black female labor as mundane and unremarkable (merely part of the surroundings), Childress's startling theater pieces had to push uphill against these widespread racialized monoliths that deny black female subjectivity and the crucial role that black women have played in modernity's construction.[24] The fact that Childress's late productions were viewed as quaint anachronistic throw-backs in light of the more bombastic and often violent offerings by male Black Arts playwrights reveals that her texts' import is widely misunderstood. We recognize today that her offerings are revolutionary, mainly because they call for deep-seated, radical social change not only in the material world of valuation but also in the audience's imaginative reach by dramatizing a staged realignment between traditional Western theatrical center (white and or male) and margin (black women) to center (black women placed in transit with others) and margin (black vernacular practice and also the disguised acting center).

Furthermore, Childress does not employ nationalism's battering ram to instigate change but stimulates the intellect and raises consciousness levels by expanding the African-American break to a much broader national cultural base. To her, conversion happens through practice and reading, not through visually based identification; it is, therefore, a learned behavior. In place of absorption, the consumer learns to travel beyond personal desire. To concretize this effort, we locate the sage advice about the American theater that Childress supplies through her characters' dialogue. As Julia Augustine avers, "nobody comes in my house without my permission," which means, according to Tomorrow Marie, that the American theater will have to meet black women somewhere on the outskirts, somewhere between objectification and autonomy. Doing so will transform generic boundaries by opening possibilities for each emblem from Julia Augustine to Herman to Tomorrow to "re-write" the lines. Arguably, Childress's daring ambition to force the American theater, including its audience, to reinvent themselves has carried a penalty—relative obscurity.

NOTES

[1] Barlow comments that the number of plays produced in New York started to decrease during the 1930–1931 season and continued to decline throughout the Depression and World War II. Furthermore, television and film siphoned off potential theater supporters (vii).

[2] See Quita Craig's *Black Drama of the Federal Theatre Era* for an apt treatment of black playwrights' contributions during the thirties. Although Hurston, Graham, and other black women were involved in The Federal Theater project, few works by black artists were produced, and none was solely written, produced, and directed by black women.

[3] Graham's productions include *Dust to Earth, I Gotta Home* (also known as *Elijah's Raven*), *It's Mornin'*, and *Track Thirteen*. "Her plays were given life by the Yale University Theater, the Gilpin Players of Cleveland, Ohio, the Florida A&M Players, and by a number of colleges and schools during the 1940s" (Brown-Guillory, *Wines* 81).

[4] For an account of the mock Dillard trial, see the *Tampa Florida Bulletin* on April 14, 1945.

[5] Childress's acting career lasted for over ten years during which she was featured in several ANT productions during the forties. She performed in *A Midsummer-Night's Dream*, *On Striver's Row*, *Natural Man*, and *Anna Lucasta* (Curb, *DLB 7* 118). Refer to the Schomburg Research Library for copies of these playbills.

[6] "Childress initiated Harlem's first all-union Off-Broadway contracts…" (Curb, *DLB 7* 119). Advancing humanitarian causes and the arts, she encouraged young artists and participated in numerous symposia and conferences.

[7] Even though it won an OBIE for an off-Broadway production, Brown-Guillory and others have noted that *Trouble in Mind* never made it to Broadway because Childress refused to compromise and change the script to give it the happy ending that the white producers wanted (*Their Place* 32).

[8] LaVinia Jennings notes that Childress's black female characters use anger and defiance to exorcise the psychic damage brought on by racism ("Segregated Sisterhood" 43).

[9] Specifically, for Childress and her contemporaries, one of the more salient issues for black America was how to remain optimistic when black people's future in this country seemed so dim. Hansberry pondered the issue as did black theater critic Loften Mitchell: "…since 1619, Negroes have tried every method of communication, of transformation of their situation, from petition to the vote—everything—we've tried it all; there isn't anything that hasn't been exhausted" (Hansberry, *Young, Gifted* 246). Mitchell, on the other hand, simply asks, "…At what point will America's most loyal citizen give up hope…?" (19). Each of Childress's major figures, in her own way, carries this question on her shoulders and balances between collective exhaustion and despair on one side and faith in racial uplift on the other. This is the general condition, or story that repetitiously frames each text. So, in some manner, each play repeats the same theme with the dramatic decision becoming a willful determination to press on towards progress, or if not progress, at least an undetermined future, even though the path to it has become impenetrably dense. Some could counter that this period was one of optimism for Black America because of King and the Civil Rights Movement. The point is that no one knew whether it would work or not while in the midst of it. So, those seeking reform had to have dedication to motor on and sustain the struggle. In many ways, this particular revolution really was about spiritual strength, even when the movement turned

toward more physical confrontational means.
[10] Brown-Guillory views Childress's female figures as heroines who progress through a series of epiphanies (*Their Place on the Stage* 81–93).
[11] The break, I contend, should be considered an African American mainstay and can impart anything from sass to derision, a warrior stance, directional change and rebirth as well as acquiescence, agreement and support, or, of course, any combination of complex takes on a given situation. The context imbues them with meaning, and, therefore, reading them requires that one be conversant with the socio-historical framework from whence they arise.
[12] See Gates, *The Signifying Monkey* (170–216).
[13] Gayle Austin notes *Trouble in Mind's* musical frame as well: "The play is bluesian and relies on overlapping dialogue that often conveys chaos" (59).
[14] This is not the last of Childress's pieces that revolves around music: *Gullah/Sea Island Songs* pays tribute to the Gullah people living off the coast of the Carolinas and their culture.
[15] See Eric Lott's *Love and Theft* on minstrelsy's complex consumption of various American ethnic forms.
[16] These vignettes are published in *Like One of the Family.*
[17] Childress continues to explore comedy and its inherent weaknesses and strengths. One of her last theatrical pieces is a tribute to the great black comedienne, Moms Mabley.
[18] See *Breaking Bread: Insurgent Black Intellectual Life.*
[19] It should be noted that we are never made privy to Mrs. Whitney's occupation, an omission that, I suggest, Childress toys with intentionally, daring the audience to racially profile her, an act which would align the audience with Mrs. Carter, who readily associates Mama and her progeny with the service industry.
[20] Dresner writes, "…she [Mildred] continually repudiates the mask that whites attempt to impose on her and compels them to confront the incongruity between their preconceptions and the reality of who she is" (226).
[21] Another fine example of Childress's strategy here can be found in *Like One of the Family.* Several of Mildred's white clients are surprised to find that she vigorously supports the Civil Rights Movement. Mildred's response hinges on the unasked statement and questions: "Of course I am. Why wouldn't I be? Shouldn't you be as well?" (171–173, 188–189).
[22] This list of symbols is not exhaustive. For instance, the mojo stands out in the play of that same name.
[23] See the Schomburg Library collection on nineteenth-century black women writers for examples of novels of unification, especially Frances Harper's *Iola Leroy.*
[24] Mull over the details: Irene brings Afrocentric clothing to Teddy; Wiletta informs her novice black colleague, John, how to use acting/masking to navigate his professional and personal life, and Tomorrow Marie teaches a houseload of black intellectuals how to respect the elderly and protect their African-American heritage. Moreover, Julia Augustine serves as the village leader in *Wedding Band.* She is not, as other critics have suggested, a lost member who finds her way back to the fold but operates as the fulcrum activist who forms the group's cohesiveness in the first place. Before her, there are only loosely connected domiciles/cells in the backyard where women do little to assist each other and much to tear each other down with competitive gossip (Alma Jean Billingslea-Brown argues that "Julia has acquired a certain 'exilic status'" (42), and Catherine Wiley claims that Julia's estrangement from the black community is the underlying tragedy that must be resolved by the play's end). Julia

provides the money and gifts from the heart: reciting letters, listening, telling white lies to respect someone's dignity, and divulging her own secrets to solidify confidences to transform these associations into true friendships.

FIVE

Sailing/Sealing over Ravines: Process as Constant in the Work of Adrienne Kennedy

ADRIENNE Kennedy and Alice Childress were contemporaries who were extremely involved during the sixties and seventies. However, critics often perceive of Childress as pre-Black Arts Movement and put Kennedy outside that school because she implements an expressionistic avant-garde style rather than naturalism. Purportedly, Childress is too old fashioned and Kennedy too experimental to belong to the mainstream aesthetic tradition that African American male artists of that era claimed. As I have argued in regard to Childress and will do so with Kennedy, this marginalization has had more to do with the widespread association of African American dramatic authenticity with black male angst, a scripting which requires review. I challenge Kennedy's categorization as that "other" downtown playwright who listed toward Euro-centered paradigms while African American men were conceiving the hard-edged theater that would liberate black communities and through advocacy and escalation transform the world. Kennedy shared many of the values and aspirations of the Black Arts credo: an end to systemic racism and colonialism, opportunity for an articulation of difference, and a return to ritual as the leading—because it is more inclusive—cultural form.[1]

Justification for Kennedy's placement as a writer whose contributions land afield of the "bona fide" black, largely urban, dramatic productions that saturated the American scene during the sixties and seventies hinges on her background and the manner in which her tragedies arrived on the stage. She hails from middle-class, mid-Western (Ohio) roots and began piecing together plays when she traveled through Europe and West Africa with her husband, Joe Kennedy, during the early sixties. Captivated by Africa, she admired the Kuntu art form along with the sights and sounds of the people and landscape, which gave her a sense of power and strength (Betsko and Koenig interview 248; Gavin 146). When she returned to the States, Kennedy enrolled in a workshop run by Edward Albee, and, as a result, she acquired the wherewithal and backing to go public with her art. She witnessed her first alinear tragedy's run (*Funnyhouse of a Negro*) in 1964 at the East End Theater in New York City. The fact that this playhouse is located in the Village and that the work won the Village Voice's Obie Award for 1964 has been reason enough for some to categorize her work as skirting, if not extraneous to, the Black Arts Movement.[2] The charge that her one-act installations were too personal and, therefore, incomprehensible was also cited as reason enough to discount her voice as qualified to speak for Black America: Martin Duberman accused her of being "absorbed by her fantasies" (as quoted in Gavin 160), and Seymour Rudin bemoaned her inability to use surrealism to effectively capture Black America's plight in contrast to the more accomplished results of black male playwrights such as Douglas Turner Ward and LeRoi Jones (Gavin 162). According to Clive Barnes, she deviates from Black nationalistic rhetoric by centering on whites and whiteness rather than on blackness: "She thinks black, but she remembers white" (Gavin 179). To these judges, Kennedy's early focus on middle-class and black female subjects signaled a self-centered preoccupation with modeling bourgeois behavior. They reduced, too easily, her displays of black female interior space to transparent impulse. It would take a new generation of scholars to discover that Kennedy toys with "the borders of revelation and concealment" (Benston, "Locating Kennedy" 118), a deeply inscribed African American and womanist stratagem.

Funnyhouse of a Negro is part of a sequence that Kennedy conceived during her visit to West Africa, information that she submits to fend off claims that her initial theatrical visions were constructed to imitate Albee's surrealism (Byrant-Jackson and Overbeck interview 4). The companion to this first success is *The Owl Answers*, which was staged in Boston and New York in 1965. Both illuminate the intersection between African and European history and culture (Wilkerson, "Diverse Angles" 73–4). A third play, *A Beast's Story*, was later attached to the duo, forming a trilogy that aired intermittently throughout the later sixties with showings from New York to Paris to England. *A Rat's Mass*, Kennedy's treatment of war, fascism and religion, debuted in Rome and Boston in 1966 and was later revised by La Mama in 1969 and again in 1976. The short but dense, *A Lesson in Dead Language*, surfaced in London in 1968 and back in New York at St. Mark's Church in 1971. Each of these plays was written sometime between 1962 and 1965 and may be considered as belonging to

Kennedy's early period.

By the late sixties, the Ohioan bard had turned to influential public figures: *The Lennon Play* (1968) and *Sun: A Poem for Malcolm X Inspired by His Murder* (1968). Already preoccupied with violent conflict, Kennedy addresses the Vietnam War and the manner in which it set off a chain reaction with *An Evening with Dead Essex* (1973). Rounding out this middle period, the dramatist steeps her inventions in cultural exposé: *A Movie Star Has to Star in Black and White* (1976) and *Orestes* and *Electra,* revisions of Euripides' classics. The nineties marshal in an autobiographic/reflective time for Kennedy as she splices together theatrical and literary (especially diary and epistolary) genres. Her stage pieces, *The Alexander Plays* (1992): *She Talks to Beethoven, Ohio State Murders, The Film Club (A Monologue by Suzanne Alexander)*, and *The Dramatic Circle* along with *Motherhood 2000* (1994) and *Sleep Deprivation Chamber* (co-authored with her son Adam in 1996) overlap with prose writing: *Deadly Triplets: A Theater Mystery and Journal* (1990), semi-autobiography, *People Who Led to My Plays,* (1987), and *Letter to My Students on My Sixty-First Birthday by Suzanne Alexander* (1993) to outline a familial chart that monitors how both group identity and personal subjectivity are built on a dynamic compendium of intimate intersections, worldly trends, and random coincidences. Other works include *Black Children's Day; A Lancashire Lad*, based on the life of young Charlie Chaplin; *Diary of Lights: A Musical Without Songs*; *June and Jean in Concert*, a musical adaptation of her semi-autobiography; and prose pieces, *Secret Paragraphs About My Brother*, *A Letter to Flowers*, *Sisters Etta and Ella*, and *Grendel and Grendel's Mother*.[3]

Even though she has not received the economic compensation or the popular acclaim that she deserves, this impressive list indicates that, except for part of the eighties, Kennedy has enjoyed fairly consistent productions, mostly sponsored by intellectual (art house) and academic communities that continue to revisit her work through various retrospectives. As she has completed so many shows across various periods, I don't have the space to cover each in detail. So, a few guiding generalizations are helpful. The first point that I bullet emanates from Kennedy's assertion that West Africa, for the most part, provides the shaping influence, ambiance, and structural properties for her early plays, not Western surrealism. She avows, "I would say almost every image in *Funnyhouse* took form while I was in West Africa where I became aware of masks" (Betsko and Koenig interview 248). When we examine her theatrical architecture, it is crucial that we fix masking and African mythology as the guiding, deep-seated symbolic base and, therefore, filter our perception through it before spinning out to western paradigms. Key West African traditions including Yoruban cosmology and Mande aesthetics saturate Kennedy's imagery and grant her visions a spiritual cast that would be missing if not for these soundings on ancient African deific presences and originating legends.

Second, I read Kennedy's early works as cautionary tales, not as autobiographically based (that comes later). Simply put, she, like Baraka, finds the construction of the Negro to be a key element in encroaching and seductive Western discourses. In the early period, Kennedy identifies the mining and exportation of "Negroness" as a global commodity and, therefore, a large-scale problem. We are apprised as well of Kennedy's anxiety about bourgeois culture (black and white) by way of the authorial distance that she braids into these initial pieces, a strategy that has not been commented on nearly enough. This ironic component that the playwright leans on heavily allows me to agree with both Herbert Blau and Linda Kintz—Blau arguing that *Funnyhouse of a Negro* is about a colonial mindset and Kintz countering that Kennedy airs the manner in which Western and African traditions have become intertwined inextricably in the New World, but the dominant group devalues this mixture and clings to notions of racial purity (Blau, "Ideology"; Kintz, *Subject's Tragedy*). Both views support the images and symbols that haunt Kennedy's early phase.

To fully understand this dual thrust, we must emphasize that the early compositions may examine a "colonial mindset" as Sarah, the main character from *Funnyhouse of a Negro,* exhibits a yearning for whiteness, but Kennedy emphatically does not and ascribes more to the perception that modern culture is overlapping interminably, but this complex patterning is rarely recognized. The breach between the writer and her character is immense. By spotlighting Sarah's view, the playwright deconstructs and reviles the Negro as a social holding-pen that is built by the West to concretize and naturalize whiteness, yet, while she augments the expanding impact of this plastic black mannequin, Kennedy does not devolve into an oppositional stance and aggrandize or authenticate blackness with her art. So, she is able to disclose, in one hand, what Europe has made of the other but conceal, in her other palm, what that other thinks about herself.

The "Negro" is a category that has shifted over time, bending to the dominant group's will. For clarity, we limit its usage to that Civil Rights span between the late forties and the early sixties when it flooded the public sphere. The variation that Kennedy targets specifically is the black middle-class variety that has access to mainstream higher education and fashions itself as urbane and economically and intellectually ambitious. Of course, this description is inadequate since the Negro is also dedicated to seeking out and elevating European culture as endemically preferable to her own "bastard" black traditions and aesthetics. In dominant discourses that include psychology, sociology, the law, and economics, the Negro embodies a quandary that commands study, which leads the inspector to hold it and its predicament at a distance. These fields consider Negrohood to be a temporary state that can be reformed and, ultimately, collapsed. On its left resides the untutored African and on its right the assimilated American, with a deep suntan. Once all are safely to the right, the Negro may then disappear and become a cultural relic. Therefore, the black middle-class Negro is made over by mainstream factories (state apparatus) into a go-between that spans black and white America (this practice was duplicated in some manner wherever colonialism occurred between light and dark people).[4] We must keep in mind, however, that because it is a mere proxy to bolster whiteness, the Negro as a sign obfuscates America's black middle class, which is not a monolithic block and contains radicals, conservatives, separatists, assimilationists, women, and men, Southerners, Easterners, Mid- and far westerners, straight and gay, Baptists, Muslims, Buddhists, and atheists, urban and rural. By ignoring this group's diversity, the mainstream wins several tools: a means to reject African American individuality, a new field to study, and another way to maintain discursive, social, and economic superiority over a group which is considered threatening.

To African American communities who were reawakening to self-determination in ritual and practice, the Negro symbolizes an antiquated way of doing business that holds African American people hostage by anchoring them to Euro-centric inclinations. In this sense, Sarah of *Funnyhouse* is an exaggerated effigy that stands in for an outdated model of racial transaction across color lines, a contract whereby Negroes are expected to imitate white folks in striving toward bourgeois comfort to prove that colored people can be normal and progressive, even while white officials regret that the Negro—in spite of his great exertion—can never fully blend into the bleached circle of white citizenship. This overstuffed Negro, seduced and beguiled by the offer, trades a path out of Jim Crow policies in exchange for African American's capitulation to racial and ethnic difference. He or she floods the public sphere, exacting notice in magazines, on talk shows, in the movies, and on the radio.

African Americans were at a crossroads: not yet Negro but wondering if becoming one would lead to the Promised Land. After all, the popular media saturated the newsstands and visual screens with the faces of black actors, artists, and athletes who had found safe ground by going that route. Within black communities, fissures opened as some took to Negroness while others advanced more black-centered postures. This was the nation and "the turning world" that Kennedy observed in the late fifties and early sixties as increasing numbers of African Americans finished college and pushed for civil reforms. Therefore, not only did Kennedy center the black middle class because she was from it but because it held a pivotal position in terms of the manner in which twentieth-century social reconstruction would proceed.

I belabor this second point about the Negro's far-reaching significance during the late fifties and early sixties because the pending Civil Rights Movement and debates about whether assimilation or black nationalism both on a national and a pan-African scale compelled Kennedy to address this contemporary Negro phenomenon (or Negro-building as it should be more appropriately titled) because the success or failure of Negro construction would have a great impact on whether self-determination and autonomy would continue to serve as viable options for black people. Not since the Harlem Renaissance had the black middle class been so featured in dramatizations by a major African American woman playwright. The difference, however, is that Kennedy was not pressed by economic or social obligation to lift up this particular social strata as an exemplar of what black citizens could offer. Instead, she concentrates on how a helium-filled Negro-doll is subsumed into dominant discourses in ways that could block true racial equality, not enhance it. She addresses this issue by way of repetitious thematic clustering and by contrast, using African-based modalities that, in many instances, contradict and consume Western dramatic form.

We interpret Kennedy's revelation that she is intrigued by African masks as a clue to how she envisions the performance space. Granted that there are numerous spiritual and secular roles for these artifacts across time and regional area, Yoruban and Ejagham usage that was transported to the New World via the slave trade stands out. In Yoruban rituals, the head of state, while in divine communion with ancestors and deities, may wear a special helmet that covers his head: "The veil that hangs across the wearer's face protects ordinary men and women from the searing gaze of the king in a state of ritual unity with his forbears" (Thompson 9). Ejagham-based rites include a similar covering: "[a]…constructed Janus mask, one visage staring into the future, the other at the past, symbolizing clairvoyance and presence in two worlds" (Thompson 239). The headgear shields the commoner/audience from potentially overpowering spiritual energies; the one who dons it has stepped over the boundary between the seen and the invisible, the living and the dead. This becomes a sacred and intimate chamber where a veil sets apart the "actor in the moment" from the uninitiated spectator. Kennedy certainly taps into the mask-as-protective device and positions it to partition the theater into different spheres. On stage, she inscribes the traditional Western puppet-box design as the living marionettes entertain a removed consumer. However, she inserts as well a West African-based motif that animates a chamber where regal/anointed figures reside in communion with an unseen but highly influential ancestral presence. In this guise, the theater patron is transformed into the commoner who must wait for a translation of what has transpired between host and the beyond. The stage becomes, under the mask's symbolic power, an ignited cubicle that connects heightened forces, and the mise-en-scène is tasked to buffer the full impact of these sacred combines. In layering the arena's signifying capacity, Kennedy acquires additional mobility, for she can turn one face to the West and its traditions and encode African-based ones as well. Consistent with the writer's own admission, these addresses are not equally significant because she privileges the African resonance over the Western one, just as Childress positions African American musical frames to comment on Western themes and structures. Because Kennedy activates the veil to contain and shield an animated creative dynamic, we can argue that the European-centered colonized mindset that the writer displays in *Funnyhouse* is not allowed to take over the stage but is answered by arch, African-based symbolism. So, a black face that is covered by a disguise or mask should not be read as one in submission to a master text or discourse but as a breaking interlude that grants an opportunity for the one who wears the headpiece to talk with traditions and forces that survived the Middle Passage and were further disseminated by it.

Kennedy counters Du Bois's double consciousness by suggesting that there may be little need to associate tragedy and weariness with wearing two facades. To the contrary, the imposed condition that is forced on the Negro by an alien culture can be re-scripted to signify a New World extension of West African practices that predate the slave trade. So mask-wearing may be recovered as an inspired function, not a defensive one. Applying these principles to *Funnyhouse*, I argue that it captures the Negro's perception that it is necessary to assume an imperial cultural and ethnic identity to survive and centers on a priestess who is in close dialogue with various spirits (Queen Victoria, The Father, Patrice Lumumba, the Duchess of Hapsburg, The Mother). Thus Sarah Negro is a mobile signifier that connects what happens in Africa to American events. This impression of impending colonial forces facing off against emerging combined/compounded ancient and natal ones will characterize Kennedy's work throughout the years, and in these theatrical moments of approach and retreat, fire and water, we find reference to the great Yoruba Orisha, Eshu-Elegba, the "ultimate master of potentiality" (Thompson 19). So, in place of sealed tableaus, Kennedy supplies us with plays that take off from history but are about shifting power around various sites and locations as well, exercises in potential extrications, reversals, and inversions as well as inventions, births, and naming.

Kennedy's second period orbits around concerns regarding race relations, women's roles, and social constructs, the same concerns she raised during the sixties, standing on that basic support, examinations that decode imperialism's mysterious, hypnotic seductive pull as she delves into the reasons specific individuals, in spite of the odds, have managed to see past these beguiling ideological and material traps: images of vampires and their slayers (she reaches back to *Beowulf* eventually). In this second phase, to build her shamanistic dramas, Kennedy shifts her implied audience's position from the celebrant at a masked ritual to that of black female explorers/detectives who must learn to dismantle subjugation's artificial magnetic pleasure to bare its "real face," which is, more often than not, horrendous. It becomes understandable that the writer would experiment with film during this stage because of its stature as the most intrusive and dominant cultural form for more people around the earth than any other genre, becoming capitalism's most potent enticing lure. Kennedy reads film as a New-World mythological system that un-writes older code, a genre whose devouring heart can only be exposed when the artist wraps it around or holds it against other forms. During this phase, she superimposes live performance on top of celluloid imagery to hold the tape down and arrest it and, consequently, balance off the genre's influence, a strategy that is reminiscent of Haitian Vodun art and West African Kente cloth where interwoven elements tell and retell one grand, multi-edged, interrelated narrative.

Finally, the playwright's latest direction (one can only hope that she will extend this one or move into another) has been to embark on an extended salvage mission, returning to both her own kin and widespread social and political trends to recover that which will sustain a collective liberation struggle. This period is the one that most resembles the more recognizable tactics of Black Arts Movement artists because it openly and forcefully displays with action, body language, monologue, and dialogue the writer's rage and quest after radical change. We record as well that the playwright shifts, once again, her relationship to the audience, for she no longer leads them through the doors of her own funhouse, introduces them to sacred callings, or positions them as fellow detectives. Increasingly in this latest period, Kennedy raises her performance pieces and her prose as if she were speaking to a cherished and close group or even a beloved (a daughter perhaps). Kennedy comes to write as a mother, not because she is driven to this position by social pressure as previous African American women writers were so obliged by their age's dictates but because she has found something in that role that is passionate, theatrical, and critical. Be aware that when I use the term "mother," I am referring to its African-based connotation. Not just a biological life-bearer, mother is associated, for instance, in Yoruban cosmology with the Deity Oshun, who has two sides. When pleased she is loving, comforting, and soft, but when riled at some injustice, she becomes a fearsome and fearless protector and can best even the most skilled warrior if he upsets her charges. Oshun lives in water and rules a kingdom at the bottom of the river. Thus she holds precise knowledge of the natural forces associated with rising water tables, droughts, restoration, flooding, cleansing, aquatic plant life, and the flow of time. By channeling her imaginative lens through an Oshun-like perspective, Kennedy can incite both Western discourse that often recognizes biological mothers, but, more importantly, she can call out to and resurrect an ancient African spirit, one who is known for defending her people during trying days. With Oshun's advent, we find that some of the more submerged cultural references that Kennedy interweaves so skillfully but in muted form during the sixties became formidable textual centers by the nineties, a transformation that, I would argue, came about because the playwright has identified a substantial mitigating instrument to fight colonialism: the black family, especially the female ancestral line.

To date, as a whole, Kennedy's theater is anti-progressive and apocalyptic but perversely optimistic as well. Linearity is absurd and decay or ruination is everywhere because wild space has so encroached on civilization that it is difficult to see where the boundary lies between one and the other.[5] Within the fissures caused by this slippage between polite society and the most feral, self-determined powers run the roads or routes to reform. This uncharted territory of infinite potential (Eshu Elegbara) is engaged via performance/ritual, the space where any conversion is conceivable. Even during the early years, Kennedy's works unfurl within this consciousness that no matter how tyrannical and imprisoning conditions may be, the other/victim is never entirely without hope or the ability to resist imperial processes whose ultimate aim is to contain the self within predetermined social frameworks. By the time that we arrive at her latest period, testimonial/autobiography has become a diving vessel to make sense, at least temporarily, of the huge junkyard of forces and trends, possible intersections, and blind ends that we have come to inhabit in the postmodern age. Furthermore, witnessing and personal narrative come to enhance Kennedy's performance art by slicing through the authorial distance that she so relied on during the sixties.

We investigate the manner in which the playwright's later efforts revise those that she composed earlier, an interlacing of texts that divulge semi-liberating avenues to clearer visions (less incantatory and dream-like) and greater agency. In this combination that more openly brings personal experience to bear on artistic production, Kennedy weaves African American church modalities (testimony) with tactics taken from the carnival tradition (doubling back and parody), fashioning, in the end, treatments that are frightfully direct (almost caustic) in their bid to preserve Africanist traditions while also wary of the future path in light of the massive disparity—in terms of resources—between political and economic power (the West) and cultural and spiritual power (the East). Nature, science, and the social (a Middle Passage of sorts) reside somewhere in between these oppositional sites, the spoils over which the battle is waged.

From this general description of Kennedy's various phases and the styles that distinguish each, it is clear that I read her plays as vastly communal while many of the more recent critics view them as preoccupied with psychological states. There is certainly room for either standpoint as the pieces are indeed multivocal; however, the materialist and historicist readings have been fewer in number because Kennedy was labeled an "expressionist" early on in her career mostly by white intellectuals who were familiar with that school of drama. As a result, the predominant take that has been applied to her work is psychoanalytic criticism from Freud to Lacan to Fanon. While these approaches are certainly valid and have breathed new life into Kennedy's opus by promoting various retrospectives and revivals, there is sufficient evidence sewn into the displays to suggest that the writer is wary of psychology, labeling it a colonial discourse that brings her black subjects no closer to resolutions or more fulfilling "lives." As Kimberly Benston maintains, "The very conventions of narrative intelligibility and logical design by which we habitually organize critical response are often indeed themselves the object of Kennedy's distorting critique" ("Prefacing the Subject" 113). To reposition Kennedy's work critically within various cultural traditions without turning her text over to a totalizing ideology, it makes sense to revisit the moment in which her work arrived on the stage and begin with history, making it the narrative frame, while we allow "the drama" itself a more chaotic reading.

Funnyhouse of a Negro and Baraka's *Dutchman* were both produced in 1964; the former opened on January 14 at the East End Theater, and the latter premiered on March 24 at the Cherry Lane, both located in New York City. Each piece features twenty-something, educated, urban African American leads, who are in a quandary about whether to assimilate into white, mainstream culture or pursue an African-inflected path. So we may say that each contribution dramatizes Countee Cullen's famous poem, *Heritage*, which asks, "What is Africa to me?" However, before either Sarah or Clay in each tragedy can hammer out a response, they are devoured literally and figuratively by the West. So the implication is that by wasting time pondering the question, the ability to act is surrendered. Critics have noted both the formal and thematic similarities between these two works: "[both] have focused…on the place of black thinkers in a white world, in an educational system that is always looking to Europe for directions and definition" (hooks, "Critical Reflections" 180). In terms of form, Bryant-Jackson comments that, "Kennedy follows in an absurdist tradition that includes Albee, Kopit, and Baraka" ("Travelers" 52). Despite the detail that Kennedy's opening preceded Baraka's, the point is that while reviewers recognize certain points of confluence, they have overlooked that these two compositions are so close ideologically, for each one argues that the "Negro" must go and that the beings of color who had been labeled as such by the United States and imperial Europe must begin to redefine themselves.

In both riveting enactments, we find central Negro figures, who are "disappeared" by the end because they pay far too much credence to their plight as slaves to white bourgeois culture and are, therefore, led astray. Instead, they should commemorate what is positive about their own African American heritage. Both plays harp on what the West has termed a colonized mind, a condition that is scripted to be a "disease" which must be treated. Yet, the two writers do not stop there because both predict that this reign, symbolized by a black intelligentsia in the guise of an inflated head that is limited to asking what to do about the Negro question, is coming to an end as it can no longer survive the rigorous, pressing, largely materialist concerns that have been excited by the vast lurid social sinkholes brought on by the idiosyncratic New-World phase of so-called de-colonization wedded to late capitalism. Both plays are calling for African Americans to learn how to stand somewhere else instead of deep in the cradle of white American lore that coheres around seduction scenes where the Negro is ineffectual and defenseless (even after a period of aggression as in *Native Son*, he or she is eventually detained, put on trial, executed). Baraka's piece renders metaphorically this transitional period as a moving underground subway, and Kennedy sets in relief a figurative mirrored, carnival enclosure, drawing on "…an amusement park in Cleveland that featured a 'funnyhouse' with two huge white figures perched on either side, bobbing back and forth and laughing hysterically at the confused patrons within" (Wilkerson, "Diverse Angles" 72).

We see that these two shocking works share many commonalities, but they differ in one major area. Kennedy limns a sketchy glimpse at a post-Negro moment while Baraka stops at the Negro's capitulation. This prophetic nod from Kennedy comes from her vivification of West African ritual, as the entire play may be interpreted as a masking ceremony, where the uninitiated viewer bears witness to a priestess' traveling through geographic and temporal space. From this overlay, we learn that Kennedy's piece is more than mere socio-cultural tragedy because it embraces the mystical act of crossing over. As the medium who controls these flights, Sarah leads rather than submits to her community. Yet, the point, it seems to me, is that while Sarah holds this fulcrum role, she is not aware that this vital responsibility belongs to her. Kennedy, along with other Black Arts Movement Era artists, surmises that an awakening consciousness cannot evolve without a greater and deeper grasp of African traditions. So, even though she presents a Yoruba ceremony on stage, generally, the Western audience would not recognize it as such. Kennedy had an Olympian challenge awaiting her: to teach her viewer to think of Africa.

Unfortunately, sexism rises to the fore in the manner in which these two perceptive and searing theatrical visions have been gauged. When it comes to critical interpretation, few name the black subway rider (Clay), who is murdered by the West, as an embodiment of Baraka's personal anguish, but Kennedy's art has been associated too often with neatly translucent autobiography. For example, Hatch and Shine aver that, "Her three best-known one-act plays…all center around a young girl who is torn between the paradoxes of spirit and flesh, black and white, past and present. They should be read as an Adrienne Kennedy trilogy, the story of a poet writing one long surreal fantasy about herself" (*1935–Today* 334). I recommend that, as an alternative to submerging the dramatist's past into the artistic mixture in such unmediated ways, we analyze the production as an instance where the meticulous craftswoman manipulates the viewer. As hooks so astutely states it, "Kennedy's plays always have that ritualized 'play'" ("Critical Reflections" 180) and beguile readers by their appeal to the enigmatic ("Critical Reflections" 179). If we concede this point about her early pieces being only tangentially biographical, then we are led to formulate different questions than the ones on the table currently. Instead of harping on Sarah's psychological condition and her obsession with racial monoliths, perhaps we should concentrate less on how she became so disturbed and highlight how to move on from Negroness to reveal Sarah's African role as an anointed messenger/translator, a transformation that Baraka's work has been posited as implying but not that of Kennedy. The hard-hitting, revolutionary edge of the *Dutchman* is readily discernible but that of *Funnyhouse* is not, a fact which leads us back to gender typecasting and the manner in which black female cries for resistance and rebellion have been ignored, misread, and judged indecipherable.[6] Few critics have responded directly to Kennedy's confession that she, "feel[s] tremendous rage against American society" (Bryant-Jackson and Overbeck interview 5). The critical access point becomes how has this rage been displaced onto her art?

While other, largely male, Black Arts Era writers exhibited their resentment with profanity and vociferous appeals for immediate change, Kennedy pulverized her passion and shipped out fragments of it on various vessels that she sent out across time and space to Europe, West Africa, Georgia, Ohio, Washington, D.C., and its suburbs, and New York. She writes of and in a traveling rage. These observations engender two additional assertions. First, the need to dispose of the Negro, that both playwrights set in motion, alludes to the end of the blues cycle as the dominant African American cultural vehicle with its constant rumination over tragedy (including the moments of pleasure imbedded within it) because it will no longer be as relevant in a post-Civil Rights era: Sarah's suicide is also the blues' obituary. A new modality is required, one whose concentration is on action, confrontation, and self-making, not allowing circular discourse to limit the self. Second, Kennedy's actual fan base may not be the one that she wished to reach. Many of Kennedy's pieces have played in houses that cater to white middle-class consumers (especially intellectuals); she has not, for the most part, delivered her message to a mass black audience, even though that, very likely, was the audience that she envisioned as she composed her work.

William Sonnega has warned that the politics of this phenomenon are well worth investigating. Sonnega asks "…in an institutional environment organized by rhetorical rather than actual constructions of diversity, in which the nuanced, complicated subject positions of personal experience are often strategically masked to prevent rather than promote intercultural dialogue, what effect could *Dutchman* [or *Funnyhouse*] have on the audience other than to reproduce a dominant cultural hegemony?" (83). Sonnega's warning grows especially relevant when we scan *Funnyhouse's* early reviews. Howard Tubman refers to the piece as an exploration "…into the tortured mind of a Negro who cannot bear the burden of being a Negro and who is too proud to accept the patronage of the white world," and Edith Oliver describes it as "…the last moments in the life of a tortured girl—half black, half white—who is lost in a nightmare world where black is evil and white is good." These blanket readings abnegate *Funnyhouse's* biting and critical undercurrent; therefore, it would appear that the black playwright finds herself in a bind over how to reproach successfully the very viewers that support her work while reaching out to an ideal audience that is more imagined than real. Because of this predicament, complicating the performance arena with mobile characters who glide through various figurations so that they are not easily captured/detained becomes crucial.

Kennedy taps into the dual qualities of the Yoruba Orisha, who often wear two facades, a cool and a hot side, to transmit parallel but divergent messages to its company, implied and real. In the early period, she sends her mainstream audience into her own funhouse, a series of blinds that will divert their fixation away from matters closer to black America's hearth. Another way of thinking about this scheme is to say that she uses culture/drama to ensnare her white intellectual viewer within the very holding pen that the dominant society intends for the Negro. Similar to Irigaray's recasting of Plato's cave, the funhouse or stage becomes the space where the consumer finds herself drifting about but drawn toward an inverted mirror, or, using the African American vernacular, these carnival chambers are the place to "zoom the zoomer" (see Aretha Franklin).

To the addressee in the inner circle, the writer provides a viable alternative in the form of a sacred masking ritual where the amusement park shimmers through space and time and becomes a pre-Middle Passage African compound, but this plateau can only be reached once the funhouse's other configuration has been demystified and evacuated. To tease out the contours of this dual positionality, we return to Sonnega's insightful comments, which imply that an audience comprised of people who have shared racial oppression's ponderous weight would more easily recognize the play's irony/parody and other carnival-like features because they may have had more exposure to the cultural codes that the artist taps. Because of this shared expressive familiarity, this group would be more inclined to recognize the work's analytical underpinnings that do not reinforce white supremacy. With this re-visioning in hand, we can imagine that to many ritual-goers who are conversant with the Negro's artificiality both in 1964 and today, Sarah, the chief figure in *Funnyhouse*, is an exaggeration of a type that resides in and across black villages, a blow-up that personifies the disparaging, class-and color-conscious black person who has internalized a racial hierarchy that places whiteness on the top and blackness on the bottom (Like Morrison's Mrs. Breedlove from *The Bluest Eye*). Those attendees who realize the deleterious impact of such thinking and how it can infect and deconstruct black self-love wish to deflate this mindset as it restricts African American psychological, economic, and spiritual growth. This group would not be enticed by Sarah—even to dissect her emotional and mental profile—but would be wary of her, considering her too susceptible to corruption to carry out any transformational social project. She, to them, is as naive and bloated as Ellison's Invisible Man. And, in this distance from Sarah's Negroness, a distance that I argue Kennedy shares as well, the implied enlightened spectator can begin to reflect on how to build other institutions and images that thrive outside "the funnyhouse." To this ideal viewer, the play maps a minefield of psychological racial warfare that need be circumvented and contained as a remnant from the past.

So, when the landlady announces twice at the end of the piece, "The poor bitch has hung herself," (25) this should not automatically be interpreted as a tragic moment.[7] To the contrary, this refrain heralds relief from the claustrophobia and meandering fog that the imperialistic Trojan horse, Sarah, exudes across the performance space. For the implied ideal audience who is fed up not only with subjugation from hostile dominant groups and systems but also from that levied by black proxies who are moving toward Negrohood by carrying out the hands-on, daily dirty work that prevailing social models had set in place, the hoped-for new beginning hangs, literally and figuratively, in the anticipated cleansing breeze that will gush forth once the Funnyhouse has been cleared. At best, to this group, Sarah's self-imposed plight and self-involvement comes across as entirely extravagant. We cannot forget that this work is set amidst the assassinations of Patrice Lumumba and JFK and was conceived during a period when Adrienne Kennedy was an eyewitness to great valor and great corruption in war-torn Africa on the brink of a "post-colonial" changeover.

Confirmation of the writer's authorial distance from and disdain for Sarah in her hot Negro-guise is secreted in key symbols. There are two underlying inventions that well up often during this dense one-act treatment. The first is the myth of the black Jesus that is as old as Nat Turner and is a conflation of New Testament prophecy and the East African phoenix legend that predicts eventual restoration. Basically, the myth reads that a black Jesus/savior will materialize and end racial tyranny by relighting a majestic

African past and, therefore, inspire ordinary black people to recover their magnanimous birthright. Once a global recognition of this illustrious epoch becomes common knowledge, race will become inconsequential. The ultimate reward of the prophecy's fulfillment will be peace on earth and a complete Christianizing of the world. The other major narrative that girds this play is that of American color politics which not only renders white good and black evil but also labels the shades in between, which results in mass and egregious social strata across black districts. Before the sixties' and seventies' cultural revolutions, ecru, yellow or almond-colored people often received privileges over their darker brethren. Other factors such as nose shape and size, hair texture, body build, and eye color were also weighed carefully to determine how much whiteness one could rightfully declare. What *Funnyhouse* does is bring these two mythologies into dialogue with the search for purity and recovery in Africa meeting the desire for assimilation and whiteness; both strands are then set down in America's cosmopolitan center (the play is set in Manhattan in a room in the nineties just on what would have been in 1964 near the border between white Manhattan and black Harlem).

These two directions have had a long, involved history in black intellectual thought with radicals from as far back as the eighteenth century seeking out black self-rule while hanging onto black moral superiority in the face of slavery and race-based brutality.[8] The other path has also had its followers and sees black capitulation to dominant systems as a victory. Black intellectual thought has wavered between these two major paths, sometimes splicing the two together in interesting variations. For example, some black American Muslims may look forward to a resurgence of African power (black messiahs) and applaud separatism but have little desire to elevate Christianity. Signs such as hair falling out, the numerous references to skin color, black popular magazines that feature yellow and vanilla faces, the erection of a Christian mission in the jungle, and saving the race as Biblical fulfillment reinforce through repetition the underlying knell that the play drums out for its intended sympathetic audience, one that is fatigued by and leery of these same old notes and is hungry for some symbols that break ground outside the carnival. That is: no matter the selected path, the funnyhouse continually returns to white progenitors as the basis for black response; creativity itself is posited as white owned.

As a case in point, one way to interpret the kinky hair that comes out in copious bunches is to relate it to the many chemical processes that black people use to straighten their tresses and appear more European, which also cause breakage and baldness.[9] Certainly, Kennedy's use of hair loss as an underlying emblem indicts the manner in which European aesthetics have dominated black estimations of beauty. The Christian mission in the jungle is critiqued as well by the double entendre hovering around the word "erection" that questions the sexual play/seduction of the native by the colonizer and the lure of Christianity to domesticate the Negro. Taken together, these clues indicate a critical and heated tone on the playwright's part as she parses out the major theories and strategies that have counterposed the overarching Negro Question. These markers have ordered African American maneuverability. To remove oneself from the funnyhouse requires decoding and defusing them. To stand outside a blues structure calls for an active engagement with overly familiar, popular entrenched paradigms. Therefore, we can say that Kennedy uses repetition to deconstruct itself.

The theater attendee who yearns to escape the mirrored cage must learn to scrutinize institutions, practices, and exchanges that carry traces of this capitulation to white supremacy. To the dominant culture another message is transmitted, and that is to stop recreating the Negro as a packaged good that can then be placed within familiar frames through a series of disciplining acts. We see this discursive confinement in the manner in which Sarah's white boyfriend, Raymond, and her landlady have the closing pronouncements, one claiming that Sarah commits suicide because her father did so and the other declaring that she is a funny little liar. Contradicting the miasma that forms Sarah's memories and interiority, each one assigns her life to a simple interpretation, each scrutinizes her through the lens of linear narrative, and each rewrites her past. The message is at least twofold. To the implied liberationist viewer, this play is actually celebratory and predicts the end of the Negro, pitching on its grave a West African spiritual rite. To the mainstream group, it is admonitory and advises that this distorting, penalizing space (the regulatory funnyhouse) can only exist if eyes fix it and then conceal that voyeurism through various magical techniques.

When Kennedy studied Kuntu in West Africa, the theater of masks, she committed herself to upholding this custom because its stress on duality is indispensable to black survival. One slope is indicative of the wooden veneer's cool side: an aperture to a plane where the living and dead and man and nature can engage in dialogue. However, the covering, like the Orisha who gave it to man, also has a hot function that is more worldly than spiritual, the guise that has been employed by the West: that is, the means to hide one's intentions to more easily subdue another. So veiling or performativity can be stimulating (ceremonial) and/or voracious (political). In its hot moment, it is the dominant trope of colonization. Along with its other functions, entering into the funnyhouse of the Negro entails encountering the place where imperial eyes see themselves through the distortion of their own cultural creation/covering head dress. Another way to view this concept is to note that *Funnyhouse of a Negro* is about white people. It also implicitly critiques Fanon and his preoccupation with the Negro because Fanon's delving into the manner in which Algerian patients' response to colonial violence establishes white theft and terror as the route for black subjects to enter into history. Alternatively, Kennedy's drama comments that narratives of black past and black memory are so complicated and often so lividly pulsating that no cultural form existed, at least not in 1964, to carry them. In place of telling tales, she derides Western attempts to do so. The playwright buys time with this early cycle of theatrical works as she continues to search for a conveyance that will allow her the flexibility to reveal and explore African American yearnings.

The Owl Answers, originally mounted in 1965, represents a step on this journey. Here we encounter similar conditions to that in *Funnyhouse*, both spotlighting a mixed-race female protagonist who is condemned to repeat her story from the penitentiary (Fuchs 80). Major symbols such as hair, the Bible, and masquerading recur as well. Furthermore, white figures including Shakespeare, William the Conqueror, Chaucer, and Anne Boleyn ground the Negro question, asking collectively and repeatedly, "If you are his ancestor [the white father], why are you a Negro?" (30). While there are many links between this work and Kennedy's first play, it also inverts its predecessor, with the Negro girl moving back towards Africa, not away from it (she travels on a subway to Harlem where she will meet Negro men), and she mourns the black mother's rape by the white father, in place of the yellow mother's rape by the black father, a shift that suggests that "Kennedy's travelers are existentially suspended in the historic middle passage and are headed homeward" (Bryant-Jackson 56). By rotating the lens in this manner, Kennedy is able to substitute a birdcage for her funnyhouse: both are containers, but the former is more porous because the inmate can gaze out and receive wafts of fresh air unlike the carnival vault. This choice signals a variation between the two dramas for in the first, the Negro is pure construct, voiceless and without hope of subjectivity, but here that space has been ignited with an imminent point of view.[10] We locate this budding voice's emergence in the play's details. Notice that this treatment concentrates more overtly on whiteness, revolving the father's "long, silky white hair," (31) a white Bible, and a white bird, signs which suggest a more conscious and deliberate dramatization, that common meaning is biased towards whiteness. Then, there is the owl's screech: a constant "owww," a pantheistic reframe that insinuates simultaneously a mass trauma and a mass gathering of forces. We are not certain whether the owl's song is weeping or battle cry, but, in either case, it forecasts a looming or ongoing conflict.

The playwright imparts that, while in Africa, she was awed by these magnificent birds: "The owls in the trees outside the Achimota Guest House were close, and at night, because we slept under gigantic mosquito nets, I felt enclosed in their sound…the owls sounded as if they were in the very center of the room" (*People Who Led to My Plays* 121–2). There are many references to birds in West African culture, and Kennedy was inspired by African art that features these flying bodies, "…I bought a great African mask from a vendor on the streets of Accra, of a woman with a bird flying through her forehead…" (*People Who Led* 121). This sculpture is a contemporary rendition of the Yoruba-based concept of "the bird of the head":

> This is the "bird of the head" (*eiye ororo*), enshrined in whiteness, the color of *iwa*, and in purity. It is the bird which, according to the Yoruba, God places in the head of man or woman at birth as the emblem of the mind. The image of the descent of the bird of mind fuses with the image of the coming down of God's *ashé* in feathered form (Thompson 11).

Ashé is translated loosely as potential from God that is prophetic and predictive (Thompson 9). Birds are often associated with, "the *ashé* of the 'mothers,' the most powerful elderly women with a force capable of mystically annihilating the arrogant, the selfishly rich, or other targets deserving punishment" (Thompson 7). So, we can read Kennedy's closing image of a black woman on the verge of metamorphosis into an owl as the moment when cosmic forces turn from cool to hot or from hot to cool, as Oshun, the mother-deity, rotates her other face. Framing this play as a breaking point instead of a brittle travail falls in line with the African-based cultural referents that Kennedy inserts vigilantly. In the place of pure grief, we are left with an impression of heightened, severely roused, rallying, flapping wings.

The screech (owww) portends an altered state, and it announces a desire for a better language and forms, ones that will allow Kennedy to write the stories, sounds, and visions that she is moved to dramatize. Dripping with profundity, primal force, wrath, warning, pain, defiance, this wail resonates all that "civilization" would stamp out of Negro expression. *Ashé* is represented on the stage with this owl speak. As Elinor Fuchs observes,

Kennedy deploys her masks, animal costumes, and symbols "to intensify rather than distance," (80) a strategy that reaches a melting point in *The Owl Answers*. Animals and beasts will continue to crowd Kennedy's work as safe/wild way stations somewhere between social traditions and individual testimonies, for these are the places that most often resist colonization by a master text, the places where characters can "…seek refuge from an empirical universe and solace in a metaphysical one" (Bryant-Jackson 46).

How do we "analyze" an oww or an owl? As opposed to stabilizing meaning, this syllable from a beast language can migrate through numerous significations as Bryant-Jackson suggests; its potency stems from its adaptability. At times, the owww mimics what Afrikaans, English, Dutch, Portuguese, or Spanish may have sounded like to enslaved Africans; in other places it reads like a woman being raped or giving birth that covers both physical pain and the ache of separating mother and child; sometimes it reverberates like the scratching beats of a rapturous predator stalking its prey as the colonialist would search for big game, human or otherwise; and sometimes it is the protest of that system. More often it chronicles nature reclaiming its home. I could go on, which is exactly the point: this sounding is not translatable, an aspect that promotes ritual, communal making over traditional realistic theater's cataloguing. Refuting Elinor Fuch's notion that Kennedy's "…signs may be historical, but their power is eternal. Whatever is always was and cannot be altered" (79), I find that, in a Kennedy production, signs take flight from any number of possible referents. The challenge is not to overanalyze them to the point where they become inflexible but allow them their multifaceted affect. So, if we can claim nothing more about this highly mutable beast language, we can at least argue that it puts us in step with the writer's travels as she delivers sound to us from her many station stops.[11]

The playwright's more assertive deconstructive energies take on steam as the sixties advance as she dissects whiteness, tunnels through natural sound to locate better expressive vehicles, and casts free symbols that have become fixtures in the African American intellectual lexicon. By the time she mounted *A Rat's Mass* in 1966 in Boston, she had revisited these same concerns on several occasions, each time adjusting her angle to capture a bit more of an elusive totality. This one-act dream takes up many of the issues the writer treated previously, raising the curtain on a compounded array rather than adjacent involvements. Here, the setting is post-World War II Rome when devastation and demoralization clogged the atmosphere. According to Forte, the play "…reveals the fascism of a socioeconomic structure founded on colonialism, racism, and slavery, and names the oppressors in all their guises" (166). Packed with allusions to Nazis and communions, white dresses and childbirth, the drama narrows in on brother and sister rat/people, who have lost their innocence as a result of the Great War and their complicity in it. Just as in previous creations, the performance turns around oft-mumbled refrains: "the Nazis will come" and "put a bullet in your head," the latter an existential query that plagues the surviving rats who must come to terms with not only Nazi atrocities but also their own willingness to follow corrupt leaders, leaders whose power resides somewhere between religious dogma and state mandates. The nation hovers somewhere in this space as well, a commanding institution that is personified by the feminized/Rosemary who wears a communion dress and has worms in her hair (47). It is implied that Rosemary orders Brother Rat to set upon Sister Rat, "Brother Rat: 'Rosemary said if I loved her I would do what she said'" (50). Both virgin and Medusa, Rosemary is the agent that induces and becomes the excuse for the sacrilege: incest that has led to Sister Rat's pregnancy.

The dramatic motif of vermin scrambling to find a hole once the light is lit is reminiscent of Richard Wright's *Native Son's* opening pages and, analogous to that novel, state violence spreads through the transfer of cruelty down a pyramid where it is eventually inflicted most stridently on the female body, as if the terror gathers force and strength the more frequently people are exposed to it. *The Rat's Mass* as pageant and as ritual attempts to intercede in this vicious chain but fails, ultimately, because at the end only post-apocalyptic Rosemary, the nation, a strong witch's herb, the last virgin, remains. She expunges her disciples by turning them in to the Nazis and into Nazis. Bounded by a specific time frame, this play predicts Kennedy's ensuing preoccupation with more focused and identifiable historical events.[12] Complementing this emphasis on targeted incidents, bolder revelatory sweeps arise, a modification that introduces evaluation and trial more explicitly in Kennedy's work.

We ask of this subsequent period that places "judgment" as its defining trope, who sets the agenda, decides what constitutes evidence, and charts and patrols the border between good and evil? More importantly, how can black female voices enter into the trial's arena when they have been excluded systematically as agents? Kennedy's answer, at least to the last question, rests on recording the sounds that she hears, what sticks in her subconscious, and what is left to forgetting. As she has remarked, "I started using the symbolism in my journals that came from dreams realizing that my dreams had a vitality..." (Betsko and Koenig interview 253). Trial, redefined by the writer, becomes akin to displaying and rearranging the images and ideas that have enough currency to charge her subconscious and remain with her. Kennedy is a playwright who gives credence to her instincts and one who respects the human mammal's urges while she also relies on her intellect to space out and make patterns of these hidden sensibilities. This world she places atop, alongside, over, and under traditional Western configurations of the trial, where evidence is restricted to the physical plain. By bringing together these two varied notions of "what really matters," Kennedy can put both instinctive manifestations and processed systemization on stage and, therefore, unearth the connection between imperialism and rationalism. That is, by putting rationalism into play with subconscious symbolic modalities, the drive toward order that science demands becomes more apparent in the same manner in which imperial power seeks to subjugate a lesser people. Linearity in the form of trial is held up as a colonial discourse that wears rationalism as its mask.

During this second period, history becomes contestable, and we find that random, alternative narratives, images, and symbols begin to encroach on and erase dominant constructs, but this competitive exertion is dangerous and difficult. More often than not, some figure is trying to testify with his or her intuition intact amid a noisy, profane, violent atmosphere. Reaching the microphone is often a bloody struggle in and of itself. We see this particular shift that dramatizes how laborious it is for black people to register on discursive ranges most clearly in Kennedy's 1973 *An Evening with Dead Essex,* a techno-performance that requires a projector, tape recorder, and newspaper clippings within a screening studio in New York. A black troupe has selected to document the transmutation of Mark Essex from innocent Midwestern church attendee to mass murderer who kills five people and wounds over a dozen others by firing from a New Orleans rooftop. Essex, based on a real case, was then toppled by over one hundred bullets from the police. From this basic story, the director, projectionist and actors seek to mythologize and raise Essex to heroic stature, using him to stand in for an avenging, cleansing angel who was awakened to his destiny to kill white people by the horrors that he experienced and observed during his Navy stint in the Vietnam War. The performers take his life, and more importantly his death, as a revolutionary omen that the atrocities visited on both Southeastern Asians and those Americans who were forced to attack them will return in full force: a cultural enactment of Malcolm X's famous prediction that, "The chickens always come home to roost."

In Kennedy's hands, this reproduction of Essex is more than a staging of Black Arts propaganda because her play highlights technology, rationalism, and discourse-making. She stresses that Essex cannot own his life or his death because of the overarching media-driven apparatus that corrals his story inside comprehensible narratives. Using a technique that is similar to the one that she employed in *Funnyhouse*, Kennedy designs a theatrical package that sets out ostensibly to plot character analysis but instead sheds light on how the object is contextualized and who commits this act; thus the beam bears down on the would-be wardens outside the projector rather than the product within it. *An Evening with Dead Essex* is more of a searing look at this ignited Black Arts Era group who would collect Essex's remains to canonize him than it is a true biography of Essex, whose motivations will remain inscrutable. Therefore, this piece levies a crucial critique of the Movement, which proclaimed a desire for revolution but continued to depend on dominant technologies and frameworks to bring about the social transformation that it so anticipated.

Snippets of Essex's life are thrown up against the screen's white canvas that accommodates photographs of his mother, Essex as a boy, the white Kansas faces that Essex grew up around as a child as well as images of the flag and the soldiers in Vietnam juxtaposed against shots of politicians and journalists. To this media barrage is added music: spirituals, church hymns, and contemporary sounds from Aretha Franklin and Isaac Hayes. Bible verses abound as does the singular phrase, "Christianity is the white man's religion." It is clear that this work is steeped in the same kind of African American modal groove that Kennedy has been signifying on since the sixties as Essex becomes to this director a seventies embodiment of Nat Turner, a black savior who will usher in a new age.[13] His killing spree becomes comprehensible to this performance group only if they situate it within a religious/spiritual script, a rationalization for his carnage. To illustrate, as the curtain falls, the company recites Luke 3: 3-6:

> And he came into all the country about Jordan preaching the Baptism of repentance for the remission of sins…the voice of one crying in the wilderness—Prepare ye the way of thc Lord make his paths straight…every valley shall be filled and every mountain and hill shall be brought low and the crooked place shall be made straight and the rough ways shall be made smooth and the flesh shall see the salvation of God—you know the spirit of the Lord is upon me because he hath anointed me to preach the gospel to the poor he hath sent me to heal the broken hearted—to preach deliverance to the captives and recovering of sight to the blind to set at liberty them that are bruised. To heal the brokenhearted.

On one hand, the revolutionary filmmakers are providing an alternative interpretation of Essex, enrobing him as an angry prophet who is directed by God, a myth that counters the media's portrayal of him as an animal. On the other hand, they have sentenced Essex to the old script, the repetitious screenplay that black America had built for itself from the earliest days of Negrohood, that it is the black man's destiny to save or recover the earth from the grip of idolaters and hypocrites, a Manichean struggle that parallels Frederick Douglass's fight with Covey, his white overseer, that inverts white power into black power. What is crucial, then, is that regardless of the Biblical verse's import, the revolutionary text continues to frame violence as the rubric that will engender change. The irony is that this superimposed selection counters brutality, arguing that preaching/testifying are the ameliorating tools that can usher in a new epoch, but the movement people depict Essex's bloody opera as a prophetic interstitial flare. They have elevated the gunshot to a language that is capable of blotting out the Biblical passage's mandate to heal through lamentation. The transposition of a spiritual mission into sanctioned violence mirrors how national leaders package war efforts, a tactic that is at least as old as the Crusades.

Even if Essex renounced Christianity (he is alleged to have said that it is the white man's religion), his biographers and his detractors will not allow him to live or die outside of that script. By framing him as either a martyr/savior or the Devil, Essex is denied his individuality because his historians refuse to read his life as a personalized series of compounded and complex events and reactions. In order to rationalize their own beliefs, those that take up Essex must deny him the same right.[14] Unanswered questions (was Essex really so religious as a boy? Or did he simply follow his mother to church? Did the war change him or did the racism that he experienced in Kansas predispose him to an extremist position? How did he feel about the poor or about the "enemy" that he was forced to kill?) do not get formulated because of the director's bias. With this play, Kennedy argues that in 1973, it is still nearly impossible for Essex, a black person without a construct, to reach the microphone.

Akin to the wardens that guard the funhouse, the artistic conductor readies his charge for exhibition. But, in this piece, the filmmaker actually admits art's limitation and, however briefly, probes the politics of representation: "I don't know where he [Essex] was…I'd say many places—he too was entering and leaving many places" (126). Even though the troupe continues to write on dead Essex anyway, this query breaks the seemingly inviolate looping visual/audio text, a conscious caesura of the director's authority as he yields to his figure. In this brief hiatus, the artist/revolutionary realizes that his account cannot capture what Timothy

Murray calls the "unframeable structures" (170). This honest moment is indicative of the transition between Kennedy's first and second waves, for chinks begin to appear in the armour/facades that were so solid during her early period.

The writer's move into a new stage reflects what is happening around her. Civil rights, anti-war, and women's rights gains had altered the socio-historic fabric. Analogously, seemingly sealed, impregnable discourses had begun to move off center because breaking moments brought on by historical events cast doubt on authority and portended a promise for dialogue on a broader scale. It may be significant as well that the first time we encounter an artist/master who bares his mechanism is when a formerly enslaved puppeteer operates the machine. This detail suggests that by the seventies power had been redistributed and no longer flowed out from hierarchical channels down a glacial pyramid but formed a layered, intricate topography of side and slip streams. Yet, in spite of the fact that power had become more diffuse, it continues to manifest itself as a dynamic force through trial. Under Kennedy's roof, both the state, which pumps one hundred bullets into Essex, and the Black Arts folks, who would transform him into a hero, evaluate his worth by interrogating the boundaries of what constitutes criminality. Combing through the remnants of his life, both groups select only those orts that will brace each one's ideological position: They attach their "owned" meaning to Essex's snapshots, written phrases, dog tags, and domestic clutter. Both go on to record and organize the scraps that Essex leaves behind, the former waging its inquisition via the media and the latter via a revolutionary film.

During this second stage, Kennedy increasingly incorporates technological artifacts. Holding up for inspection slides, film, and photography, the playwright concludes, after thorough investigation, that these media are often sinister because they are sentimental and enticing. Using her own experience as a gloss, she recollects how she admired cinema magazines that magnified actors' pictures with short, dense paragraphs underneath; she even longed to be in those star books (*Deadly Triplets* 99–100).[15] Later, Kennedy admits that she had been searching for a lost romanticism (*A Letter to Flowers, The Reader* 265). This confession intimates disquiet about film in its many varieties that has less to do with its omnipresence and more to do with its ability to color over pain and, therefore, make the expression of grief and suffering taboo. These issues are vented most forcefully in the 1976 *A Movie Star Has to Star in Black and White*, a play that critic Deborah Geis describes as posing "…the ambivalent spectatorial status of the African-

American woman whose subjectivity risks being undermined by her identification with an exclusionary cultural apparatus" (171). Geis argues further that movie-star fantasies originate from a Hollywood mythology that is oppressive and unassailable (171). While I agree with Geis that Kennedy posits film's potentially deleterious impact on black subjectivity, I differ in assigning cause to that harm. The matter is one of perspective. *Movie Star* is a performance piece that splices together three films, *Now Voyager*, *Viva Zapata*, and *A Place in the Sun* with three family tragedies, a wrenching divorce, a miscarriage, and an automobile accident that has left the central character's (Clara) brother in a coma. Movie scenes are superimposed on top of the hospital, the axis of this unrelenting one-act work. Other key elements are that the mother, father, Eddie (Clara's husband) and Clara, who are all African American, speak in their own voices, but Clara sometimes communes as well through the clairvoyant-like gauze of white cinema stars, Bette Davis, Jean Peters, and Shelley Winters. According to Geis, the black characters' circumstances do not live up to the blinding glamour of the white luminaries, and by dramatizing this gap between actual material conditions and Hollywood's dreamscapes, Kennedy traces a budding and potentially dangerous social hunger that has begun to reshape the modern self so that the self is aware constantly of its lack (Geis relies on Lacan).

Yet Geis's analysis rests on the postulation that the playwright superimposes the black narrative over the movies' preexisting contours; that is, the picture is the leading text and the family drama is secondary. I suggest that we invert the dynamic. In this manner, it is possible to conclude that the writer is auditioning film to see if it can become a feasible transport to portray this heartbreaking series of family disturbances. I arrive at this viewpoint for several reasons. From her first professional production, Kennedy has rolled around, in, under and on myth, interpolating pieces of it by way of images and symbols and, at other times, actually revising classical African and European versions.[16] This preoccupation suggests that she is on a modernist's search to recover something of the old wisdom that can be applied to contemporary conditions, a course that many African American writers take because they find that their early training as scholars revolves around interpreting the Bible (or other spiritual texts) and their own submerged ancestral and cultural heritage. The act of divining and salvaging sustenance from a mythological source compares to scanning film (that often relies on myth as well) for clues about the past that can be brought forward into contemporary time. The second reason why I argue that the writer examines and judges cinema through a theatrical filter has to do with her own admitted appetite for collecting and rearranging film relics during her childhood. In *People Who Led to My Plays* and elsewhere Kennedy describes how she cut out photographs of celebrities and pasted them in scrapbooks, how she amassed movie magazines and memorabilia like autographs, a practice that is indicative of the period during and after World War II from which Kennedy surfaced. America's children were enthralled with tinsel-town allure, but these same pre-teens and teens spliced and reshaped movie images to suit their own imaginative visions. A journal or scrapbook is a way to control, reorder, and own alien imagery. So, the child's *own* art book resists the cinematic text. I would even go so far as to call this an early adaptation of a hip-hop aesthetic where the compiler operates as the "mixer," who will re-juggle and re-prioritize current beats; the only difference is that in the forties young people crafted visual miscellany in lieu of sound. Cinema, under this general rubric, becomes a lost text and a series of ruins that can be snipped out, written on, and shuffled.

In *Movie Star,* Kennedy experiments by replacing popular movie lines with utterances about black familial relationships to see if the romantic airs that are caught on film can enhance what Kennedy pleads for in *Dead Essex*: the coming of peace (peace from domestic tragedy in *Movie Star*). *Movie Star* is what various critics from Pryse and Spillers to Reed and Baker would recognize as conjuring the Diaspora back into a unit, a cutting and pasting exercise that merges artistic genres to bring about familial restoration, an audition that stops short regrettably. To illustrate, we turn to the numerous instances when members from this black kinship network set up scenes and direct. Early on in the piece, the mother describes her childhood during the late nineteen twenties in segregated Georgia when white and colored signs polluted the public space (65). The mother later discloses that she preferred to remain indoors (66), and the inference is that she strays no farther than the porch because the town mandates a racial grid with only whites insulated against physical assault. Her self-imposed seclusion that is caused by this branding is contrasted to Bette Davis's repression in *Now Voyager* that develops from a controlling family dynamic that does not carry the added weight of racist or class-based terrorism. Under the black mother's gaze, Davis's situation appears mild. Other subtle comparisons color the piece such as the clear-cut heroism of Zapata as depicted in *Viva Zapata!* held in relief against the black father, a race man, who fights for equality for his people but tries suicide because he longs for the innocence, protection, and warmth of his upbringing (69). In both cases, the black family concerns are far more intense and involved than the cinematic text, a fact which indicates that film, as it stands during this era, cannot contain the overflowing domestic heartbreaks.

The callaloo of film, theater, and memoir in *Movie Star* does not lead to reconciliation and healing,[17] but it reveals painful findings that invigorate the playwright's quest for both a language and an artistic skeleton that can help her tell her stories. To elucidate this line of reasoning, I return to Geis's review, in which she argues that the African-American female subject is overcome by Hollywood tableaus because they create perfect fictive worlds that she can never inhabit. Certainly this logic can be applied to any cinema consumer to some extent, regardless of race and/or gender. Yet, I believe that the issue is not so much that film foments unattainable dreamscapes that are beyond the black subject's reach, but that films too often furnish impractical sanctuaries that allow for the deferral of African American (especially female) anger and agency. As James Snead warns, "…part of the fascination and danger of film is that it offers us large scale gestures that we feel make us important, once we repeat them" (144). The issue for black people is that the gestures that film broadcasts are not the poses that are appropriate or advantageous in light of the often-wrenching circumstances that demand redress.

Furthermore, there is a direct correlation between the beast world of Kennedy's sixties one-acts and the celluloid havens that she uses to traverse linear lines during her second period for both devices serve as temporary containers that bracket the fact that there are words that dare not be spoken because they would most likely lead to the end of the playwright's ability to mount productions and also because theatrical channels have not broadened enough to recognize these proclamations.[18] Yet, the difference between the first and second phases is that the later plays evidence Kennedy's growing awareness that these protective dens have served to limit the imaginative space that would allow her to fully announce a black subjectivity. Thus the journey through technology takes her from a keen evaluation of how the media acts on black life to awareness that these enticing images and scripts can be held at bay. This realization places the artist on an active quest to disclose the underpinnings behind this compunction to romanticize existence in order to withstand it.

The writer connects her initial musings and her 1976 imaginative frieze through her subject Clara who recites lines from *The Owl Answers*: "He came to me in the outhouse, in the garden, in the fig tree. He told me you are an owl, ow, owww, I am your beginning, ow" (76). As the "bird of the mind" approximates the gift of forethought from God to man, these moments when Clara breaks character and hoots generate a dramatic rupture where a fundamental ritual is pushing through and over the cinematic field. Mutability invades the performance space, with the African legends raining down confidence on Clara while the film stars conspire to speak on top of her voice. Thus the "oww" defies ownership and records a burgeoning self, punching holes in the movie's seamless, antiseptic black and white exterior, like the mask-maker who hollows out the wood for eyes and mouth. Pushing back the movie stars that encroach on her anguish with their smooth patter and soothing music, (62) Clara fortifies her strength each time she distances herself from this dislocating and seductive panoply that appears in fleshy form at curtain rise in the guise of the Columbia Pictures Lady (63) and then as Peters, Winters, and Davis. On each occasion when Clara forces her words and sounds into their mouths, the banality of the original script is confirmed; so much so that when Shelley Winters drowns at curtain descent, not even Clara, her writer, will save her.

Clara has evaluated cinema and found it unsuitable to bear the haunts that she is ordained to impart. Substantiation for this assessment comes not only from Winters's demise at the end of *Movie Star* but also from the final scene in *Sleep Deprivation Chamber* when the lights dim on the Kennedy family's screening of the homemade tape that documents Teddy Kennedy's brutal pounding by the Virginia police: "He remembers his family at the table in Edelstein's office watching film of his beating. The film is very dark and filled with the sounds of his screams" (72). Distinct from the bright Hollywood products, Teddy's reels are overtaken by the unforgettable sounds that overrun the image, reminiscent of the owl's cry. Therefore, to be useful, film's glossy finish has to be offset by chaotic, fierce aural stimulation as the visual text should concede primacy to sound. And, because most popular cinema rarely dares to display civilization's feral underpinnings in this manner or in any other, Kennedy relinquishes her fascination with it, considering it overwhelmingly obfuscating and fawning.

By the time that Kennedy enters her third cycle around the late eighties, she has lit on another experiment or interlude, perhaps obsession, with photographs, namely family albums. Technology that can be held in the hand and treasured as corroboration that one matters to a compassionate circle characterizes the underlying spring that runs through this latter body of works, which does not mean that Kennedy turns away from the worldly themes that she has treated up to this point. She persists in revealing and deconstructing imperialism, but the apparatus that the playwright brings to bear on large-scale social conditions is the same that she applies to her own past and her understanding of it, a marked difference from her previous stages. For instance, if we carefully analyze her early offerings, we will find that Kennedy divulges very little of her personal life. Even during the seventies with the seemingly confessional *Movie Star*, Kennedy continually diverts attention away from pivotal familial crises by splicing them with layering static. This is not the case as she moves toward heightened moments of disclosure during the last two decades or so, but even in this body of work that appears to be a series of admissions, she is careful to select the tidbits that allow her to lead/educate the reader/viewer back to his or her own life, his or her own position. What materializes out of this latter concentration is a candor that is borne of necessity, stemming, perhaps, from the writer's frustration with the critics' feeble reaction to the dynamics and issues that she had been highlighting all along. As a result, she must push harder and with more urgency, revamping her aesthetics to ensure that the viewer not only feels her rage but knows the impetus for it.

Specifically, Kennedy combines the pilgrim motif with the detective's search to create detailed geographical surveys of how an imperial will functions both politically and personally. Diagramming first and then peeling the cover off of human interaction (especially the drive to conquer) take precedence during this late phase as the writer opens the door and allows her characters to walk out of the claustrophobic rooms of her early works. With this added mobility, the artist will structure her pieces around the "long journeys [that] seemed to be part of the destiny of people" (*People Who Led* 47). Translating these forays for the theater is optimistic in that this trope may transform the performance space and imbue it with greater intimacy as the subjects on stage share their adventure with the eager cohorts in the seats. Of course, these trips are not free from conflict. There are forces—powers—that set out to frustrate the characters' expeditions after peering into the machinery that devises to imprison them, and the magicians who oil the gears do not wish to concede their secrets and lose their authority. In addition, pedestrian yearnings after closeness are complicated by both authority's attempt to orbit and control the circle and by the self's own disruptive impulse to rule (which also leads to community fragmentation). These conflicting individual urges are visible in Kennedy's art when she oscillates between whether to position her subjects as mother or daughter. During this late period, the perspective shifts between the fulcrum narrator/viewpoint of either the mother's or the daughter's location. At times, a protective, fierce, avenging parental command sweeps across the stage with the strength of a fearsome sorceress, and, at other moments, that force is upended by the female offspring who seeks definition apart from but still under the maternal script's halo.

Kennedy ponders what it means to be an African American daughter in a country where that social location is barely recognized: "...the kind [of black community] I grew up in—I respected. But it really was a very rigid childhood. I wasn't allowed to speak...I wasn't allowed to express what I was thinking...So all these people were burning inside of me" (Bryant-Jackson and Overbeck interview 5). Because African American parents and guardians before the Civil Rights Movement (and probably to a lesser degree even now) had to rein in their children to teach them to navigate and survive a hostile national geography, Kennedy's creativity is, in part, built on what bell hooks has called "talking back," a prohibited form of speech that is often deemed too rebellious or too frank for a young black subject because such articulations could lead to severe consequences (imprisonment, violence, stigmatization, or lesser sanctions).[19] Many African American children were taught to be seen and not heard, resulting in awful and gaping silences across generations, a state that is in opposition to the West African practice of ancestor-living dialogue. Therefore, "talking back" is an attempt to recover a Middle Passage loss. We can read Kennedy's comment that "I feel that my writing is an extension of my relationship with my mother, of talking with her" (Betsko and Koenig interview 247) as an observation that contemporary art should function to reconnect with a submerged cultural past. The playwright's observation secures her journey motif as a pursuit that is tethered around the daughter's pilgrimage to discover what the mother knows and spring off into her own identity from this foundation.

While this archetype is vital, it only addresses part of what happens in late Kennedy offerings. Beside or, more accurately, shadowing and striving to blot out this maturing black female detective is the mother figure whose mission revolves around securing a remedy for her children's long suffering. She is highly symbolic and fights not only for her own kin but for black collectivity as well. Hers is a voice that is not overly interested in intimacy but locates its strength in its singular ability to destroy all menacing agents. So, this sound is more revolutionary, more purely applied, and closer to the rigid text that Kennedy admitted stifled her own childhood. Thus the journey up to and through her latest stage has brought Kennedy to salvage and appreciate dual positionalities and to speak in double tongues. One side is cool like the daughter, who pursues her mother hoping to pick up enough wisdom to flourish, a voyage that celebrates and esteems the parent/ancestor. The other face is hot, vengeful, cranked up, and ready to strike, more akin to the female parent in a state of pique. Kennedy puts into "play" her own "summoned" Yoruba Orisha, Oshun, whose coming down probably started back in the sixties when she first traveled to Africa.

Retrospective and increasingly verbal and aural rather than image based, the playwright's pieces revolve around long trips, not as one embarking but as a returnee who must measure the outing's worth, its return on the resources invested in it. Evaluations that point out the failure of the Civil Rights Era and de-colonization merge with concerns about cultural imperialism as well as the dynamics of family groups, culminating in often apocalyptic scenes where subjects have to be brought back from the brink (or the ravine as Kennedy calls it in the *Ohio State Murders* 152, 169–170). Lines and characters from previous tragedies are refolded into displays that have been shaped to connote despair, madness, a general letting go of civilization for something that is considerably more humane in its random instability. In the end, even war, desolation, and anarchy are preferable to a status quo that is smug in its corruptness and has deceived itself into believing that the great social inequalities that have plagued the species have been resolved. The theatrical road that tracks these inquiries also leads to the story of a writer who eventually unpacks her own romantic leanings.

The first leg of this part of the sojourn begins around 1987 with the publication of Kennedy's memoir of sorts, *People Who Led to My Plays*, a collection of names, artifacts, and photographs that the writer encountered during her childhood, adolescence, and young adulthood. It is a gambit that signifies on autobiography by employing camouflaging techniques to conceal the personal. Exposing relatively little about her life and that of the relatives that she interacted with frequently, the writer manages to shield much of her upbringing from the reader's hunger. Kennedy declares her technique: "I simply had my character hide behind an African mask" (*People Who Led* 49). In lieu of the traditional narrative of a life, the writer cushions a compendium of black and white images of historical and home-based figures that made an impression on her by brief snippets/captions. Another way to describe the text is to say that it reads like a series of diary or journal entries where the artist has no need to explain her self to herself but is more interested in encapsulating fleeting memories that, for whatever reason, seem noteworthy to her. Not designed to furnish revelatory bits to an eager consumer, Kennedy's *People Who Led to My Plays* stimulates the reader's own associations and engagements with figures from Julius Caesar to Marian Anderson to his or her own mother. As a collection, the journal acts like ritual, bridging the writer's and reader's journeys, a structure that contradicts the closed, colonial aesthetics of traditional linear autobiography that breaks apart the subject for a willing book purchaser.

Kennedy has no desire to nor will she allow her past to be consumed, but she does put pieces of it in motion. These shards that take on magnified significance, because they are often repeated with or without variation in this late period, transform into barbed epées that peel off colonization's often seductive veneer, while they simultaneously retrieve the black family by providing testimony in oral, written, and visual guise (lines, letters, and photographs), witness that Kennedy realizes cannot stand for the truth because that cannot be captured (*People Who Led to My Plays* 86, 91).

Even though the playwright is well aware that a unified past is unrecoverable, her work yearns for a totality that is purely imaginative. This detail demands that we do not ascribe a strict modernist cast to her art (although she does enjoy a good rescue mission) because any retrieval of a whole is, ultimately, in her estimation, not only a lie but the means by which more voracious and brutal forces cover up their exploitation of more "innocent" groups. In contrast, Kennedy's texts acknowledge that the mythic patterns that drive and document human behavior are haphazard. Designs that incorporate unexpected patterns pervade African art because West Africans including those from Senegambia and the Mande people believe that, "evil travels in straight lines," and to evade, confound, and arrest it, the community must conceive artifacts with unusual arrangements (Thompson 222). Under this view, nature, checkered movement, unpredictable circumstances, and invisible directives undercut constant forces, but these interruptions are indispensable and welcome. Conflicting with prevailing Western social patterns, which are based on a patriarchy that flows straight down a hierarchy from male progenitor to male heir, West Africans display a penchant for unpredictability, so there is no pressing need to recover the kinship group as a lineal body because it is best represented by fragmentation: memories, half-buried relics, and sketchy memorabilia. Kennedy's theater adheres more often to the African model than to the traditional Western propensity for a progressivism. As Kimberly Benston observes, in Kennedy's creative world the subject is neither quite present nor absent but familiar, veiled, spectral ("Prefacing the Subject" 115).

Language, in turn, in Kennedy's hands is filtered through the haphazard and the jagged. I should add that this does not infer that all utterances in her pieces are equal. As I have mentioned, the mother's proclamations are much louder than any other; yet, there is ample room for discussion and for the kind of rituals where conversation/noise informs even a presupposing figure like an angry mamma. So we can say that during this later stage, Kennedy's literary and performance pieces become prophetic and tinged with jazz-like testimony, sometimes boisterous and unrelenting and, at others, merely fuming in the background, nevertheless, pushing out the encroaching Western lines that strive to invade her stage, patterns which she deems imposing.

Unfortunately, the intellectuals who have supported and applauded Kennedy's productions have also, through critique, smoothed out the play's jagged edges with analytic academic trowels. These treatments, however sophisticated, too often plunder and then narrativize Kennedy's past to draw straight lines between it and her characters: to effectively explain away the illogical and the feral in our culture and in her art. Highly conscious of this critical push to expunge the erratic by stripping her art bare, Kennedy counters her commentators in these post-eighties pieces by erecting barriers and applying back-sass or static. She disperses potential subjugators as well by continuing her dual thrust at both a culturally intimate audience and a more remote one: To those from home she predicts a purging hot wind while she urges her bourgeois viewer to action by holding him over the abyss.

Kennedy begins this portion of her journey with a memoir that first conceals and then randomizes the past, setting up a scenario and a geography that is ripe for a daughter/detective who must search out what these personal remnants may signify. Thus the critic finds herself situated as a follow-up researcher who needs to step in the footprints of the detective/guide who has been there before and has left bread crumbs. Reflect on Suzanne Alexander, the central figure from *Ohio State Murders* and of several other pieces from this cycle, as she reads aloud from a book on symbols, "A city should have a sacred geography never arbitrary but planned in strict accord with the dictates of a doctrine that the society upholds" (159). Urban planning is not arbitrary or purely aesthetically pleasing, but a system that fulfills state directives. Kennedy's impetus for her journey rests on unearthing colonialism's underpinnings, which she renders metaphorically as a vast city, a metropolis that levies various but consistent tyrannical acts on women and dark people. We join Suzanne on her trip to the metropolis' center.

This submerged city takes form as it rises from the depths by way of Suzanne Alexander's imaginings. She begins her adventure when she returns to the college campus/planned town that she helped to integrate during the early fifties, a period in her life that should have been idyllic but was marked instead by cruelty, ostracism and humiliation: "Their [the white coeds] way of laughing when they saw us [black coeds] coming into the lounge, then refusal to speak was a powerful language. It had devastated me" (167). Delving into those long-forgotten slights, Suzanne recalls as well how the campus terrified her, "The geography made me anxious" (152). Describing such ominous sights as, "University Hall, a vast dark structure" (152), "zigzagged streets" (152), "the ravine that would be the scene of the murder" (152), a classroom that is housed in a "temporary barrack-like structure" (153), and a row of sorority mansions that appear like a citadel (159), Suzanne ponders the threatening agents that strip her of her dreams. That her belongings were searched and that she was under the dorm monitor's constant surveillance (168), a stand-in for imperial power, add to the general ambiance that portends death and a counterclockwise turning away from democracy and equality. Further evidence to suggest that this university/urban site is designed to murder its fresh black female victims comes in the form of a constant snow and, most pronouncedly, in Suzanne's growing silence that results from the fact that she is denied entrance to the English major and is sidetracked to Elementary Education (171). Later, she is seduced and abandoned by an English instructor who fathers her twin girls; in the end, he kills them and himself.

Suzanne compares her college "education" to the experience of Thomas Hardy's Tess of the D'Urbervilles, a literary figure whose plight entails a similar loss of self inside a sinister landscape that has been rigged to trap and, ultimately, sacrifice her (154). The figurative surrender of Suzanne's twins (her creativity and future) makes it difficult for even the most recalcitrant viewer to escape the work's general message that Ohio State has retarded Suzanne's full potential. Kennedy emphasizes this institutional theft and murder more concretely when she includes the detail that the occasion for Suzanne's return to campus stems from the critic's insistence that Suzanne explain what motivates her play's violent imagery. Her answer is Ohio State, a comment that not only exposes the racist cruelty levied during the forties and fifties but also that of contemporary academics who search high [theory] and low [sociological/biographical] for explanations but do not consider how the very institutions that they serve not only torment black students but can afflict them with life-long, dread-filled nightmares. *Ohio State Murders*, therefore, is an exercise in placing the funhouse mirror on the building's exterior so that it radiates outward instead of searing the Negro flesh that resides within.

This method, akin to solar radiation, is one that Kennedy incorporates more often during her third cycle of writing. Take as another instance her 1990 prose piece, *Deadly Triplets: A Theatre Mystery and Journal*. In it she chronicles Suzanne's trip to England, where she must solve another homicide. Underneath the more recognizable mystery frame that traditionally preoccupies itself with an individual's incentives and impulses, more pressing, less localized affairs lie in wait. Suzanne ponders, "...who were these people who had conquered the world?" (106) and "Despite the enchantment, there was a subplot to England that I couldn't perceive" (124). The slaying and its solution serve as metaphors for the broader issue of how colonial systems function because Suzanne's perception grows keener, and she learns to connect many salient broad-based trends to her plight as a modern black woman: "...murder, ambition, greed, and political as well as personal power were kept fresh in my [her] mind" (119).

Each step that Suzanne takes discloses parallel dimensions that run between personal and global dynamics. In England and Ohio State, she learns how an imperial will often hides behind a labyrinth of civility and manners, a discovery that highlights both its structural flaw and strength: It is difficult to debunk because it hides behind a charming mask and takes the time to cover its tracks, but it is vulnerable because it depends on individuals to maintain its systemic functionability. Therefore, the potential exists for exceptional people to not only motor around these convoluted towns but dismantle them. For example, in both pieces there are characters such as David, Suzanne's future husband, and her Aunt Lou, in the *Ohio State Murders* and John Lennon in *Deadly Triplets* who help her fend off the devastating urban geography. These forces set the stage for Kennedy's polemic battles that surface throughout her work after 1987.

Another variation that emerges in the eighties is that even though she continues to incorporate repetition, incantatory and disruptive sounds, stream-of-consciousness, montage, doubles and feints, there are fewer occurrences of these modes and a mounting sense of urgency. Those owl noises from the sixties begin to form into clearly spoken accusations and a cry for restitution because colonial traps are not only set down in the geography but also spring from master texts. By the nineties, the playwright engages with psychology, especially the budding sub-field of colonial disorder. She treats this topic in various works but most unswervingly with *The Film Club (A Monologue by Suzanne Alexander)* and *Dramatic Circle*, a radio play based on *The Film Club*. In these terse, intentionally hysterical offerings, Suzanne Alexander awaits news from Africa about her husband, who had been missing for weeks after not returning as scheduled from a search mission to find a cure for his ailing friend, Frantz Fanon. Suzanne is pregnant and is accompanied by her sister-in-law Alice; each day they travel to the American Express office, anticipating a message. Although there is some ambiguity surrounding how Suzanne first encounters Dr. Freudenberger, we learn in both accounts that she becomes his patient (*The Dramatic Circle* suggests that he has been watching her for some time) and that he is the one to invite Suzanne and Alice to his purportedly cathartic reading group to distract them from their worries.

Freudenberger has selected Bram Stoker's *Dracula* and has slotted Suzanne and Alice Alexander to play Lucy and Mina, the vampire's victims. The analogy becomes clear when the doctor/stalker begins to drain the sisters, deliberately keeping them infirm so that he can keep them near him. Evidence of his duplicity can be found in the psychiatrist's literary choice: a hideously traumatizing tale about young women being depleted of their vitality and mothers being murdered along with their babies, not the calming narrative that would distract two women, one pregnant, who are nearly exhausted from anxiety. *Dracula* is a tale about mastery and domination, where resistance is complicated by the succubus' hypnotic skill that renders inert even the strongest will, an apt metaphor for an imperial siege.

Even more alarming is the manner in which Freudenberger's actions begin to mimic those of the demon, not that of the hero slayer, Van Helsig, that he pretends to affect during the group reading (191) or the hero/healer label that he hides behind professionally. Lurking in the garden as he watches the two women, Freudenberger, like the king vampire, can shape shift at will. Suzanne remarks to her sister, "It's shadowy but I think it's him" (189). And Alice later admits, "I had seen a figure and it had looked like Dr. Freudenberger and his hair had been white....Why would Sebastian be in our garden? What was the cause of his changed appearance?" (190). The "good" doctor conceals his identity, abilities, and intentions with physical disguise and cogent mesmerizing language. For instance, he has a logical explanation for each allegation that the women level, rationalizing his decision to read *Dracula* with the argument that it will provide a psychological brace for Suzanne to accept her husband's altered appearance after he has spent months in detention (one wonders how Freudenberger knows of David's condition and, if he has knowledge of it, why he does not share it with David's panicked loved ones). The psychiatrist also defangs his stalking with slick justification: "I wanted to appear as an apparition....To prepare Suzanne's mind for the darkness I knew she must face" (196). While outwardly simulating a sympathetic stance, the doctor's weird behavior signals that his relationship to these two women is shrouded. What is the darkness, and how does he obtain such foreknowledge that is so far beyond their ken? Neither the play nor the monologue will answer these queries, which seems to be the point: Freudenberger resides in a discursive realm that is forever beyond the Alexanders's reach, an empire that maintains rule with covertly aggressive, polished rationalism.

Accordingly, as dedicated detectives, Kennedy's lead figures in this late period release the predatory howls and grunts that escape from under the imperial mask. At one point, for instance, Freudenberger forgets himself and tells Suzanne, "Suzanne, you must not think of returning to Ghana [or your African ancestry and culture]. It might kill the baby. I forbid it." (188) But Suzanne resists his carping and controlling commands by hanging onto her own refrains, her own strengthening litanies, one from her husband and the other from Fanon: "My husband gives lectures on slave ships that crossed the Atlantic" (177, 193), and *But the war goes on and we will have to bind up for years to come the many, sometimes ineffaceable, wounds that the colonialists have inflicted on our people* (from Fanon 181, 196). In both cases, the words that comfort Suzanne revolve around black people's bold efforts to transcend through healing the cuts inflicted on them by the fallout from the Middle Passage, slavery, and African colonization by Europe. Although she does not say it directly, Suzanne is well aware that vampire bats, even in an alleged postcolonial moment, are numerous in the northern heights of London (187).

Distrust of rationalization courses through Kennedy's *Dramatic Circle*, a journey in repetition that leads the writer toward a renewed appreciation for porous revisionary historitization over the romanticism of film and linear narrative.[20] She continues to explore these issues in another of her Alexander plays, *She Talks to Beethoven*, a drama that is set as well during that pivotal time when Suzanne Alexander is separated from her husband David, who trails after Fanon in Africa. Philip Kolin has argued that this particular piece, "...offers healing consolation instead of the nightmarish world of fragmentation" (293), and that succor comes from Beethoven's symphonies. While I concur with Kolin that music soothes Suzanne (294), it does not mend or alleviate conflict entirely. Instead, the play is steeped in contestation between science and culture, documentation versus art, and female creativity held against male activity. The missing, bodiless, mythical Fanon becomes the elusive center around which these differing rubrics spin. David Alexander, Suzanne's often physically absent husband, develops a fascination for Fanon and finding him becomes David's vocation: "David traveled to Russia and then to France to meet Fanon. David and Suzanne had always traveled together, but now his research on Fanon, the trips the research required, were trips he forbade her to take. He said there was danger surrounding Fanon" (*Dramatic Circle* 183).

David is so smitten with the great thinker that he disseminates the doctor's ideas by broadcasting them over the radio. At times, Suzanne's connection to her husband is made through the tenuous thread of hearing him read Fanon's observations over the airwaves as if these words represent a secret transmission between her and her mate. Take the moment when Suzanne hears her husband's voice while she recuperates in Ghana after an unspecified illness; she listens as David announces: "Now the fragments have been put together by another self" (*She Talks to Beethoven* 140). This statement fills David with the great hope that drives him to abandon wife and country to embark on a perilous voyage that more than likely will end badly and painfully. His conviction is that science can cure the great social and psychological rifts/wounds that were brought on by the Middle Passage in the sense that, that which was dislocated, perforated, or lost can be refashioned into a whole.

Fanon, in his research on colonial "dis-eases," studied/examined and published his medical findings to discover a treatment. David Alexander clings to this optimism and uses Fanon's research methodology to help ease his wife's condition: as Suzanne languishes in her sickbed, David sketches her illness and explains surgical procedures to her (143). Endeavoring to make roadmaps from the inexplicable symptoms that manifest themselves over her body, David turns to Fanon's study on revolutionary Algerians. The irony is that his faith in science pulls David away from home and away from intimacy with his wife. So, even though Fanon and David are not as cold and manipulative as Freudenberger, there is a bond amongst the three, a tie that is comprised of a taste for rationalism to stand in the stead of and seal over home-life messiness/randomness, compiled moments of disjointed volatility.

In many respects, Beethoven represents Fanon's foil. Note that both figures craft intricate "theories" during martial times: Fanon endures Algerian and other colonial wars, and Beethoven observes Napoleon's mad march, which transformed his home city, Vienna, into "a dirty fog" (142). A friend of Beethoven's describes the composer's residence: "…his lodging was next to the city wall, and as Napoleon had ordered its destruction, blasts had just been set off under his windows" (143). The implication is that Beethoven's deafness may be related to the pounding mortar and the strain of impending hostile occupation; therefore, his case may be classified as a colonial disorder. He shares a frightening social reality with those twentieth-century Africans who were also in the grip of armed conflict to fend off imperial invaders. The musician's reaction to combat is to conceive disturbing, crashing symphonies that can drown out the gun's screeching pellets. His strength comes from cultural expression that has found a way to nod toward the unspeakable, documenting that same terrifying history for future generations. The composer translates the anger and despondency that has accumulated in Vienna's "dirty fog," a sweeping dust that includes the small and bold injustices that are levied by unsympathetic power: "He was venomous and embittered. He raged about everything and was dissatisfied with everything….He often banged his fist on the piano and made such a noise that it echoed around the room" (145). Out of the fleeting mass of sliding sounds that he can increasingly no longer annex, Beethoven produces masterpieces, ranging through notes that are crippled and deformed to his ears, reconstructing them as beautiful montage as he has little need to form the fragments into a smooth passionless bubble but allows each disconnected piece to announce his pain and agony. Suzanne finds camaraderie not in Beethoven's suaveness but in his madness and his rage.

Bryant-Jackson considers that Suzanne's conversation with the long-dead composer is an Egungun ritual where the dead are brought forth for guidance and praise (49). During these rites, the one who has passed on is cajoled by gifts and songs into returning to the earthly plain. In gratitude to the remembrance, the ancestor often bestows a bequest on the beckoner. In this instance, the composer grants Suzanne a reassuring prediction: "…David will return by morning, perhaps on the road with the musicians, perhaps even in disguise" (145). As Oracle, Beethoven seals the hope that has begun to seep from Suzanne's pores. Restoring her with the fortitude and confidence that only an unshakable, rebellious voice can furnish, the lost kinsman announces additionally art's power over science. Art can do for Suzanne what the hospital staff cannot because, encoded in Ludwig's message, is the inherent connection between creativity and masking that had preoccupied Kennedy for years. The African players who walk past Suzanne's residence symbolize alchemy or quick change that can transpose all kinds of states and faces from one locale to the next: they travel through a metaphysical portal, a clue or reassurance from Beethoven to Suzanne that her entreaties emptied into the play that she is working on do matter and are significant can even rival science.

By the end of *She Talks to Beethoven*, both partners have outside lovers: David's Fanon and Suzanne's Beethoven, a point that Kennedy reinforces with the closing line: "David's voice (*Not unlike* Beethoven's.): I knew he would console you while I was absent" (150). This doubling over and blurring suggests that the "I" is fluid, David thanking the artist for filling in, but also Beethoven pledging that he will return when David leaves again. Both can move into a fulcrum position in accord with Suzanne's requirement for intimacy because she can bring forth either one with her pen and imagination. Therefore, Suzanne learns to cope with David's obsession by finding a chemistry that she feels is as strong as his adherence to Fanon's antidote to Western intimidation. She controls her fear and her body by tapping into this well of artistic transposition (perhaps the solution to the Middle Passage's and colonialism's triage that Fanon and David search for in their copious notes and diagrams).

While there is no harmonious merging between the two chosen paths that Suzanne and David take in *She Talks to Beethoven*, there is mutual respect and a feeling that these two partners can work together, even though their trust resides in two altogether different containers. In many ways, this is one of Kennedy's more buoyant plays, not because it rests on art's ability to transcend pain but because the protagonist, Suzanne, has found a provisional resting place in the midst of social, political, and economic upheaval. Regrettably, this oasis soon evaporates as even the sign of the renowned ancestor/protector will be deconstructed (or at least gently shaken) by Kennedy. In her most recent work, traditional representation in the form of high culture (literary, musical, and dramatic genres) is examined for imperialistic residue and is set aside, ultimately, for the mundane, familial markers that record everyday living, as the writer trades in books, films, symphonies, and plays for home photographs, relics and clippings from family events, letters, even the memories of long-lost gardens. Take *June and Jean in Concert*, the only self-proclaimed musical that Kennedy has written to date, a production that is based sketchily on *People Who Led to My Plays*. That this piece spotlights her kin wrapped in a score that charts the African American musical tradition from spirituals to camp songs says much about the credence that Kennedy gives to black culture and memories.

Alongside this quick-change collection of melodies and sounds the photograph takes center stage and replaces the impersonal, big-screen celluloid that loomed over the dramatist's middle period. There are many references to snapshots in this late phase: "She [my mother] collected photographs of her and my father's youth in Atlanta and keeps them in scrapbooks so that I am able to imagine my parents as they were when they were young. She instills in me the desire to excel" (253). Other works feature the reproduced likeness's compelling, stimulating magnetism, "I [Suzanne] often found myself taking the faded letter from Gina and the four photographs out of the desk drawer, trying to make sense of them…sensing there was an incomplete mystery within them" (*Deadly Triplets* 75); "I [Suzanne] held up a photograph of my father's church" (*Sleep Deprivation Chamber* 6); and, in regard to a high school yearbook, "Their lovely faces and memories of their faces haunted me" (*Letter to My Students* 204). The visual text in Kennedy's hands is molded into an Egungun ceremony where the viewer not only peers into the past but discerns eyes staring back at her.

These crossed-over souls are drawn to the present by way of ritual. In turn, these convened spirits will bestow something on those who honor them: advice, strength, predictions, and wisdom. Echoing Beethoven, the images found in photographs sustain those who take the time to venerate them.

In the broadest sense, this concentration on the family album marks a step away from the mask as the prevailing trope in Kennedy's work. No longer will the opaque veil with its scant eye, nose, and mouth openings distinguish the manner in which she positions her performance space. In its stead, the more transparent, light-reflecting snapshot takes an honored seat, a choice that allows vision to become freer, keener, better able to roam around in the past and the associations that form it instead of floundering and grasping for a toehold behind a construct. The subject, then, begins to gel as an entity in its own right as it forms a vantage point and a voice that is not filtered through distancing mediation.

Another way to think about this "re-placement" is to imagine that with the album and the letters, the playwright brings her own implied engaged audience up on stage and begins to address her artistry to them and not the ones who watch the play from a safe distance. Returning to Sonnega's postulation that the audience that consumes "serious" black drama is often one that does not recognize its nuances and critiques, we can understand why Kennedy may be prompted to turn toward a communal circle, even if she has to invent it with pictures and letters. In fact, she begins to make more pointed references to the estrangement that comes from laboring in a space where one's life and art are continually repackaged and objectified. In *Letters to My Students on My Sixty-First Birthday*, David Alexander protests the academy's exclusivity, "Even though they honor me…this is like a white country club" (207). Later in the same piece, a white dramatist mounts a biographical play that probes and recounts Suzanne Alexander's life and career. This director incurs Suzanne's wrath because she snoops without permission, interrogates Suzanne's relatives, and even dares to question Suzanne about Suzanne's life as if the director knows more about the subject than the subject. Suzanne notes acerbically, "My life (as seen by the local playwright) was to open in fourteen days. The piece she invented was a long monologue" (224). Suzanne's censure comes from her deriding proclamation that the colonialist director has selected a simple monologue to present Suzanne, a formal choice that cancels out and overwrites Suzanne's life-long project to build art that features various angles, usually splicing several genres to follow the complexity of travel, association, and intersecting perspectives. Flattening Suzanne out to a linear narrative—pure evil in some West African cosmologies—and shaping that narrative into a traditional, realistic stage piece is an imperial act that reads/immobilizes the native to slot her into a lower social strata.

Suzanne equates this act of mastery on the part of her theatrical biographer to the simultaneous police brutality and trial that her son Teddy is facing. Although Teddy is the victim of a beating by the authorities, he is being indicted for resisting the police, an apt metaphor for his mother's relationship to her biographer/captor. At one point, Suzanne depicts blatantly the systemic pattern that grants colonial power its supremacy, "Teddy, you mean they know all your information and you know nothing of theirs?" (225). Freudenberger, the criminal justice system, and the white dramatist all govern by virtue of their ability to manipulate discourse, not only labeling Teddy as a criminal and Suzanne as a monologue but by likening the theatrical space to the same dynamics that inform juridical proceedings. The director and the officer continue to treat the Alexanders as deviant and abnormal just as Negro Sarah was deviant and abnormal to a previous generation of viewers. By revealing that the traditional performance venue is an arena where the other (or others) can be examined and judged (usually condemned), Kennedy draws a line between liberating cultural efforts and those that support the state (often through brutal repetitious displays). To locate an escape from theater's overarching trial-anchored dynamic, Kennedy continues to search out new ways to control her dramatic vehicle so that it does not mimic the encroaching design of a master class. Yet, while avoiding the genre's tendency toward hegemonic control, the writer still needs it to critique and debunk hierarchy and supremacy. So, she turns a deconstructive gaze on both history and culture, while resurrecting fragmentary imagery from hope chest memories.

Any reviewer of Kennedy's work is overwhelmed by the sheer number of floating literary, musical, and historical references, citations that indicate the far-reaching breadth of the playwright's storehouse. Certainly, during the sixties and seventies and well into the nineties, the dramatist extracts from this broad and deep knowledge base. So when the narrator declares in *A Letter to Flowers*, a prose piece that is memoir, catalog, and travel narrative, "I couldn't read any more. I recognized the Bronte material was an attempt to find a lost romanticism" (265), we pause and mark this as an indicator that Kennedy has embarked on another venture on her long voyage, for she has grown disenchanted with the very classical texts that gave her so much succor and inspiration during previous iterations. Specifically, what grows in significance as formal, set genres fall off is a series of home-spun documents. Kennedy examines everyday scraps to draw out useful bits, while discarding the rest. *A Letter* spotlights flowers and missives, evoking the image of old pressed roses hidden in obscure volumes that only hold meaning to the close friends and relatives that share special, nearly secret bonds, filigree formed over shared events and recollections. In turn, this new set of notes writes over the literary book that it invades, eventually tendering an alternative expressive form.

Mundane responsibilities hover around these "speaking mementos" as trips to the doctor with an elderly mother, challenging a neighbor who chain smokes, answering numerous phone calls that are usually from acquaintances asking for advice interrupt the writer's process. However disruptive, the abundant distractions work like a catalyst, driving the writer to revelation: "I fear succumbing to darkness as my heroines do. I can't stop thinking about Florence, Italy in the dark January New York" (*Letter to Flowers* 270), and "I tried to reread my play. And I saw more than ever my *Narrative 2000* was about succumbing to darkness, hatred and death" (283). Comparing this work and *She Talks to Beethoven*, it would appear that Kennedy begins to question the Egungun ceremony that she had previously praised. If modern art, as exemplified by her own in-process play, has exalted the passed-on world over the living, if it is filled with fleeting shadows, then what is the artist other than death's mistress? Given this reaction to writing, the artist sets out to redefine creativity, an insurrection that she shares with fellow Black Arts Movement advocates who sought vehicles that elevate the mundane over the stately. Take, for instance, what happens to narrative in *A Letter to Flowers*; it becomes encased within an epistolary frame: "I sent him [my son] a story I had written about a trip we took to Rome when he was a little boy….He showed me his portfolio. It was called Close to Nature" (262). Stories are shared with kin while the traditional theater-going audience is ignored. So she, similar to Black Arts Era dramatists, moves her show/stage within a tight-knit environment, albeit one that is more narrowly defined than the black world that these artists had in mind. For the most part, Kennedy's communiqués conjure up lush moments and are strong tributes to daily life.

In their bold endeavor to ride over colonial gazes and commands, Kennedy's flowers are no less potent a defense than revolutionary images of fire and retribution.[21] Primarily, they reverse power dynamics and take privilege away from an unseen spectator who ascribes meaning to a visual scene from a safe distance, granting that spectator immense interpretive license. Instead, "reading power" flows back toward the friend or acquaintance to whom the letter is addressed. So, the epistolary frame augments that the spectator is an interloper, for he is always already placed as a transgressing outsider who steals the subject's personal thoughts. A colonizer, like Dr. Freudenberger, can no longer hide behind the mask of objective observer but is highlighted as a thief who violates the letter and both its writer and recipient by reading it. Taking this one degree further, all reading outside a free and reciprocal exchange of ideas between mutually supportive parties becomes theft. Therefore, everyday ritual becomes equivalent to cultural liberation because "high" literary genres are tainted by and sealed within centuries of colonial piracy.

As Kennedy travels on her journey, she more frequently inserts letters into her theatrical pieces, pitting performativity against the sent message's confidential registers, the engagement resulting in a bolder, more candid structure that increasingly steps around the mask to address particular parties across time. Voice, whether in a rage or nurturing or some intricate combination of tones, speaks person to person, person to system rather than in the diffuse modalities that characterize her early work. Before delving into the specific contours of how this energy is manifested in Kennedy's latest offerings, I must highlight an additional force that, alongside imperialism, has become, in the playwright's estimate, another trend that impacts on the global community, and that is the widespread violence that erupts out of centuries of inequities. *Motherhood 2000, Letter to My Students on My Sixty-first Birthday* and *Sleep Deprivation Chamber* are loaded with apocalyptic undertones that envisage a final, savage, quickly approaching horizon, a vast, impending breach that is not entirely undesirable or unwarranted.[22] This coming shelf will create a chasm that will produce a cleansing wind, or smoke as Kennedy calls it, that will reveal, rather than cover, heretofore submerged powers: "I see smoke connects my life and work..."(*A Letter to Flowers* 277). With this tool/chisel in the form of a dense breeze, alienation and double consciousness can be defeated. I suggest further that this smoke is created, at least partially, by a bonfire of smoldering veils, a ritual that is presided over by Ellison-like invisible people who rise up from the ruins.

Several of the hallucinatory sequences in *A Letter to My Students* depict chilling scenarios that bridge mythic and material worlds. Suzanne Alexander is preoccupied with the people who live underneath the West Side Highway in New York City as she worries over her son's upcoming court case against the Virginia State Police (198). Similar to many of Kennedy's figures, the lost people who are championed by "the man with the baseball bat" are at least double-sided if not more multifaceted than that. This menacing force is both unsettling and disruptive but represents an avenger because he is both besieged and the featured social agent (reminiscent of Ogun, god of iron). For example, Suzanne dreams "…three thousand soldiers were sent to Broadway and 86th Street where the King of Spain was making fortifications….And this week 198 persons are dying of plague in Riverside Park near the Boat Basin at 79th. And Teddy [her son] died last night in the Tower where he remained under sentence of death because I don't have the right letters of character" (216). Incarcerated and failing, the beleaguered have no choice: they must fight for their survival or submit to the siege visited on them by the imperial monarch. This apparition portends revolutionary conditions as Suzanne's nightmare shifts from containment and death scenes to discord: "…the homeless man with the baseball bat is spreading garbage" (222). Once attacked and reviled, the "dispossessed" become the hunters that surge into the city's geography and begin to redraw the lines between civility and savagery. Emerging with weapons, clamoring din, and irreverence, they represent a nascent era that makes the old way of concealing virulent aggression behind a pleasant veneer obsolete. Another way to interpret this transition is to imagine that what was once carnival and peripheral has become central and decidedly non-theatrical but material, as the times have led to a future where skirmishes on hegemony will no longer be wrapped in irony, parody, or other distancing techniques.

The state of things as rendered by these disturbing vistas parallels, perhaps, Kennedy's own exhaustion of form because, by this time, she has tried nearly every genre, sifting them through her own purification chamber to recover some useful fragments that will allow her to tell the story of the Middle Passage's and colonialism's massive impact while ferreting out transcendent hatches. The last (or latest) straw is her eventual disillusionment with the epistle and is represented by the mother's unanswered letters that are sent out to various officials to secure her son's release from criminal charges. In *Letter to My Students*, the missive becomes a deeply embedded trope as Suzanne composes a bulletin that alludes to message-writing and her realization that the epistle, no matter how egalitarian a mode, only works if the recipient is predisposed to take it seriously: "I can tell Edelstein [the lawyer] thinks I may jeopardize Teddy's case by writing too many letters. He told me to write two…I have written seventeen…'You're too emotional, Mrs. Alexander,' he said, as we walked through glass offices" (209). What had once been Suzanne's means to reactivate ritual and kinship networks is stripped down to "emotionalism" by the lawyer who stands in discursively for the trial. So, as long as trials dictate credibility and norms, then letters can only register on a sub-discursive level; therefore, while Suzanne may reach her students, family and associates with her missives, she cannot use them to alter the structure of or change the court proceedings.

This reveals the personal dispatch's limitation as a form of social redress because a higher body retains the ability to authenticate or invalidate the letter's value. So, the trial maintains supremacy over the epistle by determining its worth, and it can also punish the writer for elevating it on an equal par with legal discourse, as Patrice Alexander observes in a statement mailed to her mother Suzanne concerning Teddy's police brutality/assault case: "The letters have infuriated them. And they're going to teach us a lesson" (*Sleep Deprivation Chamber* 39). Judicial discourse views these author's notes as mere arrogance, an interpretation that represents another state method that commandeers the subject's interior space.

Notwithstanding that the letter fails Kennedy and her character Suzanne, by adopting it, the playwright is able to make critical observations. As it is often associated with feminine writing from *Pamela* and Anne Bradstreet to the *Color Purple*, the letter in the West has been recognized as a woman's form for the most part. Consequently, Kennedy aligns it with mothers who send them to those under her care (children and students) or on their behalf. When the lawyer chastises Mrs. Alexander for sending out too many character references and complaints to state officials, her response is, "He judged me for being a mother" (209). Mothers send out corrective notices to billing offices, requests to teachers, and fundraising pleas to other parents and backers. That is what they do. When the lawyer de-legitimates Suzanne's central mode of conducting business and establishing order, he reduces motherhood's stature along with the domestic sphere that she commands. Therefore, Oshun, who is by this time turning out her hot face, has no other choice but to locate another type of communication if she is to fulfill her mission to "free her children from the tower."

Oshun's call for a better instrument gives rise to two strains in Kennedy's work as the letter recedes in potential: She returns to myth (which she never left, but she focuses on it more), and she summons a matrilineal line. References to myth have shaped Kennedy's creations from the sixties on, but, during the most recent years, that light-handed sounding has changed to a full-out immersion in ancient tales.[23] *Motherhood 2000* is about an avenging parent who takes part in a Miracle Play in post-apocalyptic New York to insinuate herself next to and eventually murder her son's tormentor, and *Grendel and Grendel's Mother* signifies clearly on *Beowulf.* So the emphasis is not so much on showing how the old tale is still relevant in contemporary society but locating a culture's origin and changing it at its source. In Kennedy's hands, an African American mother tunnels inside legend by killing the man who beat her son, and in *Grendel and Grendel's Mother*, another African American female figure becomes the heroine (Beowulf) by defeating the evil that threatens her clan. Under each revision, a white, male lead role is played/altered by a black woman.[24] This, I think, is a bold imaginative move that is similar to Kennedy's transforming Hollywood stars into black people during the seventies,[25] but, perhaps, an even more formidable decision in the sense that she no longer projects through imaginative transparencies but remolds the framing texts that most significantly construct any given people's symbolic universe. In many ways, legend is the closest that humans can come to God-speak. By placing her black mothers in this fulcrum position, she no longer situates them within hierarchical power dynamics but beyond and over them. This shift away from the epistle and toward and through myth endows black female subjects with an enhanced representational mobility and the potential to set things right because myth empowers them to materialize anywhere across and before history so that they can act absolutely, not in response to others.

Kennedy's reinvestment in ancient forms is accompanied by the reemergence of what Bryant-Jackson, building on Chinosole, would call a "matrilineal diaspora," a female line that traces its origins to Africa even if the connection is fragmentary and restless (56). For inherent in these resurrections of Miracle Plays and the Grendel tale lies a desire to re-center African Diaspora women as originators. We see this plan manifested in the interchange between mothers and daughters and aunts and nieces, the introduction of a twin sister in *June and Jean in Concert*, in the creation of a daughter, Patrice (after Lumumba) in *Letter to My Students*, and in the statement from Kennedy, "I feel that my writing is an extension of my relationship with my mother, of talking with her" (Betsko and Koenig interview 247). These black female characters search for missing fathers, defend sons, predict the future, teach, write, work in war plants, record family history, play all manner of music, become ancestors, tend to the sick, give comfort, and listen to endless complaint. What connects these black women is their charge to protect home in its various configurations from Africa to family to a cultural legacy.

This social placement of black women in Kennedy's art follows the arc that nineteenth-century black women writers established as they too employed literature to recast and bolster yearnings for and constructions of black homes/states. The difference, however, is that while these early artists mold perfect or utopian social centers, Kennedy utilizes her art to construct a series of mask and masking techniques to deflect attention away from the family/intimate community and channel it down a chute that leads to various blinds, using the colonizer's own morbid curiosity to steer him away from that which really matters. That is, she relied on this technique until recently as fewer diversionary culverts pop up in her work. With the rise in physical violence and the frequent coloring of that violence as white on black, the playwright begins to tool her pieces to respond to what she sees as an approaching storm of global proportions. Overall, the impression that is given by these late texts is that time is running out, and, in the rift, the opportunity exists for black female subjects to re-position themselves in the cultural strata from object (who is unaware of her cultural past) as is the case in *Funnyhouse* to anointed heroine as is the case in *Grendel and Grendel's Mother*. No longer trapped within a master's frame, black ancestors from photographs, scraps of words from letters, phone calls, and remembrance will keep alive not only a present generation of black women but the ones who came before and the ones that will follow.

Kennedy's extensive journey has brought her to a place where her art no longer requires a dominant masking trope to hide the power, courage, strength, and vision of her black female figures. I should note that Kennedy is still writing, so there is no assurance that this will be the last leg of her long trek. Given the trend, one expects that there will be additional confabs and interludes with form and voice. Whatever the vehicle, Kennedy's commitment to preserving a legacy that she holds dear has not diminished nor has the zeal with which she defends her personal past and the traditions of black life. While many of her fellow Black Arts era artists have long since moved into other fields, some even renouncing their early work, Kennedy continues to manufacture meaningful pieces that demand that Western atrocities be "re/addressed" and that she be able to live in a world where she is not put on trial categorically because of her blackness. Whether she reaches out from behind a false face, moves through transparent film, or speaks in the voice of ghosts and slayers, rage still moves the sails of Kennedy's schooner.

NOTES

[1] I am relying on Larry Neal's definition: "The Black Arts Movement is radically opposed to any concept of the artist that alienates him from his community....It envisions an art that speaks directly to the needs and aspirations of black America. In order to perform this task, the Black Arts Movement proposes a radical reordering of the Western cultural aesthetic" (62).

[2] Gavin observes that "...many in the black community, especially those active in the early black movement, criticized her theater because of her emphasis on the negative aspects of the black experience" (147). Carla McDonough notes, "...she was not initially embraced as a spokeswoman for the civil rights of blacks or for feminism...Kennedy was largely overlooked by the critical community until the 1980's" (173).

[3] Sources on Kennedy's plays and their productions include Gavin, Overbeck, and Sollors.

[4] A fine way to concretize this postulation that the Negro becomes a go-between is to consider the manner in which *The Cosby Show* functions. Critics have argued that this television panorama remains popular with white audiences because it normalizes a black family, making then appear no different than a similarly slated white family. Therefore, as norms, its characters can negotiate between both black and white worlds.

[5] Ruination is a term from the Caribbean that means a return of the land to its original state. See Michelle Cliff's *No Telephone to Heaven.*

[6] Paul Carter Harrison departs from this general trend that strips Kennedy of her revolutionary edge. He argues that both Kennedy and Baraka employ mytho-absurdist inventions to stimulate a Black Theater movement that possesses its own expressive voice ("Praise/Word" 6).

[7] All references to Kennedy's plays are from *The Adrienne Kennedy Reader.*

[8] See David Walker's *Appeal* and Martin Delany's work as paradigmatic early contributors to the black radical tradition.

[9] Kennedy mentions that, while she worked on *Funnyhouse*, she began to question European aesthetics: "In Ghana and for the rest of the thirteen month trip I stopped straightening my hair" (*The Adrienne Kennedy Reader* 27).

[10] I am reminded of Valerie Smith's essay, "Loopholes of Retreat: Architecture and Ideology in Harriet Jacobs's *Incidents in the Life of a Slave Girl.*" Smith interprets Jacobs's confinement to an attic for seven years as a metaphor for the general condition of black women in America. Even though her mobility is checked, Jacobs can survey the happenings below her, not only to observe and record/memorize them but critique them as well.

[11] African American music is filled with these strange noises from Ella's scat to Busta Rhymes' whoo-ha. They seem to be the places where untranslatable individual creativity resides.

[12] Forte comments on this pattern as well, "...these texts...send me...into history, into the critical examination of historical parameters of specific cultural conditions" (164).

[13] Wilson Jeremiah Moses has written extensively on the black prophet and his mission, otherwise known as the African American Jeremiad. Note especially Moses's *Black Messiahs and Uncle Toms.*

[14] It is clear that Kennedy is preoccupied with the manner in which revenge shapes social patterns on a local, national and global scale. During the early eighties, she adapted several of Euripides' tragedies, such as *Electra* and *Orestes*, that focus specifically on how to and who

should dispense justice. In this series, a brother and sister murder their mother (Clytemnestra) and their stepfather (Aegisthus), who both plotted against and killed their father (Agamemnon), an intrigue that was set in motion because Agamemnon sacrificed Clytemnestra's daughter Iphegenia, a literal blood-bath broken only by the wise words of aged Tyndareus: "…this chain of murder can never end since the last to kill is doomed to permanent sentence of death by revenge. …purge their guilt by banishment not death and by so they stop the cycle of revenge. …These fits of madness are what you pay for murder. Heaven itself has made you mad" (104–5).

[15] References to *Deadly Triplets* come from the University of Minnesota (1990) publication.

[16] Kennedy's mythological references are numerous. Sollors highlights the fact that *Funnyhouse of a Negro* is a rewriting of the myth of the flying African who returns home from the New World by the force of his/her will, and *The Owl Answers* taps into the story of the Greek goddess Pallas Athena who has African origins (x). She also rewrites *Beowulf* (*Grendel and Grendel's Mother*) and the tragedy of Electra and Orestes.

[17] It should be noted that even though the family does not overcome its numerous and catastrophic ruptures by the close of *Movie Star*, the mother and daughter become closer as a result of having to deal with the various tragedies that befall them: "…my mother cried in my arms outside the hospital, *We* [emphasis mine] were standing on the steps, and she shook so that I thought both of us were going to fall headlong down the steps" (78).

[18] Morrison refers to the African Diaspora's thoughts and experiences as an outlawed collection of "unspeakable things unspoken."

[19] See hooks's groundbreaking book, *Talking Back.*

[20] Confirmation that film's romanticism falls off during this trip to London can be found in the details of *The Dramatic Circle.* Alice Alexander is transformed by this waiting period as are all the Alexanders. Alice is a director, but after this interlude in London, she stops producing movies.

[21] Consider, for instance, the manner in which Suzanne Alexander braids together a testimonial honoring her family and a plea to thwart the criminalization of her son and other young black men. In a letter addressed to Virginia's Governor Wilder, Suzanne protests her son's brutal, unprovoked beating from a police officer: "We are an outstanding black American family….We are now a grieved family….Our son is being persecuted by the Arlington Police Department just as surely as happened in the Deep South in the 1930s or during Emmett Till's time" (*Sleep Deprivation Chamber* 8).

[22] This apocalyptic vision is described in various ways from plagues in Riverside Park (*Letter to My Students*) to dark ravines (*The Ohio State Murders)* to post-war open theaters built on civilization's ashes (*Motherhood* 2000) to great storms and an earthquake's epicenter (*Sleep Deprivation Chamber*).

[23] Kennedy revised Euripides' *Electra* and *Orestes* in the seventies, but these pieces did not splice together myth with personal narrative, a decision that granted them a more traditional structure. By the nineties, the writer remakes these ancient tales more liberally by breaking them apart with conscious intrusion, which results in an artistic product that turns in on and away from the original story: more carnival energy is applied to the ancient myths so that their underlying form and meaning are revised rather than merely modernized.

[24] Although a few saints are women of color, the majority are white males.
[25] Kennedy grows increasingly preoccupied with *Hamlet* during this latter period as well.

SIX

Dipped in the Pool: Shange's Choreopoems as Atlantic Crossings

IT SEEMS somewhat incongruous that this final chapter on the African American female dramatic tradition concludes with an artist who considers herself a poet, not a playwright; yet, of all the women mentioned in this study, her name is the one most readily associated with the American theater.[1] Ntozake Shange, like many of her African American female predecessors, gives birth to compositions that not only span but splice genres, so ascribing rigid disciplinary boundaries to her products would be not only inaccurate but presumptuous. Nevertheless, her contributions are crucial to a rounded understanding of what black women have done to and with American culture via its performing arts. In many ways, her puissant stage treatments that began appearing in the mid-seventies and are still revamped today trace a full circle in this African American women's tradition. Returning to the thematic and aesthetic preoccupations first treated by Pauline Hopkins during the late nineteenth century, Shange places her audience on an intertextual ride that covers stops from a black girl's backyard to specific locales in the United States such as New Orleans, Detroit, New York, Chicago, and St. Louis that have held notable cultural significance to African Americans to a multinational neighborhood comprised of women of color from Jamaica, Cuba, Nicaragua, Puerto Rico, and El Salvador to, more generally, working-class people everywhere. Here she charts both the horrific ruptures (her main trope is rape) and the triumphant re-patternings (dance/music) that derive from the Middle Passage's massive disembowelment that she views as not restricted solely to African people but globally injurious in the way that it has shaped an interlocking economic system that continues to strike and impale the world's folk.

Shange accomplishes this mission by repudiating standard Western theatrical form and supplanting it with a more nimble, dance-centered model that braids in lyrical verse with live music (if possible) and over-the-top symbols in the form of colorful costuming and unavoidable visual props. Character disappears in favor of performances that only adhere to roles long enough to deliver specific snatches of experience. Yet, even without character development, individuality is upheld. Additionally, the quick metamorphosis of choreographed line changes is evident in the structure's totality, as mood slides into posture and posture stretches into rhythm. By design, these plays are meant to be improvisational and freshly tweaked on each occurrence, comparable to the minstrel show, which is their closest relative on the theatrical ancestral tree.[2]

Shange's stage offerings, which she has dubbed choreopoems, sound on express earth-spaces that are saturated with salty weeping, death, and mayhem while they chart as well the ensuing challenge to this pain, talismans that often arrive in interwoven form: a fusion of song, choreography, cooking, and fashion. Her most sensitive and intense scrutiny rests on African American rites and practices, positioning them as touchstones for her raids into colonized sites from across the world. Given this emphasis on culture as a shield against terror or, more specifically, a way to survive it, even if temporarily, it is safe to argue that the poet practices what Paul Carter Harrison has referred to as Kuntu Drama: the use of song, dance, and drum to bring about a total engagement of body and spirit which testifies to the continuation of African people in the Americas (*Kuntu Drama* 7).

Kuntu modes bridge generations, often across appalling chasms; in step with this school, this theater entices many voices, reproduces many articulations across the performance field, be they in the guise of spoken word, percussion, flute, stringed instruments (especially bass), or rhythmic movement. Thus what operates tacitly is a perpetual ring of switched-on listeners and declarers that overlap and trade roles. The function of such energetic, diffuse instability is that it can deliver what Harrison recognizes as "the imperatives of the community's moral universe which revitalizes the features of black humanity" (19), a chorus that encircles both the living and the dead so that in Kuntu productions when figures appear to be talking aloud, in faith, they may be speaking to a spectral ancestral array.

Shange's choreopoems embed galvanized co-agents in the choir that stand next to individualized proclamations. Shange has observed that "I started writing because I had to have an answer, I had to hear a voice....And nobody was going to give it to me. So, I gave it to myself" (Blackwell interview 136). Dialogue's centrality situates Shange's orchestrations within the sacred rites classification that Harrison defines, and it further aligns ritual with prayer, prayer defined as the Africanist belief in ancestor communion that is initiated by way of ceremony (singing, choreography, drumming, and chanting). I would venture that her visions inscribe a spiritual raising that has come to be known in the African American vernacular as the "shout out," a custom of projecting out terms and slogans to mark figures, specific times, and places for posterity to let others know that *we* (the caller and the called) are alive and vibrant. So if God exists in this matrix, he/she is situated amongst the crowd and is bellowing out her sentiments and life force across the blacktop just like everyone else. During this practice, the competing noise connotes strength, not confusion or a loss of clarity because the spoken/performed phrases, lyrics, titles, general themes, symbols, and steps in the parading hail of affirmations beckon social formation through their familiarity even though that familiarity is rearranged ad infinitum. We recognize as well that, while an assuring custom, the shout out is also staunchly rebellious because it follows its own zigzagged, electrified path to create something fresh from present poses and sounds.

I insist on the "shout out" as opposed to the more frequently referenced call-and-response motif because I believe that Shange's work branches out from the latter's more staid, ordered rules. Call and response, while certainly a dialogue, implies a sequence and a protocol whereby a leader extends himself to a group, and it, in turn, replies with idioms that are predictable and easily recognized by the membership as suitable. Shouting out entails more wild vitality, more fluctuation as one is not sure what the speaker from the floor might say when she grabs the microphone, so an element of fun and surprise typifies these exchanges/performances. Also, an authorized guide is denied; no speaker has greater importance than any other. As there is no principal speaker, one may only gain props (proper respect) by levying a toast that is profound, unique, and appropriate, therefore leaving the door open to a democratic dispersal of power and an auditorium where each member can travel to the spotlight as the line between showman and consumer is blurred. Ben Bratley describes this phenomenon as an ensemble where the participants feed one another with reciprocal energy (C16).

Once this raucous conversational mode is wedded to physical gyrations that kick out from rotating compass points, it results in what has been called funk or the ultimate quick change and intentional loss of cohesion and resumption of it, a sliding maelstrom of beats and sounds that tend to hover on the bass line, patterned echoes formed by musicians who like to converse with underwater bones. As I will explore these concepts in greater detail shortly, it is sufficient to remark that funk restores the individual's sovereignty through a healing process that is set off by massive vibration: hope restored through physical and metaphysical rearrangement. Connecting this African American outlook to the American Theater grants the poet a dramatic agility that helps her to move through and around time. In the most abstract sense, Shange creates from a philosophical base that we can call funk driven, a positionality that she transmits often through shout-out inflected aesthetics.

Starting out as a poet and dancer, Shange segued into text arrangement with her emotionally taut, influential choreopoem, *for colored girls who have considered suicide/when the rainbow is enuf*, that, according to Shange's introduction, found its home in the bars, women's studies' lounges, and small performance spaces of northern California during 1974. The piece sets a collection of lyrical reflections to music and requires seven female dancers/orators, who are only identified by the color that each wears. The figures adopt various geographical locations and move through suites of loving, war, child care, estrangement, vulnerability, and awakening (Sechita, an African deity is resurrected). Each dancer/wordsmith glides in and out of the limelight as she imparts a memory and then steps back to allow the next sister to speak so that each poetess is both chorus and headliner. After a receptive and encouraging response from the many who enjoyed the play on the West Coast, in 1975 Shange transported it East, auditioning it in New York. Moving from DeMonte's bar to the Henry Street Settlement and finally on to the Booth Theater on Broadway in 1976, Shange managed to achieve what many African American female playwrights had aimed for: a commercial hit that retained the integrity and sincerity of a piece that serves black female participants first (everyone else is invited as well but is not centered as the implied recipient). Speaking to women of color with no apology for her decision to do so, Shange manufactures a show out of the situations and considerations that face young black and brown women, especially those from the working class.[3] Incorporating current speech that explores everything from black female sexuality, poverty, a love for music and dance to the Vietnam War and domestic violence, *for colored girls* ignites its audience. It is so stirring that many professional and amateur groups rushed to execute the play. College campuses, neighborhood arts centers, and local theaters mounted it, while it opened before women prisoners, concretizing it as a rite of passage for many women who had not found literary or theatrical works that treated the issues that pressed most heavily on them.[4]

It has succeeded in stirring its targeted group because it highlights marriage, relationships, child-rearing, and female self-actualization and because it weaves sound, movement, and costuming to reveal these stories. *For colored girls*, then, is a novel piece that embraces both the performers and the partakers within its formal construction: there is a place for nearly everyone from the singer to the dancer to the designer to the versifier to the woman in the bleachers who can shout out in response to the scenes. After winning an Obie in 1977 for her first stage poem, Shange followed with *a photograph: lovers in motion*, an unrelenting peek into the self-destructive and callous manner in which modern mechanical culture has resulted in care and empathy's demise, only to be replaced by exploitation and deception in professional and personal dealings. The drama was first produced in 1977 in conjunction with Joseph Papp's New York Shakespeare Festival. Next came a piece in 1978 that centers on one woman's past and her budding consciousness, *boogie woogie landscapes*.[5] Music accompanies her on her journey from childhood through the discovery that her plight is linked to a large-scale conflicts that emanate from excessive greed.

spell #7: geechee jibara quik magic trance manual for technologically stressed third world people was produced in 1979 also as part of the New York Shakespeare Festival. Maintaining the choreopoem format, *spell #7* visits the minstrel theme, masking, conjuring and the general performance imperative of the black self, given the hostile terrain in which it aspires to thrive. In this heated two-act farce, the darky is paraded, ridiculed, and then redrawn, eventually, as a necessary ingredient in a widely cast recipe concocted to stem any further packaging and sale of blackness through dominant channels. Other productions include *Mother Courage and Her Children* (1980); *Shapes, Sadness, and the Witch* (1984); *Betsy Brown: A Rhythm & Blues Musical* (1989); *From Okra to Greens/ A Different Kinda Love Story: A Play with Music & Dance* (1992); and *Love Space Demands* (1992). Shange has collaborated with Jessica Hagedorn and Thulani Nkabinde on *Where the Mississippi Meets the Amazon* (1977) and with Eric Simonson and Joseph Shabalala on *Nomathemba* (1995). In addition to these sets, she has offered us poetry and novels that include *Betsey Brown, Sassafrass, Cypress and Indigo, Liliane: Resurrection of a Daughter, Ridin' the Moon West: Word Paintings*, and *nappy edges*.

The critical reception to Shange's stage works has been mixed, nearly polarized into two camps: those who condemn her for her negative portrayal of black men (and cannot get beyond that point) and those who commend her work because of its innovative structure and its daring in introducing controversial matters like rape, drug use, child abuse, and corporate and state savagery. The former assessment that restricts itself to the poet's male characterizations has been discussed lavishly by political pundits in the form of reviewers, and I find no reason to elaborate on this train of thought, while the latter, ultimately more fruitful, tack has been taken by theater scholars. Take as proof Brown-Guillory's remark that, "Shange's theater pieces generally do not conform to traditional dramatic structure" (*Their Place* 96–97) and John Timpane's observation that the writer, "insists on the rough edge, the open, the fragment" (203). Undoubtedly, her refusal to adopt European-based dramatic arrangements has resulted in Shange's overwhelming influence that has revolutionized the American theater as she has helped to marshal in a slew of performance pieces that resist naturalism's linearity while still managing to satisfy popular tastes. Because of Shange's enterprise, the contemporary commercial theater now features routinely more alinear shows that juggle irony, music, dance, and dramatic elements. Even recent revivals such as Broadway's *Grease* and *Chicago* sift their elements through the sardonic distancing that the choreopoems hinge on and make stylish.

In spite of the generous response that the poet's art has elicited concerning its politics and structure, her intertextuality has not been commented on nearly enough. Shange began shaping texts to receive answers, the same stimulus that drove generations of African American female playwrights before her as they too interposed epistles into their scripts. Shange engages often with her "mentors," argumentative ghosts that range from chattering benevolent, uplift-minded black artists to the many misrepresentations of colored folk that have coursed through modernity. Take as a case in point, s*pell # 7*, which commences with the following stage direction, "*there is a huge black-face mask hanging from the ceiling of the theater as the audience enters. in a way the show has already begun*" (7). This looming sign does much to explain how Shange has situated her art: it implies that the contemporary imagination is yoked to a series of long-standing dominant fantasies. As she stands her choreopoem under the minstrel's awning, she admits that the American theater has imposed significant roadblocks that check her mobility, but, instead of reading the nation's cultural history as pure unmitigated tragedy, Shange re-fires this painful panoply, molding it into her own dramatic refrain.

Whether to face and reply to a supportive or a potentially ominous source, turning toward the past grants stability to her designs that would otherwise be a disconnected series of chants, poetry, dance and rituals (Brown-Guillory, *Their Place* 41). Thus, this ingrained talking back across time and space comprises Shange's narrative platform. Without this guide, the rebellious funkiness of Shange's pieces would color her work iconoclastic. So, regardless of the fact that her form rebels against linear order, the tales that she dramatizes, no matter how broadly referenced, follow the contours of that imperative to bridge generational lines as she speaks to the

American theater's past as she, simultaneously, works to overhaul it.

More embroiled than the concept of literary influence, intertextuality is about conscious co-creation, about charting the prints that have impressed the field and making a fresh vision that adds one's personalized, signature inventiveness to those pre-standing documents. In the process, new text is manufactured.[6] My interest lies in unearthing and exploring how Shange raises and sounds on American drama with a special emphasis on her engagements with other African American female playwrights. For this reason, we begin by resurrecting the nineteenth century and Pauline Hopkins's revisionary tent show, concentrating particularly on Hopkins's insistence that black female pleasure be reflected on the American stage. Shange's treatments also yearn for the advent of black female satisfaction in a more earnest and optimistic manner than any of the other twentieth-century artists in this study (Hurston strives to recover this elation too but is largely thwarted by the conventions of her age). In many ways, *spell #7* conceives anew Hopkins's *Peculiar Sam* even though there is no material evidence that Shange studied that early musical. But, in terms of their devotion to minstrelsy and distilling its still serviceable parts, the two writers enjoy a common revisionary, trickster-based take on the way in which culture is malleable enough to bend round and through the writer's pen and the performer's experience, skill and perspective.[7] That dexterity, which each views as endemic to African American practice, proudly claims music and dance as integral components in its mission to elude and repel imperial encroachment. Black female delight is written in as an imaginative mobility, a crucial tool that flaunts American imprisonment schemes that have relentlessly designated black women to predetermined geographic, cultural, and psycho-social locations.[8]

It is essential that we note that black women's kinetic defense against state conformity differs from the performance vehicles that black men typically concoct. More exactly, a greater stress on sensuality in fluid movement, costume, and visual patterning defines black female dance and spoken word in Shange's visions just as a century before Hopkins entrusts the same cadences to reflect the "laughing" frivolity of African American women in various stages of courtship rituals, a strategy that answers still-lingering presumptions that black folks are not fully human and also engages the black viewers' personal memories, whether near or distant, when culture (in various guises) allowed them to transcend the often-troubling conditions of life. Physical and aural lyricism as filtered through the black female body is wrapped in an intense celebration of, paradoxically, liberation through intimacy. Consider this gendered difference by comparing soft shoe that was made popular by black male entertainers or the awkward yet highly controlled movements of minstrel patter and even break dance today in light of the more rollicking twirls of black women dancers from Josephine Baker to Judith Jameson. For women, the body is often poised in a series of embracing gestures, extending out from arms and hips to draw the ritual attendees within the community of her circling body. Similarly, attire is more often braided into the pageant to welcome and empower the audience (Hopkins's short, sashaying skirts and Shange's swirling women in many hues).

These distinctions impact on the relationship between the participant/viewer and the dramatic scene that he or she ingests. Black male dance, that from the late nineteenth century through the early twentieth that followed the minstrel and vaudeville traditions, showcases a competition between opponents where the victor outpaces and outlasts the others on the battlefield. Numerous matches fed this combative spirit just as break dancers of the eighties vied for glory (one sees this pursuit after mastery at sporting events from end zone peacock struts to mid-air twirls on the basketball court). Expecting that the artist will prove something with his exhibition, the spectator is positioned as a respectful gazer.[9] Black female choreography, on the other hand, is less committed to besting a foe. Its overarching strains highlight the continuity between artist and participant because the movements are often meant to awaken unifying, even primal, reminiscences along with raising the pitch of the arena from mundane manners to the ecstasy that we often associate with an anticipation of sensual convergence. Keeping the audience wound somewhere in a rapturous state that hovers around a recognizable tingling, the black female hoofer finds confidence in her aptitude for revealing the interwoven patterns that discursive systems strive to disconnect. In this manner, Shange uses the sweep of an arm to travel through history and across geographic space, aligning each move—however improvisational—under the first intent's parcel.

With this emphasis on social transformation as pulled through physical movement interwoven with keen, strategic versification, both Shange and her nineteenth-century predecessor, Hopkins, bend theatrical space to fit a black female aesthetic that changes adversity into something useful. Another commonality that Shange and Hopkins hold dear is their reliance on the break to enhance their works, coloring them with more parodic and reflective undertone. In Shange's case, she applies the practice in the manner in which it is often implemented in dance: to signal a line change or variation. So, the viewer/participant is acted on in tiered fashion. The first layer introduces a step that becomes familiar through repetition, but just when the participant becomes accustomed to the "play," the break ushers in a change, and the attendee is revved up by the alteration. This pattern of acquired expertise followed by surprise and delight continues for as long as the band needs it. A shout-out inflected strategy, these physical shouts that are riddled with brief caesura can bring pleasure to the hall. Centered on delivering a spirit-lifting joy, enchantment is twirled within these breaking moments.

While a high-stepping, celebratory temper runs through both writers' works and puts them in dialogue across a century, there are, of course, major distinctions between *Peculiar Sam* and Shange's choreopoems. Sitting on the brink of expected comprehensive American reform, Hopkins could fantasize about a nation where insidious racial violence would subside so that all Americans could revel in the country's goals and prosperity. To her, progress is praiseworthy because she could imagine a place for black men and women in the American dream. Regional expositions, traveling entertainers, western expansion, and new technological and anthropological "discoveries" meant that she could and did learn more about history and her contemporary moment on a daily basis. For these reasons, an optimistic Pauline Hopkins drew African American figures who kicked up their heels to an Old Virginnie, foreseeing a bright horizon that surely had to shepherd forth better times than the slave period. After all, why should she have doubted America's great promise?[10] So when the gang strums and prances around the Canadian compound saluting gleefully their imminent return to the United States at the end of *Peculiar Sam*, and Juno yells, "I feel full," a sense of unencumbered warmth suffuse the stage, and the viewers feel invigorated and can show it by joining in, a moment that also exhibits Hopkins's conviction that black inclusion into America's citizenry would be realized.

Shange, however, could not possibly get away with such displays and be considered a serious artist because there is a much greater divide between dream and circumstance today; the intellectual is required to account for the world's atrocities, and, finally, America, at large, is still not ready for displays of black female ecstasy, conditioned as it is to recognize only squeaks and grunts from her (see Kennedy's "oww"). These conventions have become so entrenched that black women artists often censure themselves as there is a fear that representations of black female satisfaction will result in the refutation of black female pain. Therefore, we see in Shange's work sublime snapshots that are often roped in by references to cruelty and grief as though she returns her "selves" to the ground lest their wings get clipped. For instance, in *for colored girls* an account of a senior high school graduation party precedes a segment that centers on domestic dysfunction where Beau Willie, a returning veteran, drops his children from an open window. What results thematically and aesthetically is that obligatory suffering is provided a predetermined seat in the poet's panorama and becomes the most formulaic brick in her artistic foundation. The footloose improvisational flow that Hopkins implements is not available to Shange because the death of progressivism not only for black people but on a global scale has made a free-falling dramatization of a company rouse an affront. Hence, Shange patches onto Hopkins's vision reflective insertions that center on a series of mass social failures that do not completely blot out optimism but make it harder to earn.

Shange's veiled satisfaction, cloistered inside periods of "serious" dramatic recitation, held against Hopkins's bold strike to reveal black female exuberance as part of an assault on America's denial of civil rights to colored citizens speaks as well to the intensifying link between pleasure and exploitation in modern culture. Unfortunately, in the United States during slavery, the psycho-sexual master/slave dynamic produced a phenomenon whereby the owner's visual and physical gratification, be it sexual, nurturing, and/or economic, becomes connected to his and her use of the black body so that increasingly entertainment under this system becomes synonymous with making the foreign body perform the owners' lusts.[11] Hopkins could not have known the extent to which this contract of sorts would take root not only in popular culture but across the social spectrum. From a hundred year distance, Shange could not afford to be naive about or ignore the deep-seated and numerous ways in which black elation had been written over and parceled off for consumers.[12] The poet addresses this increasingly interlocking commercial cooptation in her verse, *irrepressibly bronze, beautiful & mine* from *The Love Space Demands* collection. Composed in reaction to Robert Mapplethorpe's photographs of black men that feature disembodied images of the black phallus(6), this three-part ode fills in some of the unsung traditions that black people have hewn in the face of overriding Western compulsions to define black art as merely those designs that titillate or otherwise engorge the master's appetite. (In the twentieth century, these sessions often arrive in the form of mechanical images that seize, reproduce, and trade in colored flesh.)

Each section of Shange's three-part lyric pits an alternative means by which black folk's relishing of life can be represented without that wonderment feeding a hunger that drains the source of its exhilaration. The first suite speaks of an ebony stone in the palm of a black girl's hand that represents the black man's heart (4); the second venerates poets, musicians, and writers who carry the tradition of black art with their songs (6); and the third applauds sex between black men and women, a space that is protected auspiciously by nature (7). In each case, the symbol (stone, art, sex) that carries this verdant, rapturous testimonial is ancient and prefigures and extends beyond the Mississippi, grandfather clauses, temples, books, and continental repatriation, as if the poet travels back to an age before the fracturing Middle Passage to recover the modes by which people engage with a world that does not require a mediating evaluative system, or, more precisely, she scours the various eddies of contemporary culture to locate art (local and widely proclaimed) that retains fragments from this old-time magic. Other illustrations of interpolated ancient rites are sprinkled across her writing from cooking and love-making recipes, narratives of youth that invite shared commentary, and, most emphatically, dance numbers that encourage the audience's own toe-tapping, stirring involvement. The poet weaves these heady practices into her theatrical pieces that are filled with sub-generic intervals so that moments of happiness buoy great tragedy, and wailing/mourning checks elation.

While a certain repartee between despair and celebration distinguishes Shange's creative assortment, this transfer between deeply drawn sites is not symmetrical but follows the shout-out's patterning in the sense that the spotlight may randomly rest on any given sphere at any given time, a device that lends the illusion that space is perpetually dense and in contestation, is multi-ringed. Consider, for instance, that if the occasion for Shange's *irrepressibly bronze, beautiful & mine* is an exhibit that objectifies and lacerates the black body into parts, that depiction is surely answered by her words; Mapplethorpe's photographs of containment do not disappear within her poem's boundaries. In her purview, the journey from Africa to America is very much epitomized by the convergence of two aesthetics, one that defines itself through its repeated rehearsal of domination and the other that articulates itself only through the lens of its own experience and through the metaphors granted by the natural world, the latter vein insisting, as Shange has scripted into her own performances, on ritual and audience participation to complete its meaning. This is the twentieth-century minstrel show that Shange co-creates with the old one, making theater summon and reflect the brutal root of its ascendance into American popular culture while it is bent simultaneously on broadcasting and recording an emerging elation. Both Hopkins and Shange saturate their form in varying degrees of black female joy; however, Hopkins's modified minstrel show alchemizes the Sambo into a trickster, then progressively departs from the past, but Shange's choreopoems allow history to stand while they mock it with community-based attitudes.

Certainly Shange and Hopkins share a preoccupation with structural revision, but in terms of thematic content, the poet more often retraces the ground that Alice Childress has planted on the nation's stage. Despite the fact that Childress drafts arguably more traditionally realistic treatments (I contend that she disrupts this pattern with African American modalities) while Shange builds up from a funky, down-beat arrangement, both spotlight working-class, black female figures, the role of the black artist, how dignity may be maintained in the face of malice, and how a musical tradition offers an instructional guide for survival. Recall that Childress's *Trouble in Mind* and Shange's *spell #7* visit topics pertaining to the black performers' complicity in and resistance to mainstream channels. Each searches for pockets or sanctuaries where race, class and gender are not bent through a supernumerary set of alienating molds. Additionally, both writers (one should add Hopkins to this list) take care to depict sexualized black women who live in the flesh as well as in a symbolic or rhetorical capacity. The body is not negated but is stressed as black women of different shapes, shades, and bearings literally crowd the stage. Furthermore, black female roles from Childress's Julia Augustine to Shange's Lady in Red own their sensuality by giving voice to what it means to be a modern colored woman who has not ceded her desire. This decision to activate characters who value both an intellectual and a carnal version of what it means to be black and female is a bold overriding of long-standing typecasting.

I note as well that, even though each of these writers recovers a rich buffet of black female creativity, all are conscious of the manner in which black female sexuality has been usurped by discursive channels that imprison it within the flesh trade industry. Hopkins and Childress counter this danger by alluding to a lushness that is never visually reproduced on stage (Julia's bed is sheltered by the house in which it sits, and Juno stands behind witty banter). Similarly, Shange shrouds sexuality behind dance. Determined to control the black female body's significance, each writer relies on illusionary curtains to mute black female sensuality's full impact. Shange confronts this necessity, resolving to only disclose as much as is prudently allowable: "There is a lush quality to women's sexuality that we have ignored because of the stark realities of pornography and the way men treat us as sexual objects. Hopefully, my characters bring out some of the richness and the sensuality that I think is inherent in a female existence, in a female landscape" (Betsko and Koenig interview 375). Agreeing with Shange's caution, Neal Lester postulates that even a partial exploration of black women's self-defined sexuality is a step forward because the mere act of naming autonomous black female aspirations is a challenge to the patriarchy.[13] While I concur with Lester that such demonstrations are indeed unsettling to established masculinist order, this skirmish on white male power is an ancillary offshoot to the more pressing imperative to construct a "female landscape" that can sanction and nurture black female imaginations. Forcing the theater to accept black female rhythms grants a sense of entitlement to black female participants, prompting them to secure their own "room" to invent and frolic.

This fixation on liberating black female sensuality (as opposed to eroticism) has much to do with the fact that Childress, Shange, and Hopkins reached the stage by way of performing. One can only imagine the disappointment that black female dancers, singers, and actresses experience because of the male-dominated entertainment industry's limited range of black female roles that still have not moved far from the mammy and the prostitute. To overturn these restrictions, all three writers, but especially Childress and Shange, offer employment in various specialties to black professionals in the business. Count the neighbors in Childress's *Wedding Band* and the assortment of figures in *for colored girls*, both pieces providing opportunities for numerous black thespians, instrumentalists, and crooners, a materialist response to under-representation in the live arts that puts into practice the concerns that the American Negro Theater, Childress's first artistic home, sought to address. If Shange adheres to Hopkins's high-spirited tone—with added lower modal variation—she adopts Childress's careful consideration of the systematic way in which black women have been barred from the American stage. And if Shange walks in Hopkins's steps by forming community through ritualistic celebrations of pleasurable moments, she reinforces Childress's insistence that solidarity comes through economic independence and artistic control. Savvy in both respects, the contemporary poet weds Hopkins's heady and daring claim on aesthetic innovation to Childress's demand for quantifiable reform in both the arts and in society at large.

Alongside structural, aesthetic, and political confluences, black music weighs heavily in the pageants of all three playwrights. Hopkins skims the minstrel format and further destabilizes this hodge-podge by substituting black spirituals with a martial air for the more simpering and racially offensive lyrics found in most minstrel scores. Her music features forward-seeking black Americans who have no intention of going back to slavery or old, staid white-supremacist tinged customs and practices. Childress's *Wedding Band* charts the black musical tradition of South Carolina during the early twentieth century, a symphonic drama that thematically follows the melodies' lead. To Childress, sound is order—history—and must be recorded to preserve sundry versions of America's past. Childress, like Du Bois in the *Souls of Black Folk*, finds that art, especially aural art, can stabilize a people's sense of themselves.

Shange joins this trio, but her song and sound differ significantly. Clues to how she situates music's potential come in several instances. As a dancer, she has theorized about how investing in her body's language has helped her to comprehend the Middle Passage's long-term impact: "The depth of my past waz made tangible to me in Sawyer's *Ananse*, a dance exploring the Diaspora to contemporary Senegalese music, pulling ancient trampled spirits out of present tense Afro-American Dance" (Introduction to *for colored girls* xi). This description of a mixture of fluid continuous motion as interrupted by breaking, intense New World moves becomes an apt definition of "funkiness," a term that we associate with the seventies, swaggering platform boots, and out-of-sight styles. Distilled down to its basic bits, however, the funk is very much about a search for a smooth center, given that the exigencies of the Middle Passage prevent a successful completion of that quest. What are left are periods of harmony that are cut into by sass, chaos, noise. Funk is also comprised of, "…something white people are still having a hard time duplicating" (Shange, foreword to *Three Pieces* ix). So, it represents both the struggle, admittedly futile, to return home, and, it is just plain evil (using Morrison's definition from *Sula*) for its own sake, intentionally disruptive, distinct, and singular to elude imitation and sale.

A fine illustration comes from the famed Brothers Johnson album, *Look Out for #1*, that features such hits as *Get the Funk out of My Face* and *I'll Be Good to You.* The chorus from the cut *Free and Single* revolves around a blues structure: three-line repetition with progressive variation in the last line:

> I might change/I might change, rearrange/Rearrange on you
> I might change/I might change/Rearrange Like I always do
> I might change your brain/I might change your brain/I might change your brain or rearrange all your marbles.

Funk, admittedly, takes off from the blues. However, funk revs up the somewhat laid-back style of the blues and becomes more frenetic with a greater emphasis on random, bass-driven thumps that separate the commonplace to announce the coming of change (note that the stress is not on the actual act of transformation but on heralding its arrival). Other fine examples of how funk can not only "move but remove" (Parliament/Funkadelic, "P-

Funk") are Bootsy Collins's ever-rebellious *Stretchin' out in a Rubber Band* and Parliament/ Funkadelic's pounding command to "dance my [your] way out of my [your] constrictions."[14] It should be pointed out as well that funk is not a late twentieth-century return to primitivism but is all about the future (even incorporating sci-fi tropes at times), insisting that a good solid one will ensue only from a grand dislodging of snug but tainted culverts. In particular, funk demands that social protocols and courtesies that camouflage aggressive imperialism require dismantling, deconstructive acts that will usher in the possibility for more honest repartee amongst equals.

Shange's drama taps into this recent black aesthetic not only in terms of the musical selections that accompany her pieces but by way of the choreopoems' overall design that includes customary, even hackneyed, scenes but undercuts them with the imperative to change or rearrange according to its own improvisational heart. Take *for colored girls* and the manner in which various moods butt against each other, tones that are depicted through versifying, costume, and dance, not to mention background instrumentals. Once a character seems in place (part of a blues riff), that order is either destabilized by the actress's own body or that of another "colored lady" who interrupts (breaks in) to vocalize her story. The overarching affect is an enhanced blues aesthetic like funk where lines are trod on and upset hips are shaken to the point that power is perpetually dislodged. What's remarkable about this mode is that it expands when the group pumps nutrition into it, but it also asserts that the individual is back, that the self is supreme: funk's ego is enormous and bows down to no one: God, Gods, ancestors, or the like.[15] Echoing Morrison's Eva Peace from *Sula*, it names its own universe and resists being slotted into any confining identity chiefly because it manifests itself as a voice and not as character. Invisibility grants enhanced dexterity and mobility.

The shout out is the part of funk's arsenal that carries its naming system, elevating individuals in a maelstrom of sound. One need only list the numerous floating references to great artists with signature styles to comprehend the diffuse and dense range of Shange's toasts: Etta James, Charlie Parker, Eubie Blake, The Dells, Willie Colon, Archie Shepp, Lady Day, Arsenio Rodriquez, Oliver Lake, Jackie Wilson, Chuck Berry, Lil Richard, Bob Marley, The Commodores, Fats Waller, Mahalia Jackson, The Miracles, Parliament Funkadelic, Stevie Wonder, The Stylistics, Sun-Ra, Eric Dolphy, Smokey Robinson, The Isley Brothers, Peter Tosh, and many others. There simply is no grid to follow other than that this genius courses through the African Diaspora. Invocation, random sampling, and insurgency define its contours: "I might change/I might rearrange/I might change your brain." The underlying logic is that the poet's shamanism develops from a musical tradition that is so rich and diverse that it can be reordered and reinvigorated endlessly. Hence, we can reaffirm that there are two routes inscribed in Shange's plays. One is an intertextual narrativizing undercurrent that depends on targeted dialogue across space, and the other houses the possibility of a trickster's pointed, strategic, irreverent disruption. Not viewing these divergent musical and dance-driven off-roads as at all incompatible, Shange places them as adjacent ingredients in her conjurer's bag, a set of tools that corresponds to what was unleashed during the many voyages across the Atlantic from Africa to the "New World."

Ringmaster Lou, from *spell #7* provides further hints as to what it means to deploy a funk aesthetic when he says, "i come from a family of retired sorcerers/ active houngans and pennyante fortune tellers wit 41 million spirits/ critturs and celestial bodies on our side" (8). In this choreopoem, lyrics, physical movement, and sassy retorts all land under the magician's sign (which is also the minstrel mask) as Lou opens his hands and chronicles, with barker-like shouts, the 41 million who crossed over because of slavery. His shouts awaken those same trod-on-long-dead spirits, calling them to defend their legacy. Here, Lou activates ghosts within colored culture, summoning a multi-generational plane, an act that Shange repeats across her oeuvre. For instance, in *for colored girls* we encounter a dancer in a room filled with disembodied souls, "she's dancin on beer cans & shingles/ this must be the spook house/ another song with no singers/lyrics" (3).

Arguably, Shange adds an element of the outré to her funkiness by spotlighting the many lost and restless souls who never completed the Middle Passage, bones that are yet contributing to a global remaking. Music functions to reflect this space where continuity is tempered by death and individuality is checked by gregarious spirits, a cultural universe of yells and ricochets, an unruly chorus where history enters but a solo can still register, even though it will receive, most likely, a response from some other sounding that thinks as highly of itself as the first.[16] Shange states it best when she announces, "Just because I had studied didn't mean that I had lost my voice" (Blackwell interview 135).

The writer chats with Hopkins and Childress while she chimes in on issues that Adrienne Kennedy raises as well. Facades, dreams, and the home space course through Shange's performance pieces, the same tropes that have saturated Kennedy's work for over four decades. As I have argued, masking has multiple referents in Kennedy's texts, indicating a hiding place, a sacred chamber where lines are drawn between living and the bodiless, and it also serves as a metaphor for colonization. A symbol that travels across various significations depending on who wears it, Kennedy's decorative headgear soars into that place of legends, a site that can still sow awe in a cynical world. But to Shange, the mask is much more concrete, a reminder of racial branding and barbarity, as she faces it starkly in *spell #7* where a giant minstrel head leers at the stage events and the audience. In many ways, this headpiece is a figurative racialized voyeur who surveys the colored figures below to keep them within the boundaries of his silent stare. An oft-repeated line from the play exemplifies the mask's imposition: "you're colored and you're going to love it." The audience is held equally captive by the wooden face as they are amused by the colored entertainers on the stage. Therefore, the giant plaster Sambo reinforces the realization that, traditionally, popular American theater is compartmentalized into racialized sectors with the colored flesh vulnerable to constant exposure while the white body is shielded from view, a circumstance that forces the black magician/performer/poet to enact voodoo or sly turns to dodge these segregated subdivisions.[17] The giant blackface impression also drives the consumer to recollect that modern entertainment ascended on the back of the minstrel. In fact, by purchasing a ticket, the very one that awaits the show colludes with this exploitative industry, whose antecedents originate from slavery. Shange's mask demands that the spectator confront his propensity to equate amusement with standardizing black life.

In comparison to Shange's politicized designation for the mask, Kennedy's usage is the very essence of transmutability. One is prone to reason that Kennedy's ephemeral designation is more constructive to New World African people because she deconstructs a major Western symbol that has damaged many black psyches, transmuting it into an emboldening vector of creativity. However, rather than signaling divergent philosophical bents, these artistic choices prick the critic to investigate whether Shange sinks her quick-change instrumentality in some other source, and if so to query that selection's significance. Granted that Kennedy (early Kennedy) manipulates the African mask's ambient dexterity to grant her figures flight (Sarah who is the Duchess of Hapsburg who is Queen Victoria who is the black father), we can argue that Shange fits her dance moves with a similar function: "The freedom to move in space, to demand of my own sweat a perfection that could continually be approached, though never known, waz poem to me, my body and mind ellipsing" (Shange, *for colored girls* xi). Akin to Kennedy's dream walkers who quickly peel through history's skin, Shange's gyrating limbs can carry her over temporal and topographic plains, chiefly those ranges that connect the African Diaspora from West Africa to South, Central and North America. As Brown-Guillory observes, Shange's choreography includes an assortment of moves that are endemic to the African Diaspora: acrobatic, tap dancing, Calindy dancing, Cotton Club choruses, comedic and doo-wop aesthetics (*Their Place* 72). We could add to this list Caribbean and South American (especially Brazilian, Puerto Rican and Cuban) numbers including salsa, the break-down, and Brazilian carnival moves. These steps are choreographed variously, not executed in chronological order. Instead, they wind across the floor, impressing a quick-change fluidity that insists on the overturning of barriers.

This emphasis on metaphysical travel reflects each artist's relationship to "home" as one often defines a journey through the prism of an origin and originating site. I have argued that Kennedy's imaginative travel is instigated by the compunction to protect and preserve an African American heritage and, more generally, Africanist traditions. So it makes sense that she would embrace a symbolic shield that guards the vulnerable associations that form within the Diaspora's cultural and social sphere (in this case I refer to the mask in its West African designation as the place of making or *ashé*). Thus she encloses home inside the mask and renders it invisible yet active, a strategic choice that removes it from imperial intrusion. Shange, on the other hand, is willing to reveal the black family and the structural frame that surrounds it, exposing especially childhood, the period before the subject becomes embittered by the divisive social classifications that are thrust on him or her by adults. Using dance as the reference that gestures toward this sacred ground, Shange visits Diaspora spaces that are open. We see that in most of her works, she draws the private exchanges of colored people with enough texture that they certainly register as part of the performance. But these intimate spaces are not completely exposed or vulnerable and are set down within a combined field of lyricism, music, and the fluid eloquence of the human body (*The Love Space Demands* 40). This step toward disclosure, albeit in the slippery New World aesthetic of "voodoo funkiness," reveals a decisive feeling of imaginative and material privilege, a place that recent Kennedy (given that she has relinquished the mask trope in her most current writing) now shares with Shange. What I mean by this is that even though each realizes keenly how commercial channels have curbed the public's ability to perceive black interior spaces, each continues to conceive and produce scenes that confront the seemingly insurmountable barrier of free-floating gross pigeonholing. From late Kennedy's black mother/Beowulf to Shange's dancers/oracles/sculptors, black female figures re-inherit their position as the world's myth-making helmswomen.

While Shange spins intertextual ballads with Childress and Kennedy, whose influence she has acknowledged, and while she sows common ground with Hopkins mainly through their shared signification on minstrelsy, her walk down the road with Angelina Grimké is far more circumstantial.[18] Grimké's *Rachel* came about at the behest of the NAACP and was broadcast as the first race play. Shange's work has also been buoyed and constrained by a mass social imperative: the women's movement. The mere label, feminist, has led to some reviewers' gross reduction of Shange's art into a simple opposition to black men, which it most certainly is not. William Collins calls *for colored girls* "a strong feminist statement" that delivers an outraged indictment of "the dehumanization of black women at the hands of their men." He goes on to advise that the work could benefit from a "larger vision that could encompass the whole of the black woman's experience." Bill Thompson claims that the play "denigrates black men—boldly, mockingly and effectively." Even after twenty-five years, in response to a revival of the choreopoem at the American Place in New York 2000, Lawrence Van Gelder argues that, "the men of *for colored girls* are uniformly the villains." It becomes clear that the solid correlation between this effort and the women's movement has predetermined, to a large degree, the critic's responsive capacity, locking some into assessments that converge, almost exclusively, on the disharmony between black men and black women, discounting the many pointed observations that Shange has skillfully inserted into her pieces. These evaluators who have been partially blinded by the "feminist insinuation" miss the current of black female joy and celebration that runs through the drama. Loving moments between black partners such as the segment about losing one's virginity are also edited out of the equation. What is even more egregious is that the historical context that the poet builds into each segment is ignored, as if there were no Vietnam War, no drug problem, no long-standing racism, no inequality between the sexes, and no massive poverty in the Americas that impinges on personal relationships. En masse this silencing of the play's fully-rounded resonance obscures its quick-change, multi-vocal heart, opting instead to stigmatize the writer by implying that she is nothing more than an angry woman and, therefore, her artistic offspring should be rated fittingly.

This wholesale packaging of *for colored girls* as "the black woman's chance to get even with black men" set the standard for subsequent reviews of her later installations as each one has been compared prodigiously to this first choreopoem, the columnist often searching for the alleged confrontational candor that they believe brands *for colored girls*. Douglas Keating, for instance, regrets that the poetry in *Love Space Demands* is more abstract than that found in the first piece. In effect, evaluators "de-intellectualize" *for colored girls* and then demand that Shange's subsequent works follow this model that they themselves had conjured from the shards of a rudimentary and shallow definition of feminism as solely hostility towards men. I would claim that in many ways, this first powerful theatrical composition has been exhibited, via the commentator, in a manner reminiscent of the nineteenth century's Sarah Baartman (the Hottentot Venus) traveling freak show. The only difference is that in addition to the pornographic focus on black female backside, Shange's work has been interpreted as epitomizing the Sapphire-like, uncontrollable carping that allegedly attends this "physical deformity."

If we pay closer attention to the details and to Shange's prose writing about how the theater ought to function, we receive a more impartial and accurate picture of her relation to the women's movement. While she has identified her work as women centered (about and to women), there is much confusion over what this statement implies (Grimké had a similar struggle with racial uplift ideology defining the boundaries of *Rachel*).[19] Consider that "Shange offers her piece quite literally to young black girls" (Lester, *Ntozake Shange* 27) and that she names artistic influences from around the world including Le Roi Jones, Ishmael Reed, Jessica Hagedorn, Victor Hernandez Cruz, C. L. R. James, Gloria Naylor, and June Jordon…(Betsko and Koenig interview 367–7). With her specific address and her wide-ranging pool of influences, it becomes clear that Shange runs transport between her worldly knowledge and the black heiress/participant who is just awakening to her fulcrum position in the world and her strength. So, the designation, women centered, is certainly more localized than the one implied by mostly white, middle-class feminist groups who often see themselves as within the preferred circle. That she addresses her visions to women of color and not middle-class white women whom she sometimes critiques (see *spell #7*) indicates that Shange is a womanist according to Alice Walker's definition and not a feminist, if we must apply a label at all. The poet is faced with the conundrum of how to retain her creative integrity under the encroaching shadow of a master discourse that does run parallel to her own aims on occasion but not always, just as Grimké had to parse out sixty years previously how to enhance racial uplift themes but also call for the equal inclusion and respect of black women's ideas and interests at the policy formation stage and not later as an addendum.

It is the old conundrum of how black women can put themselves first when no one else recognizes them in that position. Since neither Grimké or Shange yield to the pressure to force black female artistry to submit to an authority (in the guise of a traditional form), both risk dominant deliberation and feedback over the work's supposed incoherence or its seeming inability to explore "the real problems" head on without emotion. If black women's tears make men and white women uncomfortable, for instance, should they be edited out of a scene? Both writers seize their right, perhaps obligation, to interpret both the unpredictable life patterns that are visited on and become crucial to black female survival and the all-too-frequent brutal moments when black women realize that there is nothing left but a mess of boiling sentiments. And if black women do not mold these raw patches into art—words, songs, dances, gardens, quilts, paintings, cooking—then they lose the opportunity to take back their role as mythmaker, storyteller, and generational guide. In the process of defining what the Middle Passage has meant to women of color and more generally, the writers upset white and male advantage (Grimké gently and Shange brusquely) but do not denigrate liberation-loving people everywhere. The first step/rule upon entering Shange's women-centered environment is to shed both one's longing for supremacy and one's wish for emotional distance at the door.

Before delving into specific choreopoems, one additional qualification need be added. I have been using the term Middle Passage to refer to the trans-Atlantic crossing that brought Africans and a slaved-based social and economic system to the New World. This certainly reflects the most salient, seminal definition of the term. Yet, Shange depicts a number of subsidiary offshoots, using the "Middle Passage" as a metaphoric umbrella for a series of interconnected events that have fractured communities, cutting even deeper social striations on a vast scale. These tributary Middle Passages include the Vietnam War, the rise of the drug trade, and, in Shange's more recent offerings, AIDS. In each case, whether she imagines the original ghastly voyage across the ocean or a contemporary offshoot, these periods are characterized by the same order: rape followed by a time of drifting disorientation and finally restoration, restoration not in the sense of unity and return but as acceptance and triumph over despair and a yearning for self-mutilation. Didactic, cathartic, surly, and reaching toward jubilation or *ashé*, Shange's pieces whirl into, not away from, the Atlantic's blood-drenched epicenter. The poet explains that "I want to take them [the audience] to a place where they know that they have survived their own vulnerability and somebody else's. I think every time I can do that in America I help stop somebody from being shot…"(Jackson Bryer interview 214).

Keeping in mind the ongoing conference amongst Shange and a number of her predecessors, we turn to specific works, rooting the concept of multiple and co-constructing Middle Passages as a touchstone. There are many instances of and references to rape in Shange's texts, scenes that mark the division between security and fear, wholeness pinned next to the angry remains of a horrifying theft. Replicating the manner in which the slave trade raided Africa, these intense theatrical events not only stand alone but form into a collective declaration that speaks to the anguish that comes from a global system where violent penetration has become the norm. Thus, Shange comments that the world's economy and ensuing social structure is, by and large, a slave-based design as rape and forced servitude have become synonymous acts, a system that proceeds under a racialized order with darker people carrying the brunt of the incursion on their bodies and territory. This mechanism continues to consume labor for the purpose of its own gain. Many colored, poor, and politically powerless subjects are at risk from a machine/vessel that seizes indiscriminately their energy and talents for its own pleasure and continued heartiness. Rape has become so entrenched and so naturalized that it is acceptable for those who wield a bit of influence to pounce on those who have even less.

One sees this hierarchy of lusts most evidently in Shange's *Crack Annie*, a segment from her *Love Space Demands* collection that she produced as a choreopoem at the Crossroads Theater in New Brunswick in 1992. This scene revolves around a crack-addicted woman, who offers her seven-year-old daughter to a grown man to score a few hits of cocaine. Having seen the piece on several occasions, I can assert firmly that it leaves no room for escape; there simply is no respite from this "mother's" story of suffocating anguish. Pain is amplified so excruciatingly that it moves the audience to an assuredly selfish wish to protect against *Crack Annie's* uncapped terror where daughter, mother, and drug pusher damn each other.

This landscape reverberates in many directions and on many frequencies because beyond the mother's act of betrayal, Shange inserts an implied shadow text: the period before crack's introduction into American neighborhoods, the period before Africans were chained and dragged from home. A series of warping, intrusive events have literally sliced apart the roles and rules that would have held a West African unit together or any functioning social group for that matter. Encouragement from either female or male adults has ceased, economic self-preservation declined; the means to guard one's perimeters and/or one's body have all but disappeared, and a recognition of the individual's vitality to the unit's overall well-being has evaporated. *Crack Annie* does not live in a void. Her rape and the resulting intergenerational violation that she passes on to her daughter correlate to a capitalist system that desiccates the other to ensure its prosperity. So, it is paramount that we view this piece as more than an enactment of what happens when cheap drugs flood America. More importantly, it resonates how modern society operates as each member participates in some version of "selling the child." Slavery, including African based, the conquistadors conquering and enlisting of indigenous populations, and modern industries that steal human labor has created these dreadful splintering moments when the subject awakens to the realization that her innocence is lost, that she too must join this brutal system to survive.

Critics who have charged Shange with being harsh on black men miss the larger picture. The scene that has elicited the most criticism and the most misreading is that of Beau Willie in Shange's *for colored girls*. Beau Willie returns from the Vietnam conflict a changed man and drops his children to their death because he is frustrated with their mother's refusal to marry him. Placing this moment within its appropriate historical context, scholars Marilyn Elkins and Sandra Hollin Flowers point out the clear connection between what the war did to him and his difficulty adjusting to civilian life (Elkins 63; Flowers 53). Thus armed conflict, not the man, destroys this family's bonds. As unpleasant as it may be, this segment focuses on how black men are raped by dominant institutions, just as Crack Annie, her daughter, and the man who buys them are desecrated. There is no gender competition over who endures more in colored communities in Shange's work although she concentrates on women because she is speaking to them and to herself. In the poet's purview, we live in a civilization where the self is stripped and must learn to become an aggressor or forfeit its autonomy. Critics who ignore these overriding messages, in the words of Wahneema Lubiano, "shield the text of power," a force that in *for colored girls* comes in the form of a war that pits colored against colored, annihilating both sides in the process.

Power wields its might as well in the guise of racist immigration restrictions and high unemployment rates for non-white males, which Maxine, from *spell #7,* observes "cd drive a man to drink or to lie" (40). This line illuminates the poet's sensitivity to the various manners in which neo-slavery practices manifest themselves in national policies. Those who would denigrate Shange's work on the basis of its alleged male bashing neglect historical circumstance and limit her ability to reconstruct imaginatively what she deduces to be our foundational modern exchange model. Unfortunately these reviewers also perceive that text conceived by black women can only be literal, autobiographically based realism rather than consciously instituted figurative engagements. Crack Annie's and Beau Willie's violations parallel that of the black female artist because her range is checked by an impending hostile force in the form of the critic who guarantees his/her own entitlement in the face of the other's/writer's dismissal.

Destruction introduces fear, and fear leads to a self-imposed seizure of mobility. Lady in blue from *for colored girls* gives voice to this paralysis:

> when i walked in the pacific/ i imagined waters ancient from accra/tunis cleansin me/ feedin me/ now my ankles are coated in grey filth/ from the puddle neath the hydrant…i usedta live in the world/ now i live in harlem and my universe is six blocks (36)

Notably, the "block" refers to a prison: "on the cell block." Lady in blue's condition, then, alludes to a detainment that has landed her in America's urban jails, the resettlement pattern that many enslaved Africans have followed from home to the American south/plantation to northern and mid-western industrial towns and cities during the great migration that began in the late nineteenth century and had its greatest surge from the 1920s to the 1950s. Similar to prodded beasts, colored people have been nudged, via various forms of rape, toward more confined areas. The right to inhabit and commune with the land is wrested away by force just as the black body is desecrated; so, mass resettlement schemes represent another form of rape. This disenfranchisement ends in a loss of wealth in terms of material security and results in an additional surrender of spiritual enrichment. Shange makes this clear when she elevates the ancient home waters that symbolize renewal, rebirth, and even prescience as they provide a visionary plane in which to imagine the future (resist nihilism), but modern life has transformed the ocean's great electric force into a mere hydrant that is ineffective at purging common dirt; in fact, it has become a contributor to the filth rather than its remedy.

Certainly this is a modernist proposal that places its faith in previous civilizations' beliefs and practices; late nineteenth-century progressivism prefigures twentieth-century uplift ideology.[20] Shange's position not only debunks this faith that better days can be achieved by moving forward along the axis that has been provided by modern society, which she defines as steeped in systemic slavery, she argues that the road to liberty means going back in time to recover the pre-violation period. I should add that this does not presage complete reclamation, but it situates the past as an orienting memory, a potent amulet, as it were. Therefore, the artist's task revolves around reminding the lady in blue that she once washed in waters that could propel her across time and space. If this sacred marriage with nature and the empowering sense of self that it grants has been stolen, then it is possible to conceive of its return.

This leads us to the second strain of Shange's great Middle Passage/s reconstruction. After the rape comes a period of darkness, of bewilderment as the chattel Africans must have felt after days at sea with only brief minutes above deck and fellow Africans dying to the left and right. It is also that narrow space before death when those who had managed to jump into the ocean in defiance of the owner labored to swim back to their birthright only to succumb to the tide. Analogous to a moving void, this trope references the condition of colored folks who have not yet awakened to their full potential. Dim-lit sets pervade Shange's installations: "…for certain characters I can't [look at the audience] because they're doing such awful stuff I have to just be talking to black space" (Bryer interview 220).

Beau Willie, Crack Annie, and the entirety of *A Photograph: Lovers in Motion* reside in this watery dark room's boundaries. Photographic development makes for a handy metaphor that clarifies how contemporary Western culture has recast the Atlantic abyss via technology. Antitheses such as life/death, light/dark, liberty/detention are mass produced by way of a chemical process that turns the improvisational into formulaic, canned objects. Previously, I mentioned that tragic deliberations are the more rote components in Shange's dramas, seemingly inserted to detract from an unfettered display of black female pleasure (that could be misread as pornographic). Here we arrive at another possible explanation for these intense but expected, repetitious moments of tragedy. They act like burning fluids that etch an indelible image on our consciousness; they are a reminder of stasis, of what it means to be fixed to history's underside. Consequently, Shange makes them formulaic to mirror the manner in which modern life often feels banal and impenetrable.

We see this effect most pronouncedly in *A Photograph*, a treatment that sheds light on two black men and three black women who become involved in each other's lives to varying degrees. Sean, the photographer, uses his male heterosexual privilege to center himself, while the others envelope him like satellite moons. Michael, the dancer, is next in line because she has brokered a strong connection to Sean, but she attempts to seduce his other lover behind his back: Claire, the model/kept woman. When Sean catches her in the act, Michael quickly shifts the blame to Claire. Nevada represents the financially successful bourgeois black woman who backs Sean but cannot win his affection, and Earl, Sean's male friend, may now be interested in Nevada after breaking up with Claire (Earl is not fully aware of the extent of the relationship between Sean and Claire). There is evidence as well that Earl may have homoerotic desires for Sean. In short, each figure in this play wears a disguise, what Shange refers to as "fronting." She connects this generally accepted, nationwide tendency to dissemble to the country's sadism, theorizing that one of the reasons why so many people are murdered in our nation is because Americans "front" all the time (Bryer interview 214).

The photograph and this deceptive act are both equivalent to the dead space between worlds that the Middle Passage encompasses, an unreadable gap between old world and new mores. The entire cast of *A Photograph* reflects this cavity as each performs a hackneyed part (angry black male artist, sensitive female artist, black party girl, black uptight middle-class lady, and fawning black male sycophant), but no subject is truly rounded or proceeds from his or her own self-named dreams. Not only has the funk left the immediate stage, the play pantomimes how these chilling spells of detachment can last over centuries. An extension of the original condition whereby African bones were driven to an unsettled grave, Sean, Michael, Claire, Nevada, and Earl continue to pass through as mere shadows to richer selves, or, as Shange has commented, "...michael/sean/claire/nevada/earl are afflicted with the kinds of insecurities & delusions only available to those who learned themselves thru the traumas of racism" (*three pieces* xiv–xv). What brands them as particularly American is their ability to convert their acumen for deception into social currency. Earl and Nevada maneuver to trade their cash for the raw talent that they believe Sean, Michael, and Claire possess. In the midst of this industrial clearinghouse, intimacy and mutual concern evaporate. Thus the title, *A Photograph: Lovers in Motion* is an oxymoron as the snapshot burns and seals the lovers into a system that barters manufactured artificial emotions for an image.

This drama is extremely bleak with few breathing spaces or inspirational moments, a terrifying depiction of the Middle Passage's massive consequences. In outlining this desolate interval, Shange constructs intertextual bridges that span other dramatists' pieces and her own work. Chiefly, Shange's *Photograph* calls upon Alice Childress's *Wine in the Wilderness*, another play that spotlights artistic reproduction and framing. We remember that Childress foregrounds a triptych of portraits capturing black female figures in various stages to articulate how male artists during the Black Power era objectified and commercialized black women. Shange pivots on Childress's powerful symbol by exploring how mechanical duplication has a knack for transforming kinetic individuality into something tame, predictable, and hollow. This instance of intertextuality identifies the image's paramount figurative function. So, once we filter this choreopoem through *Wine*, we become more attuned and alert to the snapshots that preside over events in Shange's piece. Parallel to the minstrel mask that overshadows the crowd in *spell #7*, the pictures establish the tone. Voyeuristic, teeming souvenirs of conquests line the artist's lair, auguring that the being or beings that reside within are thrill seekers and collectors, a band of predators that fight over their possessions, tokens, and pecking order. Resembling Shakespeare's haunted ghosts in castles, the pictures here predict the violent unrest that erupts from unjust, often savage raids on natural and social harmony. So, even before the spectators learn of the characters' abusive and deceitful behavior, they expect some form of man-made cruelty to be linked to his use of technology.

In addition to chiming in on Childress's play, Shange's *A Photograph* also reaches out to *for colored girls*, a poem that declares, by its very title, to be about suicide. *A Photograph* fills in the missing analysis and provides the necessary addendum that living in confining social roles that have been handed over by imposing scripts (American fronting) is just as much a relinquishing of vitality as is the loss of a pulse.[21] We can observe that these two works comment on each other: *for colored girls* chooses life and independent signatures, but the "lovers in motion" lean toward self-inflicted death as they cling to a blues cycle that does not eventually spin off into the kind of self-reflection that can lead to a triumph over the circumstances of birth and history. This exploration of communal dysfunction dramatizes what it means to be adrift and underscores how this condition continues to be reproduced in various guises. As Shange's art names it, the world still conforms tenaciously to a slave-based ethos. Dismantling such an entrenched global mode of operation rests on recognizing through ritual both the various tributary, contemporary Middle Passages and the various phases embedded within each of these terrifying iterations. In the case of the aforementioned choreopoem, the poet targets that period succeeding the rape but before a reformation of terms and restorative forces. As logic dictates, people have to grow conscious of their plight before they can repair it. So, just as Kennedy encodes a great deal of authorial distance between herself and her characters to broadcast that the Negro must depart, Shange places this crew at arm's length to exhibit how they thrive on dissimulation rather than on mutual support and honesty, a group that represents what is undesirable and unhealthy. If Kennedy calls for the Negro's demise, Shange envisions a world without fronting.

Even though I strongly disagree with Timothy Murray that *A Photograph* features, "redemption, retrieval, and reclamation," (172) he names the keys to re-appropriation that crop up in Shange's other dancing poems. There are instants that adhere to this third movement across the Middle Passage: an eventual acceptance of displacement and a will to subsume and transform the best shards that are formed by dis-location. I should add that, while the poet includes triumphs, we should not forget that these periods are tempered by the reasoning that unless the pressing slavery-based archetype is surrendered, a cycle of rape, disassociation, and recovery will continue as each succeeding generation will be plagued by its own middle passages. Under the shadow of this impending absurd and obscene closed loop, the difference between a blues versus a funk-geared response is that the funketeer places her faith in her individuality and the chaotic pattern of the universe to eventually find a way out even if that liberating avenue is not clear at the present moment. Furthermore, a funk performance may excite others to start moving as well. Countless souls start trying to shake off their own body cuffs. Impulse is always double, traveling towards a crowd but away from it as well. Critic John Timpane views this phenomenon in Shange's art as, "ambivalence and paradox" (198). Her work seizes its right to be multi-directional, to double-back, sass, reverberate, and change. This structural choice that may include, for instance, a nostalgic scene about loving in the back seat of a car that switches quickly into domestic violence (*for colored girls*) reproduces the random pattern of African American female living.

Keeping in mind that triumph is muted by imminent danger, we turn to the places in Shange's art where she documents a series of guides and recipes on how to withstand rape and stormy nights in the ocean. First, she recognizes that physical intimacy alone is no longer strong enough to wage the numerous funky battles that will liberate the world from dividing itself into a stand-off between slaves and masters. The domestic/courtship theme that has ruled black women's art is not nimble enough to unseat this entrenched social patterning and, therefore, has to be replaced by something else. Shange suggests several options. Anger is a way to soften the ties between subjugated people and the state that they inhabit just as the remembrance of pain and collective atrocity provides clarity in visualizing a peaceful future. In addition, a celebration/shout out of one's intellectual and cultural heritage will also assist in securing a path beyond distress, and, finally, conjuration, carnival, and magic can provide temporary sanctuaries to allow for ideas to be incubated and hatched.

The poet's work is replete with interludes that focus on this third Middle Passage spiral that represents an upswing from the rib-crushing claustrophobia of the first two strains. She adopts the term, "combat breath" (foreword to *Three Pieces* xii–xiii) to convey flattening oppressive symbolic codes and language with an undercutting mode that weaves together rage, spoken and written word, and the body's sublingual sputtering, fuming utterances. Other movements to Shange's suite, however, turn the voice and dance toward praise songs that chronicle individuality's triumph and rejoice in what has been salvaged. She summarizes this sentiment with the previously mentioned revelation to interviewer Henry Blackwell that, "Just because I had studied didn't mean that I had lost my voice" (135), an observation that not only represents the artist's personal relationship to her craft but stands as well for the mass loss and subsequent buoyancy of African culture after a most horrendous submergence. The notion that a besieged voice/aesthetic can survive in the midst of master discourses' imposition speaks to the manner in which Shange positions her art as a defender and protector of an endangered legacy. Like Du Bois before her and other black modern visionaries like Hurston and Hughes, she sets out to record the sounds and, more importantly to her, the rhythmic patterns of black folks' hungers. So, the cultural and intellectual heritage that matters most to this late-day poet is the one that pays tribute to and absorbs its commands from the masses, not the elite, which explains her emphasis on musicians, dancers, and popular legends rather than on academic, legal, or other remote channels.

We see homage to homespun contributions throughout Shange's work, but she venerates them most vigorously in *spell #7* when Lou, the ringmaster, commands his fellow revelers—performers and audience—"to be colored and love it." Here he conjures up the "hoodoo" that black people must perform daily: to build with culture the illusion of passion, a trick, if executed successfully, that will convince even the secret-sharer that she/he is better off. Under the sway of the MC's voice, the New World African "...does become One. With everything...does feel Holy like God. But is only the bass drums, and the bush and the Dawn and Desperadoes that can cast that kind of magic" (Borbon from Lennox Brown's *Devil Mas': A Play in Three Acts* 219). Under Lou's incantation a temporary syncretism is achieved that, although different from a pre-Middle Passage accord, spins a provisional unified field.

Shamanism not seduction rises as the key trope, a noteworthy modification in the black female dramatic tradition. This claim warrants further explanation because, on the surface, it contradicts what I have been positing about Shange's concentration on black female sensuality. The poet drenches her drama in sexy, heightened allusions to good, earthy loving, most certainly overheated, even a little kinky. Yet, she also retreats from these steamy displays, an oscillation that she reflects with several lines from *boogie woogie landscpes*: "...but holding soft & close/means danger/makes you see red/to orange/to make fury to champion the tendermost" (119). While the poet treats intimacy between black partners repeatedly, these sensual unveilings also remind her of the dominant taboos that mark their occurrence as salacious. So black sensuality and black rage—not at each other but directed toward a panoptic Western gaze—often commingle. Even the most precious private interludes between black subjects are vulnerable to this intrusion that leads double consciousness into the bedroom. Aware of this potential incursion, Shange hedges or shields portrayals of black love. The artist peppers her visions with sexy bits, but these "revelations" are placed within a meta-text that reads comprehensive discursive patterns. Consider that she has yet to compose a production that exclusively or primarily centers on the courtship theme, a choice that early African American women playwrights Hopkins, Grimké, Hurston, Miller, Spence, and Childress selected to various degrees. Alternatively, the choreopoem's form along with its lyrical content transposes the wooing game into sharp social critique as the "love scenes" are framed by annotations that check their ability to speak on their own. Consider that *A Photograph* spins out from a series of interrupted love connections and *boogie woogie landscapes* bounces a lush black female sensuality that is represented by dance and music against the mandate that self-defense classes are needed to prevent rape (123). From *for colored girls* to *the love space demands*, the poet curbs heated intermingling with circumstances that either bracket flirtation within a nostalgic and, therefore, temporally remote bubble or tinge it with loneliness' tragic overtones.[22]

In Shange's plays, the breaks that interrupt the wooing are often emotionally colored red or orange—the hues of rage, passion, and fire—and costuming becomes responsible for specifying that what was once restorative (the reconstitution of the home through coupling) has become a hot topic embroiled in turmoil and politics. Characters from *spell #7* express this issue most cogently through their attire. Employing fashion to announce insurgency, they shout, "we dress up" (18). Putting on one's finest threads to go out in public means jumping into a verbose speaking costume, a funky undertaking. As the poet professes, "…we are a people of color, with color. We cula ful: yellow, violet, green, orange, pink, and always black" (*See No Evil* 49). Funk, when determined by clothing, equates to those moments when anger overlaps pleasure, just as the bright rags that Shange's characters throw on their backs declare both unfettered exhilaration and battle reveille.

Shange's crimson and hot pink dresses and whistling hems answer as well Kennedy's concerns about the colonization of the black home space, Kennedy (early on) protecting it with her masks but Shange aware that it is already too late to fend off the invasion. The poet counters dominant incursions with a collection of aesthetic masquerades, selecting a more fluid substance in the form of silky fabric over a wooden, head-covering. Rather than a capitulation to despair over the state of colored people, Shange's ever-bright couture asserts defiance most assuredly but also amplifies pleasure (and anger), making them all hyperbolic. This theatrical device pulls a sensual lushness out from fetid air. The invitation to put on one's glam rags is instructive and provides a clear passage out from suicide's, conformity's, or nihilism's lure just as Gwendolyn Brooks suggests with her poems about street artists whose palette is a daring clothing arsenal.[23]

In terms of its material purpose, by centering fabric, Shange can introduce yet another cultural viewpoint into her performance's communal hub that already features dancers, musicians, and actors. These apt, often over-the-top togs reinforce the music's and the form's funkiness by challenging dominant predictions that the besieged will fold under the weight of constant affronts and assaults on their territories and bodies. In the same vein as the vibrating hips that relax psychological warfare's chains, the brazen skirts, bright stripes and even high-puffed wigs (*spell #7)* reconstitute authority's polarities by giving those who are under stress another lexicon in the guise of "loud," back-sassing threads, drapes that confirm the Brothers Johnson's famed lyric, "I might change, rearrange…."

Accepting that the rape has already occurred and will be, most likely, ongoing, concealment offers no succor nor does it stimulate Shange's endeavors. Instead, she mourns and celebrates, in the manner of a New Orleans wake, the Middle Passage while she strives to recover and record the places and times when creativity can be achieved outside the boundaries of commodity markets. As Maxine from *spell #7* phrases it:

> …i had a baptists child's version of high mass for the slaves in new orleans whom i had read abt/ & i tried to grow watermelons and rice for the dead slaves from the east. as a child i took on the burden of easing the ghost-colored-folks' souls & trying hard to keep up with the affairs of my own colored world (50)

Shange's writing exists within the same sphere as the Baptist child's high mass that pays tribute to an ancestral presence from the East. Crafting her work from the position of daughter and heir, her pieces exalt ritual, reading, and inventiveness. Consider that many of the poet's works refer to farming or food preparation as essential practices that bridge the living and the dead, a way to imbue the earth with communicative spiritual properties, making it into a telephone of sorts. Certainly, this high mass with its emphasis on gathering sustenance from the ground and converting its issue to bring about social restoration are the tools of the black shaman, forces which Shange taps into and signifies on with her ritualistic theater. In this manner, dancing, lyrical/rhythmic poetry, and vibrant dress are like this offering of watermelon and rice, cultural rites that result from a distilling of the natural world to produce ceremonial elements. Shange says it best when she describes what it means to pick up the pen:

> Writing is for most people a cerebral activity. For me it is a very rhythmic and visceral experience. Dance clears my mind of verbal images and allows me to understand the planet the way I imagine atomic particles experience space. I am not bogged down with the implications of language. I am only involved in the implication of movement which later on, when I do start to write, become manifest in the rhythms of my poetry. (Betsko and Koenig interview 365)

Connecting the desire to uplift a people to this quest to break language away from mechanical imagery makes Shange a deconstructionist. Wrestling against a symbolic order that is manifested in the language while simultaneously recovering and memorializing lost cultures in that same language with the breaking addition of ethnically inflected semiotic signs drawn from dance, fashion, culinary skills, and magic results in, at least for Shange, a theatrical style that is all about conversation. Some voices mock, others confirm, testify, praise, and chant, each so profound that it "…transcend[s] temporal and physical boundaries" (Lester, *Shange* 46).

Shange's choreopoems revolutionized the theater and opened the door for such satirists and experimentalists as George Wolfe and Suzan-Lori Parks, and others who have produced a spate of revisionary and improvisational plays that not only scrutinize and toy with the minstrel but such luminaries as Uncle Tom and Aunt Jemima.[24] Today's African-American drama routinely splices irony and sharp wit with music and conflict-laden dialogue, a strategy that the most noted craftsman of the age, August Wilson, weaves through his more traditionally structured multi-act plays. This splattering of erupting sidebar elements has become so commonplace in black theater that the audience has come to welcome its intrusion. For example, blaring trumpets, overwrought piano playing and rocking blues mark several of Wilson's offerings (*Fences, The Piano Lesson*, and *Ma Rainey's Black Bottom*), noise that is integral to the play and does not appear arbitrarily disruptive but part of the compendium that comprises each work's historical, symbolic, and spiritual resonance. These contemporary innovations rest on Shange's foundationally novel writing process that incorporates discussions with other artists and with the dancer that is Shange. Because of her labor, the American theater has learned to appreciate new breaking forms. Connoisseurs of black performances have come to expect deviation from the traditional three-or five-act European construction, anticipating in its place, bits of funkiness thrown in at key spots, caesura that invite audience participation, carnivalesque back-track and reverberations, black bodies that revel in stepping limbs or pull those same arms, legs, torsos, necks, thighs, and hips through tense gestures that point toward some unfinished pain. These elements pan through the creative space to dislodge a Euro-centric familiarity in favor of a Middle Passage-inflected chaotic unpredictability.

Ironically, these contemporary formal revisions are conjured by way of salvaging acts that seize upon minstrelsy as a progenitor, implementing its mobile, open-mouthed format: the singing, dancing, and intentional and strategic broken speech. Other kernels are combed along the way from ancient myths (African, early English, and Greek), new-world myths (tall tales, slave narratives, literary/dramatic hybrids, and frontier narratives) to historical pageants, passion plays, African masking rituals, and expressionist drama. To these ingredients, African American women writers add their own panache and healthy store of culturally specific aesthetics (shout outs, dance moves, emotionally laden epiphanies, advance and retreat, comedy, and sensuality). The question remains as to whether these heady century-long invigorating sparks will continue given the current dire economic straits that have hampered, for the most part, the kind of climate that supports play writing especially that by black women who often have to labor outside the institutional networks that are available to mainstream artists. The widescale production of works by black women has certainly not increased significantly with few shows reaching the Great Way.[25] Many of the black-owned and-operated community theaters established over the past half-century have closed or are experiencing tough financial times. Similarly, black institutions such as colleges and universities and uplift organizations find that they can no longer justify huge budget appropriations for the arts, and formally segregated high schools that promoted both black writers and performers are no longer preoccupied exclusively with developing cultural outlets for African Americans and showcasing the students' and teachers' talent. Yet, if the history of black women playwrights affirms anything, it predicts that black women and theater will remain inseparable. No matter how small or how imagined the audience has to be, the imperative to craft art will prevail. As Shange claims, sometimes black women write under the auspices of talking out loud to find answers, and if that dialogue to one's people, or self (or other selves) produces theater, then let it wax.

NOTES

[1] Shange has taken up the poet's mantle, claiming that, "…most activity that takes place on our stages [is] overwhelmingly shallow/stilted & imitative. that is probably one of the reasons i insist on calling myself a poet or writer/rather than a playwright" (foreword to *Three Pieces* ix).

[2] Shange selected from several poems when she first began performing *for colored girls* in northern California in the mid-seventies, substituting pieces at will (introduction xiii).

[3] In an interview with Henry Blackwell, Shange admits that, "In most of my work, I'm talking to women, because I'm talking to myself when I write" (137).

[4] *for colored girls* has played in front of incarcerated women at the New Jersey Correctional Institute for Women, Riker's Island, Bedford Hills Prison, and Essex County Prison (Waldron).

[5] *boogie woogie landscapes* started out at the Public Theater on December 18, 1978, then moved to the Symphony Space Theater to benefit the Frank Silvera Writers' Workshop, a Harlem group that provided a training ground for black playwrights (Fraser).

[6] See Michael Awkward's study on intertextuality in the African American female literary tradition: *Inspiring Influences*.

[7] Shange reasons that, "the minstrel may be 'banned' as racist/but the minstrel is more powerful in his deformities than our alleged rejection of him" (foreword to *three pieces* xiii).

[8] Visualize Harriet Jacobs's seven-year stay in her grandmother's attic. Escaping these compact holding pens requires a certain type of psychological and imaginative agility, what Houston Baker refers to as "To Move without Moving" (in *Black Literature and Literary Theory*). Ralph Ellison describes a similar African-American attitude with the phrase "change the joke and slip the yoke" (*Shadow and Act* 45–59).

[9] Eric Lott maintains that minstrelsy not only mocked black bodies and aesthetics but also displayed white admiration for black culture. In mimicking certain belligerent and non-conformist stances that had been coded as black, white youth were able to explore their own dissatisfaction with modern institutions and politics. See *Love and Theft*.

[10] Hopkins came to doubt America's promise as lynching and other horrendous crimes became more commonplace by the turn of the century. Her writing reflects this shift as she turns to novels by 1899 to wage her often-scathing indictment of state-sponsored genocide and segregationist policies.

[11] Filmmaker Issac Julien has commented on this connection, especially in terms of racialized sado-masochistic and voyeuristic images in the visual arts (*Darker Side of Black*).

[12] A fine story that explores this dynamic is Alice Walker's *1955* that is based on Elvis Presley's rise to fame on the back of songs first performed by Big Mama Thornton.

[13] "Filled with the Holy Ghost: Sexual Dimension and Dimensions of Sexuality in the Theater of Ntozake Shange" in *Black Women Playwrights* highlights this issue.

[14] Shange pays tribute to George Clinton, an original "funkateer" and leader of the group, Parliament Funkadelic, when she charges writers to figure out ways to represent on the page Clinton's command to seize the opportunity to dance one's way out of one's constrictions (foreword to *three pieces* xi).

[15] To receive a glimpse of Shange's commitment to individuality, review her essay, *takin a*

solo/a poetic possibility/a poetic imperative (*See No Evil* 26–33).

[16] This design shows up very well in *for colored girls* when the dancers swing in and out of the spotlight. The productions that I have attended feature overlapping moments when several voices can be heard at once. Even the ever-mobile costumes appear to be holding conversations. Music, preferably live, concurrently adds its strains to the mélange.

[17] Unfortunately, some reviewers have managed to disregard Shange's gigantic minstrel mask and, accordingly, misread the play. Take, as a case in point, Richard Eder's claim that the work explores the relationship of black men and women primarily and is in no sense a "piece about show business."

[18] Shange names Childress as an influence (Betsko and Koenig interview 367) and refers to Kennedy's *Rat's Mass* (*See No Evil* 29).

[19] On several occasions, Shange has professed a woman-centered base for her writing. See her interview with Lester Neal and her interview with herself.

[20] Music critic Nelson George discusses uplift ideology's demise in his book, *The Death of Rhythm and Blues*. He argues that budding post-Vietnam War, post-Civil Rights era genres like rap and house music have edged out rhythm and blues' dominance because African Americans have lost faith in the American Dream.

[21] In opposition to what I am arguing, critic Timothy Murray views Michael as an offsetting presence: "As Shange's visionary of moving dreams, Michael confirms that her art is framed in pathos, in struggle, in vulnerable openness" (168). To the contrary, I envision this character as predisposed to deceive just as she and the other figures feed themselves by taking something away from another quadrant. Only collectively and cooperatively can they find the road that leads out of the drama's overarching frame.

[22] The examples are numerous: Fay's story in *spell #7* (21–23), *boogie woogie landscapes* (122–124), and Lady in Red's recitation from *colored girls* (31–35).

[23] I refer to Gwendolyn Brooks' *The Sundays of Satin Legs Smith* in particular.

[24] See pieces by Robert Alexander and Breena Clarke and Glenda Dickerson.

[25] Anna Devere Smith, Susan-Lori Parks, and Robbie McCauley are exceptions.

AFTERWORD

THIS POSTSCRIPT connects what I have gleaned from my concentration on the African American female dramatic tradition to more recent discussions on the general state of black theater. It proposes some means by which we critics, aficionados, and consumers can encourage play composition by black artists and subsequent productions, especially those pieces that explore areas beyond today's formulaic black gospel, comedy, and conventional heavy-handed morality dramas.[1] The first step involves establishing more sophisticated analytical frames that do not view these works, either individually or collectively, as transparent, primarily experientially based naturalism. While we can credit the academy with spearheading a revisionary thrust over the last twenty-five years that has resulted in articles and books on the subject, there is a conspicuous gap between these measured responses and the commentator who writes for a newspaper or a magazine. Furthermore, if we compare these two evaluative outlets, it becomes apparent that the reviewer has far more influence over whether a certain show or ones of a similar ilk will either make it to the stage or endure more than a few nights. Unfortunately, these judges that retain more immediate power over a theater piece evidence a less firm grip on the alternative aesthetics and viewpoints that exceed predictable conventions, knowledge that should inform their assessments. So what often ensues is that productions by black writers are held up against Euro-centric standards, and the columnist interprets any creative difference from these rules as either incomprehensible or something requiring correction. More specifically, within Western theater discourse, the Negro has been assigned very limited but established roles that generally discount a black female presence while it fires the black male image into something at once excessive and ineffectual. While these long-standing demarcations are slowly breaking down as more black journalists have entered the marketplace, they continue to impact directly on how reporters see black play.

Reviews that too easily connect the black writer's biographical data to the stage show are especially suspicious. These readings that submerge the offering inside the black artist's personal experience negate the fact that she has applied an imaginative process to her composition that includes her reading of the traditions that she engages as well as her general position on modern life. One is reminded of Kennedy's insightful emphasis in the *Alexander Plays* on would-be colonizers' ferreting out the intimate details of writer/character Suzanne Alexander's past, or Kennedy's tongue-in-cheek reply in the form of *People Who Led to My Plays* to the question, who influenced you as a writer? (As if that information could result in a simple, linear answer.) In place of analytical models that unabashedly chain the creator's personal history to her artistic vision, I suggest that we assume these relationships are so highly mediated as to make attempts at charting clear lines between the writer's life and her product futile and, ultimately, insupportable. It is far more rewarding to concentrate on the intertextual bridges that the treatments establish with other cultural issues and with events. This study has focused on what African American women writers have said to each other with a few major, American-born racialized types entering the conversation. Other examinations that explore how this tradition converses with drama from the Caribbean and Africa as well with other closely related genres such as the circus, tent shows, and music concerts would surely enhance this study.

We should assume that black women writers are astute observers of global and national trends and highlight how these happenings impact on the daily circumstances of black people. This may seem an obvious statement, but all too often examiners have side-stepped the political terrain in which these works are carefully placed and have opted instead to gather them under the slice-of-life category that restricts the artistic resonance to the so-called "natural drama" found in black social groups. To the contrary, theater by black women often contains an intricate layering of text and subtexts that speak directly to an implied core of sympathetic and intimate viewers but also signify on consumers who are less familiar with the flashing bobs and weaves of black survival. Pushing and pulling against preconceived notions, black women playwrights rely on quick-change methodologies to move them beyond constraining boundaries. Therefore, it is crucial that we create a critical language that can log how these offerings can be celebratory and inviting, at times, but, at other moments or simultaneously, may be hostile, even repellent, intentionally exposing the audience to the particular circumstances that surround women of color in the material world: beset and besieged but trying to maintain communities and joy nevertheless. In fact, the media journalist is targeted as a recipient of some of these barbed messages in post-fifties pieces by black women playwrights as code is sent to him through the dialogue and the embroiled structure. Generally, these communiqués call for greater sensitivity to ethnic, gender, class and racial difference and demand that the theater stop reflecting racist and sexist master fantasies.[2]

Moreover, because plays by black women are often constructed to reach disparate audience subgroups, they come across as volatile, a condition that some critics label as excessive emotional exaggeration. However, this instability is inserted to deconstruct dramatic structure that does not serve black female artists' creative requirements.[3] So if there are radical shifts in mood or jagged or odd transpositions of character, they comprise part of an overarching thrust to dislodge sealed categorization and staid tableaus. By attributing this radical charge to an unreflective seeping sentimentality or pathos, the assessor denies the intellectual labor that black female playwrights invest in and inject into their pieces. Pauline Hopkins studied Black Nationalism and kept abreast of Africa's liberation efforts; Angelina Grimké was steeped in information about the abolitionist and Civil Rights Movement; Shirley Graham held an advanced degree in musicology: Hurston took to anthropology on a graduate level; Marita Bonner studied the German language and culture at Radcliffe. Each of the playwrights in this study is well read and diligently committed to philosophy from all walks of life. This drive to keep informed that includes a wide range of interdisciplinary engagement represents a far cry from the predominant journalistic notions that these women write from a narrowly bounded channel of personal experience. To the contrary, these tradition bearers evidence a deep reflection on world events and patterns and a zeal for bettering them. Therefore, to do justice to these works, they should be treated as part of a broad cultural collage that, through exchange, moves back and forth, through and over historical time. Considering that a deeply contemplative base reinforces the African American women's dramatic tradition and allows for open but intense evaluations that do not flatten the plays into manageable, transparent, and disconnected installations, one can view them as ongoing conversations that center on how to bend the theatrical platform to reflect autonomous black-owned desire, a project that began in earnest in the nineteenth century.[4] Unfortunately, there are few cases today when reporters take the time to determine how productions by black women fit into this overarching schema.

This disregard that does not appreciate that this body of works constitutes a tradition (one that certainly intersects with many different ideas, practices, and artistic modes) returns us to materialist concerns. There are very few black male or black female theater critics, and those who report on these stage pieces by black women are associated often in some manner with higher education and write for an academic circle even though they may write for mainstream publications as well (see Glenda Dickerson, Elizabeth

Brown-Guillory, Margaret Wilkerson, bell hooks, and Michelle Wallace). The issue of who owns the critical apparatus hangs over black theater's future. James Snead has written that in Western popular culture, drama is formed by the contrast of light and dark, and Hollywood paints black to appear very black (146). Snead's words underscore how blackness has been placed as a foil to normalized "whiteness." This associative link has enabled white imaginations and wills to continue owning dark skin by way of cultural representation and critical discourse. Modern black theater as scripted by both men and women has struggled since its inception to re-appropriate and redefine blackness. This battle has not only been levied via the actual pieces that appear on the stage, which often enact a repossession of black bodies and expression, but also through an insistent cry for black ownership of buildings, companies, journals, and newspapers.

Defenders of black theater have noticed that in the past ten years or more these spaces are disappearing at an alarming rate, some of them directly citing the move toward multiculturalism in the fine arts as the culprit. "The nineties found financial support shifted away from ethno-specific arts programs in favor of funding the agglutinated Other, newly marginalized as the multi-cultural experience" (Harrison, "Crisis" 573). This funding shift away from black theaters and companies toward white-owned regional theaters that promise multi-cultural installations has left black-owned theaters anemically struggling to cover expenses and, therefore, unable to plan for the future. Other less fortunate units have had to close their doors, making Glenda Dickerson's astute observation "...if you own a piece of property, they can't put you off" (212) increasingly apt. This opinion is shared by many black writers, directors, theater owners, performers, and critics including August Wilson, who has debated the issue contentiously and publicly with Robert Brustein, setting off an uproar that may actually reinvigorate black arts.[5] Of course, the bottom line is that federal funding, because of conservative changes in government policy and priorities, has declined, and resources that were once adequate are now scarce.

In the midst of these depressing economic times, the worry about multi-cultural theater elevation over that which is owned and controlled by specific racial and ethnic groups is at least twofold. James Moy has pointed out that when racially or ethnically branded others are allotted roles in mainstream productions, racial markers do not altogether disappear but are broken apart into elements that continue to "circulate freely" in an "increasingly dense hypertext" that houses a "new theoretical order," where the representations of people of color contain "elemental traces of the stereotype" (199). Because of this residue, performances by people of color are stifled by the floating, always-already scraps that contain difference. This realignment is more likely to occur when the play is originally intended for an all-white cast and a person of color receives a role in it. Once she enters the production, the screen in her corner shifts toward racial typecasting. The other likelihood is that a character is predetermined to be from a specific ethnic or racial group other than white and middle or upper class. In this case, Moy implies that through the very script, the character may likely be tinged with accretion from these stereotypes. In both cases, whether through the live performance's shading or through the actual stage directions and dialogue, whiteness remains central and invisible as those who are not spin out from that omnipresent principle.

Another related trouble spot is the multi-cultural compilation that either contains several vignettes about different ethnic/racial groups, or it covers several divergent groups under one sweeping gesture. In these instances, there may be so many competing aesthetics and themes that what may happen to fend off a Babel-like incomprehensibility is a fall back to what Paul Harrison calls "a Eurocentric universe of apocalyptic alienation" ("Crisis" 574). I agree with Harrison that this is certainly a credible point because black drama is so diffuse, so primed for quick change, that mixing it with two or three other renditions does not leave enough space or opportunity to explore thoroughly even one imaginative vision. Mull over, for instance, Caribbean scholar and writer Honor Ford-Smith's projection of what good Jamaican performance art should encompass: "Street theater, forum theater, conventional three-act plays and poetic dramas need to mix with dub poetry, cabaret and Sunday-afternoon yard concerts" (194). If black drama from its various Diasporic locations should incorporate such energetic and distinct styles, how can it retain its integrity to its own expressive community sandwiched between several other glimpses into "ethnic culture"? The representations of hybridity that already exist in colored cultures may be lost if too many ethnic scenes are crowded under one roof. Furthermore, smoothing out the already discrete but dialogic bridges found in black theater (as well as from other minority groups) will assuredly end in a return to white-owned essentialism or towards alienated sound bites that no one can really absorb.

In the face of these issues, I posit my final observation, which is merely that theater for and by people of the African Diaspora is still very much needed in the United States. In this nation where literacy is high and African Americans spend millions of dollars each year on books by black authors whose narratives feature black subjects, book clubs, bookstores, poetry readings, and even writer's groups are accessible if not plentiful in some areas (add on-line chat rooms and other Internet forums). While I applaud this surging interest in printed texts, it cannot in and of itself transport black culture, which Shange reminds us banks on singing, dancing, and costuming—whether we like to admit it or not. That is, certain African American rituals are performance based and can only be passed on through some form of theater. Overall, these modes preserve a spirituality that is built on dialogue across distances and temporal locations, a loosely defined communion with ancestral forces, a repartee that is driven by the artist's and implied ideal audience's belief that some tribute is owed to those who have gone on before.

Working in tandem with this ceremonial function, inherently, black theater embraces revolution. While black male writers have succeeded to some degree in clearing a dramatic space that forecasts and demands radical change because of the contributions of Neal, Baraka, Bullins, and others in the sixties and seventies, black women playwrights labor to deliver their message as their precarious position in American society at large determines how their work is interpreted/translated, even if they quite firmly stipulate change with their texts. For example, Angelina Grimké pressed for lynching's cessation with *Rachel* by depicting a mother's boycott, but it was years before critics could decipher this underlying mandate, instead converging on the main character's "nervous condition." So, what is germane is that no matter the ideological underpinnings, products by black women are often stripped of their political edge by critics who resist their call for wide-scale transformation. Also, because of gender-based restrictions, no matter how much a woman writer seethes and assertively employs her pen to correct injustices, she is compelled too often to convey these desires within proper and decorous (feminine) aesthetics. So, offerings by black women dramatists often blend a forecast for revolution within muted, subtle sub-textual pockets. However, just because black women writers have been forced to subdue, to some degree, the radical thrust of their plays does not mean that we should ignore it. The bottom line is that we can only reach Kennedy's evocative "the coming of peace" (*Dead Essex)* after much turmoil and strain, exertion that has been documented by the African American female dramatist's tradition if we listen and look for it. Theater is the place where this skirmish that first began during the Middle Passage finds an artistic home, a site that will survive until social equality renders it superfluous.

NOTES

[1] Gates refers to these plays as the Chitlin Circuit. While this seems a rather judgmental appellation, I agree that the works under this umbrella do not stray from a pre-rehearsed series of themes that revolve around the saving of lost souls and the girl next door getting her man. I suggest that further study of these plays may prove revealing, especially an exploration of why certain topics have arisen as integrally comforting to black communities at this particular point in history.

[2] See, in particular, Childress's *Trouble in Mind*, Kennedy's *Alexander Plays*, and Shange's *spell #7*.

[3] Grimké's *Rachel* is a prime example of a text that uses a shattering sentimentality to effect material reform.

[4] It should be noted that the most recent academic work on black women's drama is promising. Please see the works cited for an extensive list of these treatments. However, the reviews, for the most part, tend to be reactionary: love/hate toss-ups that show very little evidence that the commentator has done any research about the tradition as a whole or even about the specific interests of the playwright beyond an individual work.

[5] See the town hall debate: *On Cultural Power: The August Wilson/Robert Brustein Discussion.*

WORKS CITED

Primary Sources

Alexander, Robert. *I Ain't Yo Uncle: The New Jack Uncle Tom's Cabin*. Woodstock: Dramatic Publishing, 1996.

Bonner, Marita. *Exit: An Illusion. Black Female Playwrights: An Anthology of Plays before 1950*. Ed. Kathy Perkins. Bloomington, Indiana: Indiana University Press, 1990. 200–205.

———. *Frye Street and Environs: The Collected Works of Marita Bonner Occomy*. Eds. Joyce Flynn and Joyce Occomy Stricklin. Boston: Beacon Press, 1987.

———. *The Pot Maker. The Opportunity Reader*. Ed. Sondra Kathryn Wilson. New York: Random House, 1999. 241–249.

———. *The Purple Flower. Black Theatre USA, The Early Period, 1847–1938*. Eds. James Hatch and Ted Shine. New York: The Free Press, 1996. 207–212.

Brown, Lennox. *Devil Mas': A Play in Three Acts. Kuntu Drama*. Ed. Paul Carter Harrison. New York: Grove Press, 1974.

Brown, William Wells. *The Escape; or, A Leap for Freedom. Black Theatre USA, The Early Period, 1847–1938*. Eds. James Hatch and Ted Shine. New York: The Free Press, 1996. 37–60.

Burrill, Mary P. *Aftermath. Black Theatre USA, The Early Period 1847–1938*. Eds. James Hatch and Ted Shine. New York: The Free Press, 1996. 176–182.

———. *They That Sit in Darkness. Black Female Playwrights: An Anthology of Plays before 1950*. Ed. Kathy Perkins. Bloomington, Indiana: Indiana University Press, 1990. 67–79.

Childress, Alice. *Florence, A One-Act Play. Wines in the Wilderness: Plays by African American Women from the Harlem Renaissance to the Present*. Ed. Elizabeth Brown-Guillory. New York: Greenwood, 1990. 111–121.

———. *Like One of the Family*. Boston: Beacon Press, 1986.

———. *Mojo and String: Two Plays*. New York: Dramatists Play Service, 1971.

———. *Trouble in Mind: A Comedy-Drama in Two Acts. Plays by American Women: 1930–1960*. Ed. Judith E. Barlow. New York: Applause, 1994. 469–542.

———. *Wedding Band: A Love/Hate Story in Black and White*. New York: French, 1973.

———. *Wine in the Wilderness*. New York: Dramatists Play Service, 1969.

Clarke, Breena, and Glenda Dickerson. *Re/membering Aunt Jemima. Colored Contradictions*. Eds. Harry J. Elam Jr. and Robert Alexander. New York: Penguin Books, 1996. 141–172.

Du Bois, W.E.B. *The Star of Ethiopia. Black Theatre USA, The Early Period 1847–1938*. Eds. James Hatch and Ted Shine. New York: The Free Press, 1996. 89–92.

Dunbar-Nelson, Alice. *Mine Eyes Have Seen. Black Theatre USA, The Early Period, 1847–1938*. Eds. James Hatch and Ted Shine. New York: The Free Press, 1996. 170–174.

Duncan, Thelma Myrtle. *Sacrifice. Plays and Pageants from the Life of the Negro*. Compiled by Willis Richardson. 1930. Reprint, Jackson: University of Mississippi, 1993. 3–24.

Gaines-Shelton, Ruth Ada. *The Church Fight. Black Theatre USA, The Early Period, 1847–1938*. Eds. James Hatch and Ted Shine. New York: The Free Press, 1996. 194–196.

Graham, Shirley. *It's Morning. Black Female Playwrights: An Anthology of Plays before 1950*. Ed. Kathy Perkins. Bloomington, Indiana: Indiana University Press, 1990. 211–224.

———. *Tom-Tom. The Roots of African American Drama*. Eds. Leo Hamalian and James Hatch. Detroit: Wayne State University Press, 1991. 238–286.

Grimké, Angelina. *Rachel. Black Theatre USA, The Early Period, 1847–1938*. Eds. James Hatch and Ted Shine. New York: The Free Press, 1996. 135–168.

———. *Selected Works of Angelina Weld Grimké*. Ed. Carolivia Herron. Oxford: Oxford University Press, 1991.

Guinn, Dorothy, C. *Out of the Dark. Plays and Pageants from the Life of the Negro*. Compiled by Willis Richardson. 1930. Reprint, Jackson: University of Mississippi, 1993. 305–330.

Gunner, Frances. *The Light of the Women. Plays and Pageants from the Life of the Negro*. Compiled by Willis Richardson. 1930. Reprint, Jackson: University of Mississippi, 1993. 333–342.

Hansberry, Lorraine. *Les Blancs: The Collected Last Plays of Lorraine Hansberry*. Ed. Robert Nemiroff. New York: Random House, 1972.

———. *A Raisin in the Sun*. New York: New American Library, 1966.

Hopkins, Pauline. "Famous Women of the Negro Race." *Colored American*. 4 (November 1901): 45–53; 4 (February 1902): 211–233; 4 (April 1902): 366–371; 5 (May 1902): 41–46; 5 (June 1902): 125–130; 5 (July 1902): 206–213; 5 (August 1902): 273–277; 5 (September 1902): 445–450; 5 (October 1902): 362–367.

———. *Peculiar Sam, or The Underground Railroad, A Musical Drama in Four Acts. The Roots of African American Drama*. Eds. Leo Hamalian and James Hatch. Detroit: Wayne State University Press, 1991. 100–123.

Hurston, Zora Neale. *Color Struck. Black Female Playwrights: An Anthology of Plays before 1950*. Ed. Kathy Perkins. Bloomington, Indiana: Indiana University Press, 1990. 89–102.

———. *The First One. Black Female Playwrights: An Anthology of Plays before 1950*. Ed. Kathy Perkins. Bloomington, Indiana: Indiana University Press, 1990. 80–88.

Hurston, Zora Neale, and Langston Hughes. *Mule Bone*. New York: Harper, 1991.

Johnson, Georgia Douglas. *Blue Blood. Black Female Playwrights: An Anthology of Plays before 1950*. Ed. Kathy Perkins. Bloomington, Indiana: Indiana University Press, 1990. 38–46.

———. *Frederick Douglass. Negro History in Thirteen Plays*. Eds. Willis Richardson and May Miller. Washington, D.C.: Associated Press, 1935. 143–165.

———. *Blue-Eyed Black Boy. Black Female Playwrights: An Anthology of Plays before 1950*. Ed. Kathy Perkins. Bloomington, Indiana: Indiana University Press, 1990. 47–51.

———. *Plumes: A Folk Tragedy. Black Female Playwrights: An Anthology of Plays before 1950*. Ed. Kathy Perkins. Bloomington, Indiana: Indiana University Press, 1990. 24–30.

———. *Safe. Wines in the Wilderness: Plays by African American Women from the Harlem Renaissance to the Present*. Ed. Elizabeth Brown-Guillory. New York: Greenwood, 1990. 26–32.

———. *A Sunday Morning in the South. Black Theatre USA, The Early Period, 1847–1938*. Eds. James Hatch and Ted Shine. New York: The Free Press, 1996. 233–237.

———. *William and Ellen Craft. Negro History in Thirteen Plays*. Eds.Willis Richardson and May Miller. Washington, D.C: Associated Press, 1935. 164–186.

Jones, Leroi [Imamu Amiri Baraka]. *Dutchman and the Slave*. New York: Morrow, William and Company, 1976.

Kennedy, Adam P., and Adrienne Kennedy. *Sleep Deprivation Chamber*. New York: Theatre Communications Group, 1996.

Kennedy, Adrienne. *Adrienne Kennedy in One Act*. Minneapolis: University of Minnesota Press, 1988.

———. *An Adrienne Kennedy Reader*. Ed. Werner Sollors. Minneapolis: University of Minnesota Press, 2001.

———. *The Alexander Plays*. Minneapolis: University of Minnesota Press, 1992.

———. *Deadly Triplets: A Theatre Mystery and Journal*. Minneapolis: University of Minnesota Press, 1990.

———. *An Evening with Dead Essex. Theater*. 9.2 (1978): 66–78.

———. *People Who Led to My Plays*. New York: Theatre Communications Group, 1987.

Miller, May. *Christophe's Daughters. Black Female Playwrights: An Anthology of Plays before 1950*. Ed. Kathy Perkins. Bloomington Indiana: Indiana University Press, 1990. 166–175.

———. *Graven Images. Black Theatre USA, The Early Period 1847 to 1938*. Eds. James Hatch and Ted Shine. New York: The Free Press, 1996. 335–341.

———. *Harriet Tubman. Black Female Playwrights: An Anthology of Plays before 1950*. Ed. Kathy Perkins. Bloomington, Indiana: Indiana University Press, 1990. 176–185.

———. *Nails and Thorns. The Roots of African American Drama*. Eds. Leo Hamalian and James Hatch. Detroit: Wayne State University Press, 1991. 310–327.

———. *Riding the Goat. Black Female Playwrights: An Anthology of Plays before 1950*. Ed. Kathy Perkins. Bloomington, Indiana: Indiana University Press, 1990. 153–165.

———. *Sojourner Truth. Negro History in Thirteen Plays*. Eds. Willis Richardson and May Miller. Washington, D.C.: Associated Press, 1935. 313–333.

———. *Stragglers in the Dust. Black Female Playwrights: An Anthology of Plays before 1950*. Ed. Kathy Perkins. Bloomington, Indiana: Indiana University Press, 1990. 145–152.

Shange, Ntozake. *From Okra to Greens/ A Different Kinda Love Story: A Play/with Music & Dance*. New York: Samuel French, 1985.

———. *for colored girls who have considered suicide when the rainbow is enuf*. New York: Collier Books, 1989.

———. *Love Space Demands (a continuing saga)*. New York: St. Martin's Press, 1991.

———. *nappy edges*. New York: Methuen, 1987.

———. *See No Evil: Prefaces, Essays & Accounts, 1976-1983*. San Francisco: Momo's Press, 1984.

———. *three pieces: spell #7; a photograph: lovers in motion; boogie woogie landscapes*. New York: Penguin Books, 1982.

Spence, Eulalie. *Her. Black Female Playwrights: An Anthology of Plays before 1950*. Ed. Kathy Perkins. Bloomington, Indiana: Indiana University Press, 1990. 132–140.

———. *Episode. Wines in the Wilderness*. Ed. Elizabeth Brown-Guillory. New York: Praeger, 1990. 51–60.

———. *Fool's Errand. Black Female Playwrights: An Anthology of Plays before 1950*. Ed. Kathy Perkins. Bloomington, Indiana: Indiana University Press, 1990. 119–131.

———. *Foreign Mail*. New York: French, 1927.

———. *Hot Stuff. Wines in the Wilderness*. Ed. Elizabeth Brown-Guillory. New York: Praeger, 1990. 43–50.

———. *The Starter. Plays of Negro Life*. Eds. Alain Locke and Montgomery Gregory. New York: Harper Brothers, 1927. 205–214.

———. *Undertow. Black Theatre USA, The Early Period 1847 to 1938*. Eds. James Hatch and Ted Shine. New York: The Free Press, 1996. 199–205.

Tillman, Katherine D. Chapman. *Aunt Betsy's Thanksgiving. The Roots of African American Drama*. Eds. Leo Hamalian and James Hatch. Detroit: Wayne State University Press, 1991. 126–133.

Williams, Tennessee. *Cat on a Hot Tin Roof*. New York: New American Library, 1989.

———. *The Glass Menagerie*. New York: New Directions, 1999.

———. *A Streetcar Named Desire*. New York: New American Library, 1989.

Wilson, August. *Fences*. New York: Plume, 1986.

———. *Ma Rainey's Black Bottom*. New York: Plume, 1985.

———. *The Piano Lesson*. New York: Plume, 1990.

Wolfe, George. *The Colored Museum*. New York: Grove, 1988.

Secondary Sources

Abramson, Doris E. "Angelina Weld Grimké, Mary Burrill, Georgia Douglas Johnson, and Marita Bonner." *Sage*. 2.1 (1985): 9–13.

Allen, Carol. *Black Women Intellectuals: Strategies of Nation, Family and Neighborhood in the Works of Pauline Hopkins, Jessie Fauset and Marita Bonner*. New York: Garland, 1998.

———. "Snapping Frontiers: Lynching Photography, Then and Now." *Spectacular Savagery*. Ed. Barbara Lewis.

Ammons, Elizabeth. "*Winona*, Bakhtin, and Hopkins in the Twenty-First Century." *The Unruly Voice*. Ed. John Cullen Gruesser. Urbana: University of Illinois Press, 1996. 211–220.

Anderson, Lisa M. *Mammies No More: The Changing Image of Black Women on Stage and Screen*. Lanham, MD: Rowman and Littlefield Publishers, 1997.

Archer, Leonard. *Black Images in American Theater*. Nashville: Pageant Press, 1973.

Austin, Gayle. "Alice Childress: Black Women Playwright as Feminist Critic." *Southern Quarterly*. 25.3 (1987): 53–62.

Awkwar ichael. *Inspiring Influences*. New York: Columbia University Press, 1989.

on. *Blues, Ideology, and Afro-American Literature*. Chicago: Chicago University , 1984.

nism and the Harlem Renaissance. Chicago: Chicago University Press, 1987.

ve Without Moving." *Black Literature and Literary Theory*. Ed. Henry Louis r. New York: Routledge, 1984. 221–248.

———. *Workings of the Spirit*. Chicago: Chicago University Press, 1991.

Barlow, Judith, ed. *Plays by American Women: 1930–1960*. New York: Applause Publisher, 1994.

Barnes, Clive. "A *Rat's Mass* Weaves Drama of Poetic Fabric." Review of *A Rat's Mass* by Adrienne Kennedy. *New York Times*, 1 November 1969, 39.

Barth, Jonathan. *Lost in the Funhouse*. New York: Bantam Books, 1979.

Bean, Annemarie. "Black Minstrelsy and Double Inversion, Circa 1890." *African American Performance and Theater History*. Eds. Harry J. Elam and David Krasner. New York: Oxford UP, 2001. 171–191.

Benjamin, Walter. *Illuminations*. Ed. Hannah Arendt. Trans. Harry Zohn. New York: Schocken, 1969.

Benston, Kimberly. "The Aesthetic of Modern Black Drama: From Mimesis to Methexis." *The Theatre of Black Americans: A Collection of Critical Essays*. Ed. Errol Hill. New York: Applause Theatre Book Publishers, 1987. 61–78.

———. "Locating Adrienne Kennedy: Prefacing the Subject." *Intersecting Boundaries: The Theater of Adrienne Kennedy*. Eds. Paul K. Bryant-Jackson and Lois More Overbeck. Minneapolis: University of Minnesota Press, 1992. 113–130.

———. "*Cities in Bezique*: Adrienne Kennedy's Expressionistic Vision." *College Language Association Journal*. 20.2 (1976): 235–244.

Betsko, Kathleen, and Rachel Koenig. *Interviews with Contemporary Women Playwrights*. New York: Beech Tree Books, 1987.

Bigsby, C.W.E. *A Critical Introduction to Twentieth-Century American Drama: Beyond Broadway*. New York: Cambridge University Press, 1985.

Billingslea-Brown, Alma Jean. "The 'Blight of Legalized Limitation' in Alice Childress's *Wedding Band*." *Law and Literature*. Eds. Bruce Rockwood and Roberta Kevelson. New York: Peter Lang, 1996. 39–51.

Blackwell, Henry. "An Interview with Ntozake Shange." *Black American Literature Forum*. 13.4 (1979): 134–138.

Blau, Herbert. *The Eye of Prey: Subversions of the Postmodern*. Bloomington: Indiana University Press, 1987.

———. "Ideology and Performance." *Theatre Journal*. 35.4 (1983): 441–460.

Bogle, Donald. *Brown Sugar: Eighty Years of America's Black Female Superstars*. New York: daCapo Press, 1980.

———. *Toms, Coons, Mulattoes, Mammies, and Bucks: An Interpretive History of Blacks in American Films*. New York: The Viking Press, 1973.

Boskin, Joseph. *Sambo: The Rise and Demise of an American Jester*. New York: Oxford University Press, 1986.

Bradstreet, Anne. "To My Dear Children." *The Works of Anne Bradstreet*. Ed. Jeannine Hensley. Cambridge: Belknap Press, 1967. 240–245.

Brantley, Ben. "7 Sisters Still Reflect Rainbow's Colors." Review of *for colored girls* by Ntozake Shange. *New York Times*, 26 June 1995, C11+.

Brecht, Bertolt. *Brecht on Theater*. Trans. and Ed. John Willett. New York: Hill and Wang, 1964.

Brooks, Gwendolyn. "The Sundays of Satin-Legs Smith." *Selected Poems*. New York: Perennial Classics, 1999. 12–18.

Brooks, Kristina. "Mammies, Bucks and Wenches: Minstrelsy, Racial Pornography, and Racial Politics in Pauline Hopkins's *Hagar's Daughter*." *The Unruly Voice*. Ed. John Cullen Gruesser. Urbana: University of Illinois Press, 1996. 119–157.

Brown, E. Barnsley. "Celebrating the (Extra)Ordinary." *Black Women Playwrights*. Ed. Carol P. Marsh-Lockett. New York: Garland, 1999. 131–153.

Brown, Janet. *Feminist Drama: Definition and Critical Analysis*. Metuchen: Scarecrow Press, 1979.

Brown, Wesley. *Darktown Strutters*. New York: Cane Hill, 1994.

Brown-Guillory, Elizabeth. *Their Place on the Stage: Black Women Playwrights in America*. New York: Praeger, 1990.

———. *Wines in the Wilderness: An Anthology of Plays before 1950*. New York: Praeger, 1990.

Browne, Ray B. "Shakespeare in American Vaudeville and Negro Minstrelsy." *American Quarterly*. 12.3 (1960): 374–391.

Bryant-Jackson, Paul K. "Kennedy's Travelers in the American and African Continuum." *Intersecting Boundaries: The Theater of Adrienne Kennedy*. Eds. Paul K. Bryant-Jackson and Lois More Overbeck. Minneapolis: University of Minnesota Press, 1992. 45–57.

Bryant-Jackson, Paul K., and Lois More Overbeck. "Adrienne Kennedy: An Interview." *Intersecting Boundaries: The Theater of Adrienne Kennedy*. Minneapolis: University of Minnesota Press, 1992. 3–12.

———. *Intersecting Boundaries: The Theater of Adrienne Kennedy*. Minneapolis: University of Minnesota Press, 1992.

Bryer, Jackson, ed. *The Playwright's Art: Conversations with Contemporary American Dramatists*. New Brunswick: Rutgers University Press, 1995.

Burke, Sally. *American Feminist Playwrights: A Critical History*. New York: Twayne, 1996.

Butler, Judith. "Performative Acts and Gender Constitution." *Performing Feminisms*. Ed. Sue-Ellen Case. Baltimore: Johns Hopkins Press, 1990. 270–282.

Carter, Steven R. *Hansberry's Drama: Commitment amid Complexity*. New York: Meridian, 1993.

Case, Sue-Ellen. *Feminism and Theatre*. New York: Methuen, 1988.

Childress, Alice. "But I Do My Thing." *New York Times*, 2 February 1969, D9.

———. "For a Negro Theatre." *Masses and Mainstream* 4 (1951): 61–64.

———. "Keynote Address." *International Women Playwrights: Voices of Identity and Transformation—Proceedings of the First International Women Playwrights Conference, October 18–23, 1988*. Metuchen: Scarecrow Press, 1993. N. p.

———. "Negro Woman in Literature." *Freedomways*. 6 (1966): 14–19.

———. "Why Talk About That?" *Negro Digest*. 16 (April 1967): 17–21.

Cliff, Michelle. *No Telephone to Heaven*. New York: Plume, 1996.

Collins, Bootsy. "Stretchin' Out in a Rubber Band" by W. Collins and G. Clinton. *Stretchin' Out in Booty's Rubber Band*. Warner Brothers Recording, 1976.

Collins, Patricia Hill. *Black Feminist Thought: Knowledge, Consciousness, and the Politics of Empowerment,* 2nd edition. New York: Routledge Press, 2000.

Collins, William B. "A Strong Protest of Black Men—by Black Women." Review of *for colored girls* by Ntozake Shange. *Philadelphia Inquirer*, 29 Mar. 1978, B4.

Craig, Quita. *Black Drama of the Federal Theatre Era: Beyond the Formal Horizon*. Amherst: University of Massachusetts Press, 1980.

Cripps, Thomas. *Slow Fade to Black: The Negro in American Film, 1900–1942*. New York: Oxford University Press, 1977.

Cronacher, Karen. "Unmasking the Minstrel Mask's Black Magic in Ntozake Shange's *spell #7*." *Theater Journal*. 44 (1992): 177–193.

Cullen, Countee. "Heritage." *The Black Poets.* Ed. Dudley Randall. New York: Bantam Books, 1971. 95–98.

Curb, Rosemary. "Alice Childress." *Dictionary of Literary Biography: Twentieth-Century American Dramatists.* Volume 7. Ed. John MacNicholas. Detroit: Gale Research, 1981. 118–124.

———. "An Unfashionable Tragedy of American Racism: Alice Childress's *Wedding Band.*" *MELUS.* 7 (1980): 57–68.

Dance, Daryl. Ed. *Honey, Hush!: An Anthology of African American Women's Humor.* New York: Norton, 1998.

Delany, Martin R. *The Condition, Elevation, Emigration and Destiny of the Colored People of the United States.* Black Classics Press, 1996.

Diamond, Elin. "Brechtian Theory/Feminist Theory: Toward a Gestic Feminist Criticism." *The Drama Review.* 32.1 (1989): 168–180.

———. "(In)Visible Bodies in Churchill's Theater." *Making a Spectacle: Feminist Essays on Contemporary Women's Theater.* Ed. Lynda Hart. Ann Arbor: The University of Michigan Press, 1989. 92–105.

———. "Rethinking Identification: Kennedy, Freud, Brecht." *The Pushcart Prize xvii, 1992–1993: Best of the Small Press.* Ed. Bill Henderson. Wainscott: Pushcart Press. 86–99.

Dickerson, Glenda. "A Womanist African-American Theater." *Performing Feminisms.* Ed. Sue-Ellen Case. Baltimore: Johns Hopkins Press, 1990. 109–118.

———. In *International Women Playwrights: Voices of Identity and Transformation—Proceedings of the First International Women Playwrights Conference, October 18–23, 1988.* Metuchen: Scarecrow Press, 1993. N. p.

Dillon, John. "Alice Childress' *Wedding Band* at the Milwaukee Repertory Theater: A Photo Essay." *Studies in American Drama, 1945–Present.* 4 (1989): 129–141.

Douglass, Frederick. *Narrative of the Life of Frederick Douglass, An American Slave: Written by Himself.* Eds. John Blassingame, John R. McKingan, Peter R. Hinks. New Haven: Yale University Press, 2001.

Dresner, Zita. "Alice Childress's *Like One of the Family: Domestic and Undomesticated Domestic Humor.*" *Look Who's Laughing.* Ed. Gail Finney. Langhorne: Gordon and Breach, 1994. 221–229.

Duberman, Martin. "Black Theater." *Partisan Review.* 36.3 (1969): 483–500.

Du Bois, W.E.B. "Editing the *Crisis.*" *The Crisis Reader.* Ed. Sondra Kathryn Wilson. New York: Random House, 1999. xxviii–xxix.

———. "Krigwa Little Theatre." *Crisis.* 32 (1926): 135.

———. *The Souls of Black Folk.* New York: Bantam, 1969.

Eder, Richard. "Stage: Ntozake Shange in her *spell #7* at Public." Review of *spell #7* by Ntozake Shange. *New York Times*, 4 June, 1979, C13.

Elam, Harry J. Jr., and David Krasner, eds. *African American Performance and Theater History: A Critical Reader.* New York: Oxford University Press, 2001.

Elkins, Marilyn. "Sicker than a Rabid Dog: African American Women Playwrights Look at War." *Black Women Playwrights.* Ed. Carol P. Marsh-Lockett. New York: Garland, 1999. 55–68.

Ellison, Ralph. *The Invisible Man.* New York: Vintage Books, 1972.

———. *Shadow and Act.* New York: Random House, 1953.

Fabre, Genevieve. *Drumbeats, Masks and Metaphor: Contemporary Afro-American Theatre.* Cambridge: Harvard University Press, 1983.

Fanon, Franz. *Black Skin, White Mask.* 1967. Trans. Charles Lam Markham. New York: Grove, 1991.

———. *Toward the African Revolution.* 1967. Trans. Haakon Chevalier. New York: Grove, 1988.

Fletcher, Winona. "Georgia Douglass Johnson." *Dictionary of Literary Biography: Afro-American Writers Before the Harlem Renaissance.* Vol. 50. Ed. Trudier Harris. Detroit: Gale Research Company, 1986. 153–164.

Flowers, Sandra Hollin. "Colored Girls: Textbook for the Eighties." *Black American Literature Forum.* 15.2 (1981): 51–54.

Ford-Smith, Honor. *International Women Playwrights: Voices of Identity and Transformation—Proceedings of the First International Women Playwrights Conference, October 18–23, 1988.* Metuchen: Scarecrow Press, 1993. N. p.

Foreman, Ellen. "The Negro Ensemble Company: A Transcendent Vision." *The Theatre of Black Americans: A Collection of Critical Essays.* Ed. Errol Hill. New York: Applause Theatre Book Publishers, 1987. 270–282.

Forte, Jeanie. "Kennedy's Body Politic: The Mulatta, Menses, and the Medusa." *Intersecting Boundaries: The Theater of Adrienne Kennedy.* Eds. Paul K. Bryant-Jackson and Lois More Overbeck. Minneapolis: University of Minnesota Press, 1992. 157–169.

———. "Women's Performance Art." *Performing Feminisms.* Ed. Sue-Ellen Case. Baltimore: Johns Hopkins Press, 1990. 251–269.

Foucault, Michel. *Discipline and Punish.* 1975. Translator Alan Sheridan. New York: Random House, 1979.

Franklin, Aretha. "Who's Zooming Who?" Arista Records, 1985.

Fraser, C. Gerald. "New Shange Play Will Aid Writers' Workshop." *New York Times.* 25 June 1979, C16.

Fuchs, Elinor. "Adrienne Kennedy and the First Avant-Garde." *Intersecting Boundaries: The Theater of Adrienne Kennedy.* Eds. Paul K. Bryant-Jackson and Lois More Overbeck. Minneapolis: University of Minnesota Press, 1992. 76–84.

Garner, Stanton B. *Bodied Spaces: Phenomenology and Performance in Contemporary Drama.* Ithaca: Cornell University Press, 1994.

Gates, Henry Louis, Jr. "The Chitlin Circuit." *African American Performance and Theater History: A Critical Reader.* Eds. Harry Elam Jr. and David Krasner. New York: Oxford University Press, 2001. 132–148.

———. ed. *Zora Neale Hurston, Eulalie Spence, Marita Bonner, and Others; The Prize Plays and Other One-Acts Published in Periodicals.* New York: G.K. Hall Publishers, 1996.

———. *The Signifying Monkey.* New York: Oxford University Press, 1988.

———. "A Tragedy of Negro Life." *Mule Bone.* New York: Harper, 1991. 5–24.

Gavin, Christy, ed. *African American Women Playwrights: A Research Guide.* New York: Garland, 1999.

Geis, Deborah. *Postmodern Theatric[k]s Monologue in Contemporary American Drama.* Ann Arbor: University of Michigan, 1995.

———. "'A Spectator Watching My Life': Adrienne Kennedy's *A Movie Star Has to Star in Black and White.*" *Intersecting Boundaries: The Theater of Adrienne Kennedy.* Eds. Paul K. Bryant-Jackson and Lois More Overbeck. Minneapolis: University of Minnesota Press, 1992. 170–178.

George, Nelson. *The Death of Rhythm and Blues.* New York: Penguin, 1988.

Gilman, Sander L. "Black Bodies, White Bodies: Toward an Iconography of Female Sexuality in Late Nineteenth-Century Art, Medicine, and Literature." *Race, Writing and Difference*. Ed. Henry Louis Gates, Jr. Chicago: University of Chicago Press, 1986. 223–261.

Gilmore, Paul. "'De Genewine Artekil': William Wells Brown, Blackface Minstrelsy, and Abolitionism." *American Literature*. 69.4 (1997): 743–780.

Glassberg, David. *American Historical Pageantry: The Uses of Tradition in the Early Twentieth Century*. Chapel Hill: University of North Carolina Press, 1990.

Gray, Christine R. Introduction to *Plays and Pageants from the Life of the Negro*. Compiled by Willis Richardson. 1930. Reprint, Jackson: University of Mississippi Press, 1993. vii–xli.

———. "*Mara*, Angelina Grimké's Other Play." *Black Women Playwrights*. Ed. Carol P. Marsh-Lockett. NY: Garland, 1999. 69–85.

Green, Michael. "Angelina Weld Grimké." *Dictionary of Literary Biography: Afro-American Writers Before the Harlem Renaissance*. Vol. 50. Ed. Trudier Harris. Detroit: Gale Research Company, 1986. 149–155.

Hall, Stuart. *Stuart Hall: Critical Dialogues in Cultural Studies*. Eds. D. Morley and K.H. Chen. London: Routledge, 1996.

Hamalian, Leo, and James V. Hatch, eds. *The Roots of African American Drama: An Anthology of Early Plays, 1858–1938*. Detroit: Wayne State University Press, 1991.

Hansberry, Lorraine. *To Be Young, Gifted and Black*. New York: Signet, 1970.

Hardy, Thomas. *Tess of the D'Urbervilles*. 1891. New York: Modern Library, 1998.

Harper, Frances. *Iola Leroy*. New York: Oxford University Press, 1988.

Harris, Trudier. "Alice Childress." *Dictionary of Literary Biography: Afro-American Writers after 1955: Dramatists and Prose Writers*. Vol. 38. Eds. Thadious Davis and Trudier Harris. Detroit: Gale Research, 1985. 66–79.

———. "Before the Strength, the Pain." *Black Women Playwrights*. Ed. Carol P. Marsh-Lockett. New York: Garland, 1999. 25–42.

———. Introduction to *Like One of the Family*, by Alice Childress. Boston: Beacon Press, 1986.

Harrison, Daphne. *Black Pearls: Blues Queens of the 1920's*. New Brunswick: Rutgers University Press, 1988.

Harrison, Paul Carter. "The Crisis of Black Identity." *African American Review*. 31.4 (1997): 567–578.

———, ed. *Kuntu Drama: Plays of the African Continuum*. New York: Grove Press, 1974.

———. "Praise/Word." *Black Theatre: Ritual Performance in the African Diaspora*. Eds. Paul Carter Harrison, et al. Philadelphia: Temple University Press, 2002. 1–10.

Harrison, Paul Carter, Victor Leo Walker II, and Gus Edwards, eds. *Black Theatre: Ritual Performance in the African Diaspora*. Philadelphia: Temple University Press, 2002.

Haskins, James. *Black Theater in America*. New York: Thomas Y. Crowell, 1982.

Hatch, James. Introduction to *Lost Plays of the Harlem Renaissance 1920–1940*, edited by James V. Hatch and Leo Hamalian. Detroit: Wayne State University Press, 1996. 9–20.

———. "Some African Influences on the Afro-American Theater." *The Theater of Black Americans: A Collection of Critical Essays*. Ed. Errol Hill. New York: Applause Theatre Book Publishers, 1987. 13–29.

Hatch, James, and Ted Shine, eds. *Black Theatre USA, The Early Period, 1847–1938*. New York: The Free Press, 1996.

———, eds. *Black Theatre USA: 1935–Today*. New York: The Free Press, 1996.
Hawthorne, Nathaniel. *The Scarlet Letter*. Oxford: Oxford World Classics, 1998.
———. "Young Goodman Browne." *Nathaniel Hawthorne's Tales*. Ed. James McIntosh. New York: W.W. Norton, 1987. 65–75.
Hay, Samuel A. *African American Theater: An Historical and Critical Analysis*. Cambridge: Cambridge University Press, 1994.
Hill, Errol, ed. *The Theatre of Black Americans: A Collection of Critical Essays*. New York: Applause Theatre Book Publishers, 1987.
Himes, Chester. *The Gold Dream*. New York: Thunder's Mouth Press, 1960.
Hine, Darlene Clark, and Kathleen Thompson, eds. *A Shining Thread of Hope: The History of Black Women in America*. New York: Broadway Books, 1999.
Holliday, Polly. "I Remember Alice Childress." *The Southern Quarterly*. 25.3 (1987): 63–65.
Holloway, Karla. *Passed On: African American Mourning Stories*. Durham: Duke University Press, 2002.
hooks, bell. "Critical Reflections: Adrienne Kennedy, the Writer, the Work." *Intersecting Boundaries: The Theater of Adrienne Kennedy*. Eds. Paul K. Bryant-Jackson and Lois More Overbeck. Minneapolis: University of Minnesota Press, 1992. 179–185.
———. *Talking Back*. Boston: South End Press, 1989.
hooks, bell, and Cornel West. *Breaking Bread: Insurgent Black Intellectual Life*. Boston: South End Press, 1991.
Hull, Gloria T. *Color, Sex, and Poetry: Three Women Writers of the Harlem Renaissance*. Bloomington: Indiana University Press, 1987.
Hurston, Zora Neale. *Dust Tracks on the Road*. New York: HarperCollins, 1996.
———. "What It Means to be Colored Me." *I Love Myself When I Am Laughing...and Then Again When I Am Looking Mean and Impressive: A Zora Neale Hurston Reader*. Ed. Alice Walker. New York: The Feminist Press, 1989. 152–155.
Irigaray, Luce. *Speculum of the Other Woman*. Trans. Gillian C. Gill. Ithaca: Cornell University Press, 1985.
Jacobs, Harriet. *Incidents in the Life of a Slave Girl*. New York: Washington Square Press, 2003.
Jackson, Pamela Faith, and Karimah eds. *Black Comedy: 9 Plays*. New York: Applause Books, 1997.
James, Rick. "Fire and Desire." By Rick James. *Street Songs*. Motown Records, 1981.
Jennings, La Vinia Delois. *Alice Childress*. New York: Twayne, 1995.
———. "Segregated Sisterhood." *Black Women Playwrights*. Ed. Carol P. Marsh-Lockett. New York: Garland, 1999. 43–53.
Johnson, Brothers. "Free and Single." By Louis Johnson and George Johnson. *Look out for #1*. A&M Records, 1976.
Julien, Issac. Director. *Darker Side of Black*. Filmmakers Library, 1993.
Keating, Douglas J. "Shange Voices Her Concerns in New Work." *Philadelphia Inquirer*. 20 Feb. 1993, D10.
Kennedy, Adrienne. "Adrienne Kennedy: An Interview." With Paul K. Bryant-Jackson and Lois More Overbeck. *Intersecting Boundaries: The Theater of Adrienne Kennedy*. Eds. Paul K. Bryant-Jackson and Lois More Overbeck. Minneapolis: University of Minnesota Press, 1992. 3–12.
Kintz, Linda. "The Sanitized Spectacle: What's Birth Got to Do with It? Adrienne Kennedy's *A Movie Star Has to Star in Black and White*." *Theatre Journal*. 44 (1992): 67–86.

———. *The Subject's Tragedy: Political Poetics, Feminist Theory and Drama.* Ann Arbor: The University of Michigan Press, 1992.

Kolin, Philip C. "Orpheus Ascending: Music, Race and Gender in Adrienne Kennedy's *She Talks to Beethoven.*" *African American Review.* 28.2 (1994): 292–304.

Krasner, David. *Resistance, Parody, and Double Consciousness in African American Theatre, 1895–1910.* New York: St. Martin's Press, 1997.

Kupa, Kushauri. "Close-Up: The New York Scene." *Black Theatre.* 6 (1972): 38–40.

Larsen, Nella. *An Intimation of Things Distant: The Collected Fiction of Nella Larsen.* Ed. Charles Larson. New York: Anchor Books, 1989.

Lhamon, W.T. Jr. *Raising Cain: Blackface Performance from Jim Crow to Hip Hop.* Cambridge: Harvard University Press, 1998.

Lester, Neal. "At the Heart of Shange's Feminism: An Interview." *Black American Literature Forum.* 24 (1990): 717–730.

———. "Filled with the Holy Ghost: Sexual Dimension and Dimensions of Sexuality in the Theater of Ntozake Shange." *Black Women Playwrights.* Ed. Carol P. Marsh-Lockett. New York: Garland, 1999. 193–211.

———. *Ntozake Shange: A Critical Study of the Plays.* New York: Garland, 1995.

Liddell, Janice Lee. "The Discourse of Intercourse." *Black Women Playwrights.* Ed. Carol P. Marsh-Lockett. New York: Garland, 1999. 155–171.

Lott, Eric. *Love and Theft: Blackface Minstrelsy and the American Working Class.* New York: Oxford University Press, 1993.

———. "The Seeming Counterfeit: Racial Politics and the Early Blackface Minstrelsy." *American Quarterly.* 43.2 (1991): 223–254.

Lowell, Sandra. Rev. of *Mojo* and *String* by Alice Childress. *Los Angeles Times.* 13 Oct. 1978, sec. 4: 28+.

Maguire, Roberta. "Alice Childress." *The Playwright's Art: Conversations with Contemporary American Dramatists.* Ed. Jackson R. Bryer. New Brunswick: Rutgers University Press, 1995. 48–69.

Maraini, Dacia. *International Women Playwrights: Voices of Identity and Transformation—Proceedings of the First International Women Playwrights Conference, October 18–23, 1988.* Metuchen: Scarecrow Press, 1993. N. p.

Marsh-Lockett, Carol P., ed. *Black Women Playwrights: Visions on the American Stage.* New York: Garland, 1999.

———. "Other Scribbling Women: African-American Female Dramatists." *Black Women Playwrights.* Ed. Carol P. Marsh-Lockett. New York: Garland, 1999. 3–12.

McDonough, Carla J. "The Nightmare of History: Conceptions of Sexuality in Adrienne Kennedy's *Funnyhouse of a Negro.*" *Black Women Playwrights.* Ed. Carol P. Marsh-Lockett. New York: Garland, 1999. 173–192.

McDowell, Deborah. "Viewing the Remains: Black Funerals/Black Families in Contemporary Photojournalism." Paper presented at the annual Paumanok Lecture, Long Island University, Brooklyn, New York, March 1998.

McKay, Nellie. "'What Were They Saying?': Black Women Playwrights of the Harlem Renaissance." *The Harlem Renaissance Re-examined.* Ed. Victor Kramer. New York: AMS, 1987. 129–147.

Meigs, Susan E. "No Place but the Funnyhouse: The Struggle for Identity in Three Adrienne Kennedy Plays." *Modern American Drama: The Female Canon.* Ed. June Schlueter. Rutherford: Fairleigh Dickinson University Press, 1990. 172–183.

Melville, Herman. "*Benito Cereno*." *The Heath Anthology of American Literature*. Vol. 1. Ed. Paul Lauter. 2nd edition. Lexington: D.C. Heath and Company, 1994. 2497–2554.

Miller, Adam David. "It's a Long Way to St. Louis: Notes on the Audience for Black Drama." *The Theatre of Black Americans: A Collection of Critical Essays*. Ed. Errol Hill. New York: Applause Theatre Book Publishers, 1987. 301–306.

Miller, Jeanne-Marie A. "Black Women Playwrights from Grimké to Shange: Selected Synopses of Their Works." *But Some of Us Are Brave: Black Women's Studies*. Eds. Gloria T. Hull, P.B. Scott, and Barbara Smith. Old Westbury: Feminist Press, 1982. 280–296.

Mitchell, Loften. *Black Drama*. San Francisco: Leswing Press, 1967.

Molette, Barbara. "They Speak: Who Listens?" *Black World*. 25 (1976): 28–34.

Morales, Donald M. "Do Black Theatre Institutions Translate into Great Drama?" *African American Review*. 31.4 (1997): 633–637.

Morrison, Toni. *Beloved*. New York: Knopf, 1987.

———. *The Bluest Eye*. New York: Washington Square Press, 1970.

———. *Paradise*. New York: Plume, 1999.

———. *Playing in the Dark: Whiteness and the Literary Imagination*. Cambridge: Harvard University Press, 1992.

———. *Song of Solomon*. New York: Plume, 1987.

———. *Sula*. New York: Plume, 1982.

———. "Unspeakable Things Unspoken: the Afro-American Presence in American Literature." *Michigan Quarterly Review*. 28:1 (1989): 1–34.

Moses, Wilson Jeremiah. *Black Messiahs and Uncle Toms: Social and Literary Manipulations of a Religious Myth*. University Park: Penn State Press, 1993.

Moy, James S. "Asian American Visibility: Touring Fierce Racial Geographies." *Staging Difference: Cultural Pluralism in American Theatre and Drama*. Ed. Marc Maufort. New York: Peter Lang, 1995. 191-200.

Murray, Timothy. "Facing the Camera's Eye: Black and White Terrain in Women's Drama." *Modern Drama*. 28.1 (March 1985): 110–124. Reprinted in *Reading Black, Reading Feminist: A Critical Anthology*. Ed. Henry Louis Gates, Jr. New York: Meridian, 1990. 155–175.

Neal, Larry. *Visions of a Liberated* Future. Ed. Michael Schwartz. New York: Thunder's Mouth Press, 1989.

Oliver, Edith. "Theater Review: Off Broadway." Review of *Funnyhouse of a Negro* by Adrienne Kennedy. *The New Yorker* 25 January 1969, 77–78.

Overbeck, Lois More. "The Life of the Work: A Preliminary Sketch." *Intersecting Boundaries: The Theater of Adrienne Kennedy*. Eds. Paul K. Bryant-Jackson and Lois More Overbeck. Minneapolis: University of Minnesota Press, 1992. 21–41.

Painter, Nell Irvin. *Sojourner Truth: A Life, A Symbol*. New York: Norton, 1997.

Parliament/Funkadelic. "Flashlight." By G. Clinton, B. Worrell and W. Collins. *Funkentelechy vs. the Placebo Syndrome*. Casablanca Records, 1977.

Patterson, Martha. "Remaking the Minstrel: Pauline Hopkins's *Peculiar Sam* and the Post-Reconstruction Black Subject." *Black Women Playwrights*. Ed. Carol P. Marsh-Lockett. New York: Garland, 1999. 13–24.

Pawley, Thomas D. "The Black Theatre Audience." *The Theatre of Black Americans: A Collection of Critical Essays*. Ed. Errol Hill. New York: Applause Theatre Book Publishers, 1987. 307–317.

Petrushevskaya, Liudmila. *International Women Playwrights: Voices of Identity and Transformation—Proceedings of the First International Women Playwrights Conference, October 18–23, 1988*. Metuchen: Scarecrow Press, 1993. N. p.

Perkins, Kathy A., ed. *Black Female Playwrights: An Anthology of Plays Before 1950*. Bloomington Indiana: Indiana University Press, 1990.

Peters, Ida. "Colored Girls…No Lynching of Black Men: Trazana Beverley." *The Afro-American*. (February 21–25, 1978): 7.

Peterson, Bernard L. *Early Black American Playwrights and Dramatic Writers: A Biographical Directory and Catalog of Plays, Films, and Broadcasting Scripts*. Westport: Greenwood, 1990.

———. *A Century of Musicals in Black and White*. Westport: Greenwood, 1993.

Poussaint, Alvin, and James Comer. *Raising Black Children: Two Leading Psychiatrists Confront the Educational, Social, and Emotional Problems Facing Black Children*. New York: Plume, 1992.

Pryse, Marjorie, and Hortense Spillers. *Conjuring*. Bloomington: Indiana University Press, 1985.

Reed, Ishmael. *Flight to Canada*. New York: Scribner, 1998.

———. *Mumbo Jumbo*. New York: Scribner, 1996.

———. "Neo-Hoodoo Manifesto." *The Norton Anthology of African American Literature*. Eds. Henry Louis Gates, et al. New York: Norton, 1997. 2297–2301.

Richards, Sandra L. "Conflicting Impulses in the Plays of Ntozake Shange." *Black American Literature Forum*. 17.2 (1983): 73–78.

———. "Under the Trickster's Sign: Toward a Reading of Ntozake Shange and Femi Osofisan." *Critical Theory and Performance*. Eds. Janelle G. Reinelt and Joseph R. Roach. Ann Arbor: University of Michigan, 1992. 65–78.

Richardson, Willis, compiler. *Plays and Pageants from the Life of the Negro*. 1930. Reprint, Jackson: University Press of Mississippi, 1993.

Robinson, Marc. *The Other American Drama*. Cambridge: Cambridge University Press, 1994.

Rudin, Seymour. "Theater Chronicle." *Massachusetts Review*. 10 (1969): 583–593.

Sampson, Henry T. *Blacks in Blackface: A Source Book on Early Black Musical Shows*. Metuchen: Scarecrow Press, 1980.

Sanders, Leslie Catherine. *The Development of Black Theater in America*. Baton Rouge: Louisiana State University Press, 1988.

Schroeder, Patricia R. "Re-reading Alice Childress." *Staging Difference: Cultural Pluralism in American Theater and Drama*. Ed. Marc Maufort. New York: Peter Lang, 1995. 323–337.

Shange, Ntozake. "Ntozake Shange Interviews Herself." *Ms*. 6 (1977): 35, 70–72.

———. *See No Evil*. San Francisco: Momo's Press, 1984.

Smith, Valerie. "Loopholes of Retreat: Architecture and Ideology in Harriet Jacobs' *Incidents in the Life of a Slave Girl*." *Reading Black, Reading Feminist*. Ed. Henry Louis Gates, Jr. New York: Meridian Press, 1990. 212–226.

Snead, James. "Repetition as a Figure of Black Culture." *Black Literature and Literary Theory*. Ed. Henry Louis Gates. New York: Routledge, 1984. 59–79.

———. *White Screens Black Images*. New York: Routledge, 1994.

Sollors, Werner. Introduction to *The Adrienne Kennedy Reader*. Minneapolis: University of Minnesota Press, 2001.

Sonnega, William. "Beyond a Liberal Audience." *African American Performance and Theater History*. Eds. Harry J. Elam, Jr. and David Krasner. Oxford: Oxford University Press, 2001. 81–98.

Southern, Eileen. *Nineteenth-Century African American Musical Theater, Vol. 9*. New York: Garland, 1994.

Soyinka, Wole. "The Fourth Stage: Through the Mysteries of Ogun to the Origin of Yoruba Tragedy." *Black Theatre: Ritual Performance in the African Diaspora*. Eds. Paul Carter Harrison et al. Philadelphia: Temple University Press, 2002. 140–152.

Spillers, Hortense. "Cross-Currents, Discontinuities." *Conjuring*. Eds. Marjorie Pryse and Hortense Spillers. Bloomington: Indiana University Press, 1985. 249–261.

———. "Mama's Baby, Papa's Maybe: An American Grammar Book." *Literary Theory: An Anthology*. Eds. Julie Rivkin and Michael Ryan. Malden: Blackwell Publishers, 1998. 656–672.

Spivak, Gayatri. "Can the Subaltern Speak?" *Marxism and the Interpretation of Culture*. Eds. Larry Grossberg and Cary Nelson. Urbana: University of Illinois Press, 1988. 271–313.

Stack, Carol D. *All Our Kin: Strategies for Survival in a Black Community*. New York: Harper and Row, 1974.

Staples, Robert. "The Myth of Black Macho: A Response to Angry Black Feminists." *Black Scholar*. 10 (1979): 24–32.

Stephens, Judith L. "Anti-Lynch Plays by African-American Women: Race, Gender, and Social Protest in American Drama." *African American Review*. 26.2 (1992): 329–339.

Storm, William. "Reactions of a Highly-Strung Girl: Psychology and Dramatic Representation in Angelina W. Grimke's *Rachel*." *African American Review*. 27.3 (1993): 461–470.

Stowe, Harriet Beecher. *Uncle Tom's Cabin: Authoritative Text, Backgrounds and Contexts, Criticism*. Ed. Elizabeth Ammons. New York: Norton, 1993.

Sullivan, Megan. "Folk Plays, Home Girls, and Back Talk: Georgia Douglas Johnson and Women of the Harlem Renaissance." *College Language Association Journal*. 38.4 (1995): 404–419.

Tanner, Jo A. *Dusky Maidens: The Odyssey of the Early Black Dramatic Actress*. Westport: Greenwood Press, 1992.

Tate, Claudia. *Domestic Allegories of Political Desire: The Black Heroine's Text at the Turn of the Century*. New York: Oxford University Press, 1992.

Taubman, Howard. "Adrienne Kennedy Play Opens at East End." Review of *Funnyhouse of a Negro* by Adrienne Kennedy. *New York Times*, 15 January 1964, 25.

Terry-Morgan, Elmo. "Noise/Funk: Fo' Real Black Theatre on 'Da Great White Way." *African American Review*. 31.4 (1997): 677–686.

Thompson, Bill. "*Colored Girls* and black men." Review of *for colored girls* by Ntozake Shange. *Philadelphia Inquirer*, 2 April 1978, L1+.

Thompson, Robert Farris. "An Aesthetic of the Cool: West African Dance." *The Theatre of Black Americans: A Collection of Critical Essays*. Ed. Errol Hill. New York: Applause Theatre Book Publishers, 1987. 99–111.

Timpane, John. "'The Poetry of a Moment': Politics and the Open Form in the Drama of Ntozake Shange." *Modern American Drama: The Female Canon*. Ed. June Schlueter. Rutherford: Fairleigh Dickinson University Press, 1990. 198–206.

Toll, Robert. *Blacking Up: The Minstrel Show in Nineteenth Century America*. New York: Oxford University Press, 1974.

Toomer, Jean. *Cane*. 1923. New York: Liveright, 1974.

Traylor, Eleanor. "Two Afro-American Contributions to Dramatic Form." *The Theatre of Black Americans: A Collection of Critical Essays*. Ed. Errol Hill. New York: Applause Theatre Book Publishers, 1987. 45–60.

Van Gelder, Lawrence. "For Some Girls a Rainbow May Still Not Be Enough." Review of *for colored girls* Ntozake Shange. *New York Times*, 13 June 2000, late ed., sec. E: 5.

Waldron, Ann. "These Stone Walls Are Not a Prison for Papp's Musical." *Philadelphia Inquirer* 25 December 1977, G1+.

Walker, David. *Appeal, in Four Articles; Together with a Preamble, to the Coloured Citizens of the World*. New York: Hill and Wang, 1995.

Walker, Alice. "1955." *You Can't Keep a Good Woman Down*. New York: Harvest Books, 1981. 3–20.

Wall, Cheryl. "Poets and Versifiers, Singers and Signifiers." *Women, the Arts and the 1920's in Paris and New York*. Eds. Kenneth Wheeler and Virginia Lussier. New Brunswick: Transaction Books, 1982. 74–98.

———. *Women of the Harlem Renaissance*. Bloomington: Indiana University Press, 1995.

Warren, Kenneth W. *Black and White Strangers: Race and American Literary Realism*. Chicago: University of Chicago Press, 1995.

Washington, Booker T. "Atlanta Exposition Address." 18 Sept. 1895. Reprinted in *The Booker T. Washington Papers*. Ed. Louis R. Harlan et al., Vol. 3. Urbana: University of Illinois Press, 1974. 584–587.

Washington, Mary Helen. "Ntozake Shange." *The Playwright's Art: Conversations with Contemporary American Dramatists*. Ed. Jackson R. Bryer. New Brunswick: Rutgers University Press, 1995. 205–220.

Watkins, Mel. *On the Real Side*. New York: Simon and Schuster, 1994.

West, Cornel. "Black Strivings in a Twilight Civilization." *The Cornel West Reader*. New York: Perseus Books Group, 1999. 87–118.

———. "Nietzsche's Prefiguration of Postmodern American Philosophy." *The Cornel West Reader*. New York: Perseus Books Group, 1999. 188–210.

Wickham, Glynne. *A History of the Theater*, 2nd edition. London: Phaidon Press, 1992.

Wiley, Catherine. "Whose Name, Whose Protection: Reading Alice Childress's *Wedding Band*." *Modern American Drama: The Female Canon*. Ed. June Schlueter. London: Associated University Press, 1990. 184–197.

Wilkerson, Margaret B. "Diverse Angles of Vision: Two Black Women Playwrights." *Intersecting Boundaries: The Theater of Adrienne Kennedy*. Eds. Paul K. Bryant-Jackson and Lois More Overbeck. Minneapolis: University of Minnesota Press, 1992. 58–75.

———. "Music as Metaphor: New Plays of Black Women." *Making a Spectacle: Feminist Essays on Contemporary Women's Theatre*. Ann Arbor: University of Michigan Press, 1989. 61–75.

———, ed. *Nine Plays by Black Women*. New York: Mentor (Penguin), 1986.

Williams, Judith. "Uncle Tom's Women." *African American Performance and Theater History*. Eds. Harry Elam and David Krasner. New York: Oxford University Press, 2001. 19–39.

Williams, Mance. *Black Theatre in the 1960s and 1970s: A Historical-Critical Analysis of the Movement*. Westport: Greenwood Press, 1985.

Williams, Raymond. "Ideological State Apparatuses." *Literary Theory: An Anthology*. Eds. Julie Rivkin and Michael Ryan. Malden: Blackwell Publishers, 1998. 294–304.

Wilson, August, and Robert Brustein. "On Cultural Power." Town Hall Debate, New York City, January 1997.

Wilson, Sondra Kathryn. Ed. *The Crisis Reader: Stories, Poetry, and Essays from the N.A.A.C.P.'s* Crisis *Magazine*. New York: Modern Library, 1999.

———. Ed. *The Opportunity Reader: Stories, Poetry, and Essays from the Urban League's* Opportunity *Magazine*. New York: Modern Library, 1999.

Woll, Allen. *Black Musical Theater: From Coontown to Dreamgirls*. Baton Rouge: Louisiana State University Press, 1989.

———. *Dictionary of Black Theatre*. Westport: Greenwood Press, 1983.

Wright, Richard. *Native Son*. New York: HarperPerennial, 1993.

INDEX

A

B

C

D

G

H

I

J

K

L

Q

R

S

V

W